AFRICANS ABROAD

A Documentary History of the Black Diaspora in Asia, Latin America, and the Caribbean During the Age of Slavery

AFRICANS ABROAD

A Documentary History of the Black Diaspora in Asia, Latin America, and the Caribbean During the Age of Slavery

Graham W. Irwin

New York ■ Columbia University Press ■ *1977*

Library of Congress Cataloging in Publication Data
Main entry under title:

Africans abroad.

Bibliography: p.
Includes index.
1. Slavery—History. 2. Blacks—History.
I. Irwin, Graham W.
HT861.A4 301.45'19'6 77-457
ISBN 0-231-03936-0
ISBN 0-231-03937-9 pbk.

Columbia University Press
New York Guildford, Surrey

Printed in the United States of America

CONTENTS

PREFACE

THE ENFORCED EXPATRIATION over many centuries of millions of Africans from their homeland to the Americas, Europe, and Asia—the "Black Diaspora," as it is sometimes called—is one of the most important mass movements of population in history. It is also one of the least understood.

The chief reason for this is that the source materials on which any account of the Black Diaspora must be based are fragmentary and often highly obscure. There is little direct evidence of any kind, since in slavery times almost all the Africans who left their homelands for overseas were nonliterate. Moreover, in the countries to which they were taken they constituted for centuries the most oppressed and exploited element in society. Very few even of those who could write left a record of their lives behind them, since the system denied them the means of self-expression.

For the bulk of his information, therefore, the historian of the African experience outside Africa has to rely on what nonblacks have said over time about blacks. Because of the nature of the relationship between the two—a relationship in which the masters were almost always white and the slaves were always black—most of what the nonblacks recorded was prejudiced, much of it was ill-informed, and some of it was deliberately falsified. Indeed, during the age of slavery fair-minded reporting of the African experience was hardly possible for nonblacks. If a slavemaster admitted that Africans and persons of African descent had a history and culture of their own that was worthy of notice, he struck away one of the main props of slavery as an institution. It used to be held that Africans were fitted to be slaves (and therefore might legitimately be enslaved) precisely because in their own continent they had not advanced to a stage of development that the rest of the world could accept as "civilized."

As far as Africa itself is concerned, the situation is today much changed. A great deal is now known about African history in the precolonial period, and it is no longer possible for even the most prejudiced observer to deny to Africa a past of which all blacks, whether of the continent or of the Diaspora, may be proud. But the history of the African experience outside Africa, except for certain areas and periods, has not yet been subjected to the same intensive scrutiny.

This book samples the materials by means of which such a history might be written. The sources assembled here are not comprehensive, in the sense that they do not illustrate all facets of the African experience overseas. No attempt has been made, for example, to cover either modern Europe or North America. In the case of Europe, although much valuable work has been done in recent years on Africans in Britain, the subject as a whole has barely begun to be investigated. In the case of North America, the opposite is true; the outpouring, since the increase in interest in Black Studies in the United States in the 1960s and 1970s, of monographs, texts, and books of readings on "Afro-American History" has been so vast that to try to duplicate them seemed unnecessary. The intention has rather been to portray the African experience in those areas of the world which up to now have been relatively neglected, at least in the English-speaking world, and which lend themselves to a reasonably full treatment within the limits of a single volume.

In "source books" the problem of trying to achieve consistency of transliteration becomes almost unmanageable when quotations from sources in different languages and dating from different eras are brought together in one book. In the case of Arabic it is only recently that the representation in Roman script of words in that language has become standardized; in earlier times a wide variety of accent marks and diacritics was used. I have not changed the spelling of Arabic words in the extracts reproduced below but, for greater ease of reading, I have taken the liberty of modernizing the diacritics when quoting from older sources, altering, for example, 'á' and 'â' to 'ā' throughout.

I am grateful to my colleagues Douglas M. Dunlop and Ainslie T. Embree for advice on the Middle Eastern and Indian sections respectively, and to C. Diane Christensen, who helped me choose the Latin American selections. My thanks are also due to Marion Berdecio, Edward B. Cone, D. M. Dunlop, Rudolf Perina, Hasan Shuraydi, J. W. Smit, and Elise P. Wright, who made translations for me from Arabic, Spanish, Portuguese, French, German, and Dutch sources.

September 1976 G.W.I.

ACKNOWLEDGMENTS

I WISH TO THANK the following for permission to quote from copyright works:

No. 1: from Eugen Strouhal, "Evidence of the Early Penetration of Negroes into Prehistoric Egypt," *Journal of African History* (1970), 12(1): 4–7; reprinted by permission of The Cambridge University Press, New York.

No. 2: from Guy Brunton and Gertrude Caton-Thompson, *The Badarian Civilization and Predynastic Remains near Badari* (London: Quaritch, 1928), pp. 40–42; courtesy of Miss G. Caton-Thompson and Department of Egyptology, University College, London.

No. 3: from E. A. Wallis Budge, *The Egyptian Sûdân: Its History and Monuments* (2 vols.; London: Kegan Paul, 1907), 1:559–60; reprinted by permission of Routledge & Kegan Paul, Ltd., London.

No. 6: from C. H. Oldfather, trans., *Diodorus Siculus, Library of History* (Cambridge, Mass.: Harvard University Press, 1935), pp. 89–95, 97–99, 101–3 (extracts); reprinted by permission of Harvard University Press, Cambridge, Mass. (Loeb Classical Library).

No. 7: from James Henry Breasted, *Ancient Records of Egypt* (5 vols.; Chicago: University of Chicago Press, 1906–7), 4:418–19, 421–23, 425–27, 429, 443–44 (extracts); reprinted by permission of The University of Chicago Press, Chicago.

No. 8: from Keith Irvine, *The Rise of the Colored Races* (New York:

Norton, 1970), pp. 14–19; reprinted by permission of W. W. Norton & Company, Inc., New York. Copyright © 1970 by Keith Irvine.

No. 10: from Frank M. Snowden, *Blacks in Antiquity: Ethiopians in the Greco-Roman Empire* (Cambridge, Mass.: The Belknap Press of Harvard University Press), pp. 216–18; reprinted by permission of the publishers. Copyright © 1970 by the President and Fellows of Harvard College.

No. 11: from Erich F. Schmidt, *Persepolis. I: Structures. Reliefs. Inscriptions* (Chicago: University of Chicago Press, 1953), p. 90; reprinted by permission of The University of Chicago Press, Chicago.

No. 12: from H. B. Dewing, trans., *Procopius,* Vol. I, Book 1, sect. 20 (Loeb Classical Library; London: Heinemann, 1914); reprinted by permission of Harvard University Press, Cambridge Mass., and William Heinemann, London.

No. 14: from Ignaz Goldziher, *A Short History of Classical Arabic Literature. Translated, revised, and enlarged by Joseph DeSomogyi* (Hildesheim: Olms, 1966); reprinted by permission of Georg Olms Verlag, Hildesheim, Federal Republic of Germany. Copyright © 1966 Ignaz Goldziher.

No. 16: from Henry Cassels Kay, ed., *Yaman: Its Early Mediaeval History. By Najm ad-Din 'Omārah al-Ḥakami* (London: Arnold, 1892), pp. 20–22; reprinted by permission of Edward Arnold (publishers), Ltd., London.

No. 17: from Muḥammad ibn Ṣaṣrā, *A Chronicle of Damascus 1389–1397,* edited and translated by W. M. Brinner (2 vols.; Berkeley and Los Angeles: University of California Press, 1963), 1:278; originally published by the University of California Press; reprinted by permission of The Regents of the University of California.

No. 24: from Theodore Nöldeke, *Sketches from Eastern History,* translated by John Sutherland Black (London: A. & C. Black, 1892), ch. 5; reprinted by permission of Adam and Charles Black, Publishers, London.

No. 26: from Nassiri Khosran, *Sefer Nameh: Relation du voyage de Nassiri Khosran en Syrie, en Palestine, en Égypte, en Arabie et en Perse, pendant les années de Hégire 437–444 (1035–1040)*, edited and translated by Charles Schéfer (Paris: Leroux, 1881), pp. 227–28; reproduced in English translation by permission of Presses Universitaires de France, Paris.

No. 27: from Ṣā'id al-Andalusī, *Kitāb Tabaḳāt al-Umam* (*Livre des catégories des nations*), translated by Régis Blachère (Paris: Larose, 1935), pp. 36–38; reproduced in English translation by permission of Éditions G.-P. Maisonneuve et Larose, Paris.

No. 28: from Peter Quennell, trans., *The Book of the Marvels of India* (London: Routledge, 1928), pp. 44–52; reprinted by permission of Routledge & Kegan Paul, Ltd., London.

No. 29: from Charles Pellat, *The Life and Works of Jāḥiẓ: Translations of Selected Texts,* translated by D. M. Hawke (London: Routledge & Kegan Paul, 1969; Berkeley and Los Angeles: University of California Press, 1969), pp. 195–97; reprinted by permission of Routledge & Kegan Paul, Ltd., London, and The University of California Press, Berkeley and Los Angeles.

No. 30: from Bernard Lewis, *Race and Color in Islam* (New York: Harper and Row, 1971), pp. 18–29, 38, 64–78; reprinted by permission of the publisher. Copyright © 1970, 1971 by Bernard Lewis.

No. 31 (a): from H. A. R. Gibb, trans., vols. 3 and 4 of *The Travels of Ibn Baṭṭūṭa A.D. 1325–1354* (Cambridge: Cambridge University Press for the Hakluyt Society, 1971), 3:631; reprinted by permission of the Hakluyt Society, c/o British Museum, London.

No. 32: from *The Cambridge History of India* (6 vols.; Cambridge: The University Press, 1922–37), 3:268–69; reprinted by permission of The Cambridge University Press, New York.

No. 33: from G. Yazdani, *Bidar: Its History and Monuments* (London: Oxford University Press, 1947), pp. 180–81; reprinted by permission of The Oxford University Press, Oxford.

No. 34: from W. Ph. Coolhaas, ed., *Pieter van den Broecke in Azië* (2 vols.; The Hague: Nijhoff, 1962–3), 1:146–51; reproduced in English translation by permission of Martinus Nijhoff's Boekhandel en Uitgeversmaatschappij B.V., The Hague.

Nos. 70 and 77: from Arthur Ramos, *The Negro in Brazil* (Washington, D.C.: Associated Publishers, 1939), pp. 24–41 and 66–79; reprinted by permission of The Associated Publishers, Inc., Washington, D.C.

Introduction

AFRICA AND THE ANCIENT WORLD

EGYPT

THE STUDENT of the African experience outside Africa must begin his search in ancient Egypt. The nature and degree of the Egyptian contribution to the world of antiquity has long been a matter of bitter controversy. Some scholars have sought to prove that all science and philosophy began in the land of the pharaohs. Others have denied the Egyptians primacy in anything, save an early form of writing and a certain competence in practical geometry, developed in response to the need to mark out agricultural fields afresh after the annual inundations of the River Nile. No one, however, has disputed the fact that ancient Egypt possessed one of the oldest seats of civilization in the world or that its inhabitants traveled widely and influenced their neighbors.

The question arises, therefore, Of what physical type were the ancient Egyptians? There can be no argument about the civilization of Egypt being an African civilization; the facts of geography make it so. But were the inhabitants of the valley and delta of the Nile in ancient times black?

A second and equally fundamental question is: What contribution was made to the civilization of ancient Egypt by Africa south of the Sahara, including Nubia and Ethiopia? Until recently this question was usually put the other way. Scholars were more interested in the diffusion of Egyptian culture to the rest of Africa [1] than in the possibility of traffic in the reverse direction. But there is a growing realization that Black Africa's influence on ancient Egypt was greater than has been thought, particularly in the predynastic period.

Answers to these questions may be sought in three main ways. First, the archaeological record has to be examined—the graves and tombs, wall paintings, sculptures, and monumental architecture of Egypt, Nubia, and Ethiopia. Second, the written record must be searched. This involves the study not only of the inscriptions and papyri that survive in northeastern Africa itself but also of the works of contemporary travelers, geographers, and historians (writing mostly in Greek and Latin) who were familiar with the area. Finally, comparisons have to be made between the cultural heritages of the lands on either side of the Sahara to determine, where possible, priority of invention or innovation.

1 Black Badarians

"Predynastic" is a term used by Egyptologists to signify the period before Upper and Lower Egypt were united under the pharaohs into one kingdom. It was followed by the thirty dynasties, or sequences of rulers, into which Egyptian history has traditionally been divided.

The predynastic period consists of three main chronological phases: Badarian, Amratean (or Naqada I), and Gerzean (or Naqada II). Of these the first, or Badarian, which may be dated to c.6000–4000 B.C., is unique in that an exceptionally large number of skull finds are associated with it. Because of this profusion of fossil remains, physical anthropologists working on the Badarian materials have been able to quantify the results of their cranial measurements and arrive at conclusions about the race of the Badarians that have a reasonable claim to validity in that the sample employed is adequately large.

■

With the aim of elucidating the question of the morphological character of the Badarians, I studied both available Badarian series, the first one in the Duckworth Laboratory at Cambridge (53 skulls), and the second one in the Institute of Anatomy at Kasr El-Aini, University of Cairo (64 skulls), making a total of 117 skulls of adult and juvenile individuals. . . .

Of the total of 117 skulls, 15 were found to be markedly Europoid, 9 of these were of the gracile Mediterranean type . . . 6 were of very robust structure reminiscent of the North African Cromagnon type. Eight skulls were clearly Negroid . . . and were close to the Negro types occurring in East Africa. The majority of 94 skulls showed mixed Europoid-Negroid features in different combinations and with different shares of both major race components. In one-third of them the Europoid, in the other third the Negroid, features were dominant. The last third showed both components, either well balanced or with characters of the neutral range, common to both racial groups. We may conclude that the share of both components was nearly the same, with some overweight to the Europoid side.

In some of the Badarian crania hair was preserved, thanks to good conditions in the desert sand. In the first series, according to the description of the excavators, they were curly in 6 cases, wavy in 33 cases, and straight in 10 cases. They were black in 16 samples, dark brown in 11, brown in 12, light brown in 1, and gray in 11 cases. . . .

I was able to take samples of seven of the racially mixed Badarian individuals which were macroscopically curly (spirals of 10–20 mm in diameter) or wavy (25–35 mm). They were studied microscopically by S. Tittlebachová from the Institute of Anthropology of the Charles University, who found in five out of seven samples a change in the thickness of the hair in the course of its length, sometimes with a simultaneous narrowing of the hair pith. The outline of the cross-sections of the hairs was flattened, with indices ranging from 35 to 65. These peculiarities also show the Negroid influence among the Badarians. . . .

[Thus] the Negroid component among the Badarians is anthropologically well based. Even though the share of "pure" Negroes is small (6.8 percent), being half that of the Europoid forms (12.9 percent), the high majority of mixed forms (80.3 percent) suggests a long-lasting dispersion of Negroid genes in the population. It can be interpreted by the supposition that the mixture of both components began many generations previously. . . .

We still do not know exactly when neolithic farmers first settled in the Nile Valley, nor from whence they came. A date in the sixth millennium B.C. is most likely and the sources of the settlement may probably be found in the eastern Mediterranean area. At the same period, however, with the beginning of the Makalian wet phase, the Negro population of the Sudanic savannah belt would have started its movement towards the north, into Saharan latitudes, which then, for the last time, became open to human occupation. Maybe some of these emigrant groups penetrated down the Nile as far as Upper Egypt, thus providing one of the oldest known biological contacts between the Negroids and Europoids, the ultimate evidence of which appears some 1,000–1,500 years later in skeletons preserved in the Badarian cemeteries.

In this connection, we have to mention that Egyptologists have found in the Badarian and other predynastic cultures of Upper Egypt some material and ideological evidence of southern or Sudanic African elements. The Badarian pottery is connected with the pottery of the Khartoum neolithic culture, which originated probably from the ceramics of the Early Khartoum culture. Some authors postulate the direct derivation of Badarian pottery from the Khartoum neolithic pottery. While in Egypt pottery of this type was later replaced by other ceramic forms, often under the influence of the Middle East, in the Sudan this archaic pottery persisted for a long time, and was from there later introduced on several occasions by southern immigrants into Nubia and even (though in small quantities) into Egypt. Fishing hooks were also found in Badari, typologically similar to Khartoum neolithic hooks, but more developed, and therefore probably younger. To this connection between the Khartoum neolithic and Badarian cultures it is necessary to add that, according to present—unfortunately still very poor—evidence, the population of the Khartoum neolithic was Negroid.

Badarian flint instruments are of surprisingly poor quality. They were made from free-lying boulders, regardless of the fact that in the living area of the Badarians plenty of superb flints could have been collected from the limestone layers. This provides an argument for the arrival of Badarian people from an area lacking limestones with flints, e.g., from more southern areas, where, starting with 25° N. latitude in the Eastern Desert and Esna in the Nile Valley, the limestone relief comes to an end.

In some of the Badarian graves, conical buttons made from fine polished ceramics were found which were probably worn in the earlobes or in the nasal wings. . . . The custom of wearing ornaments in the nose or ears can be considered in this region also as being of African origin.

In the predynastic cultures of Upper Egypt Aldred found evidence of the cult of celestial and astral deities, as well as of the idea of the leader (later the deified king), and the "rainmaker." This is also an old African conception, which may be connected with the original home of the Upper Egyptian population (or part of it) in a region depending more on rainfall than on the Nile floods. Ritual killing of the leaders in the time of their decreased strength, known also from predynastic Egypt, has analogies in the historic and even in the recent Sudan.

SOURCE: Eugen Strouhal, "Evidence of the Early Penetration of Negroes into Prehistoric Egypt," *Journal of African History* (1971), 12(1):4–7 (extracts; footnotes omitted).

2 Badarian Culture

Badāri, from which the Badarian culture takes its name, is a village in Upper Egypt, some miles east of the Nile at Asyūṭ. The men and women who lived there some 8,000 to 6,000 years ago [2] were members of what is probably the oldest black African civilization of which we have definite record.

As we have seen, the evidence of the Badarians' skull measurements has enabled scientists to tell a great deal about their race. But the graves from which these skulls came have also yielded a wealth of information about Badarian culture. Like other peoples of the time the Badarians believed in an afterlife. In consequence, they customarily placed a man's belongings in his grave alongside his corpse, with the object of preventing his ghost from returning to haunt the living and perhaps also of helping him to survive in the next world. From artifacts found in graves archaeologists have been able to reconstruct many details of the Badarian way of life.

■

The climate in those days seems to have been colder than it is now, if we may judge from the amount of fur worn; sometimes we find two skin garments; and the hair is nearly always on the inside for warmth. The Nile Valley was largely occupied by swamps, evidenced by the profusion of rush or reed matting; the fact that villages were placed on the desert spurs also indicates that there was not overmuch habitable land on the lower levels. Hippopotami and crocodiles abounded. The fauna of the desert was probably much the same as it was in early historic times; it included the ostrich. No doubt there was much more vegetation then than now, and there is a possibility that the Badarian cattle may have found pasture in what is now desert. Remains of rough stone walls on the high desert near the great *wadi* may be parts of fences or cattle enclosures. . . .

We do not know what kind of house or shelter the Badarian made for himself. We may imagine that wattle was the mainstay of the walls; it may have been covered with mud, skins, or matting. We found no hut circles in the Badarian villages; huts were probably therefore more in the nature of shelters. If we can take the graves as imitations of living habitations, then sticks and matting would have been the materials used. No wonder the Badarians slept in fur.

Their clothing was of woven material, probably a coarse linen, in addition to the skins. This took the form of a kilt, or of a longer garment. As at the present day, the head was well wrapped up at night, if we may take the burial garments as being those worn by the living during sleep. Over the linen, when occasion demanded, the skin garments were worn, sometimes sewn, sometimes with leather fringes, sometimes a single pelt; but they were never ornamented with patterns in beads. Goat and antelope seem to have furnished the majority of these; but finer fur, like a black cat's, might be worn on occasions. These skin garments were more usual with men than with women; doubtless they required more protection when out hunting and cattle tending than the more sheltered wives. The Badarian does not seem to have made himself sandals.

Like most primitive Africans, he was fond of ornaments in the shape of necklaces, bracelets, and anklets. Men affected the single large bead at the neck or on the arm; and, when they could afford the luxury, wore ropes of greenish-blue beads round the waist. Women and children had necklaces of beads and shells, and young girls liked girdles and headbands of shells. Both sexes were fond of large ivory bracelets which were worn in numbers on the forearm. Ear-studs seem to have been usual ornaments; and even a pale-green nose-stud was thought attractive, a very African touch. We may not be far wrong if we suppose that the Badarians were sufficiently civilized to carry handkerchiefs.

The eyes were painted round with green malachite ointment; everyone ground and mixed his own. The castor plant, which grew wild, supplied them with oil to lubricate their skins, or to fill their lamps. Men wore their hair long, according to modern European ideas; women sometimes plaited theirs, or twisted the tresses, or even had curly fringes; but they never grew it longer than eight inches or so. Combs were worn as ornaments. The men were clean-shaven, or beardless.

There was no scarcity of food; apart from herds of oxen, sheep, and goats which we may suppose to have been domesticated, game abounded; birds and fish were also plentiful. The crocodile was made use of, though we cannot say it was eaten. Cereals were known, but what species is uncertain. Husks were found with the deposit of saw-edged flints, and also in one of the cooking pots. The grain was perhaps pulled up, as the usual Predynastic sickle-flints are not found, and the saw-edged knives would not be very suitable for reaping. The grain was stored in clay bins; and made into bread, apparent remains of which are found in graves. Porridge no doubt was a common form of food, and was ladled out of the pots with large dippers or spoons, which could be carried hung from the belt.

In hunting, arrows with flint heads were the common weapons. We have no information at present as to how they were projected; no bows have been found. If they existed, they have either left no trace in the graves, or, as is more likely, they were considered too valuable to be buried. . . .

The principal industries were potmaking, flint chipping, tanning, weaving, basket- and matmaking. It was in the manufacture of pottery that the Badarian especially excelled. Not only was it made in great quantities, but the finer qualities were never equalled in later times in the Nile Valley. The best vases are extraordinary for the thinness and excellence of the ware, and for the high finish of the delicately rippled or smooth surfaces. . . .

Leather work was carried on with considerable skill. For softening the hides, we can see the Badarians using some of the many hard stone rubbers which are so often found. The bone awls were for piercing the leather; and the sewing was done with bone needles.

Copper borers were also much prized for some such purpose, or perhaps for the piercing of the steatite beads, if these were made locally and not imported.

Of trade we have ample evidence. It is a matter of dispute from what neighboring lands certain materials and objects come; but it is quite certain that they were not found or manufactured locally. The basalt vases were probably traded up the river from the Delta region or from the northwest. Elephant ivory may have been local, but was more likely imported from the south. Shells came in quantities from the Red Sea shores. Turquoise possibly came from Sinai; copper from the north. A Syrian connection is suggested for the four-handled pot of hard pink ware. The black pottery, with white incised designs, may have come directly from the west, or indirectly from the south; and the celts suggest intercourse in the same directions. The porphyry slabs are like the later ones in Nubia, but the material could have come from the Red Sea mountains. The glazed steatite beads, found in such profusion, can hardly have been made locally. We see, then, that the Badarians were not an isolated tribe, but were in contact with the cultures of countries on all sides of them. Nor were they nomads; their pots, some of them both large and fragile, were absolutely unsuitable for the use of wanderers. . . .

Of the everyday religion of the Badarians we know very little. That they had a belief in the efficacy of amulets we know from the animals' heads found on the bodies; the gazelle and the hippopotamus had attributes which it was desired to acquire by magical means, or they were objects of veneration and could afford the wearer protection. We may infer that certain animals were revered, from the fact that their bodies are found buried in certain select areas of the cemetery and with as much care as human beings. The dog or jackal, the ox, sheep, and goat, are thus found wrapped in matting and even in linen. . . .

That there was a belief in survival after death is obvious from the food offerings placed in the graves. The deceased were wrapped in their everyday clothes and laid down as if sleeping, covered by what may have been a replica of their home; and with them were placed their toilet objects and implements of craft. For some reason, it was considered desirable that they should look towards the setting sun. The purpose of placing objects with the dead was either that their spirits could pass over into the spirit-world with their owner, or, more likely, that the ghost who haunted the grave would find everything that he wanted there and not return to his abode and trouble his family.

SOURCE: Guy Brunton and Gertrude Caton-Thompson, *The Badarian Civilization and Predynastic Remains near Badari* (London: Quaritch, 1928), pp. 40–42 (extracts).

3 Black Egyptians: Rulers

The contention that the ancient Egyptians were black not only rests on the deductions of physical anthropologists; it also derives from references in classical literature and from the fact that many of the statues and portraits of the rulers of the country in Pharaonic times show "Negroid" characteristics. Among the more famous personages who have been identified as African are the Pharaoh Zoser and Imhotep, his chief minister and the father of medicine, the Pharaohs Amenemhet I, Sesostris I, Thutmose III, and Rameses II, and Queens Nefertari, Hatshepsut, and Nefertiti. One modern writer has dryly observed that, before the passage of the Civil Rights Act of 1964, "not one of the Egyptian Pharaohs could have bought a cup of coffee in a white drug store in the Southern states of the U.S.A." [3]

On this matter hard evidence is not easy to obtain. For every authority who sees the face of the Sphinx of Gizeh as "unquestionably Negroid," there is another who as forcefully denies that there is anything African about the Sphinx at all. Nevertheless, inscriptions exist that tend to prove not only that there were blacks in the service of the state at all levels, including the highest, but that these individuals were aware of their racial origin and took pride in it. An example is King Rā-Neḥsi of the XIIIth Dynasty.

■

Towards the close of the XIIIth Dynasty there reigned in the Delta a king who styled himself "King of the South and North, Rā-Neḥsi," or "Neḥsi-Rā." Now the word "Neḥsi" means "Black," or "Negro"; therefore this king's name means "the Negro of Rā." It is quite certain that he was a king of foreign extraction, for the sign stands after his name, and as he is styled in an inscription at Tanis, "the Royal son Neḥsi," it is probable that he was in reality a black man, and a son of one of the kings of Egypt who led expeditions into the Sūdān, and that he had by some means established himself, by virtue of his descent, on the throne of Egypt.

SOURCE: E. A. Wallis Budge, *The Egyptian Sûdân: Its History and Monuments* (2 vols.; London: Kegan Paul, 1907), 1:559–60.

4 Black Egyptians: Soldiers

Another example of blacks in the service of the Egyptian state is provided by the Nubian mercenaries of Gebelein. The description given below refers to the First Intermediate Period, i.e., to the interregnum between the Old and Middle Kingdoms. Gebelein was a garrison town in Upper Egypt.

■

We know that during the later half of the Old Kingdom Nubians were employed by the Egyptians for domestic service . . . and in the army. . . . But the chief point of interest does not lie in the fact that the Nubians had stelae of their own; nor is it surprising, in a period when "foreigners had become people everywhere" * that these mercenaries became Egyptianized to the extent that they equipped themselves with funerary stelae made by the local craftsmen, and that they frequently adopted Egyptian names. What is more remarkable is the fact that those who could afford a funerary monument had themselves represented as Nubians, both in person and in costume. To explain why they retained their ethnic identity as fully as they did, it is perhaps only necessary to point out that Gebelein was not a very great distance from their homeland . . . it also seems likely that the Nubians enjoyed considerable prestige among the Upper Egyptians at Gebelein on account of their prowess as hunters and warriors, and accordingly would have taken some pride in showing themselves as they actually looked. . . .

* The ancient Egyptians regarded only themselves as "people"; "foreigners" became "people" by being Egyptianized. ED.

We are, in fact, reasonably sure that Nubians were employed as mercenaries by virtually every group that took part in the struggles preceding Egypt's reunification, but there is no indication that they were anywhere so well established as they were at Gebelein.

SOURCE: Henry George Fischer, "The Nubian Mercenaries of Gebelein during the First Intermediate Period," *Kush* (1961), 9:76–78 (extracts).

5 Herodotus on Egypt

Of all the references in classical literature that bear on the problem of race in ancient Egypt, the most important, and certainly the most frequently cited, are contained in the Second Book of the *History* of Herodotus of Halicarnassus. Herodotus wrote his *History* about 450 B.C. He visited Egypt, and thus had the advantage of personal observation; however, his knowledge of Egyptian history was derived almost entirely from priests of the local religion, and some authorities claim that these men exaggerated the glories of their country's past in order to impress an unsuspecting foreigner. On the other hand, modern scholars are continually being surprised at how often their researches confirm the general accuracy of Herodotus' observations on the Mediterranean world he knew.

■

The Egyptians, they said, were the first to discover the solar year, and to portion out its course into twelve parts. They obtained this knowledge from the stars. . . . The Egyptians, they went on to affirm, first brought into use the names of the twelve gods, which the Greeks adopted from them; and first erected altars, images, and temples to the Gods; and also first engraved upon stone the figures of animals. In most of these cases they proved to me that what they said was true. And they told me that the first man who ruled over Egypt was Mên, and that in his time all Egypt, except the Thebaic canton, was a marsh. . . .

The following tale is commonly told in Egypt concerning the oracle of Dodôna in Greece, and that of Ammon in Libya. My informants on the point were the priests of Jupiter at Thebes. They said "that two of the sacred women were once carried off from Thebes by the Phoenicians, and that the story went that one of them was sold into Libya, and the other into Greece, and these women were the first founders of the oracles in the two countries." On my inquiring how they came to know so exactly what became of the women, they answered, "that diligent search had been made after them at the time, but that it had not been found possible to discover where they were; afterwards, however, they received the information which they had given me."

This was what I heard from the priests at Thebes; at Dodôna, however, the women who deliver the oracles relate the matter as follows: "Two black doves flew away from Egyptian Thebes, and while one directed its flight to Libya, the other came to them. She alighted on an oak, and sitting there began to speak with a human voice, and told them that on the spot where she was, there should henceforth be an oracle of Jove. . . ."

The Dodoneans called the women doves because they were foreigners, and seemed to them to make a noise like birds. After a while the dove spoke with a human voice, because the women, whose foreign talk had previously sounded to them like the chattering of a bird, acquired the power of speaking what they could understand. For how can it be conceived possible that a dove should really speak with the voice of a man? Lastly, by calling the dove black the Dodoneans indicated that the woman was an Egyptian. . . .

Next, they [i.e., the priests at Thebes] read me from a papyrus the names of three hundred and thirty monarchs, who (they said) were [Mên's] successors upon the throne. In this number of generations there were eighteen Ethiopian kings, and one queen who was a native; all the rest were kings and Egyptians. . . .

There can be no doubt that the Colchians are an Egyptian race. Before I heard any mention of the fact from others, I had remarked it myself. After the thought had struck me, I made enquiries on the subject both in Colchis and in Egypt, and I found that the Colchians had a more distinct recollection of the Egyptians, than the Egyptians had of them. Still the Egyptians said that they believed the Colchians to be descended from the army of Sesostris. My own conjectures were founded, first, on the fact that they are black-skinned and have woolly hair, which certainly amounts to but little since several other nations are so too; but further and more especially, on the circumstance that the Colchians, the Egyptians, and the Ethiopians, are the only nations who have practiced circumcision from the earliest times. . . . I will add a further proof of the identity of the Egyptians and the Colchians. These two nations weave their linen in exactly the same way, and this is a way entirely unknown to the rest of the world; they also in their whole mode of life and in their language resemble one another.

SOURCE: George Rawlinson, ed. and trans., *History of Herodotus* (4 vols.; London: Murray, 1880), 2:4, 54, 55, 57, 100, 102, 104, 105 (extracts).

ETHIOPIA

6 "The Customs of the Ethiopians"

The civilization of Kush in Nubia was centered first on Napata and later on a more southerly capital at Meroë. It flourished for more than a thousand years. Though subjected to a strong Egyptian cultural imprint during the early centuries of its existence, it became a distinctively African civilization—the oldest, next to Egypt, in the continent's history.

Today, we refer to this civilization as "Kushite" or "Meroitic." To the Greeks and Romans, however, all black- and dark-skinned races living in Africa were "Ethiopians." The people described in the extracts printed below were not inhabitants of the region now known as Ethiopia, but rather of Meroë, capital of Kush.

Diodorus Siculus, or Diodorus of Sicily, wrote a history of the world covering the period from the beginning of time to 59 B.C. His comments on "the Ethiopians," which appear in Book 3 of his *Library of History,* were derived partly from older authors, including Herodotus, Hecataeus of Abdera, and Agatharchides of Cnidus, and partly from his own contacts with Africans he met in the Nile Valley during his visit to Egypt in 60–57 B.C.; but mostly they were based on information supplied to him by Egyptian priests. Many scholars believe that Diodorus accepted too uncritically what the priests told him, and did not understand their motives for telling him what they did. By the time he visited Egypt the priestly class there had lost most of its power. It looked back, somewhat wistfully, to a time when kings had been better supporters of the traditional Egyptian religion than, in the Hellenized Egypt of the first century B.C., they had become. What the priests provided to Diodorus, it has been said, was "a blend of obsolete practices at Meroë and reliable memories of the reign of the Nubian kings who had conquered Egypt in the name of Amun and whose piety was legendary." [4]

Nevertheless, the account that Diodorus gives of "the Ethiopians" is important on two counts. It is the most categorical statement in classical literature of the pre-eminence of black Africans as "the first of all men." And it is the source most frequently cited by those who claim that Africa south of the Sahara exerted a decisive influence on Egypt, and hence on Greece and Rome, in the fields of religion and culture.

■

1. . . . In this present Book we shall . . . describe the Ethiopians. . . .

2. Now the Ethiopians, as historians relate, were the first of all men and the proofs of this statement, they say, are manifest. For that they did not come into their land as immigrants from abroad but were natives of it and so justly bear the name of "autochthones" is, they maintain, conceded by practically all men; furthermore, that those who dwell beneath the noonday sun were, in all likelihood, the first to be generated by the earth, is clear to all; since, inasmuch as it was the warmth of the sun which, at the generation of the universe, dried up the earth when it was still wet and impregnated it with life, it is reasonable to suppose that the region which was nearest the sun was the first to bring forth living creatures. And they say that they were the first to be taught to honor the gods and to hold sacrifices and processions and festivals and the other rites by which men honor the deity; and that in consequence their piety has been published abroad among all men, and it is generally held that the sacrifices practiced among the Ethiopians are those which are the most pleasing to heaven. As witness to this they call upon the poet who is perhaps the oldest and certainly the most venerated among the

Greeks; for in the *Iliad* * he represents both Zeus and the rest of the gods with him as absent on a visit to Ethiopia to share in the sacrifices and the banquet which were given annually by the Ethiopians for all the gods together:

> For Zeus had yesterday to Ocean's bounds
> Set forth to feast with Ethiop's faultless men,
> And he was followed there by all the gods.

And they state that, by reason of their piety towards the deity, they manifestly enjoy the favor of the gods, inasmuch as they have never experienced the rule of an invader from abroad; for from all time they have enjoyed a state of freedom and of peace one with another, and although many and powerful rulers have made war upon them, not one of these has succeeded in his undertaking.

3. Cambyses,† for instance, they say, who made war upon them with a great force, both lost all his army and was himself exposed to the greatest peril; Semiramis also, who through the magnitude of her undertakings and achievements has become renowned, after advancing a short distance into Ethiopia gave up her campaign against the whole nation; and Heracles and Dionysus, although they visited all the inhabited earth, failed to subdue the Ethiopians alone who dwell above Egypt, both because of the piety of these men and because of the insurmountable difficulties involved in the attempt.

They say that the Egyptians are colonists sent out by the Ethiopians, Osiris having been the leader of the colony. For, speaking generally, what is now Egypt, they maintain, was not land but sea when in the beginning the universe was being formed; afterwards, however, as the Nile during the times of its inundation carried down the mud from Ethiopia, land was gradually built up from the deposit. Also the statement that all the land of the Egyptians is alluvial silt deposited by the river receives the clearest proof, in their opinion, from what takes place at the outlets of the Nile; for as each year new mud is continually gathered together at the mouths of the river, the sea is observed being thrust back by the deposited silt and the land receiving the increase. And the larger part of the customs of the Egyptians are, they hold, Ethiopian, the colonists still preserving their ancient manners. For instance, the belief that their kings are

* Book 1, 423–24. TRANS. † See Herodotus, 3, 25. TRANS.

gods, the very special attention which they pay to their burials, and many other matters of a similar nature are Ethiopian practices, while the shapes of their statues and the forms of their letters are Ethiopian; for of the two kinds of writing * which the Egyptians have, that which is known as "popular" (demotic) is learned by everyone, while that which is called "sacred" † is understood only by the priests of the Egyptians, who learn it from their fathers as one of the things which are not divulged, but among the Ethiopians everyone uses these forms of letters. Furthermore, the orders of the priests, they maintain, have much the same position among both peoples; for all are clean ‡ who are engaged in the service of the gods, keeping themselves shaven, like the Ethiopian priests, and having the same dress and form of staff, which is shaped like a plow and is carried by their kings, who wear high felt hats which end in a knob at the top and are circled by the serpents which they call asps; and this symbol appears to carry the thought that it will be the lot of those who shall dare to attack the king to encounter death-carrying stings.§ Many other things are also told by them concerning their own antiquity and the colony which they sent out that became the Egyptians. . . .

5. As for the customs of the Ethiopians, not a few of them are thought to differ greatly from those of the rest of mankind, this being especially true of those which concern the selection of their kings. The priests, for instance, first choose out the noblest men from their own number, and whichever one from this group the god may select, as he is borne about in a procession in accordance with a certain practice of theirs, him the multitude take for their king; and straightway it both worships and honors him like a god, believing that the sovereignty has been entrusted to him by Divine Providence. And the king who has been thus chosen both follows a regimen which has been fixed in accordance with the laws and performs all his other deeds in accordance with the ancestral custom, according neither favor nor punishment to anyone contrary to the usage which has been approved among them from the beginning. It is also a cus-

* There were, in fact, three kinds of Egyptian writing: 1) the hieroglyphic, 2) the hieratic, and 3) the demotic. Like Herodotus, Diodorus does not distinguish between the first two. TRANS.

† Now commonly called the "hieratic." TRANS.

‡ I.e., they observe certain rites and practices of purification. TRANS.

§ The snake was the sacred uraeus, the symbol of the Northern Kingdom. TRANS.

tom of theirs that the king shall put no one of his subjects to death, not even if a man shall have been condemned to death and is considered deserving of punishment, but that he shall send to the transgressor one of his attendants bearing a token of death; and the guilty person, on seeing the warning, immediately retires from his home and removes himself from life. Moreover, for a man to flee from his own into a neighboring country and thus by moving away from his native land to pay the penalty of his transgression as is the custom among the Greeks, is permissible under no circumstances. . . .

6. Of all their customs the most astonishing is that which obtains in connection with the death of their kings. For the priests at Meroë who spend their time in the worship of the gods and the rites which do them honor, being the greatest and most powerful order, whenever the idea comes to them, dispatch a messenger to the king with orders that he die. For the gods, they add, have revealed this to them, and it must be that the command of the immortals should in no wise be disregarded by one of mortal frame. And this order they accompany with other arguments, such as are accepted by a simple-minded nature, which has been bred in a custom that is both ancient and difficult to eradicate and which knows no argument that can be set in opposition to commands enforced by no compulsion. Now in former times the kings would obey the priests, having been overcome, not by arms nor by force, but because their reasoning powers had been put under a constraint by their very superstition; but during the reign of the second Ptolemy the king of the Ethiopians, Ergamenes, who had had a Greek education and had studied philosophy, was the first to have the courage to disdain the command. For assuming a spirit which became the position of a king he entered with his soldiers into the unapproachable place where stood, as it turned out, the golden shrine of the Ethiopians, put the priests to the sword, and after abolishing this custom thereafter ordered affairs after his own will.

SOURCE: C. H. Oldfather, trans., *Diodorus Siculus, Library of History* (Cambridge, Mass.: Harvard University Press, 1935), Book 3 (extracts).

7 The Triumph of Piankhi

In 1862 a pink granite slab, 18 meters high, was discovered in the ruins of the temple of Gebel Barkel (Napata) in Nubia. Now in the Cairo Museum, it has become known as the Piankhi Stela.* It describes the campaign by means of which the forces of Piankhi, King of Kush, won control over Lower Egypt.

The sequence of events that culminated in the "Ethiopian domination" in Egypt began in the mid-eighth century B.C. Piankhi's father, Kashta, invaded Upper Egypt from Kush and drove the ruling Pharaoh, Osorkon III, north into the Delta. When Piankhi succeeded Kashta in about 751, he dispatched an army to complete the conquest. By the time of Kashta and Piankhi a united Egypt existed only in name, and the Kushite troops were able to overcome the princes of the Delta (or the "Northland" as the inscriptions of the Piankhi Stela have it) one by one. The final stages of the operation were commanded by Piankhi himself. When the last of the Delta princes, Tefnakhte of Sais, made his submission, Piankhi was master of the whole of Egypt. After his death he was recognized by the state historians of Egypt as a pharaoh of the XXIIId Dynasty.

The Ethiopian domination begun by Piankhi continued until the end of the XXVth Dynasty—with one short break because Bocchoris, the sole ruler of the XXIVth, was not a Kushite—a total period of nearly a century. The early years of the XXVth Dynasty were fairly peaceful. But by the time of the dynasty's fourth pharaoh, Taharka (Tirhakah in the Bible), the threat of the rising power of Assyria began to be felt in the Nile Delta. Taharka and his successor, Tanutamon, were able to resist a number of Assyrian invasions, but in 667 B.C. the great conqueror, Ashurbanipal, drove the Ethiopians out of both Lower and Upper Egypt, sacked Thebes, and established his

* A *stela,* or stele, is an upright stone slab embellished with carving and inscriptions. In ancient Egypt steles were often used by rulers and others to record their achievements for the benefit of posterity. Ed.

own rule. From this time onward the kingdom of Kush was confined to Nubia.

■

Year 21, first month of the first season, under the majesty of the King of Upper and Lower Egypt, Meriamon-Piankhi, living forever.

Command which my majesty speaks: "Hear of what I did, more than the ancestors. I am a king, divine emanation, living image of Atum, who came forth from the womb, adorned as a ruler, of whom those greater than he were afraid; whose father knew, and whose mother recognized that he would rule in the egg, the Good God, beloved of the gods, achieving with his hands, Meriamon-Piankhi. . . .

Then his majesty sent an army to Egypt, charging them earnestly: "Delay not day nor night, as at a game of draughts; but fight ye on sight. Force battle upon him from afar. If he says to the infantry and chariotry of another city, 'Hasten'; then ye shall abide until his army comes, that ye may fight as he says. But if his allies be in another city, then let one hasten to them; these princes, whom he has brought for his support: Libyans and favorite soldiers, force battle upon them first. . . . When ye arrive at Thebes, before Karnak, ye shall enter into the water, ye shall bathe in the river, ye shall dress in fine linen; unstring the bow, loosen the arrow. Let not the chief boast as a mighty man; there is no strength to the mighty without him (Amon). He maketh the weak-armed into the strong-armed, so that multitudes flee from the feeble, and one alone taketh a thousand men. Sprinkle yourselves with the water of his altars, sniff the ground before him. Say ye to him, 'Give to us the way, that we may fight in the shadow of thy sword. As for the generation whom thou hast sent out, when its attack occurs, multitudes flee before it.' "

Then they threw themselves upon their bellies before his majesty, saying: "It is thy name which endues us with might, and thy counsel is the mooring-post of thy army; thy bread is in our bellies on every march, thy beer quenches our thirst. It is thy valor that giveth us might, and there is strength at the remembrance of thy name; for no army prevails whose commander is a coward. Who is thy equal therein? Thou art a victorious king, achieving with his hands, chief of the work of war."

They sailed downstream, they arrived at Thebes, they did according to all that his majesty had said. [Piankhi's army wins battles against the "men of the Northland" at Thebes, Heracleopolis, and Per-peg, and besieges Hermopolis.]

They sent a report to the majesty of the King of Upper and Lower Egypt, Meriamon-Piankhi, given life, on every conflict which they had fought, and on every victory of his majesty.

Then his majesty was enraged thereat like a panther, saying: "Have they allowed a remnant of the army of the Northland to remain? allowing him that went forth of them to go forth, to tell of his campaign? not causing their death, in order to destroy the last of them? I swear: as Re loves me! As my father Amon favors me! I will myself go northward, that I may destroy that which he has done, that I may make him turn back from fighting, forever. . . ."

Then the army, which was there in Egypt, heard of the wrath which his majesty felt toward them. Then they fought against Per-Mezed of the Oxyrhynchite nome, they took it like a flood of water, and they sent to his majesty; but his heart was not satisfied therewith.

Then they fought against Tetehen, great in might. They found it filled with soldiers, with every valiant man of the Northland. Then the battering-ram was employed against it, its wall was overthrown, and a great slaughter was made among them, of unknown number; also the son of the chief of Me, Tefnakhte. Then they sent to his majesty concerning it, but his heart was not satisfied therewith.

Then they fought against Hatbenu, its interior was breached, the army of his majesty entered into it. Then they sent to his majesty, but his heart was not satisfied therewith. . . .

First month of the first season, ninth day; his majesty went northward to Thebes, and completed the Feast of Amon at the Feast of Opet. His majesty sailed northward to the city of the Hare nome (Hermopolis); his majesty came forth from the cabin of the ship, the horses were yoked up, the chariot was mounted, the terror of his majesty reached to the end of the Asiatics, every heart was heavy with the fear of him. [King Namlot, one of the princes of the Northland, surrenders Hermopolis to Piankhi.].

His majesty proceeded to the house of King Namlot, he entered every chamber of the king's house, his treasury and his magazines. He caused that there be brought to him the king's wives and king's daughters; they saluted his majesty in the fashion of women, but his majesty turned not his face to them.

His majesty proceeded to the stables of the horses and the quarters of the foals. When he saw that they had suffered hunger, he said: "I swear, as Re loves me, and as my nostrils are rejuvenated with life, it is more grievous in my heart that my horses have suffered hunger, than any evil deed that thou hast done, in the prosecution of thy desire. . . ." [The remaining kings of the Northland surrender to Piankhi and swear allegiance to him.]

Then the ships were laden with silver, gold, copper, clothing, and everything of the Northland, every product of Syria, and all sweet woods of God's Land. His majesty sailed upstream, with glad heart, the shores on his either side were jubilating. West and east, they seized the [effaced], jubilating in the presence of his majesty; singing and jubilating as they said: "O mighty, mighty Ruler, Piankhi, O mighty Ruler; thou comest, having gained the dominion of the Northland. Thou makest bulls into women. Happy the heart of the mother who bore thee, and the man who begat thee. Those who are in the valley give to her praise, the cow that hath borne a bull. Thou art unto eternity, thy might endureth, O Ruler, beloved of Thebes."

SOURCE: James Henry Breasted, *Ancient Records of Egypt* (5 vols.; Chicago: University of Chicago Press, 1906–7), 4:418–44 (extracts; footnotes omitted).

AFRICANS IN CLASSICAL ANTIQUITY

8 Color and Race in Greece and Rome

In classical Greece and Rome color consciousness existed, but it was not the overwhelming fact of life that it later became in the Christian West. Distinctions between different kinds of men were drawn, but these were based on categories like "civilized" and "uncivilized," and "Greeks" (and later "Romans") as against "barbarians."

Nor were Africans by any means singled out as especially barbarous. On the contrary they were thought of, at least initially, as favored of the gods and among the foremost of mankind.

Here is a recent summary of Greek and Roman attitudes toward Africans and Africa in ancient times.

■

The Greeks, of course, primarily through their special relationship with Egypt, were well acquainted with black- and brown-skinned peoples, and also knew much of other lands. Here again it is Herodotus who can provide us with further insights. In discussing the reasons for which, in his opinion, the Nile waters could not be formed of melted snow, he put forward three arguments, one of which was that in the land out of which the Nile flows "the natives of the country are black with the heat." The comment is interesting for two reasons. The first is that it confirms that in the fifth century B.C. the peoples who lived in those regions were indeed black. Today this may seem to us a truism. Yet in the tenth century B.C. the black Queen of Sheba (or Sabaea), from whom the Ethiopians claim descent, then ruled not in Africa, but over the southern part of the Arabian peninsula. The second is that the comment of Herodotus reveals something of his own belief—and presumably that of his Sophoclean contemporaries—concerning the reason for the difference in the color of men's skins. This belief was that skin color was due to environment, and not to any qualitative difference.

The Greeks, indeed, tended to divide humanity into two groups—Greeks and Barbarians. An expression of Greek sentiment on the subject of Barbarians—who were distinguished principally by being unacquainted with the Greek language—is to be found in the writings of Euripides, in which this passage occurs: "It accords with the fitness of things that Barbarians should be subject to Greeks, for Greeks are free men and Barbarians are slaves by nature." Although four out of five of the population of ancient Greece were slaves, the blacks among them were not sufficiently numerous to attract any particular attention. The criteria for enslavement remained mainly political or cultural, rather than physical. In that eotechnic age,* when wind, water, and muscle were the sole generators of power, slavery was considered a practical necessity, and knew no color line. . . .

The Greeks derived not only some proportion of their religion, but also their knowledge of astronomy from Kush and/or Ethiopia, via Egypt. It was the remoteness of Ethiopians and others that led to their being regarded as Barbarians. Who, whether black or white, being situated far from Greece could be regarded as other than unfortunate? The Greek poet Menander, writing of the unimportance of pedigree in comparison with moral qualities, says:

> The man whose natural bent is good,
> He, mother, he, though Aethiop, is nobly born.
> A Scyth, you say? Pest! Anarcharsis was a Scyth!

* Lewis Mumford's term for the age when wind was the main source of power.

The geographer Ptolemy placed the "uncivilized" blacks who lived beyond Napata and Kush at one pole, and Scythians at the other. The uncultured habits of these tribes, he said, were attributable to the fact that in their homes they were continually oppressed by the heat, just as the behavior of the savage Scyths was due to the fact that they had to endure constant cold.

The black Africans were also known to the Greeks as soldiers who had fought against them in both the Trojan and the Persian wars. (Memnon, who had fought on the Trojan side, and who killed Antilochus, son of Nestor, and was himself killed by Achilles, was an Ethiopian). Quintus of Smyrna wrote that the Ethiopians at Troy excelled in battle. Certainly African troops were widely used as auxiliaries in the ancient world. The high esteem in which Odysseus held Eurybates of the "woolly hair" and the "sable skin" and the rank that he gave him as one of his heralds is also worth noting.

As in Egypt, so in Greece, depictions of both white and black individuals have come down to us from the artists of ancient days, although such Greek examples are considerably less numerous than those from Egypt. Some of the coinage of Phocis, Delphi, Lesbos, and Athens bears the head of a black African who, according to some, was Delphos, the founder of Delphi, himself.

SKIN COLOR AND THE ROMANS

It was in the Roman civilization, rather than in the Egyptian or Greek, that the greater degree of international contact, both at home and abroad, appears to have taken place. The reputation of the Roman Empire has continued to exercise a compelling influence upon the pattern of history down to our own times. Have not certain Frenchmen, Britons, Italians, and Americans of our own century tended to view their respective nations as the destined "heirs of Rome"? The puissance of Rome's example is due, in effect, to its universalism.

How, then, could an Empire claiming universality not have knowledge of even the remotest places or peoples? Such knowledge, that is, as lay within its power to acquire. Northern Africa, from Mauritania to Egypt, had, by 30 B.C., become subject to Roman rule. Further south and east, however, the traces of the limits of Roman power and knowledge are less discernible. But the Romans are known to have been more knowledgeable about black Africa than was previously suspected. As Richard Jobson, the seventeenth-century English trader, eloquently commented, "The Romans, careful Relaters of their great victories, doe speak little of the interior parts of Affrica." The Carthaginians, in earlier times, did much to bar the trans-Sahara trade to them. Later, however, in the first century A.D., after the reduction of Carthage, and after the conclusion of an alliance between the Romans and their former enemies, the Libyan tribe of the Garamantes, more than one Roman expedition marched south across the desert. Suetonius Paulinus is believed to have reached the headwaters of streams that are tributary to the Niger itself.[5] How far Septimus Flaccus penetrated into the "country of the black men" nobody can now tell. Julius Maternus and his men, accompanied by the King of the Garamantes, proceeded "toward the Aethiopians"; after four months of traveling they arrived at Agisymba, "a district or province of the Ethiopians where rhinoceroses congregate," which has been identified with the Lake Chad area.

It has been suggested that the custom, found in some parts of West Africa, of constructing an "atrium," or large entrance hall, in the houses of the more important personalities, as well as the widespread West African custom of offering libations to ancestors, have much in common with Roman practice. The fashion of wearing sandals and a cloth draped like a toga, followed by Ashanti and some other West African groups, provides an even more obvious parallel. Roman beads are also reported to have been discovered in the tombs of the Ashanti kings.

On the Nile the Romans were for a relatively long period in communication with Kush, where, in 23 B.C., the Roman general Petronius conducted a punitive campaign after the Kushites had raided Philae and Aswan and pulled down the statues of the Emperor Augustus. A bronze head of Augustus was found hidden beneath the floor of the former royal palace of Meroë, once the capital of Kush, about fifty years ago. The Emperor Nero also sent two centurions to visit the Sudan and to report to him whether it was worth conquering. After reportedly traveling the entire length of the Nile, the centurions returned to Rome and told Nero that it was not. . . .

In Rome, and in the Empire itself, we hear little of any repugnance for dark-skinned Africans. Rome, the greatest city of the ancient world, was also its melting pot. Herodian, writing in the third century A.D., called the population of Rome "variegated and commingled," and related how the Emperor Constantine stared at the sight of the Roman people, commenting on "how swiftly every type of man on earth congregates at Rome." "The hub of the globe," "the inn of the world,"—such were the expressions used to describe the Rome of those days. Cicero himself stated that immigration "overflowed Rome and blended her blood with that of every race" of the ancient world.

Ludwig Friedlander writes that

> At Rome the gabble of a hundred speeches might be heard, the shapes and garb of every race rubbed shoulders. Moorish slaves led elephants from out of the Emperor's stables. There a troop of blond Germans of the Emperor's Life Guards were exercising in gleaming armor. The Egyptians, with shaven heads, in sweeping linen robes, were carrying the goddess Isis in procession. Behind a Greek professor a young Nubian was carrying his scrolls of books. Oriental princes . . . tattooed savages from Britain staring their eyes out at the marvels of the new world all about them.[6]

And again:

> Roman courtesans received according to Martial visits from Parthians, Germans, Cilicians, Cappadocians, Egyptians, Nubians, Jews, Dacians, and Alani. At Augustus' spectacle of a naval battle (2 B.C.), Ovid says the whole world was in Rome; at the consecration of the Flavian amphitheater according to Martial, spectators foregathered from the farthest regions, Sarmatians, Sigambians, Arabians, Sabaeans, and Aethiopians.

Comparing the Roman Empire to empires of our own day, we must conclude that the barriers of color, language, and habits we know today were unknown in the Roman world. Similarly, just as barriers exist in modern times which were not there before, so in the ancient world forces for unity were at work which today have grown fainter under the insistent pressure of modern technological culture with its scarcely concealed impatience with the survivals of past eras. Lord Bryce . . . sensed a connection between African tribal customs and those of the ancient world. "How thankful we should be, we men of the nineteenth century, if a Roman had taken the trouble fully to investigate the habits of our Celtic forefathers!" he remarked to H. A. Junod, the Swiss anthropologist. Leo Frobenius, in his *Voice of Africa,* also noted similarities between the religion of the Yorubas of West Africa and the pre-Christian religion of the ancient world. Like the Etruscans, the Yoruba built their temples on a plan divided into sixteen different quarters, and divided the horizon into sixteen sections for the purpose of divination. Sir James Frazer was also among those who first noted the close connection between ancient classical studies and modern anthropology. Contemporary educators in West Africa have more than once noted the ease with which their African students have understood passages in the Greek classics which have given considerable trouble to European or American schoolchildren. The metaphysical framework, no less than the technical one, was similar, and the imbalance of our own days had not yet occurred.

Yet if Rome did not know domination based on color, it knew and practiced domination based on conquest. Slavery in Rome, as in Greece, was an accepted norm—and yet was quite different in character to that which, over a thousand years later, sprang up in Europe and the Americas.

Under the Roman slave system a large proportion of physicians and sculptors were slaves, as also were some distinguished authors, not to speak of lesser literary lights, many imported from Greece. The well-known proposal that slaves should be distinguished by special dress, which was rejected lest they should become overly conscious of their overwhelming numerical strength and plot to seize the city, is also additional evidence that slaves were not marked out by color. Montesquieu, in the eighteenth century, commented on the unselective aspect of slavery in Rome. "There was a great circulation of men from all the universe," he wrote. "Rome received them as slaves and sent them back Romans."

As in Greece, slaves were to be found of every skin color. Nobody suggested that it should be otherwise; nor did anyone suggest that a system that was so self-evidently necessary to civilization at that time be abolished.

So far as the Roman Empire was concerned, men with dark skins as well as those with white could aspire to the most eminent of positions. Septimus Severus, Emperor of Rome from A.D. 193–211, who was born in Tripolitania, is said to have been at least partially of black African origin. He died at York, in England, where he had been reorganizing the Roman defenses against the Scottish tribes.

His son Caracalla, whose mother was Syrian, succeeded him, and is credited with having done much to make possible the granting of Roman citizenship to men of all origins, instead of on the more restrictive basis previously practiced.

In the religious domain, Egyptian religion, in pre-Christian times, was immensely popular in Rome. Among the Christians a most notable African was Saint Augustine, himself a Berber, who was born in Carthage.

There can, in sum, remain little doubt that in antiquity skin color was by no means invested with the emotional significance that has in more recent times become attached to it. One would hardly wish to claim that antiquity constituted, from the social point of view, a "golden age." Despite its more renowned virtues and values it was anything but that. But the curse of acute color-consciousness, attended by all the raw passions and social problems that cluster around it—that, at least, antiquity was spared.

SOURCE: Keith Irvine, *The Rise of the Colored Races* (New York: Norton, 1970), pp. 14–19.

9 Roman Knowledge of Black Africa

By the time of the Roman Empire the outside world's knowledge of sub-Saharan Africa was increasing rapidly. North Africa and Egypt were both included within the Empire's frontiers, and it was natural that prudent and ambitious officials in these areas should direct expeditions southward. One of these expeditions, as pointed out above, may have reached the Niger.

Nevertheless, the extent of reliable and factual knowledge of Black Africa possessed by the Romans should not be exaggerated. When they speculated about the lands beyond the limes, they tended to give their imaginations full rein. The following extract comes from a compendium of scientific and geographic information compiled by a Roman encyclopedist, Pliny the Elder, in the first century A.D. This work, the *Historia Naturalis,* retained its authority well into the European Middle Ages and beyond. It, and books like it, therefore helped to mold the attitude of the Western world toward sub-Saharan Africa for over a thousand years. When Shakespeare has Othello speak of "men whose heads do grow beneath their shoulders" inhabiting Africa, it is obvious that his image is derived from Pliny's description of the "Blemmyae" in the *Historia Naturalis.*

■

If we pass through the interior of Africa in a southerly direction, beyond the Gaetuli, we shall find, first of all the Liby-Egyptians, and then the country where the Leucaethiopians dwell.* Beyond these are the Nigritae, nations of Aethiopia, so called from the river Nigris, the Gymnetes,† surnamed Parusii, and, on the very margin of the ocean, the Perorsi. . . . After passing all these places, there are vast deserts towards the east until we come to the Garamantes,‡ the Augylae, and the Troglodytae. . . . The river Nigris has the same characteristics as the Nile; it produces the calamus, the papyrus, and just the same animals, and it rises at the same seasons of the year. Its source is between the Tarraelian Aethiopians and the Oecalicae. Magium, the city of the latter people, has been placed by some writers amid the deserts, and, next to them the Atlantes; then the Aegipani, the Blemmyae,§ the Gamphasantes, the Satyri, and the Himantopodes.

The Atlantes, if we believe what is said, have lost all characteristics of humanity; for there is no mode of distinguishing each other among them by names, and as they look upon the rising and the setting sun, they give utterance to direful imprecations against it, as being deadly to themselves and their lands; nor are they visited with dreams, like the rest of mortals. The Troglodytae make excavations in the earth, which serve them for dwellings; the flesh of serpents is their food; they have no articulate voice, but only utter a kind of squeaking noise; and thus are they utterly destitute of all means of communication by language. The Garamantes have no institution of marriage among them, and live in promiscuous concubinage with their women. The Augylae worship no deities but the gods of the in-

* Or, "white Aethiopians." TRANS.

† From Gk. *gymnos,* "naked." TRANS.

‡ Inhabitants of the region today called the Fezzan. TRANS.

§ A nomadic people, frequently met with in the classical accounts. They lived in and near Nubia. TRANS.

fernal regions. The Gamphasantes, who go naked, and are unacquainted with war, hold no intercourse whatever with strangers. The Blemmyae are said to have no heads, their mouths and eyes being seated in their breasts. The Satyri,* beyond their figure, have nothing in common with the manners of the human race, and the form of the Aegipani † is such as is commonly represented in paintings. The Himantopodes are a race of people with feet resembling thongs, upon which they move along by nature with a serpentine, crawling kind of gait. The Pharusii, descended from the ancient Persians, are said to have been the companions of Hercules when on his expedition to the Hesperides. Beyond the above, I have met with nothing relative to Africa worthy of mention.

SOURCE: Caius Plinius Secundus, *The Natural History* (John Bostock and H. T. Riley, trans. 6 vols.; London: Bohn, 1855–57), 1: Book 5, ch. 8 (extracts; some footnotes omitted).

10. The Individual African Contribution

Consideration was given above to the degree of influence exerted by Black Africa on Egypt, and hence on the civilization of the rest of the ancient world. Some of the difficulties of interpretation presented by this problem were also pointed out. It is even harder to estimate the extent of the contribution to antiquity of individual Africans. Precisely because of the lack of a color bar in Greece and Rome, a man was valued for himself and his achievements rather than by reference to his country or continent of origin. The question of his race did not necessarily arise.

The fact that he was colored did not, for example hinder the career of the comic playwright, Terence. Born in Carthage and brought to Rome as a slave while still a child, Terence (Publius Terentius Afer) obtained an excellent education in both Greek and Latin and established himself as the greatest man of the theater of

* So-called from their supposed resemblance in form to the satyrs of ancient mythology who were represented as little hairy men with horns, long ears, and tails. TRANS.

† Creatures that were half-goat, half-man. TRANS.

his day. That he was not only born in Africa but was in fact black is suggested both by his cognomen, "Afer" (the African), which would not have been given to a white man, and by the fact that the historian Suetonius described him as *colore fusco,* that is, "swarthy" or "dark-complexioned." He acquired an estate, married his daughter to a Roman knight, and died, a successful man, in 159 B.C.[7] The contemporary records refer to him as a playwright, not as an African or black playwright.

The standard work on the African contribution to the Greek and Roman worlds is *Blacks in Antiquity,* by Frank M. Snowden, chairman of the classics department at Howard University. The conclusion to this work is reproduced below.

■

The first Ethiopians to appear in Greek literature were Homer's blameless Ethiopians. Dear to the gods and renowned for their piety and justice, Ethiopians enjoyed the favor of divine visits. High-souled Ethiopians, according to Hesiod, were among the descendants of the almighty son of Kronos. Xenophanes, the first European to contrast the physical characteristics of Negroes and whites, described Ethiopians and Thracians as he saw them and implied nothing as to the superiority or inferiority of either, whether physical, aesthetic, mental, or moral. Like Xenophanes, the artists who fashioned Janiform Negro-white heads depicted accurately what they saw. In short, those Greeks who first described and depicted dark or Negroid peoples did so without bias.

The early, unbiased approach toward colored peoples adumbrated what was to follow. Long after the Ethiopian was divested of any romanticization stemming from a mythological aura and long after he was well known to the Greeks and Romans, whether in Africa or in various parts of the classical world, antipathy because of color did not arise. The Greco-Roman view of blacks was no romantic idealization of distant, unknown peoples but a fundamental rejection of color as a criterion for evaluating men.

Scientists, in their environmental explanation of the origin of racial differences, developed no special theory as to inferior dark or black peoples and attached no stigma to color. The Thracian-Ethiopian contrast of Xenophanes became, in the hands of the environmentalists and other observers on racial differences, a Scythian-Ethiopian *topos*. This antithesis provided a medium for statements of conviction that race is of no consequence in judging man's worth. Though a man comes from faraway Scythia or distant Ethiopia, though a man is physically different from the Greek or Roman as the blackest Ethiopian or the blondest Scythian, such distinctions are trifles. It is intrinsic merit, says Menander, that counts. Similarly, the early Church embraced both Scythian and Ethiopian. It was the *Ethiopian,* the blackest and remotest of men, who was selected as an important symbol of Christianity's mission—by Ethiopians, all nations were signified; Christ came into the world to make blacks white.

That classical and early Christian views of Ethiopians were no theoretical pronouncements is amply demonstrated by the experience of Ethiopians in many regions of the Greco-Roman world. The Ethiopian was no rarity among classical peoples. Whether he came as slave, prisoner of war, ambassador, or adventurer, he experienced no exclusion because of his color. If Ethiopians were slaves, manumission and a career open to talent were available to them in the same way as to others of foreign extraction. If the Ethiopian excelled as charioteer, pugilist, or actor, he was celebrated by the poet or depicted by the artist. In fact, for centuries the black man appealed to artists who found in him an attractive model. Neither servile descent nor humble origin was a barrier to acceptance in artistic or literary circles. A former slave from Carthage, the dark- or black-skinned Terence received a social and literary recognition comparable to that later accorded Horace, whose father was a freedman, probably of Italian stock. References to race mixture of blacks and whites were not accompanied by strictures on miscegenation. Ethiopian blood was interfused with that of others. The Ethiopian worshipped Isis at the same shrine as other *Isiaci.* He was sought as a brother in Christ. Both the devotees of Isis and the converts of Christianity continued the tradition of Homer's gods, who knew no color line.

How much of the Greco-Roman attitude toward Ethiopians was a result of the original unprejudiced approach to colored peoples reflected in the environmental explanations of racial differences; how much is to be attributed to understandings developed through contacts between blacks and whites over many centuries; how much is to be explained by the fact that darker races were not the only or the largest part of enslaved peoples; or how much may have derived from the refusal of Christians to recognize color as a criterion for acceptance as a brother in Christ—all this is difficult to determine. There is nothing in the evidence, however, to suggest that the ancient Greek or Roman established color as an obstacle to integration into society.

The relationship of blacks and whites continues to be a critical problem of the twentieth century. Not without meaning for this vital question is the experience of the Ethiopian in classical antiquity—the first major encounter in European records of blacks in a predominantly white society. The Greeks and Romans counted black peoples in.

SOURCE: Frank M. Snowden, *Blacks in Antiquity: Ethiopians in the Greco-Roman Experience* (Cambridge, Mass.: Harvard University Press, 1970), pp. 216–18.

Part One

AFRICANS IN ASIA

THE MIDDLE EAST BEFORE ISLAM

11 The Stairway at Persepolis

The Apadama or audience hall at Persepolis, the capital of the Achaemenian kings of ancient Persia, was built about 470 B.C. The remains of the building still stand. Part of the decoration provided by Xerxes' sculptors for the stepped retaining walls ("stairways") of the terrace leading to the Apadana on its north and east sides consists of near-duplicate sets of pictorial bas-reliefs, one for each wall. Each set shows twenty-three groups of representatives greeting their ruler on the occasion of the festival associated with the vernal equinox. The representatives come from remote parts of the empire, and carry in their hands tribute and gifts typical of their homelands.[1]

The last group in each set depicts, quite unmistakably, Africans from south of the Sahara. Since no part of sub-Saharan Africa was ever within the Achaemenian Empire, the "Negroid" delegation leader of the description given below could not have been a tribute-bearer. He is likely to have been the head of a diplomatic mission, coming perhaps from Kush or "Ethiopia." [2] He would bear gifts, since present giving between rulers was customary in those days.

And an embassy from Africa to Persia would have had a point to it, since there were "Ethiopians" serving in Xerxes' army.[3] The following description is of the twenty-third panel on the eastern stairway (which is better preserved than the northern). This carving, made at Persepolis nearly two and a half millennia ago, is in all probability the oldest record of black Africans in Asia.

■

Delegation No. 23: The Ethiopians. *Eastern stairway* . . . Median usher. Unnamed delegation leader and two attendants with Negroid features and hair. All are bareheaded and wear skirt reaching from waist to ankles, with ribbed band along vertical edge suggesting embroidery or the like. Scarf with ribbed edge draped over leader's upper body and left shoulder; right shoulder and arm bare. Bands, perhaps connected with skirt, extend over both shoulders of two attendants; end of band projects from back of neck. Leader and first attendant wear stereotyped sandals provided with heel guard and two cross-straps connected by lengthwise strap; second attendant barefooted. Tribute: vessel with lid, problematical contents; elephant tusk carried on shoulder of second attendant, who in addition leads an okapi.

SOURCE: Erich F. Schmidt, *Persepolis. I: Structures. Reliefs. Inscriptions* (Chicago: University of Chicago Press, 1953), p. 90.

12 The Homeritae of Arabia Felix

For thousands of years southwestern Arabia, or the Yemen (the Romans called the region "Arabia Felix"), has had close links with the Horn of Africa. It was immigrants from the Yemen who, about the first century A.D., created the kingdom of Aksum in northern Ethiopia. By the mid-fourth century Aksum was strong enough to challenge and destroy the ancient Nubian empire of Meroë or Kush, and become the most powerful state on either side of the southern Red Sea. At this period the Aksumite kings often intervened, at times decisively, in the affairs of their south Arabian homeland.[4]

The most important of these interventions occurred in the sixth century A.D. King Kālēb (Caleb), or Amda, of Aksum—his Greek name was Elesbaas or Hellestheaeus (Hellestheaios)—sent a powerful expeditionary force against Dhu Nuwas, king of the Yemen, in the year 523. Dhu Nuwas belonged to the dynasty of the Himyarites which had united the independent states of southwestern Arabia under one rule in the third century. The Himyarites were known to the Greeks and Romans as the "Homeritae."

The following account of the Aksumite invasion of the Yemen is by the historian Procopius. Procopius was born in the late fifth century A.D. in Caesarea in Palestine. In 527 he moved to Constantinople and was appointed legal adviser and private secretary to Belisarius, commander of the armies of Justinian I, who ruled the Eastern Roman Empire from 527 to 565. Procopius was an eyewitness of Belisarius' campaigns in northern Africa, Italy, and Asia, and had an intimate knowledge of Eastern Roman diplomacy. He saw the Aksumite invasion of Arabia as simply one incident in the long struggle, then going on, between Rome and Persia. The Christians of Byzantium hoped to win the support of the Christians of Aksum and the Yemen against the pagan Persians, but in this they were to be disappointed.

■

Hellestheaeus, the king of the Aethiopians, who was a Christian and a most devoted adherent of this faith, discovered that a number of the Homeritae on the opposite mainland were oppressing the Christians there outrageously; many of these rascals were Jews, and many of them held in reverence the old faith which men of the present day call Hellenic. He therefore collected a fleet of ships and an army and came against them, and he conquered them in battle and slew both the king and many of the Homeritae. He then set up in his stead a Christian king, a Homerite by birth, by name Esimiphaeus, and, after ordaining that he should pay tribute to the Aethiopians every year, he returned to his home. In this Aethiopian army many slaves and all who were readily disposed to crime were quite unwilling to follow the king back, but were left behind and remained there because of their desire for the land of the Homeritae; for it is an extremely goodly land.

These fellows at a time not long after this, in company with certain others, rose against the king Esimiphaeus and put him in confinement in one of the fortresses there, and established another king over the Homeritae, Abramus by name. Now this Abramus was a Christian, but a slave of a Roman citizen who was engaged in the business of shipping in the city of Adulis in Aethiopia. When Hellestheaeus learned this, he was eager to punish Abramus together with those who had revolted with him for their injustice to Esimiphaeus, and he sent against them an army of three thousand men with one of his relatives as commander. This army, once there, was no longer willing to return home, but they wished to remain where they were in a goodly land, and so without the knowledge of their commander they opened negotiations with Abramus; then when they came to an engagement with their opponents, just as the fighting began, they killed their commander and joined the ranks of the enemy, and so remained there. But Hellestheaeus was greatly moved with anger and sent still another army against them; this force engaged with Abramus and his men, and, after suffering a severe defeat in the battle, straightway returned home. Thereafter the king of the Aethiopians became afraid, and sent no further expeditions against Abramus. After the death of Hellestheaeus, Abramus agreed to pay tribute to the king of the Aethiopians who succeeded him, and in this way strengthened his rule. But this happened at a later time.

At that time, when Hellestheaeus was reigning over the Aethiopians, and Esimiphaeus over the Homeritae, the Emperor Justinian sent an ambassador, Julianus, demanding that both nations on account of their community of religion should make common cause with the Romans in the war against the Persians; for he purposed that the Aethiopians, by purchasing silk from India and selling it among the Romans, might themselves gain much money, while causing the Romans to profit in only one way, namely, that they be no longer compelled to pay over their money to their enemy. (This is the silk of which they are accustomed to make the garments which of old the Greeks called Medic, but which at the present time they name "seric."*) As for the Homeritae, it was desired that they should establish Caisus, the fugitive, as captain over the Maddeni,

* In Latin *serica,* as coming from the Chinese (Seres). TRANS.

and with a great army of their own people and of the Maddene Saracens make an invasion of the land of the Persians. This Caisus was by birth of the captain's rank and an exceptionally able warrior, but he had killed one of the relatives of Esimiphaeus and was a fugitive in a land which is utterly destitute of human habitation. So each king, promising to put this demand into effect, dismissed the ambassador, but neither one of them did the things agreed upon by them. For it was impossible for the Aethiopians to buy silk from the Indians, for the Persian merchants always locate themselves at the very harbors where the Indian ships first put in (since they inhabit the adjoining country), and are accustomed to buy the whole cargoes; and it seemed to the Homeritae a difficult thing to cross a country which was a desert and which extended so far that a long time was required for the journey across it, and then to go against a people much more warlike than themselves. Later on Abramus, too, when at length he had established his power most securely, promised the Emperor Justinian many times to invade the land of Persia, but only once began the journey and then straightway turned back. Such then were the relations which the Romans had with the Aethiopians and the Homeritae.

SOURCE: H. B. Dewing, trans., *Procopius* (7 vols.; London: William Heinemann, 1914–40), 1: "History of the Wars," Book 1, sect. 20.

13 The Aksumite Conquest of the Yemen

Procopius, the Roman historian, saw the Aksumite invasion of the Yemen and the wars that resulted from it as a small drama played out in a distant land. From his standpoint the conflict turned out to be of no great concern to his masters in Constantinople. But the inhabitants of the Yemen, participants in the actual struggle, naturally viewed the matter differently. For them sixth-century southwestern Arabia was the scene of a major religious civil war.

Exactly when Christianity entered the Yemen is unknown. The legends say that St. Thomas the Apostle preached in Arabia Felix on his way to India. What is certain is that by the sixth century A.D. the new religion had won many adherents. Churches and monasteries had been built, and perhaps a majority of the monied and merchant classes were Christian.

Locked in fierce competition with the Christians for religious supremacy in the Yemen were the Jews. Persecuted by the Romans, who massacred hundreds of thousands of them, the Jews had fled toward the extremities of the world of antiquity, particularly to Mesopotamia and Arabia. In these regions they had built many prosperous communities, some of which may fairly be described as kingdoms.[5] There was thus political and commercial as well as religious rivalry between the Christians and Jews of Arabia. King Abū Karib of the Himyarite dynasty, who unified southwestern Arabia in the third century, had embraced Judaism after his successful attack on Medina in the Hijaz, then a predominantly Jewish city. From his time onward the Himyarite kings appear to have alternated a policy of toleration for all religions with savage persecution of Christians. The last Himyarite king, Dhū Nuwās (Dthoo Nowās), who came to the throne in 490 and who had to face the final and most serious assault from Aksum in 525, was an adherent of Judaism and a religious fanatic. His actions suggest that he hoped to extirpate Christianity from his dominions altogether.

By the early part of the sixth century Aksum, too, had been Christian—at least so far as the beliefs of its ruling class were concerned—for nearly 200 years. In those days it was a recognized obligation of Christian princes to come to the rescue of their coreligionists in neighboring lands when the latter were suffering persecution. Thus King Kālēb's conquest of the Yemen was not undertaken solely for the glory and profit of Aksum, and certainly not at the behest of an Eastern Roman Emperor; it was one incident, though a decisive one, in a south Arabian religious war.

The dynasty established by the renegade Aksumite commander Abrahā (Abramus in Procopius) lasted only until 575, in which year a Persian army conquered the Yemen. In the seventh century the whole of Arabia came under the sway of the Arab Empire, and both Christianity and Judaism were displaced by Islam.

The *History of Arabia Felix or Yemen* compiled more than a century ago by Robert Playfair, an official of the British Indian government stationed in Aden, is mainly derived from Arabic and Greek authorities. Playfair indiscriminately mixes fact and fancy, and his history need not therefore be taken as "true," but it provides a fascinating picture of a time when Black Africa exercised power in Asia.[6]

■

Dthoo Nowās was . . . proclaimed sovereign of Yemen. He reigned from A.D. 490 to A.D. 525, and became a zealous partisan of Judaism, which, in consequence, made great progress in his day. His conversion is ascribed by some to his having witnessed the fire consecrated to a demon extinguished by a Jewish teacher reading several passages from the Pentateuch over it; and by others to his having acquired a predilection for that religion when on a visit to Yathrib, then partly inhabited by Jews and partly by heathen. On his change of religion he assumed the name of Yoosoof.

The religious fanaticism and natural cruelty of Dthoo Nowās led him to persecute in a most unrelenting manner all the Christians within his dominions, who had of late greatly increased in number; and the Roman merchants engaged in the Ethiopian trade were amongst the first to feel its effects. But the great atrocity of his reign . . . was a fearful act of barbarity, committed upon the Beni Thāleb tribe at Nejrān, who had embraced the religion of Christ at the preaching of a Syrian. The punishment which this crime entailed upon him was commensurate with its enormity—no less than the entire extinction of the Himyarite dynasty.

The legend of the conversion of the Beni Thāleb is as follows:—There was in Syria a very pious Christian named Fumiyoon, who led an ascetic life, and traveled about from place to place, leaving each residence as the fame of his virtues, and the efficacy of his prayers, became known. He had a faithful disciple named Sāleh, who followed him in all his wanderings. On leaving one place, where the report of his cures had made the people importunate, they traveled over a part of Arabia, till they were met by a party of Bedouins, who took them prisoners, and conveyed them to Nejrān, where they sold them as slaves.

Fumiyoon was purchased by one of the principal men of the town. On retiring to rest for the night, he began to pray, and immediately a supernatural light filled the apartment. This miracle led his master to make inquiries regarding the Christian religion: his slave replied,—"My God is the only God; His alone is the power and majesty; the palm-tree which you worship is devoid of power, and would be immediately destroyed were I to invoke against it the God whom I serve." His master replied,—"Pray then to your God to destroy the object of our worship, and we will embrace yours."

Fumiyoon prayed, and a speedy answer was vouchsafed to his supplication; for God sent a scorching wind, which dried up the roots of the tree, and it fell;—whereupon most of the inhabitants of Nejrān embraced Christianity.

Another tradition is related by Ibn Ishāk. A young man, named Abdulla, the son of Thāmir, witnessing the prayers of a holy man, also styled Fumiyoon, was much struck with the spectacle, and, becoming a disciple of the stranger, eventually became a Christian. He discovered the "great name of God," whereby miracles are wrought, by writing various names on arrows, and shooting them into the fire one after another; all were burnt excepting that whereon was inscribed the great name, which passed through the fire uninjured.

Having acquired this knowledge, he went about healing the sick, upon the condition that they abjured idolatry and embraced his religion: thus all the people in Nejrān who were afflicted with any disease were healed, and renounced paganism.

The prince of the district summoned Abdulla, and accusing him of corrupting the minds of his subjects, ordered him to be thrown from a precipice—but he fell down unhurt; he was then flung into a pit of water, but with the same result: at last Abdulla informed the prince that he had no power against him unless he embraced the Christian religion. The latter repeated the protestation of faith, and then struck Abdulla slightly with a cane, whereupon he fell down lifeless, and the prince died at the same moment. The greater number of the inhabitants of Nejrān were struck at this occurrence, and changed their religion for that of Christ.

Upon the pretext of the murder of two Jews by the people of Nejrān, Dthoo Nowās took up arms against them, and besieged the city with 120,000 men; but failing to take it by force, he had recourse to stratagem. He assured the inhabitants, upon oath, that no evil should happen to them if they opened their gates: upon the faith of this assurance they surrendered; but no sooner had Dthoo Nowās entered the town, than he plundered it, and gave the inhabitants their choice between Judaism and death.

They preferred the latter: accordingly large pits were dug, and filled with burning fuel, and all who refused to abjure their faith, amounting, it is said, to 20,000, including priests, monks, consecrated virgins, and matrons, who had embraced a monastic life, were either cast into the flames or slain by the sword. Amongst the victims was the chief man of the town, whom Mahomedan writers call Abdulla the son of Thāmir, and ecclesiastical historians Aretas the son of Calib, by which name he has been admitted into the Roman calendar of saints. Little doubt exists that these two names represent the same individual, since Abdulla certainly belonged to the family of Hārith the son of Käab, and it is probable that the former was his proper or Christian name, and the latter that of his family.

The heroism of a Nejranite matron, and of her son, who threw themselves into the flames, gave rise to the following fable, recorded by El-Masäoodi:—a woman, with a child of seven months, refused to abjure her religion; she was taken to the burning pit, and when she was frightened, God gave speech to her infant, and it said,—"Go on, mother, in thy faith! thou wilt not meet a fire after this." They both perished in the flames.

The Tobba next caused the ashes of the bishop Paul, who had died some time before, to be disinterred, and scattered to the winds; after which he retired with his army to Sanäa.

This tragedy obtained for Dthoo Nowās the epithet of "the lord of the burning pit," and the fidelity of the martyrs, or "brethren of the pit," is commended in the Korān, where an anathema is pronounced on their persecutor.

According to Greek and Syrian writers, an embassy had been sent about this time by Justin I to the "mondār" or king of the Arabs of Heera, to endeavor to detach them from their dependence on Persia; a presbyter named Abraham, the son of Euphrasius, was charged with the mission. When he reached the camp of the Arab chief, a messenger had just arrived from the Himyarite king, detailing the success of his measures for exterminating the Christians, and suggesting the adoption of similar ones at Heera. The bishop immediately wrote a full account of the tragedy to the emperor, and implored him to take up the cause of the martyrs.

It is also related by Mahomedan historians, that Doos Dthoo Thālibān, one of the few Christians of Nejrān who had escaped the persecution of the Himyarite monarch, traversed Arabia, Syria, and Asia Minor, and at last reached the Court of Constantinople, where he implored the emperor to espouse the cause of his persecuted brethren in Yemen. Justin was well disposed to listen favorably to this appeal; but the distance of Arabia, as well as the political state of his own dominions, prevented his personal interference; he however wrote letters to the king of Abyssinia, requesting him to send troops into Yemen for the punishment of Dthoo Nowās.

The sovereign who reigned in Abyssinia at this time was a Christian; he is styled by the Greek writers Elisbaas, and by the Ethiopians Caleb, or Amda. Agreeably to the request of Justin, he commenced to make warlike preparations for the conquest of Yemen. He caused seven hundred small vessels to be constructed, and in addition to these, he was furnished by the Roman emperor with large ships from the Egyptian ports in the Red Sea. In this fleet he embarked his army, which amounted to 60,000 men, and, crossing over the Arabian Gulf, landed them at the port of Ghalifica.

Dthoo Nowās, on the first intimation of the approaching invasion, had applied for assistance to the Kails and Dthoos, who were tributary to him. These refused to send contingents to his army, but declared that each would defend his own territories. Notwithstanding this defection, the Himyarite prince succeeded in raising a considerable army, with which he marched to oppose the advance of the army. He encountered the Abyssinian army, under Aryāt,* shortly after its disembarkation; a battle ensued on the sea coast, in which the Himyarites were entirely defeated. The Tobba fled from the field of battle, but, being closely pursued and hemmed in by his enemies, he leaped his horse into the sea and was drowned.

Aryāt then penetrated into Yemen almost unopposed; Dthafār, which was unprepared for a siege, immediately surrendered to him;—in a very short time he subdued the greater part of the country, and, in order to make his conquest more secure, razed the walls of some of the most important fortresses.

One Himyarite prince, by the name of Dthoo Jadān, for some time disputed the advance of the Abyssinians. He received the appellation of Dthoo Jadān from having a remarkably sweet voice, and it is said that he was the first who cultivated the art of singing in Yemen.

* Called "Esimiphaeus" by Procopius. Ed.

After a battle with Aryāt, in which he was completely routed, he followed the example of his predecessor, and destroyed himself, by plunging into the sea.

Several Himyarite kings are mentioned by Arab historians as having reigned subsequent to the conquest of Yemen by the Abyssinians. Amongst these are Marthād the son of Dthoo Jadān, and another is Alkāma Dthoo Keefān, the son of Sharaheel, the son of Dthoo Jadān, who governed the district of Hamdān, by the people of which he was slain. It is probable either that the country was not entirely subdued, or that some Himyarite princes continued to rule as vassals of the king of Abyssinia.

Thus terminated the Himyarite dynasty, which had ruled in Yemen for two thousand years. Its power had long been on the decline, but its downfall was accelerated by the intolerance of the Jewish Tobbas, which induced them to persecute with unrelenting fury the disciples of Jesus. These latter, neglecting the precepts of their divine Master, were in many instances only too ready to repay by equally bitter persecutions the injuries they had received at the hands of the Jews; and to this circumstance may be attributed in some measure the shortness of their rule.

In consequence of the brilliant victories of Aryāt, he was confirmed in the government of Yemen, and reigned as viceroy of the Negāshi * or king of Abyssinia from A.D. 525 to A.D. 537. It is said by several Arabian historians that he received orders from his master to destroy a third part of the country of the Himyarites, to massacre a third of the males, and to send a third part of the females in captivity to Abyssinia; and it is related that he executed these cruel instructions, at least in part.

He also enriched the chiefs of the army with the spoils of Yemen, to the entire exclusion of the soldiery, whom he taxed with the most arduous duties, employing them on various public works, without supplying them with the bare necessaries of life. They soon began to manifest their discontent at this treatment, and recognized Abrahā as their chief. This Abrahā was a Christian; he had been the slave of a Roman merchant at Adulis, and had afterwards risen to high rank in the Abyssinian army.

Aryāt marched at the head of such of his troops as remained

* I.e., *negusa nagast,* the title of the kings of Aksum, later to become one of the titles, "King of Kings," of the Emperors of Ethiopia; in English often transliterated as "Negus." ED.

faithful to him against his rival: when the two parties met, it was proposed by Abrahā that, instead of hazarding a civil war, and permitting the soldiers to destroy each other, the question should be decided by single combat. To this Aryāt agreed, and the two champions prepared for the conflict. Abrahā was short and corpulent, while his antagonist was tall, strong, and well made. The latter was the first to strike his adversary with a pike, but, missing his aim, instead of cleaving his skull, he only succeeded in slightly wounding his forehead and nose, the latter of which was slit open. This wound afterwards left a deep scar, which procured for Abrahā the title of El-Ashram, or "the split-nosed." Abrahā had an attendant with him, named Atwāda, who, seeing his master wounded, flew to his assistance, and slew Aryāt; whereupon, although the victory had been obtained by treachery, all the troops went over to Abrahā, who thus became ruler of Yemen without opposition. He reigned from A.D. 537 to A.D. 570.

Abrahā, in his gratitude, is said to have offered to comply with any desire which this slave might express; the latter requested that no bride in Yemen should be conducted to the bridegroom, until he had enjoyed her. The viceroy considered himself bound to fulfill his promise, and the request was granted. The slave was subsequently slain by a bridegroom whom he had insulted, and Abrahā had no desire to avenge his death, which rather gratified him.

When the intelligence of the murder of Aryāt reached the ears of the Negāshi, he vowed, in the first transports of his rage, that he would never lay aside his arms until he had trampled under his feet the land of Abrahā, till he had stained his hands in his blood, and had dragged him by the hair of the head. Abrahā no sooner heard of this, than he caused a sack to be filled with earth, he suffered himself to be bled, and filled a small bottle with his blood, to which he added some locks of hair, cut from his head. These he enclosed in a rich casket, and sent them to Negāshi, with a letter to the following effect:—"O king! Aryāt and I were both thy servants; he merited his death, by tyranny and injustice. Empty, therefore, the earth out of this sack, and tread it beneath thy feet—it is the land of Himyar; stain thy hands with my blood, which is contained in this bottle; and drag with thy hand this hair, which I have myself cut from my head: thus, having fulfilled thine oath, turn away from me thine anger, for I am still one of thy servants!" The king was appeased, and confirmed Abrahā in the government of Yemen, after he had solemnly promised forever to continue his tribute to the Abyssinian crown.

Abrahā followed the example of his predecessor, in oppressing the Himyarites: amongst other outrages, he is said to have carried off Rihana, wife of Aboo Mourra Saif, the son of Dthoo Yazan, by whom he had a son, called Maadi Karib. She afterwards bore a son and a daughter to Abrahā, named Masrook and Bessasa. Abrahā already had, by another wife, two sons, named Amooda and Yaskoom; the former of whom, after having been admitted by his father to a share in the government, made himself so unpopular, through tyranny and oppression, that he was assassinated. Abrahā, not being of a sanguinary nature, did not avenge the murder of his son.

The reign of Abrahā was favorable to the extension of Christianity in Yemen: a bishop, whom the patriarch of Alexandria had sent there, and whom the Roman church reckons in her catalogue of saints as St. Gregentius, fixed his residence at Dthafār. He drew up a code of laws, which was published by the viceroy. The harsh measures which had been adopted toward the Jews and other enemies of Christianity were succeeded by others more consonant to the mild spirit of that religion; the unbelievers were challenged to public disputations with St. Gregentius, in the royal hall, in the city of Dthafār; the viceroy and his nobles were present, and a learned Rabbi named Herbanus was chosen to advocate the cause of Judaism. The dispute lasted three days, and resulted in the conversion of Herbanus and many of his followers to Christianity. The religious zeal of Gregentius was powerfully seconded by Abrahā, who is universally allowed by Greek and Arabian authors to have been a just prince, a zealous Christian, and charitable to the needy and unfortunate.

Abrahā is said to have built a church at Sanäa, which was the wonder of the age. The emperor of Rome and the king of Abyssinia supplied marble and workmen for its construction, and it is related by Nowairi that, when completed, a pearl was placed on the altar, of such brilliancy that, on the darkest night, objects were clearly seen by its light! The viceroy, deeply grieved to see the vast multitudes who still performed their idol worship at the Käaba of Mecca, endeavored to substitute his church for the object of their superstitious reverence,—probably, also, he wished to divert the valuable trade of

Mecca to his own territories; but his persuasions were without avail, and the Arabs would not abandon their ancient customs. He accordingly issued an order, that all Arabs in the neighborhood should perform the pilgrimage to his church at Sanäa; he also sent missionaries to the Hejāz and Nejd, to invite the inhabitants of those parts to visit it, and he wrote to Negāshi, and told him that he intended forcing the Arabs to abandon the Käaba, and substitute this temple as the object of their pilgrimage.

This design was speedily known throughout Arabia, and excited the indignation of all the pagan tribes, but especially of the custodians of the Käaba, who foresaw that the prosperity of this new Christian church would overthrow their own greatness. Accordingly, on the arrival of Abrahā's messengers in the Hejāz, they were badly received, and one was murdered by a man of the tribe of Kināna.

Another man of the same tribe was bribed by the guardians of the Käaba, and, having proceeded to Sanäa, was successful in obtaining employment in the church. Seizing the opportunity of the preparation for a high festival, he entered the sacred edifice by night, and defiled it with filth. The wrath of Abrahā was inflamed at this indignity, and having discovered the author of it, he vowed to take signal vengeance, by the total destruction of Mecca and its Käaba.

He accordingly collected an army of 40,000 men, and having headed it, mounted on a white elephant of great size and beauty, he proceeded against Mecca.

He routed in a single battle the inhabitants of the Tehāma, who had refused to transfer their religious allegiance to Sanäa, and he seized all the cattle in the neighborhood of Tāef, amongst which were two hundred camels belonging to Abd-el-Motalib ibn Hasjemi, the grandfather of Mahommed, who was then chief of the Koraish, and guardian of the sacred temple. The appearance of this formidable army before Mecca spread the direst consternation amongst the Koraish, who in vain offered Abrahā large sums of money to induce him to abandon his designs. Abd-el-Motalib begged for an interview with the viceroy; he was admitted into his presence, and treated with every mark of honorable distinction; but the chief had only come to ask restoration of his plundered camels. Abrahā asked why he made so insignificant a request, and abstained from interceding on behalf of the Käaba. Abd-el-Motalib replied that the camels were his own property, while the temple belonged to the gods, who would assuredly protect it, as they had always hitherto done. The camels were restored, but the temple was left to the protection of its own sanctity.

On the nearer approach of Abrahā, the Koraish, and all the inhabitants of Mecca, retired to the mountains and fortresses in its vicinity, after first having implored the aid of their gods in a pathetic hymn.

According to Mahomedan authors, the deities were not importuned in vain; and the Christian army, after having approached the walls of Mecca, was destroyed in a miraculous manner: Abrahā advanced on his famous elephant Mahmood, but, though it evinced readiness to move in every other direction, it could not be induced to enter the sacred walls; the other elephants, thirteen in number, evinced the same reluctance. At length, a dense flight of birds from the sea coast, called Ababeel, overspread the hostile force: each carried three small pebbles, of the size of a lentil, one in each claw, and one in the beak, which they let fall with such violence as to pierce through the armor of the soldiers, killing both men and elephants. Most of the invaders who escaped death by this means perished in the desert, and Abrahā, with a very small remnant of his army, reached Sanäa, where he soon after died of a loathsome disease.

These events, well known in Arabian history as "the war of the elephant," took place in the same year as that which gave birth to Mahommed. It has been suggested that the fable of the birds was invented by the prophet himself, in order to augment the national reverence for the Käaba, and that the Christian host was destroyed by an epidemic disease, most probably smallpox. Others have imagined that they perished from want of provisions, or were destroyed by the Koraish, who, lining the hills above the passes leading to the city, discharged stones upon the assailants.

Abrahā was succeeded by his son Yascoom, by Rihāna, wife of Saif the Himyarite. He reigned two years, namely from A.D 570 to A.D. 572. Arabian authors accuse him of cruelty and tyrannic oppression, and narrate that under him the Abyssinians ravished the women, killed the men, and made slaves of the children. This cruelty inclined many to seek the protection of the Koraish, whose victory over his predecessor had raised them in importance in the estimation of Arab tribes. The Greek writers, on the other hand, styled him Serdius or Serdeed, and inform us that he resembled his father in justice and piety.

Masrook succeeded his brother Yascoom, whose tyranny he emulated and surpassed; he reigned, according to Masäoodi, for three years, namely from A.D. 572 to A.D. 575, and was the last of the Abyssinians who governed Yemen.

The advantages to the Negāshi from the conquest of this province appear to have been very trifling; for the troops sent over became so enamoured of the country that they permanently settled there, and soon broke every tie, save a nominal allegiance to the parent state. Their rulers, too, assumed the manners and style of royalty, and considered themselves almost in the light of independent princes.

SOURCE: Robert L. Playfair, *A History of Arabia Felix or Yemen* (Bombay, 1859; repr., St. Leonards: Ad Orientem, 1970), pp. 62–71.

14 The Story of 'Antara

The warrior-poet 'Antara, hero of Arab chivalry, had an African mother and an Arab father. He lived in central Arabia in the sixth century A.D. Few details of his life are known for certain.[7] His exploits are described at length in the famous epic, *Sīrat 'Antar,* but these are often fantastical and many of them are additions to the original tale contributed by generations of story-tellers during a period of at least 500 years after 'Antara's death.[8] Nevertheless, there was a historical 'Antara, and his life provides proof that a man of mixed race could, in pre-Islamic times, achieve distinction and status in the Arab world.

■

The Arabs, proud of their pure descent, call some of their heroes of antiquity, those descended from an Arab father and a Negro mother, "the Ravens of the Arabs" (*aghribat al-'arab*), because of their dark complexion inherited from their mothers. Tha'abbaṭa Sharran himself was ranked among them, but the most famous of the Ravens of the Arabs was 'Antara ibn Shaddād, of the tribe of 'Abs, whose mother was an Ethiopian black slave. He lived in the time of the fights called Dāḥis-Ghabrā which raged for eleven years between the tribes of 'Abs and Abū Dhubyān. These fights were due to a dispute involving a race between two horses, Dāḥis and Ghabrā, on which occasion the tribe of 'Abs accused the tribe of Dhubyān of having had recourse to stratagems to assure the victory of their horse. In these fights 'Antara fought in the ranks of his paternal tribe of 'Abs, and won glory for his kinsmen by his valor. Moreover, he also prevailed over his personal enemies, and nobody could be equal to him in valor and strength although he was the son of a slave woman, and as such not acknowledged by his proud tribesmen as their equal: for which an act of individual emancipation would have been necessary, and this was denied him. Of course, his adverse status profoundly affected the mind of the black hero. He loved his niece 'Abla. According to Arab custom, he could have asked for the hand of his niece but he was denied this because a free daughter of the tribe could not marry the son of a slave, since in the view of the Arabs the husband was expected to be at least of the same rank as his wife. This slight greatly exacerbated [sic] 'Antara who had saved his tribe from many dangers. When the men of the tribe of 'Abs once more needed his helping hand he refused them indignantly, saying: "The slave is not for fighting; he is only needed to milk the camels and tie up their udders." Upon that he was declared free and was admitted into his tribe.

'Antara sang his fights, vicissitudes, and love for 'Abla in many *qaṣīdas* which are considered by the Arabs as the pearls of their poetry. In the most famous of his *qaṣīdas,* which is one of the finest specimens of pagan Arab poetry, he boasted of the heroic feats he did for his tribe, and related his love for 'Abla in the most sentimental manner. It begins thus:

Hal ghadara 'sh-shu 'arā'u min mutaraddami
am hal 'arafta 'd-dāra ba^{c}da tawahhumi

(Did the poets leave to me anything to be patched; or do you still recognize the [pristine] abode after their guess?)

'Antara is the national hero of the Arabs. The Arab story-tellers sang many a sumptuous narrative about him, recounting his vicissitudes and struggles which finally earned social recognition for him and the hand of 'Abla. In these romantic narratives the hero of the desert performs his feats not only in the Arabian Peninsula but also in such distant, fabulous lands as India, Persia, and Greece: everywhere he prevailed in his duels with ogres and demons; alone he defeated whole armies with the strength of his arm and the courage of his heart. There were special reciters of 'Antara's feats (*al-'Antariyya*) whose duty it was to fascinate their audiences by reciting the romance of chivalry; the verses interwoven with the romance were accompanied on the rebec (*rabāb*). The cycle of romance entitled *Qiṣṣa 'Antara* ("The Story of Antara") is one of the most widely read books of the Arabs.

SOURCE: Ignace Goldziher, *A Short History of Classical Arabic Literature* Joseph DeSomogyi, trans. and rev. (Hildesheim: Olms, 1966), pp. 14–15.

BLACKS IN THE ISLAMIC WORLD

FROM THE BIRTH of Islam in the seventh century to the early twentieth century the vast majority of Africans who lived in, or were brought into, the Muslim Middle East were slaves. Among them there were some, mostly mulattos, who became freedmen, and as time went on there was an increasing number of descendants of both slaves and freedmen among the population. The freedmen (and women) and their offspring were naturally better off than the slaves, but all—slave and free, men and women—were alike in that they were subjected by the rest of the population to a greater or lesser degree of social discrimination. This was sometimes because of their status or origin and sometimes because of their color; often it was because of both. In this respect the attitudes of the Muslim Middle East in medieval and early modern times do not compare favorably with those of the classical world of Greece and Rome, when discrimination based on race or color was rare (see Introduction).

On the other hand, it was possible for Africans and persons of African descent living under Arab, and, later, Turkish rule to attain positions of distinction and even of authority. This was conspicuously true of those who, because of the superior status of their fathers, began life at the top of the social or political ladder; some of the best-known reigning monarchs of the Middle East and northern Africa, including many of the 'Abbasīd caliphs, were the sons of African slave concubines. But it was also true of slaves and freedmen of the lowliest origin. Such men could, if they possessed outstanding piety, unusual intellectual ability, marked artistic talent, or noteworthy military or diplomatic skills, achieve the highest rank and often commanded enormous popular esteem.

Selections 15 to 22, printed below, provide examples of black "success stories" from the period of medieval Islam. The men described are of African origin, and all attracted the attention, for various reasons and in various ways, of their contemporaries. They are representative only, for there must have been many other black divines, scholars, lawyers, entertainers, and the like, of whom no record has been preserved. And they are also profoundly unrepresentative, for clearly these stories describe the achievements of the fortunate ones. In noting their success we must not forget that almost all Middle Eastern blacks in historic times lived out their lives not as favored notables but as maidservants and concubines, eunuchs, traders, artisans, and agricultural laborers. About these humbler people we know a good deal in the mass, but of their individual life histories nothing at all.

15 Sa'īd ibn Misjaḥ, the Singer

The *Kitāb al-Aghānī* (Book of Songs), from which the following extract is taken, took its author, Abu 'l-Faraj al-Iṣfahānī (897–967), fifty years to compile. It is a collection of songs, with their texts and melodies, but it is also a mine of information about the authors of the songs and the singers who performed them. Sa'īd ibn Misjaḥ was considered the greatest musician of his century. This anecdote, which he tells himself, is set in Damascus, and shows not only the color-consciousness of his Arab hosts but also their embarrassment when their prejudices are revealed.

■

"Kind sirs, is there one among you who will offer hospitality to a stranger from al-Ḥijāz?" They looked at each other, for they had an appointment to visit a singing-girl called Barq al-Ufuq, and were reluctant [to comply with my request]. But one, who feared censure, said: "I shall give you hospitality," and to his friends he said: "You proceed, I shall go with my guest." So we went to the singing-girl's house.

When lunch was served, I said to them: "I am a black man. There may be some among you who find me offensive. Therefore I shall sit and eat apart." I rose [and sat apart]. They felt ashamed, and sent me something to eat. When they got to drinking, I spoke as before, and they acted as before.

Two singing-girls appeared, sat on a bed, sang until the evening, and disappeared. Then a beautiful singing-girl appeared, accompanied by the other two, and sat on the bed; the others sat below her, one to the right of the bed, the second to the left. . . . I recited this verse:

Is it a sun, or the lamps of a church, that appeared
Behind the curtain, or are you dreaming?

The singing-girl was furious, and said: "Shall this black man be permitted to utter parables about me?" The company looked at me disapprovingly, and tried to calm her down. She sang another melody and I said: "You have done well, by God!" Her owner was furious and said: "Shall a black man like this behave in this bold fashion to my slave-girl?" The youth who had offered me hospitality said to me: "Rise and go to my lodging. You have become burdensome to the company." I started to leave, but the company, fearing censure, said to me: "It is better that you stay and behave better." So I stayed. When the singing-girl sang another melody, I said: "O whore! You have sung that wrong." And I proceeded to sing the melody. The girl jumped up and said to her owner: "This, by God, is Abū 'Uthmān Sa'īd b. Musajjiḥ!" * I said: "Certainly I am he, by God! By God, I shall not stay among you!"

SOURCE: Abu 'l-Faraj al-Iṣfahānī, *Kitāb al-Aghānī* (Book of Songs), 3:87. Translated for the present volume by Hasan Shuraydi.

* Or, Misjaḥ. ED.

16 Faraj as-Saḥrati, the Benefactor

This is a story of the youth of ʻAlī ibn Muḥammad aṣ-Ṣulayḥi, who became ruler of southwestern Arabia in 1063. It was told by the leading Arabic historian of the early Muslim period in the Yemen, ʻUmārah al-Ḥakami (c. 1121/22–1159/60).

The hero of the tale, the Abyssinian (Ethiopian) Faraj as-Saḥrati, who befriends the young aṣ-Ṣulayḥi, appears to have been a very wealthy man. He was one of many Africans permanently resident in the Yemen at this period. Some of them were descendants of the survivors of the Aksumite invasions of the pre-Islamic time; others had come to the Yemen since, voluntarily as soldiers and merchants and involuntarily as slaves. Many were in positions of power and authority. From 1018–19 to 1159–60, for example, the kings of Zabīd, the town within whose walls the house of Faraj as-Saḥrati lay, were of Ethiopian origin.

■

Ḳāḍi ʻOmar ibn al-Murajjal, who bore the surname of the Hanafite and belonged to that school of religion, and who was a distinguished scholar . . . said that near the gate of Zabīd, within the walls, there was the house of an Abyssinian of the name of Faraj as-Saḥrati (the Sahrite), a man of benevolence and of exceeding charity. Whoever entered his mosque he welcomed and entertained. His thoughts were occupied with his guests, and he was in the habit of entering the mosque and of making private inquiries respecting them, without the knowledge of his agents and servants. He went forth one night and found in the mosque a person occupied in reading the Ḳur'ān. He questioned him touching his evening meal, and the man in reply recited the following lines of al-Mutanabbi:-

Who hath taught the mutilated negro the performance of generous deeds?—
His noble-minded masters or his enslaved forefathers?

The Abyssinian took the man with him. He led him to the chief room of his house, and treated him with the most liberal hospitality.

He asked his guest the reason for his journey to Tihāmah. Aṣ-Ṣulayḥi replied that he had a paternal [*read* maternal] uncle named Shihāb, whose daughter Asmā had few equals in beauty, and was unmatched in literary culture and intelligence. He had asked her in marriage, and had been met with a demand for dowry exceeding in its amount the bounds of moderation, her mother urging that she should be married to none other but to one of the Hamdanite Kings of Ṣan'ā, or to one of the kings of the family of the Banu Kurandi in Mikhlāf Ja'far. They, in short, exacted a sum which it was wholly beyond his power to command. He was now, he added, on his way either to the Banu Ma'n at Aden, or to the Banu Kurandi in the district of al-Ma'āfir. The Ḳā'id Faraj as-Saḥrati, continued the narrator, supplied him with a large sum of money, double the amount that aṣ-Ṣulayḥi actually paid. The bride and bridegroom were equipped on a scale such as kings strive to provide when allying themselves with women of the most noble lineage. Aṣ-Ṣulayḥi returned, by direction of the Abyssinian, to his uncle, and married Asmā.

SOURCE: Henry Cassels Kay, ed., *Yaman: Its Early Mediaeval History. By Najm ad-Din 'Omārah al-Ḥakami* (London: Arnold, 1892), pp. 20–22.

17 The Pious Rainmaker

This account of an anonymous African "rainmaker" in Medina comes from Muḥammad ibn Ṣaṣrā's description of late fourteenth-century Damascus. There are many similar stories in the Arabic literature of the period. It may be that they reflect the medieval Muslim world's knowledge of the African institution of divine kingship. Many rulers in the savanna regions of east and northeast Africa were believed to possess power over the elements and to be able to cause rain to fall in time of drought.

■

The author of the book *al-Kanz al-maṭlūb fī manāqib al-Ḥabasa wal-Nūb* related on the authority of Ibn al-Munkadir, saying, "Rain was withheld from us in Medina in a certain year." He said, "The people went out to ask for rain, but no rain came, and they returned. When night came, I went to perform the late evening prayer in the mosque of the messenger of God—may God bless him and give him peace—I leaned against a wall and no one saw me. There came a black man, his [features] overcome by paleness, wearing a woolen cloak, and with a woolen garment about his neck. He went forward, performed a two-*rak'ā prayer,** and sat down. Then he said while I was listening, 'O Lord, the people of the sanctuary of Thy Prophet went out to ask for water, and Thou didst not give them water. I adjure Thee to give them water!' " Ibn al-Munkadir said, "I thought, he is mad! But by God, no sooner had he put down his hand than I heard the sound of thunder, and it rained." He continued, "When he heard the rain, he praised God the Exalted with praises the like of which I had never heard. Then he said, 'Who am I, and what am I, O Lord, that Thou didst answer me?' He then arose and continued praying until we performed the morning prayer, and he performed it with us. When the prayer leader gave the final salutation, he arose and went out, and I went out in order to know who he was. He raised his garments to wade through the water, and I followed him, lifting my garments, wading after him, and I did not know where he went."

SOURCE: Muḥammad ibn Ṣaṣrā, *A Chronicle of Damascus 1389–1397,* W. M. Brinner, ed. and trans. (2 vols.; Berkeley and Los Angeles: University of California Press, 1963), 1:278.

18 Abū Ruwaim Nāfē, the Ḳur'ān-reader

Aḥmad ibn Muḥammad ibn Khallikān compiled the *Wafayāt al-a'yān wa-anbā' abnā' al-zamān* (known as the *Biographical Dictionary*) at Cairo during the mid-thirteenth century. The next three extracts are taken from this work.

■

Abū Ruwaim Nāfē, the son of Abd ar-Rahmān Ibn Abi Nuaim and a *mawla* † of Jawana Ibn Shaūb as-Shijāi, was a native of Me-

* The term *rak'ā* is applied to the middle part of the *ṣalāt,* or sequence of ritual prayers offered by Muslims in the mosque. A "two-*rak'ā* prayer" would be that portion of the ritual known as the *ṣalāt al-fajr.* ED.

† I.e., *mawlā* = "freed slave." TRANS.

dina and one of the seven principal *Koran-readers.* He was the *imām* * of the people of Medina; they conformed to his manner of reading and adopted the readings he preferred. He belonged to the third class (*or generation*) after the Companions (*of Muḥammad*) and filled the office of *muhtasib* †. . . . His humor was facetious and his complexion dark, extremely dark.

SOURCE: Baron Mac Guckin de Slane, trans., *Ibn Khallikan's Biographical Dictionary* (4 vols.; London: Oriental Translation Fund, 1842–71; repr., New York: Johnson Reprint Corp., 1961), 3:522–23.

19 Sa'īd ibn Jubair, the Tābi'

The word "*tābi'* " (pl. *tābi'ūn*) means "follower" or "disciple." In the Muslim tradition it is given to those who came after the Aṣḥāb, the Companions of the Prophet; the *tābi'ūn* are those of the next generation or contemporaries of the Prophet who did not know him.[9] Sa'īd ibn Jubair's birthplace, Kūfa, was a city in 'Irāḳ, on the western arm of the Euphrates, south of the ruins of Babylon.

■

Abū Abd Allah (some say Abū Muhammad) Saīd Ibn Jubair Ibn Hishām, surnamed al-Asadi, was a black and a client by enfranchisement to the tribe of Wāliba Ibn al-Harith, a branch of that of Asad Ibn Khuzaima. This eminent *Tābī* was a native of Kūfa; he acquired his learning under the tuition of Ibn Abbās and Abd Allah Ibn Omar, the former of whom told him one day to teach the Traditions. "I teach the Traditions?" exclaimed Saīd, "and you here!"—"Is it not a favor which God grants you," replied Ibn Abbās, "in procuring you the opportunity of teaching them in my presence? for if you do it right, it is well; and if you make mistakes, I correct you." When Ibn Abbās lost his sight, Saīd was inscribed on the list of the *muftis,* an honor which he had always refused to accept, and which now

* The word *imām* designates the person who presides at the public prayer; but, in the present case, it appears to signify "oracle, a person whose opinions were of the highest authority." TRANS.

† *Muḥtasib* = "censor," an officer appointed by the Caliph or his *wazīr* to oversee public morals. TRANS.

gave him great dissatisfaction. . . . It is related by Ismaīl Ibn Abd al-Malik * that Saīd Ibn Jubair once acted for them as imām in the month of Ramadān, and that one night he recited the Koran according to the reading of Abd Allah Ibn Otba Ibn Musūd; † another night, according to that of Zaid Ibn Thābit; following thus, each successive night, a different mode of reading. A person having once asked Saīd to put down for him in writing the explanation of the Koran, he flew into a passion and exclaimed: "I should rather be palsied in one half of my body than do so." It was said by Khasīf that the best acquainted among the *Tābīs* with the laws of divorce was Saīd Ibn al-Musaiyab,—with the rites of the Pilgrimage, Atā,—with the distinction between what was lawful and what was forbidden, Tawūs,—and with the interpretation of the Koran, Abū 'l-Hajjāj Mujāhid Ibn Jubair, but he observed that Saīd Ibn Jubair had a more general knowledge than them all of the whole of these sciences. . . .

It is related by Muhammad Ibn Habīb that when Saīd Ibn Jubair was at Ispahan, they asked to hear from him the Traditions, but he would not communicate any to them, yet when he returned to Kūfa he taught them publicly; on this some one said to him: "Abū Muhammad! you would not teach the Traditions when at Ispahan, and here you are now, teaching them in Kūfa!" Saīd replied: *"Set forth your wares where you are best known."*

Saīd joined Abd ar-Rahmān Ibn Muhammad Ibn al-Ashāth Ibn Kais in his revolt against Abd al-Malik Ibn Marwān. When Ibn al-Ashāth lost his life after the defeat of his partisans at Dair al-Jamājim, Saīd fled to Mekka, but was arrested by Khālid Ibn Abd Allāh al-Kasri, the governor of that city, and sent to al-Hajjāj Ibn Yūsuf with Ismaīl Ibn Awsat al-Bajali. Al-Hajjāj, on seeing him, said: "Wretch, son of Wretched! didst thou not come to Kūfa when a vile Arab of the desert was imām there, and did I not put thee in his place?"—"Yes."—"And did not I appoint thee kādi? and when the people of Kūfa murmured and said that none but an Arab of the desert was fit for that office, did I not replace thee by Abū Borda Ibn Abi Mūsa, ordering him, however, not to decide any

* This Ismaīl was probably a son of Abd al-Malik Ibn Marwān, the fifth Omaiyide Khalif. TRANS.

† This was a nephew of the celebrated Koran reader Abd Allah Ibn Masūd. His father, Otba, was one of the Ansars. TRANS.

question without consulting thee?"—"Yes."—"Did I not admit thee to my evening parties as a companion, though the company were all Arab chieftains?"—"Yes."—"The first time I saw thee, did I not give thee one hundred thousand dirhims to distribute among the needy, without questioning thee afterwards about the manner in which the money was employed?"—"Yes."—"What then made thee revolt against me?"—"An oath which bound me to Ibn al-Ashāth." Here al-Hajjāj grew angry and said, after a pause: "And before that, were thou not bound by an oath to the Commander of the faithful, Abd al-Malik? By Allah! I shall put thee to death; guard, strike off his head." This passed in the month of Shābān, A.H. 95 (April–May, A.D. 714), or 94, at Wāsit, outside of which place Saīd was interred; his tomb is still visited by pilgrims. . . .

When al-Hasan al-Basri was informed that Saīd Ibn Jubair had been put to death by al-Hajjāj, he exclaimed: "O God! be [turned] against this reprobate of [the tribe of] Thakīf! Almighty God! if there be any persons on earth, from east to west, who were accessory to his death, lay them prostrate into fires of hell!" It is related that al-Hajjāj, when on the point of death, would faint away, and on recovering, cry out: "But what business has Saīd Ibn Jubair with me?" The report was, that whenever he fell asleep during his last illness, he saw Saīd come up and seize him by the girdle, saying: "Enemy of God, arise! why didst thou murder me?" On which he would awake in terror and exclaim: "What business has Saīd Ibn Jubair with me?" It is related also that a person saw al-Hajjāj in a dream, after his death, and asked him what God had done to him. "He put me to death," replied al-Hajjāj, "once for each person whom I put to death, and seventy times for Saīd Ibn Jubair."—The *shaikh* Abū Ishak as-Shīrāzi mentions in his book, entitled *al-Huhaddab,* that Saīd Ibn Jubair could play at chess with his back turned to the chessboard.

SOURCE: De Slane, *Ibn Khallikan,* 1:564–68.

20 ‘Aṭā’ ibn Abī Rabāḥ, the Mufti

‘Aṭā’ ibn Abī Rabāḥ was born in southern Arabia of Nubian parents. He moved to Mecca and became a famous teacher and jurisconsult there. In his later years “his reputation spread far beyond Mecca,” [10] and important scholars like Abū Ḥanīfa are said to have been present at his lectures.[11]

‘Aṭā’ was a *tābi‘*, like Sa‘īd ibn Jubair, and also a *mawlā*, or freed slave. The *fatwās* referred to in this account of his life are opinions on points of law. In Islam, the person who gives a *fatwā* is known as a *mufti*.

■

Abū Muḥammad ‘Aṭā Ibn Abī Rabāḥ Aslam (or Sālim) Ibn Ṣafwān was a mulatto, born at al-Janad, and a *mawlā* to the Fihr family of Makkah, or to the family of Juman: some, however, considered him as a *mawlā* to Abū Maysarah al-Fihri. He held a high rank at Makkah as a jurisconsult, a *tābi‘*, and a devout ascetic, and he derived [his knowledge of the law and the Traditions] from the lips of Jābir Ibn ‘Abd Allāh al-Anṣārī, ‘Abd Allāh Ibn ‘Abbās, ‘Abd Allāh Ibn al-Zubayr, and many others of Muḥammad’s Companions. His own authority as a traditionist was cited by ‘Amr Ibn Dīnār, al-Zuhrī, Qatādah, Mālik Ibn Dīnār, al-Ā‘mash, al-Awzā‘i, and great number of others who had heard him teach. The office of *mufti* at Makkah devolved to him and to Mujāhid and was filled by them whilst they lived. Qatādah declared him to be the most learned of all men in the rites of the pilgrimage, and Ibrāhīm Ibn ‘Umar Ibn Kaysān said: “I remember that, in the time of Umayyids, a crier was ordered by them to proclaim to the pilgrims that no one should apply for *fatwās* to any person but ‘Aṭā Ibn Abī Rabāḥ. . . .

‘Aṭā was black in color, blind of an eye, flatnosed, having the use of only one arm, lame of a leg, and woolly-haired; when advanced in life he lost the use of sight. Sulaymān Ibn Rafī‘ said: “I went into the Sacred Mosque and saw all the people assembled around some person, and on looking to see who it was, behold! there was ‘Aṭā sitting on the ground and looking like a black crow." He died A.H. 115 (A.C. 733–4); some say 114, at the age of eighty-eight years. It is related however, by Ibn Abī Laylā, that 'Aṭā performed the pilgrimage seventy times and lived to the age of one hundred.

SOURCE: S. Moinal Haq, ed., *Ibn Khallikan's Wafayāt al-A'yān wa Anbā' abnā' al-Zamān (M. de Slane's English Translation)* (5 vols.; Karachi: Pakistan Historical Society, 1961–70), 3:248–50 (extracts; footnotes omitted).

21 Ibrāhīm ibn al-Mahdī, the Caliph

'Abd al-Raḥmān ibn al-Jawsī (1126–1200) was a famous preacher, jurisconsult, traditionist, historian, and polemicist of Baghdād. He wrote extensively about Africans and had a high opinion of them, citing the Abyssinians as possessing "abundant generosity, beauty of person, little arrogance, much laughter, pleasant breath, readiness of expression, and sweetness of speech." He believed that a white man could claim no superiority over a black by reason of his color; superiority in a man was "only owing to the fear of God."

The following brief biographical sketch is taken from one of al-Jawsī's writings on "The Excellence of the Blacks." Its subject, Ibrāhīm ibn al-Mahdī (779–839), was proclaimed caliph in Baghdād by the opponents of a rival candidate, al-Ma'mūn, and received the oath of allegiance in the Great Mosque on July 24, 817, taking the regnal name of al-Mubārak. He failed, however, to win the support of certain powerful provincial governors, and had to resign his office in June 819. He lived in hiding for some years, but was captured by agents of al-Ma'mūn in 825. After a brief period of imprisonment he was pardoned, and spent the rest of his life as a courtier in Baghdād and in Sāmarrā.

The fame of Ibrāhīm ibn al-Mahdī does not, however, rest on his political achievements, which were meager. Rather he is remembered as a musician of extraordinary talent. He had "a magnificent voice of tremendous power, with a compass of three octaves," and was "one of the most proficient of mankind in the art of the notes (*nagham*), in the knowledge of the rhythms (*īqā'āt*), and in performing on stringed instruments." [12] In his approach to music he appears to have been a conscious innovator, almost a revolutionary. He pioneered a "romantic" style of performance which challenged the "classical" manner of singing in vogue at court at that time. He suppressed notes and altered musical passages as he thought fit, and, when reproved, answered: "I am a king, and the son of a king; I sing just as the whim of my fancy takes me." [13] Many anecdotes attest to his impish humor, his extreme prodigality, and his delight in besting rivals in musical compositions.[14]

All the surviving traditions about Ibrāhīm ibn al-Mahdī concur in describing his skin color as black. Yet precisely how he came by this distinction is uncertain. His mother is said to have been "a concubine of Daylamī origin, named Shikla." [15] The district of Daylam, which is in northwestern Iran, did not have a significant African population in the eighth century A.D., and the probability that Ibrāhīm derived his color from his mother may be regarded as slight. Did he then obtain it from his father? Al-Mahdī was the son of the caliph al-Manṣūr and his wife, Umm Mūsā, who came from the family of the ancient Himyarite kings of southern Arabia, while the mother of al-Manṣūr (Ibrāhīm's grandfather) was of North African Berber origin. Both of these women could well have had a black African genetic inheritance.

However this may be, the career of Ibrāhīm ibn al-Mahdī demonstrates that it was not only 'Abbāsids "of African origin" who could attain the highest office in the Muslim world, but also the "very black in color."

■

[Ibrāhīm ibn al-Mahdī] was very black in color. He was an excellent, sound man, with a pleasant [gift for] poetry. Allegiance was done to him as Caliph. The reason was that 'Alī ibn Mūsā ar-Riḍā was done allegiance to by al-Ma'mūn as Caliph. The 'Abbāsids, however, were angry, and said: "The rule shall not pass from our hands." So they did allegiance to Ibrāhīm and his name was invoked in the pulpits, and he got possession of Kūfah and the Sawād.* 'Alī

* I.e., ancient Chaldaea. TRANS.

ibn Mūsā ar-Riḍā died. Al-Ma'mūn returned, and the cause of Ibrāhīm became weak. The people deserted him, and he went into concealment, remaining so for six years, four months, and ten days. When he was tired of being in concealment, he wrote to al-Ma'mūn: "Vengeance is secured by punishment, but forgiveness is nearer to piety. He who is deceived in what is held out to him by way of hope [pits himself] against the hostility of time. Allāh has placed the Commander of the Faithful above all pardoners, just as He has placed all sinners below him. So if he [i.e., the Commander of the Faithful] pardons, it is by his grace, and if he punishes, it is by his right." Al-Ma'mūn wrote his judgment [qaḍāhu] below, and said in it: "Power takes away resentment, and repentance in intention suffices." Ibrāhīm entered his presence and said: "If I am guilty, my luck has gone wrong. Lay aside much punishment. Say as Yūsuf said to the sons of Jacob, when they came to him, 'There is no reproach.' " . . .

Ibrāhīm ibn al-Mahdī died in the year 224 [A.D. 838], and [the Caliph] al-Mu'taṣim prayed over him [at his funeral].

SOURCE: Ibn al-Jawzī, "Tanwīr al-Ghabash fī Faḍl as-Sūdān wa'l-Ḥabash" (Illumination of the Darkness on the Excellence of the Blacks and the Abyssinians), ch. 19. Ms. Gotha, 1692; translated for the present volume by Douglas M. Dunlop.

22 Farhan, the Hospitable Amīr

In the eighteenth and nineteenth centuries observers continued to be struck by the large numbers of Africans and persons of African origin holding positions of dignity and power in the Muslim world. The "chief of the black eunuchs" at Constantinople, capital of the Ottoman Empire, in the first decade of the nineteenth century, was "richly dressed, mounted upon a magnificent horse, similar to that of the Sultan, and surrounded by his servants on foot. In passing, he made continued bows to the right and left, with so exact a precision that he might have been taken for an automaton. . . . [He] wore the same mark of distinction in his turban as the Grand Visier." [16] A traveler on the coast of Arabia in 1777 was told that, at that time, the occupant of the highly important post of *sharīf* of Mecca was "as black as a negro." [17] And in the 1830s 'Alī Mansūr, ruler of Ṣan'ā', capital of the Yemen, whose mother was Ethiopian, appeared to a visiting Englishman as "a young man, perhaps twenty-four years of age" with "a very dark complexion" and "dressed in a crimson silk robe with a white turban, wound round a flat gold cloth cap, and a dagger studded with jewels." [18]

An unusually full description of one of these well-placed Africans is included in the memoirs of the Danish traveler Carsten Niebuhr. In 1761 a party of five Danes, with Niebuhr at their head, left Copenhagen on a scientific exploring trip to the Middle East and India. Niebuhr alone survived the journey and later published two volumes recounting his experiences; his narrative has long been accepted as a model of accuracy and candor. When early in their expedition he and his companions arrived at Loheia (Luḥaiya) on the southeast coast of the Red Sea, they were warmly welcomed by the port governor, an African slave named Farhan. The account Niebuhr gives of his and his friends' reception by this black *amīr* of Loheia not only shows how an African of servile origin could rise to a position of power in the Muslim world but also portrays a man so confident of himself and of his authority that he could risk treating infidel strangers generously. Extracts from Niebuhr's description of his stay in Loheia follow.

Not all foreigners received this kind of welcome from black officials in Arabia. Half a century later Dominigo Badia y Leblich, a Spanish army officer posing as a Muslim, was given a quite different reception by the African governor of the Port of Jiddah (Judda). This governor, formerly slave to a *sharīf* of Mecca, tried to obtain one of the Spaniard's camel-saddles as a free gift, disputed with him in the mosque over the placing of a prayer rug, and generally sought to make his visit as brief and uncomfortable as possible.[19]

Africans in authority in the Middle East in the eighteenth and nineteenth centuries fall into two main categories. There were those who inherited a high status, usually as sons of Arab rulers by black concubines, and capitalized on it. Then there were Africans of more lowly origin—slaves and the descendants of slaves—who owed nothing to powerful fathers, having achieved distinction because of their own talents and capabilities. The literature of the period contains numerous examples of men from both groups.

■

Dola, or *Emir,* is the title which the Arabs give to the governors of cities. He of Loheia was an Emir, and his name was *Farhan.* He was a native of Africa, and entirely black; but he had been brought into Arabia in his youth, and sold to a man of rank, who was since dead, after having occupied one of the first offices in the service of the Imam. He had given young Farhan a good education, and had obtained for him a small office, in which he gave so much satisfaction, that his merit soon raised him to be Dola of a considerable city. We found him to possess the dignified politeness of a nobleman, the strictest integrity, and the candid benevolence of a true friend to mankind. . . .

Hitherto, this governor had known no Europeans but India merchants. He was surprised, when he understood, from the letters, that one of us was a physician; another in search of plants; and a third, an observer of stars. Struck with this singularity, and supposing that we might not be in very great haste, he proposed to us to stay some time at Loheia, offering to send us to Mokha upon his own camels. . . .

We no longer hesitated to quit the vessel. The captain, not having taken the precaution to exact payment for our passage, when we came first on board, now applied to the governor, begging him to compel us to pay in full for our passage to Hodeida. The Emir generously replied, that he would pay his demand from his own purse, if we refused; and the merchant Maechsen made the same promise. We did not put the generosity of our Arabian friends to the trial; but felt ourselves deeply indebted to them for their offers and services.

When we spoke of the conveyance of our baggage to the shore, the Emir sent his own boat for it; and, to spare us all trouble, directed the merchant's clerk to satisfy the officers of the customs. In the evening, he sent us an excellent sheep, as a present of welcome, and accompanied it with a letter, in which he called us his guests, and assured us of his friendship. His boat having only mat sails, moved so slowly, that we could not bring all our effects on shore in one day, which gave us some concern, lest we might lose what remained behind, or be robbed of what lay on shore. The Emir, understanding that we were uneasy upon this head, immediately sent some soldiers to guard our baggage. . . .

When we sent to take leave of our friend Emir Farhan, he was indisposed, and we could not see him. But when he heard that we had determined to set out, he desired that we would come to him very late in the evening. We found him in company with several Arabs; before him lay an English telescope which I had lent him, a piece of silk stuff, and a parcel of crowns. He would return me my telescope, but I insisted that he should keep it; which, after long refusal, he at last, with visible satisfaction, consented to do. The piece of silk, with twenty crowns, were a present intended for our physician; and the rest of the crowns he pressed us to accept, in order to pay the hire for our asses and camels.

SOURCE: Carsten Niebuhr, *Travels through Arabia, and Other Countries in the East* (2 vols.; Edinburgh: G. Mudie, 1792), 1: 247–50, 263–64. (Extracts.)

THE REVOLT OF THE ZANJ

MOST BLACK SLAVES in the Muslim world were household servants, artisans, traders, musicians, and the like. The majority shared intimately in the lives of the families to which they were attached, and they were generally well treated. They had little occasion to associate together in large numbers. Thus the opportunity, as well perhaps as the motivation, for revolt were not often present.

Outbreaks by black slaves, however, did occur. In Medina in Arabia in 762 the soldiers of the city's garrison angered the local storekeepers, many of whom were Africans, by commandeering goods without paying for them, and tension between the two groups began to rise. One day, when a soldier tried to "buy" meat from a black butcher without offering money in exchange, the butcher and his assistants attacked the soldier and killed him. Immediately a trumpet-call sounded—it must have been a prearranged signal—and a general assault on the military began. The insurgents were eventually pacified by the "earnest persuasion" of the nonblack inhabitants of the city, who acted as mediators not because they favored the soldiers but because they feared punishment by the government of the Caliph.[20]

The Medina incident of 762 was a revolt by blacks, but it was not a "slave revolt" in the usual sense of the term. The blacks who attacked the military garrison were not all slaves; many were free, and the strong feeling of solidarity between the two groups is a striking feature of the affair.[21] Further, the rebellion was an expression of resentment against illegal commercial practices. It was not directed against a slave-owning class—indeed, slaves and slaveowners, blacks and whites, appear to have made common cause against a garrison that was not only behaving oppressively but was foreign. (Most of the soldiers were Persians.)

To find what may be called true slave revolts by blacks in the Muslim Middle East we have to turn to the area of the Persian Gulf. There slaves from Africa were known as Zanj.[22] Between the seventh and ninth centuries Zanj gang-laborers worked the salt-marshes near Baṣra in ʿIrāḳ. The very heavy work these slaves performed, the use of overseers or "taskmasters," and the large number of slaves involved created conditions similar in all essential respects to those which existed on the plantations of the New World in later times. As in the Americas, intolerable conditions of servitude produced frequent revolts and attempted revolts. The salt-marshes of Baṣra and their environs were the scene of several serious rebellions, beginning in the late seventh century.

23 Sīr Zanjī, Lion of the Zanj

The first Zanj rebellion, which was on a small scale, occurred in 689–90,[23] but a more serious revolt took place in 694–95. For the details of this second and larger outbreak we are dependent on an account written by Aḥmad ibn Yaḥyā al-Balādhurī, who lived 200 years after the event in Baghdād. Al-Balādhurī gives the authorities for his statements at what we regard today as unnecessary length, and he fails to create a synthesis out of his facts. As a result his narrative is, in places, somewhat hard to understand. But in al-Balādhurī we can see at least the outline of the heroic figure of Sīr Zanjī (Shīrazanjī), "the Lion of the Zanj," who defied the Arab Empire and won praise from his enemies for his valor.

■

Rawḥ b. 'Abd al-Mu'min al-Muqri' told me that he heard 'Alī b. Naṣīr al-Jahḍamī, quoting Jarīr b. Ḥāzim, who was quoting from his uncle aṣ-Ṣa'b b. Zayd, say that the Zanj gathered in great numbers by the Euphrates near Baṣra. When people complained about what the Zanj had brought upon them, [al-Ḥajjāj] organized a large army and attacked them. They were scattered, and some of them were crucified and killed.

When 'Abdallāh b. al-Jārūd, together with a group of 'Irāḳī notables, rose against al-Ḥajjāj, while the latter was in Rustaqābādh, the Zanj rebelled again. A great many of them gathered by the Euphrates and chose one of themselves, known as Riyāḥ Shīrazanjī—Shīrazanjī means 'Lion of the Zanj'—as their leader. When al-Ḥajjāj had completed the destruction of those who had rebelled against him in Rustaqābādh and returned to Baṣra, he dispatched an army against [the forces of Shīranzanjī] and killed them.

Rawḥ b. 'Abd al-Mu'min told me, on the authority of his uncle, Ibn Hishām, that Suḥaym b. Ḥafṣ and others said: The Zanj rebelled by the Euphrates during the governorship of al-Ḥajjāj, when Ziyad b. ''Amr al-'Atakī was the prefect of the Baṣra police. Ziyād, under orders from al-Ḥajjāj, dispatched an army of Baṣran fighters under the leadership of his son Ḥafṣ to engage them. He fought with them, but they killed him and defeated his followers. The governor of Ubulla at that time was Kurāz b. Mālik as-Sulamī, and then al-Fihrī.

Rawḥ b. al-Walīd b. Hishām b. Qaḥdham said: Shīrazanjī rebelled by the Euphrates, being joined by many of the Zanj as well as by a group of the people of al-Kallā',* and others, who were white. The governor of Ubulla then was Kurāz as-Sulamī; that was when al-Ḥajjāj went to Rustaqābādh. Shīrazanjī wrote to Kurāz as-Sulamī: "Now then! the time for Sikka, Mother of the Faithful, to give birth has come. So send your wife to serve as a midwife! Salām!" Kurāz fled, abandoning his post, and entered Baṣra.

Ziyād b. 'Amr al-'Atakī, prefect of the Baṣra police during the governorship of al-Ḥajjāj, dispatched an army under the leadership of his son Ḥafṣ to fight Shīrazanjī. The latter fought Ḥafṣ hard, killed him, and defeated his followers. Thus Shīrazanjī became strong. When al-Ḥajjāj returned to Baṣra, he said to the Baṣrans:

* A part of the town of Baṣra. TRANS.

"Your slaves and workmen, witnessing your disobedience, have followed your example. By God! if you do not fight these dogs and rid me of them, I shall destroy your palm trees* and bring upon you what you deserve—the confiscation of your goods and the destruction of your lives." People from every fifth of the [five] fifths of Baṣra answered his call.

Joining them to a group of soldiers, he appointed Kurāz b. Mālik as-Sulamī as their leader. Kurāz fought [the Zanj] until they came to the deserts of Dawraq. He attacked them there, killing Shīrazanjī and all the Zanj save a few.

He [Rawḥ b. al-Walīd] said: Jarīr said of al-Akhṭal,

> Seek not [noble] maternal uncles in Taghlib,†
> The Zanj have nobler maternal uncles than they.

But Sunayḥ b. Riyāḥ, client of the Banū Sāma b. Lu'ay, opposed this, saying:

> If you met the Zanj in war,
> You would find them leaders and brave men.
> They killed Ibn 'Amr when he attacked them;‡
> He learnt that the lances of the Zanj are long!
> Ibn 'Ijl, as you know, is one of them;
> He outshone other men with his magnanimity and good deeds;
> And Banū al-Ḥubāb, too, who are known for their generosity and bravery
> In winter when the wind is blowing from the northward.§
> And Banū Zabība; 'Antar and Harāsa;
> And Sulayk, who suffers hardships well.
> The Prophet has acknowledged the liberality of the Zanj,
> And their bravery when they fight the enemy.‖

* Literally, "I shall cut off the head and cut out the heart of the palm tree so that it dries up." TRANS.

† The tribe of al-Akhṭal. TRANS.

‡ Literally, "when he desired their lances." TRANS.

§ A reference to the common statement that, in the life of the Bedouin, generosity is most appreciated when the weather is cold. TRANS.

‖ By Ibn 'Amr, the poet means Ziyād b. 'Amr, and by Ibn 'Ijl he means 'Abd Allāh b. Khāzim as-Sulamī, whose mother was black. 'Umayr b. al-Ḥubāb's mother was

SOURCE: Al-Balādhurī, *Ansāb al-Ashrāf,* pp. 303–7 (extracts). Translated for the present volume by Hasan Shuraydi.

24 A Servile War in the East

The main Zanj revolt lasted for fifteen years, from 868 to 883. By the late ninth century the 'Abbāsid Caliphate had fallen into a state of near-anarchy, and provincial rebellions, led by military leaders whose troops were loyal to their officers rather than to the Caliphs in Baghdād, had become common. Thus, when the Zanj rose against their masters in 868, theirs was but one of several challenges to the government and the more difficult to deal with in consequence. Of all these outbreaks the Zanj revolt was probably seen by Baghdād as the most dangerous. For a time the black slave insurgents held much of southern 'Irāḳ and southwestern Persia as well as the city of Baṣra, which enabled them temporarily to cut Baghdād's economic lifeline to the Persian Gulf and the East.

The commander-in-chief of the Zanj forces was white, possibly an Arab. His real name is believed to have been Bihbūdh, but he is known to history as 'Alī b. Muḥammad al-Zanjī and also as Sāhib al-Zanj ("Lord of the Zanj").[24] The evidence is strong that he had little personal sympathy for the cause of the oppressed black slaves of the Baṣra salt-marshes. Rather he sought to use them to further his own designs and did not turn to them for support until after he had vainly tried to persuade several other groups, none of them black, to join him in rebellion against the 'Abbāsids.[25] On the other hand, he was a Khārijī, that is, a member of an egalitarian Muslim sect which held, among other beliefs, that the best man available should be chosen as Caliph, "even though he be a black slave." [26] This fact may have helped 'Alī to be accepted as their leader by the Baṣra blacks.

The end of the "revolt of the Zanj" brought an almost complete

---

black, as also was Sulayk's mother, Sulaka. In the phrase, "The Prophet has acknowledged the liberality of the Zanj," the poet is referring to the tradition that the prophet said of the blacks: "They had two good qualities: generosity and helpfulness." TRANS.

decimation of the African slaves of southern 'Irāḳ. Survivors of the slaughter were either recruited into local armies or returned to the land as gang-slaves on small agricultural holdings. Permitted concentrations of slaves in one place were much smaller than they had been in the past.

Theodore Nöldeke's article, "A Servile War in the East," is reproduced below. Though written at the end of the nineteenth century, it is the most comprehensive treatment of the subject that has yet appeared in English.[27]

■

Immediately after the tragic night in which the Caliph Mutawakkil was murdered at the instigation of his own son (11th or 12th December 861), the proud fabric of the Abbāsid empire—already greatly shaken—began to collapse. The troops, Turkish and others, raised and deposed the Caliphs; the generals, for the most part quondam slaves, like those whom they commanded, strove for a mastery which in turn was often dependent on the humors of the soldiery. In the provinces new rulers arose, who did not always think it necessary to acknowledge the Caliph as lord, even in name. Claimants belonging to the house of Alī had success in some places. In the great towns of the Tigris region there were serious popular tumults. Peace and security were enjoyed only in those districts where a governor, practically independent, held firm and strict rule.

This circumstance alone makes it in some degree intelligible how a clever and unscrupulous adventurer, leaning for support on the most despised class of the population, should have been able, not far from the heart of the empire, to set up a rule which for a long time was the terror of the surrounding regions, and only yielded at last, after nearly fourteen years of effort on the part of the caliphate, which had in the meanwhile recovered a little of its former strength.

Alī, son of Mohammed, a native of the large village of Verzenīn, not far from the modern Teherān, gave himself out to be a descendant of Alī and his wife Fātima, the daughter of the Prophet. The claim may have been just; the descendants of Alī by that time were reckoned by thousands, and were very far from being, all of them, persons of distinction. It is, of course, equally possible that his alleged descent was a mere invention. According to some authorities his family belonged to Bahrein, a district of northeastern Arabia, and was a branch of the tribe of Abdalkais, which had its seat there. In any case, he passed for a man of Arab blood. Before he became known to the world, Alī is said, among other adventures, to have gone about for a while in Bahrein, seeking a following there. This statement is made extremely probable by the fact that several of his principal followers belonged to that district, though it is far removed from the world's highways, and but seldom mentioned in history; among these was the black freedman, Sulaimān, son of Jāmi, one of his most capable generals. The ambitious Alī, utilizing the prevailing anarchy, next sought to secure a footing in Basra. This great commercial city, next to Bagdad the most important place in the central provinces, was suffering much at that time from the conflicts of two parties, to all appearance the inhabitants of two different quarters of the town. Yet Alī gained little here; some of his followers, and even the members of his own family, were thrown into prison, a lot which he himself escaped only by flight to Bagdad. But soon afterwards, in connection with a change of governor, new disturbances broke out in Basra, the prisons were broken, and Alī was soon again on the spot. He had already thoroughly surveyed the ground for his plans.

We are very imperfectly acquainted with the scene of the occurrences which I am about to relate. Even if the modern condition of these parts admitted of being represented on maps much more closely than defective surveys allow, and were the surveys better, they would not help us very much, for the whole face of the land has greatly changed since the times we write of. At that time the Euphrates in the lowest part of its course discharged itself into a region of lake and marsh, connected with the sea by a number of tidal channels. The most important of these waters was near Basra, which lay farther to the west than the modern much smaller city of the same name (Bussorah). That place and its immediate neighborhood was intersected by innumerable canals (more than 120,000, it is asserted). The chief arm of the Tigris was at that time the southward flowing, now called Shatt al Hai, upon which stood the city of Wāsit. Farther down, the stream must have turned towards the southeast. The present main arm, whose main course is to the southeast, was at that time dry, or had a very limited volume of water. The lowest part of the Tigris was connected with the stream on which Basra stood by numerous canals, some of them navigable to large sea-going ships. All these waters were reached by the tide. Floods and broken embankments had even by that time converted much arable land into marshes; while, on the other hand, by drainage and embanking, many pieces of land had been reclaimed. Since that time, in common with all the rest of Irāk (Babylonia), this southern portion, in a very conspicuous degree, has been so grievously wasted and neglected, that the forces of nature have entirely gained the upper hand. What was a smiling country has been turned into a wilderness by the spread of the marshes, or by the silting up and stoppage of the drainage channels. The rivers have in part quite changed their beds. On this account we can follow only in a vague way the very precise topographical details which our sources give in describing the campaigns against Alī and his bands.

At no great distance eastward from Basra there were extensive flats, traversed by ditches, in which great numbers of black slaves, mostly from the east coast of Africa, the land of the Zenj,* were employed by rich entrepreneurs of the city in digging away the nitrous surface soil, so as to lay bare the fruitful ground underneath, and at the same time to obtain the saltpeter that occurred in the upper stratum. An industry of such magnitude in the open country is seldom met with in the East. The work in such a case is very hard, and the supervision must be strict. The feeling of affection which in the East binds the slave very closely to the family in which he lives and has grown up, is here altogether wanting. On the other hand, among such masses of slaves working together there easily springs up a certain community of feeling, a common sense of embitterment against their masters, and, under favorable circumstances, a consciousness of their own strength; thus are combined the conditions of a powerful insurrection. So it was in the servile wars of the last century of the Roman republic, and so it was here. Alī recognized the strength latent in those black slaves. The fact that he was able to set this strength in motion, and that he developed it into a terrible power which required long time and the very greatest exertions to overcome it, conclusively shows that he was a man of genius. The "leader of the Zenj," the "Alid," or the "false Alid," plays a very great part in the annals of his time—such a part, indeed, that it is easy to understand why our main informant, Tabarī, should by pre-

*Or, Zanj. Ed.

ference call him "the abominable one," "the wicked one," or "the traitor."

Once before in Babylonia a talented and unscrupulous Arab had utilized a time of internal confusion to raise a sovereignty on religious pretexts by the aid of a despised class; the cunning Mokhtār had appealed to the Persian or half-Persian population of the great cities, particularly Cufa, upon whom the dominant Arabs in those early days of Islam looked down with supreme contempt (685–687 A.D.). But our hero went much deeper, and maintained himself much longer, than Moktār.

Before openly declaring himself, Alī had sought out from among the lowest strata of the population and the freedmen in particular, suitable tools for the execution of his plans. In the beginning of September 869 he betook himself, at first under the guise of business agent for a princely family, to the saltpeter district, and began at once to rouse the slaves. Saturday, 10th September 869, is reckoned as the date at which he openly declared himself. He represented to the negro slaves how badly they were being treated, and promised them, if they joined him, freedom, wealth, and—slaves. In other words, he did not preach universal equality and well-being, but reserved the supremacy for the particular class to which he addressed himself. All this, of course, was clothed in religious forms. He proclaimed the restoration of true legality. None but those who followed himself were believers, or entitled to claim the heavenly and earthly rights of the true Moslem. Alī thus appealed at once to the nobler and to the more vulgar feelings of the rudest masses, and with complete success. We may accept the statement that he gave himself out for inspired; at any rate to the blacks he seemed to be a messenger of God. That he himself believed in his own heavenly vocation is hardly to be assumed; all that we know of him bespeaks a very cool understanding. We learn much more, it is true, about his warlike deeds than about his true character; religious fancy has often great influence even upon coolly calculating natures, and in the East especially it is very difficult to draw the line between self-deception and imposition upon others. That Alī was sincere when he betook himself to astrology in important crises need not be doubted, for this superstition at that time held sway over even the clearest heads with hardly an exception.

Since the rebel leader claimed, as we have seen, to be descended from Alī, Mohammed's son-in-law, we should naturally have expected to find him, like other Alids, appealing to the divine right of his house, and coming forward as founder of a sect of Shīites. But instead of this he declared himself for the doctrine of those most decided enemies of Shīite legitimism, the Kharijites or Zealots, who held the first two Caliphs alone to have been lawful, and rejected Othmān and Alī alike, because they had adopted wordly views; who demanded that none but "the best man" should wield the sovereignty, "though he were an Abyssinian slave"; who, moreover, in their ethical rigorism regarded as idolatry every grave sin, and most of all, of course, opposition to their own doctrine as the true Islam; and who accordingly regarded all their Moslem enemies, with their wives and families, as lawfully given over to the sword or to slavery. One of the most prominent officers of the negro leader preached in this sense in Basra when it was taken; the same idea lent fury to his black troops; and even his banner bore the text of the Koran which had been one of the chief watchwords of the old death-defying Karijites. It was certainly also with a purpose that he called himself upon this banner simply, "Alī, son of Mohammed," without allusion to his high descent. With this it agrees that an original document of the period shortly after his death designates him as a Kharijite. His choice of party was in the highest degree appropriate. The slaves were easily gained by a strong personality who could condescend to them, but they were not to be inspired with enthusiasm for a mystical hereditary claim. But that they themselves were the true believers and the lawful destroyers or masters of all others, the blacks were ready to believe; and they acted accordingly. Perhaps their leader took this also into account, that in Basra (on the lower classes of which place he seems at first to have reckoned), the Shīite doctrine was at that time very unpopular, quite the opposite of what it was in Cufa, the old rival of Basra. From what has been said it will be abundantly clear why Karmat, one of the founders of the Karmatians, an extreme Shīite sect which was destined soon after this to fill the whole Mohammedan world with fear and dismay, should, on religious grounds, have decided not to connect himself with the negro leader, however useful this association might otherwise have been to him.

The nature of the ground was highly favorable to a rising of the kind. Indeed, some forty years before this, in the marshes between

Wāsit and Basra, the Gypsies (Zutt) settled there had, augmented by offscourings of humanity brought together from all quarters, lived the life, first of robbers, and afterwards of declared rebels, and were only after the greatest exertion compelled to capitulate; yet these were people who neither in courage nor in numbers could be compared to the East Africans, and that, too, at a time when the caliphate was still in reality a world empire.

Of the beginning of the negro insurrection we have exceptionally minute details from the accounts of eyewitnesses. We learn how one band of slaves after another—a troop of fifty, a troop of five hundred, and so forth—obeyed the call of the new Messiah. We even know the names of those slaves who incited their companions to join the rebel leader. As was natural, their wrath was directed, not merely against their masters, who were mostly absent, but even more against the taskmasters, all of them, we may suppose, themselves slaves or at most freedmen. Yet the leader spared their lives and let them go, after they had first been soundly beaten by their former subordinates. The owners more than once begged him to let them have their slaves back again, promising him amnesty and five gold pieces per head; but he refused all offers; and when the blacks began to show uneasiness about such negotiations, he solemnly pledged himself never to betray them, and to further their best interests. This oath he kept.

The most numerous class of these negroes—the Zenj, properly so called—were almost all of them ignorant of Arabic; for during their common labors in the open air they had had no occasion to learn this language, though the Oriental black, for the most part, very readily drops his mother tongue to take up that of his master. With these, accordingly, Alī had to use an interpreter. But others of the negroes—those from more northern countries (Nubia and the like)—already spoke Arabic. With the saltpeter workers were undoubtedly associated many fugitive slaves from the villages and towns, and probably all sorts of fair-skinned people as well, but apparently few representatives of the urban proletariat. A valuable accession to their strength was contributed by the black soldiers who, especially after defeats, went over to the Zenj from the government troops. So, for example, at the very outset a division of the army fell upon the almost unarmed rebels, but was beaten; whereupon three hundred blacks at once went over to the latter.

Unfortunately we possess practically no particulars as to the internal arrangements of this singular State, composed of fanatical warriors or robbers who once had been, for the most part, Negro slaves. With regard to their great achievements in war, it is to be remembered that they were excellently led; that they fought upon a favorable and familiar soil, full of marshes and canals, of which they thoroughly knew how to take advantage, while the enemy was equipped for an altogether different kind of fighting; and, finally, that the East African blacks, as a rule, are brave. It was not without reason that many negroes were at that time enrolled in the troops of the empire; even at present the black regiments of the Khedive are much more serviceable than those raised in Egypt. We know, too, that the negro leader * maintained strict discipline.

It would seem that he had exerted himself to win over the villagers also, who for the most part, if not altogether, were dependent on aristocratic or wealthy masters. Perhaps he was more successful in this than our authorities say. He sometimes gave up hostile villages to plunder; but the provisioning of his large masses of men was probably, to a considerable extent, made easier for him through the connivance of the peasants. And when, at the very outset, he allowed a band of Mecca pilgrims to pass unharmed, this action was not only sagacious, but also in accordance with the doctrine which he professed.

Hardly had the slaves' revolt declared itself when troops were sent for its suppression; but within a few weeks the Zenj had gained several victories. The imperial armies were, it may be presumed, not large enough, and were badly led; the enemy, as was natural, was underrated. Here, at the outset, we find the Zenj's peculiar mode of fighting,—namely, out of concealed side-channels, heavily overgrown with reeds, to fall suddenly upon the rear of the enemy's troops as they rowed along. In this war it is the regular thing that a number of the vanquished are drowned. The leader of the Zenj was always well served by his scouts.

Of the booty taken in the first encounters, the most important part consisted of arms. Prisoners were remorselessly put to death. In fact, according to Kharijite doctrine, they were unbelievers, and worthy

* I.e., 'Alī b. Muḥammad. "Leader of the Negroes" is meant, rather than "negro leader." Ed.

of death; while the women and the children, as non-Moslems, were made slaves. When at last the negro chief had defeated an army consisting principally of inhabitants of Basra, he marched in person against that town; he calculated, it would seem, that one of the two town parties, with which he had frequently had dealings, would declare itself for him; but in this he was deceived. The people, high and low, stood together. They faced him on Sunday, 23rd October 869 (full six weeks only after the date of his first rising), and completely shattered his army; he himself barely escaped death, fighting bravely. But the citizen-army, though it had manfully defended hearth and home, was hardly fit to take the offensive, and certainly had no leader who could be matched with Alī, who quickly rallied his followers. When, on the second day, the first division of the Basrans was advancing by water, bodies of Zenj posted in ambush on both sides of the canal fell upon their rear. Some vessels capsized. The negroes fought with fury; their women threw bricks. Those also who were advancing by land were involved in the disaster; many were killed or drowned. The defeat of the townspeople was complete. A large number of members of the ruling family even, descendants of Sulaimān, the brother of the first two Abbāsid Caliphs, perished. Alī caused a whole ship to be laden with heads of the slain and sent along a canal to Basra. His associates now urged him immediately to fall upon the town; but his reply was, that they ought to be glad that they might now count upon peace for some time, so far as the Basrans were concerned. He had in the meanwhile no doubt satisfied himself that he had no substantial following in Basra, and still felt himself too weak to make himself master of the great city.

After these events the Zenj chief caused to be established, on a suitable dry spot, impregnated with salt and thus without vegetation, a settlement of his blacks, which he exchanged for another in the following year. His people reared huts of palm branches, we may suppose, or perhaps of mud. The "palaces" of the chief and of his principal officers, the prisons for the numerous captives, the mosques, and some other public buildings which were gradually added, may in some cases have been relatively handsome and internally adorned with the spoils of the enemy, but their material was certainly, at best, sun-dried brick. In the broader sense, the city finally, founded, called Mokhtāra ("the elect city"), covered a large area, and included extensive fields and palm groves. It lay somewhat below Basra, abutted on the west bank of the Tigris, and was intersected by the canal Nahr Abilkhasīb, the main direction of whose course was from north to south (or perhaps from northeast to southwest); other canals also surrounded, or, we may suppose, traversed it. With the complete change of the water-courses in that region, it is hardly likely that its site will ever be exactly made out.

The inhabitants of this ephemeral capital for the most part, doubtless, drew the necessaries of life from the immediate neighborhood. Yet they were also dependent to some extent on imports; so that in the end, when the blockade was fully established and all communications cut off, they were reduced to great extremity. Until then traders and Bedouins had ventured to bring provisions to the negro city even in full sight of the hostile army. The dates grown there served, in part at least, as payment for the Bedouins. But as the home consumption of this chief article of produce hardly left much over for trade, we must assume that the dealers who thus risked their lives for the sake of gain must have been paid for the flour, fish, and other provisions which they brought with articles of plunder, and with money that had been accumulated by plunder and taxation, or rather blackmail.

At the pressing entreaty of the terrified Basrans the government sent the Turkish general Jolān. For six months he lay in camp face to face with the Zenj. His troops, consisting mostly of horsemen, could not move freely over the ground, thickly planted as it was with date-palms and other trees, and broken up by water-courses. At last a night attack by the negroes upon the entrenched camp made such an impression upon his soldiers, that Jolān judged it expedient to withdraw to Basra. Previously to this an attack of the Basrans had been victoriously repelled by the Zenj. The latter now grew so bold that they seized upon a fleet of twenty-four vessels bound for Basra; much blood was shed in this action, and the booty, including many captive women and children, was very great. On Wednesday, 19th June 870, they attacked the flourishing town of Obolla, which lay four hours from Basra, on the Tigris (approximately on the site of the modern Bussorah), and captured it after a brief struggle, in which the commandant fell along with his son. The slaughter was great: many were drowned; the city, built of wood, fell a prey to the flames. The fall of Obolla had such an effect upon the inhabitants of Abbādān, a town on an island at the mouth of the Tigris, that they made their submission to the Zenj; in doing so they had to deliver up their slaves and all their arms; the former augmenting the fighting strength of the victors. Hereupon the negro chief sent an army far into Khūzistān (Susiana), the adjoining country on the east. Wherever submission was not made, fire and sword did their work. On Monday, 14th August, the capital Ahwāz (on the stream now known as the Kārūn) was taken. The garrison of this important place had prudently withdrawn, and this doubtless secured for the inhabitants a milder treatment. But, of course, all the property of the government and of the governor, who with his people had remained at his post, was confiscated.

Thus, then, within less than a year an adventurer at the head of negro slaves had taken considerable cities, made himself master of the mouth of the Tigris, and gained control of wide territories. Even the disturbance to commerce was very serious. The communications of Bagdad, the world-city, were broken, and its victualing rendered a matter of difficulty. Basra trembled at the fate of Obolla. Matters certainly could never have gone quite so far, if in the meantime the greatest confusion had not prevailed at the then residence of the Caliph, Sāmarrā (on the Tigris, some three days' journey above Bagdad). At the very time of the fall of Obolla the disputes of those in authority had led to the death, after less than a year's reign, of the pious Caliph Muhtadī, and the proclamation of his cousin Motamid as Caliph. But this was the beginning of an improved state of affairs. For though Motamid was not at all such a sovereign as the times demanded, yet his brother Mowaffak,* who in reality held the reins of government, leaving to the Caliph only the honor and luxury of the exalted position, had intelligence and perseverance enough gradually to restore the power of the dynasty, in the central provinces at least. At first, indeed, he had too much on hand elsewhere to be able to think of the Zenj, but in the early summer of 871 he had got so far as to send against them an army under the command of his chamberlain Saīd. Saīd at first inflicted serious losses on them, but in the end suffered a disastrous defeat through a night attack. He was recalled, but his successor fared no better. Five hundred heads of soldiers of his were exhibited in the immediate neighborhood of Basra; many were drowned. In Susiana, too, a general of

* Al-Muwaffaḳ, brother of the Caliph, al-Mu'tamid, and the savior of the 'Abbāsid state. Ed.

the blacks had fought with success, but their chief called him back to cut off the Basrans anew from communication with the Tigris, which had recently been reopened for them by the imperial troops. This done, the Zenj for some time pressed hard on Basra itself, which had but an inadequate garrison, was torn by party dissensions, and was suffering from dearth. The negroes were joined by a number of Bedouins. Great as is the contempt with which the genuine Arab regards the black, the prospect of plunder, and the plunder of so rich a town as Basra, is an attraction which the hungry son of the desert cannot resist. These Bedouins were not equal to the Zenj, either in bravery or in loyalty; but they were valuable to the chief, as supplying him with a body of cavalry. On the 7th September 871, during the Friday service, the negro general Mohallabī, with these Arab horsemen and with black foot soldiers, penetrated into the city, but retired once more, after setting fire to it in several places. It was not till Monday that the Zenj took full possession. The massacre that followed was frightful. It is even alleged that many inhabitants were induced, by offers of quarter, to gather together at certain places, where they could more easily be cut down. The chief had vowed direst vengeance on the city which had deceived his hopes. His general Alī, son of Abbān, had allowed a deputation from one of the parties of the town to approach his chief with prayers for quarter; but he would not admit them to his presence, and superseded the general by a less softhearted man. The brutal negro slaves waded in the blood of the free men. The lowest estimate places the number of the slain in Basra at 300,000. The captured women and children were carried into slavery. The noblest women of the houses of Alī and of the reigning house of Abbās were sold to the highest bidder. Many negroes are said to have received as many as ten slaves, or more, for their share.[28]

But a permanent occupation of the great city was not feasible. It was forthwith evacuated, and the army, which, immediately after the arrival of the shocking tidings, had been despatched from the capital, under Mowallad, against the Zenj, was able, in conjunction with the remains of the troops already in the district, to occupy Basra and Obolla without striking a blow. Many inhabitants who had been lucky enough to escape gathered together once more in Basra. But when Mowallad proceeded further against the Zenj, he was, like his predecessors, defeated in a night attack, and compelled to withdraw again to the neighborhood of the town. In Susiana likewise the fortunes of war, after some fluctuations, proved favorable to the Zenj.

Mowaffak himself now advanced with a brilliant force to the neighborhood of the negro city; but this also suffered defeat (29th April 872). The mortal wound of Moflih, the actual commander, seems to have thrown the soldiers into confusion at once. Mowaffak remained in the district of Obolla, keeping the Zenj steadily in his eye. In one of the battles of this period one of their best generals, Yahyā of Bahrein, was wounded and made prisoner. He was brought to Sāmarrā, and there, in the brutal and cowardly fashion then customary in the treatment of prominent captive rebels, was led about on a camel for exhibition before being cruelly put to death in the presence of the Caliph.

After Mowaffak's troops had somewhat recovered from the severe sicknesses from which they had suffered in those hot marshy regions, and had repaired their equipment, he again marched against the enemy; but although he occasionally gained some advantage and succeeded in rescuing captive women and children, he in the end sustained another reverse; and, to add to his misfortunes, his camp took fire and was burned. Towards the beginning of full summer, accordingly, he found himself compelled to quit the proper seat of war, and to withdraw to Wāsit. His army melted away almost entirely, and he himself, in January 873, returned to Sāmarrā, leaving Mowallad behind him in Wāsit. The expedition on which such great hopes had been built had come to nothing; yet it had not been wholly vain, for Mowaffak had come to know the enemy more perfectly, and had seen more clearly how he was to be reached.

After the imperial army had left the field, the negro chief again sent considerable forces into Susiana, who, with some trouble, succeeded a second time in taking Ahwāz, the capital (beginning of May 873). Several prisoners of distinction, who had fallen into the hands of the victors there, had their lives spared by the chief, doubtless with a view to heavy ransoms. The expeditions of the Zenj into the neighboring countries, be it noted, were designed less for the acquisition of permanent possessions than to procure food and booty, perhaps also to inspire terror in the enemy. The Zenj leader may sometimes have dreamt of conquests on the grand scale, but in the end he always recognized that he and his negroes were safe only among their marshes and ditches.

A new army, dispatched from the capital, ultimately defeated the Zenj in Susiana, and drove them out of the country. Other armies pressed on them from other quarters, and sought to cut off their supplies. The principal leader in these enterprises was one of the most powerful men in the empire—Mūsā the Turk, son of Boghā, who had left Sāmarrā in September 873. Still nothing decisive took place.

A considerable interval passes, during which we learn nothing of the Zenj. Meanwhile, they were aided by a rising to which they had not contributed, and which had not them in view. For when a rebel, who had made himself master of Persia proper (Persis), had vanquished one of the subordinates of Mūsā, the latter found himself uncomfortable in Wāsit, and begged to be relieved of his post (spring 875). Provisionally, Mowaffak undertook, nominally at least, the government of Mūsā's provinces along with the war against the Zenj. The latter had meanwhile taken Ahwāz a third time, and had proved disastrous occupants. They had to be left alone, for now a quite new and very dangerous enemy made a diversion in their favor. Yakūb, son of Laith, the coppersmith (Saffār), who had conquered for himself a great empire in the East, aiming also at the possession of the central lands of the caliphate, forced his way through Persia and Susiana and advanced upon Bagdad. But between Wāsit and the capital he was met by Mowaffak with the imperial army, and decisively defeated (April 876).

The Zenj, of course, took advantage of the withdrawal of troops from the lower Tigris, every available soldier being required against the coppersmith. They extended themselves farther to the north, where the Arab tribes who had their settlements in the marshy districts to the south of Wāsit lent them a helping hand. Isolated efforts to drive them back had no result. The negro king now seriously exerted himself to become sovereign of Susiana. A Kurdish upstart, Mohammed, son of Obaidallāh, who, under Yakūb as his superior, had made himself master of part of that province, became his ally, but with no sincere intentions. The two armies parted, and consequently the Zenj were defeated by the imperial troops, especially as a number of Bedouins had gone over to the latter. The *Societas malorum* had not held good. Yet the government derived no substantial benefit; in the long run the Zenj retained, even in these regions, the upper hand. All sorts of troubles, and, in particular, the threatening proximity of Yakūb, who would not be propitiated by Mowaffak, and who might break out again at any moment, sufficiently explain why nothing considerable was attempted against them. For the inhabitants of those countries this must have been a dreadful time. Yakūb peremptorily rejected the alliance tendered by the chief of the Zenj, yet, at last, without definite agreement, a truce was established between the two enemies of Mowaffak. But after Yakūb's death (4th June 879) the imperial regent quickly induced his successor, his brother Amr, to conclude a peace. Meanwhile, he made him very great concessions, in order that in his great expedition against the blacks his left flank and his rear might remain covered.

In 878 the Zenj succeeded in capturing Wāsit and other cities of Babylonia; the customary atrocities were, of course, not wanting. But in the end not even Wāsit was held; Mowaffak's lieutenant again forced the Zenj back to bounds. The latter continued to make plundering and devastating incursions; in 879 they ventured as far as Jarjarāyā, less than seventy miles below Bagdad, so that the terrified inhabitants of the country fled for refuge to the capital.

In Susiana, Tekīn the general opposed the Zenj with vigor, and relieved the great city of Shūshter, which they were besieging, but afterwards entered into negotiations with them. When these became known, one portion of his army went over to the enemy, another joined Mohammed, son of Obaidallāh. Such things throw a strange light upon the discipline and loyalty of the imperial army. After much fighting and conference the Kurdish Mohammed had at last to bring himself to recognize the supremacy of the negro chief, to surrender to him a part of his territory, along with the important town of Rāmhormuz, and to pay tribute; but even now he continued to act in a thoroughly untrustworthy manner, and caused all kinds of mischief to the Zenj.

In any case, the power of the Zenj was now (879) greater than ever. But it was at this point that the tide really began to turn. Mowaffak's position had gradually grown stronger, and the death of Yakūb had given him a free hand. He now no longer delayed to summon all his resources for making an end of the black robber-scourge. In doing so he proceeded with great deliberation and unwonted caution. He had learned wisdom at last, from many failures of the imperial troops, which, in part, had followed close on brilliant victories. He now knew that it was impossible to get at these amphibians in the same way as enemies on firm accessible soil are reached. His preparations for a decisive campaign against the Zenj would require to be of a quite peculiar character, and in the campaign itself it would be of supreme importance, along with bravery, to exercise all caution. A great general with similar resources at his command would certainly have annihilated the blacks much more quickly than Mowaffak did; the latter in the campaign plays the part rather of the prudent statesman who acts only with hesitation, does not place much at stake, and strives towards his end slowly, if surely.

The task of expelling the Zenj from the northern territories near Wāsit was entrusted by Mowaffak, in the first instance, to his son Abul Abbās (afterwards Caliph Motadid), who was now but twenty-three years old. In November or December 879 the troops and ships of the latter were reviewed by his father near Bagdad. The fleet consisted of very diverse kinds of craft, but all of them rowing vessels. The largest served partly for transport, partly as floating fortresses; a smaller kind, of which some were mentioned as carrying twenty, and others as carrying forty rowers, seem chiefly to have been used for attack. The young prince justified the confidence reposed in him. He gave battle repeatedly with success, and, though operations had often to be suspended, the Zenj were steadily compelled to give place. One of their captains was taken and pardoned; this is the first instance of the application of a new policy which was to gain over the officers and soldiers of the rebel. This course, more astute than heroic, had great success. In proportion as the situation of the negro chief grew serious, his subordinates were more ready to desert him, and, instead of continuing to endure the dangers and privations of a siege, to accept from Mowaffak amnesty, honors, rewards. Care was taken to make the deserters in their robes of honor conspicuous, so that the rebels might be able to see them. Their prince, of course, did all he could on the other side to check the falling away. Thus, we are told that he caused "the son of the king of the Zenj" to be put to death, because he had heard that he proposed to go over to the enemy. Of this real negro prince we would gladly know more. The prisoners taken by the imperial troops were, as a rule, killed. Abul Abbās distinguished himself personally by his bravery. In one of the battles twenty arrows were found sticking in the coat of felt which he wore over his breastplate. Almost a year passed before Mowaffak in person appeared with a great army on the scene (Tuesday, 11th October 880). The first result of consequence was the capture of the city of Manīa, built by the Zenj not very far from Wāsit, when five thousand captive women and children were restored to freedom. The liberation of great masses of women and children becomes an occurrence of increasing frequency as one place after another is taken from the possession of the negroes. At every advance Mowaffak was very careful to secure his rearward communications, and to make it impossible for the blacks to attack him from behind. This rendered necessary, among other things, much river engineering, making and breaking of dams. The regent thereupon again left the campaign for a time in the hands of his son, and marched towards Susiana (Friday, 6th January 881), to clear that portion of the empire. This was quickly done, and without much trouble, for the negro chief himself had given orders to evacuate the territory which was not to be definitively held, so as to concentrate his whole power. On their march back the Zenj continued to loot some villages, although these had made their submission to the chief. Several bands cut off from the main army asked and obtained pardon. That honest Kurd Mohammed naturally made his peace with Mowaffak without delay, and was received into favor. On Saturday, 18th February 881, Mowaffak again joined his son Abul Abbās and his other son Hārūn, whom he had sent on before with his army from Wāsit towards the south, and the united hosts advanced.

The negroes were now confined to their own proper territory in and around Mokhtāra. Before the attack on this place began, Mowaffak sent once more a solemn summons to the rebel calling upon him to surrender, and promising him a full pardon if he obeyed. It need not be said that such a demand had no effect. Bad as the position of the Zenj chief was,—and it grew worse every day,—he could not stoop to become a pensioner of the Caliph. Moreover, it was at any moment possible that troubles in Bagdad or Sāmarrā, or the appearance of some dangerous rebel in one of the provinces, might compel the persistent adversary to abandon the siege and all that he had gained. Some of his officers were less steadfast. The desertion of these to the regent, who received them with open arms, began with his first approach, and went on repeating itself to the end of the bloody tragedy. Many soldiers also went over. Mowaffak so arranged that the negroes in his army tempted those of the enemy over to his side. All so inclined were forthwith enrolled in his ranks. Naturally, no one dreamed for a moment of considering the claims of their former masters upon these slaves. In this way the negro chief found many of his best forces gradually drawn away from himself and augmenting the strength of the enemy; this they did less by their direct fighting capacity than by their accurate acquaintance with the localities and with the whole condition of things. To the cause of the Zenj it was, moreover, highly prejudicial that their leader had to become ever-more mistrustful of his subordinates. In fact, several of his best colleagues, in whom he had placed perfect confidence, abandoned him, though others held by him to the death. The amnesty was extended also to those Bedouins who shall fall away from the Zenj. On the other hand, a leader of the negroes, who had been made a prisoner, when it was proved that he had treated women who had fallen into his hands with singular atrocity, was put to a painful death. In other cases also, cruel punishments were sometimes inflicted on prisoners.

The city of Mokhtāra, the siege of which henceforward constitutes the whole war, was protected, not only by water-courses and dams, but also by a variety of fortifications properly so called. It even had catapults upon its walls. During the course of the long siege new defensive works of various kinds continued to be erected, and artificial inundations were also resorted to. Nor was there any lack of boats, and still less of men, though we may take it that the number of 300,000 fighting men claimed for the negro leader is greatly exaggerated. The Zenj may very well have outnumbered their assailants, whose strength is given at 50,000, at least at the beginning of the struggle; but the latter were, on the whole, certainly much better equipped, better fed, and continually recruited by newly arriving troops. Mowaffak, however, had so little thought of taking Mokhtāra by sudden attack, that in front of the place, though judiciously separated from it by the breadth of the river, he built for himself on the east bank of the Tigris a city-camp, which he named after himself Mowaffakīya. The matter of supreme importance was to cut off the supplies of the Zenj, and to secure his own. In Mowaffakīya a lively trade sprang up: he even caused money to be coined there. But the Zenj still showed themselves very troublesome enemies, and occasionally captured transports that had been destined for the imperial troops. It was not until a new fleet arrived from the Persian coast that intercourse with the outer world was made almost impossible for the negroes; and henceforward provisions could only be introduced occasionally and by stealth. For the Bedouins, who had still been venturesome enough to supply the Zenj with various kinds of food in exchange for dates, Mowaffak established an easy and safe market in Basra. Thus gradually the scarcity of food began to be keenly felt among the blacks, and the supply of bread virtually ceased. Nevertheless, they held out bravely; and in the numerous collisions which took place, as our authorities make plain, notwithstanding their highly official coloring, the imperialists had by no means always the best of it.

Towards the end of July 881 the troops succeeded in forcing their way into Mokhtāra, and had begun their work of destruction with fire and sword, but the same evening they again abandoned their capture. The same thing frequently recurred; moreover, the invading troops were more than once again driven out by the Zenj. At a comparatively late stage of the siege (end of 882) Mowaffak found himself under the necessity of again removing his base, which he had recently advanced to the western bank of the Tigris, back to the eastern, so troublesome had the Zenj proved themselves to be. The main action was, moreover, more than once interrupted; as, for example, from the end of summer 881 till October of that year. In their assaults on the town the besiegers specially directed their efforts to destruction of the defensive works, so that several approaches lay open in a way that did not admit of their being again closed; they also set themselves as much as possible to clear away the obstacles—bridges, dams, chains—which the besieged had introduced to prevent the entrance of great ships into the waterways, and especially into the main canal—the Nahr Abilhasīb. In these operations the tide proved sometimes a help, sometimes a hindrance; it frequently happened that the ebb would leave the vessels high and dry on the sand. As the opposing parties were often quite near one another, separated only, it might be, by narrow ditches, wounds were frequent. In addition to the ordinary weapons of war, molten lead was hurled against the foe. The besiegers had also with them "naphtha men," who threw Greek fire at the Zenj or their works. Fireships were also sometimes used against the bridges. Occasionally the assailants made way far into the city; on Monday, 10th December 882, they in this manner destroyed the building which "the abominable ones called their mosque," but which the Faithful naturally regarded as nothing better than a synagogue of Satan. But in this particular attack Mowaffak himself was seriously wounded with an arrow, shot by a quondam Byzantine slave; and as he did not spare himself, his wound grew alarmingly worse. Operations were on this account suspended for a considerable time, and many became so filled with fear that they quitted Mowaffakīya. And in the meanwhile an untoward circumstance of another kind arose. The Caliph Motamid manifested an inclination to free himself from the tutelage of his brother, and (in the beginning of December 882) quitted Sāmarrā, to take refuge with Ibn Tūlūn, the vassal prince of Egypt. But the governor of Bagdad, Ibn Kondāj, who held by Mowaffak, intercepted the Caliph and brought him back to the residency (middle of February 883). For this service Mowaffak loaded Ibn Kondāj with honors. The wretched Caliph had even to submit so far as to cause Ibn Tūlūn, whom he had just been regarding as his liberator, to be cursed from every pulpit as a rebel against the ordinance of God; nay, his own son, designated to be his successor (though afterwards compelled to surrender his right), had to be the first solemnly to pronounce this curse. We can easily understand how in these circumstances Mowaffak was pressingly urged to abandon his camp for a while and betake himself to the center of the empire; but he continued steadfast in his task. What he had neither heroic courage nor brilliant generalship to achieve, he effected by caution and perserverance.

The Zenj leader utilized to the utmost the truce that had been thus forced upon his assailants, to place his defensive works in as complete repair as possible, or even to strengthen them still further. It is certain, too, that he was adequately informed by his spies and scouts as to the seriousness of Mowaffak's then position, both personally and politically, and he may well have cherished new hopes; but in February 883 he was again sorely pressed: his own palace was plundered and burnt, and he himself exposed to great danger. In March and April the illness of Mowaffak rendered necessary another cessation of the attack, but from the end of April onwards the struggle was seldom intermitted for any time. The rebel chief transferred the center of his defense from the west to the east side of the main canal, though without wholly abandoning the former.

The desertions of his officers went on increasing. It is alleged that even his own son opened negotiations with Mowaffak; these, however, we may conjecture to have been quite hollow. But, among others, Shibl, a former slave, one of his most prominent lieutenants, went over to Mowaffak, and allowed himself forthwith to be sent directly against his old comrades. To another of these people, Sharānī, whose wicked deeds had been many, there was at first an inclination to refuse pardon; but, in order not to scare his accomplices, he too was at last accepted, and received a rich reward for his treachery. The official account gives us a touching scene, in which Mowaffak, shortly before the last decisive struggle, solemnly admonishes the deserters to make good their evil deeds by bravery and fidelity; and this, deeply moved, they promised to do.

In the actual encounters the Zenj still continued to show great courage. The imperialists were not now, it is true, invariably forced to give up again in the evening the ground they had gained during the day; yet even in the great battle of Tuesday, 21st May 883, in which the harem of the negro chief, with more than a hundred women and children, had been sacked, and Prince Abul Abbās, in his advance, had burned great stores of grain, the assailants found themselves at last so hard pressed by the blacks that Mowaffak judged it advisable to withdraw them to his ships. He did not yet feel himself strong enough to deliver the mortal blow. But now new reinforcements were continually coming in, though indeed, for the most part, these did nothing more than repair the continual losses through battle and sickness. Among the newcomers were numerous volunteers, who, from religious motives, entered upon the holy war against the heretics. An event of very special importance was the separation from his master of Lūlū, the commander in Northern Syria of the forces of Ibn Tūlūn, the ruler of Egypt mentioned above; he entered into negotiations with Mowaffak, of which the result was that with a considerable army behind him he joined the latter on Thursday, 11th July 883. The preparations for a decisive assault were now complete; transport ships for large masses of troops were in immediate readiness, and the great waterways of the hostile territory were by this time so entirely free of all obstacles as to be passable at all states of the tide. Mowaffak is said to have brought more than 50,000 men into the great battle of Monday, 5th August, while yet leaving a large number behind in Mowaffakīya. After a severe struggle the whole city was taken. The negro chief fled; but as the imperialists, instead of pursuing him keenly, occupied themselves with plunder, and by becoming scattered, exposed themselves to the danger of surprise, a withdrawal was again in the end found necessary, and Alī returned once more to the city. The respite, however, was but short. The final assault was delivered on Saturday, 11th August 883. From the first the advanced troops broke up the Zenj. Their leader was separated from his companions; Sulaimān, son of Jāmi, along with others, was made prisoner. A section of the Zenj, indeed, drove back the enemy once more, but this was of no avail; in a little news was brought that the rebel chief was dead, and one of Lūlū's people almost immediately confirmed this intelligence by bringing in his head. It is not certain how he met his death. Perhaps we may venture to believe [the statement of Hamza Isfahānī] that he poisoned himself. According to another story, he perished in flight. That he did not fall in battle is further indicated by the circumstance that none of our authorities, with all their fullness, speak of any combatant as having sought to obtain the royal reward for slaying the archrebel. Death by his own hand seems the most appropriate to the nature of the man; at the same time, I am free to confess that we can form a tolerably vivid picture of him only if we bring a good deal of fancy into play.

When Mowaffak saw the head of his enemy, he threw himself upon the ground in an attitude of worship, full of thankfulness to God. The example was followed by officers and troops. It would almost seem as if without the energy of Lūlū the mortal struggle of the Zenj might have been still further protracted. This is not indeed exactly what is said by the history, written as it is entirely in the government sense, but there is evidence for it in a couplet which the soldiers sang, to the effect that—

> Beyond all doubt, say what you choose,
> The victory was all Lūlū's.

On this and the following days some thousands of Zenj surrendered themselves, and were pardoned; it would have been a senseless thing to have driven the last remnants of the enemy to desperation, especially when they could be utilized as soldiers. Others, again, fared badly who had fled into the desert, some dying of thirst, and some being made slaves by the Bedouins. Yet a number of blacks still remained unsubdued, and from the swampy thickets to the west of Basra, whither they had a considerable time before been sent by the negro chief, continued to carry on their robberies and murders. Mowaffak was on the point of sending a division against them, when they, too, made their submission. When they showed themselves, their good condition struck the beholders; they had not gone through the hardships of the long siege.

The son of the rebel chief and five of his high commanders had fallen alive into the hands of the victors. They were kept in prison in Wāsit until one day the negroes there once more raised an insurrection, and by acclamation chose the first-named as their chief. The prisoners were then beheaded (885). The bowman who had hit Mowaffak was recognized far away from the seat of war at Rāmhormuz in Susiana, and brought to Mowaffak, who handed him over to his son Abul Abbās to be put to death.

Mowaffak remained for a considerable time in the city he had founded, to bring matters into order. A general proclamation was issued, that all who had fled through fear of the Zenj should return to their homes. Many betook themselves to Mowaffakīya, but this city also had only an ephemeral existence; even the geographers of the following century no longer mention it. The great trading city of Basra, which once more rose to prosperity, proved too powerful a rival for its neighbor.

Abul Abbās arrived in Bagdad, the capital, with the head of the negro leader displayed on a pole, on Saturday, 23rd November 883.

Thus ended one of the bloodiest and most destructive rebellions which the history of Western Asia records. Its consequences must long have continued to be felt, and it can hardly be doubted that the cities and regions of the lower Tigris never entirely recovered from the injuries which they at that time suffered.

SOURCE: Theodore Nöldeke, "A Servile War in the East," *Sketches from Eastern History*, John Sutherland Black, trans. (London: A. & C. Black, 1892; repr., Beirut: Khayats, 1963), pp. 146–75 (footnotes omitted).

25 The Revolt according to al-Ṭabarī

Theodore Nöldeke's account of the Revolt of the Zanj of 868–883 relies mainly on the work of Abū Ja'far Muḥammad al-Ṭabarī (c.839–923). Al-Ṭabarī was one of the greatest of the Arab historians of medieval times. What he had to say about the Zanj Revolt (which happened during his lifetime) was included in his world history, *Ta'rikh al-rusul wa 'l-mulūk,* extracts from which follow.

As an orthodox Sunnī and supporter of the Baghdād regime, al-Ṭabarī cannot bring himself to mention the name of 'Alī b. Muḥammad, the leader of the revolt, who to him was a heretic and a rebel. He sometimes refers to 'Alī as "the Chief," but most often abusively, as "God's Enemy," "the Wicked One," "the Dissolute One," and "the Traitor."

■

It was related of Rayḥān ibn Ṣāliḥ, one of the slaves of the Shuwarjīyīn and the first among them to follow him [i.e., the Chief], that he said: "I was in charge of my master's slaves; I would bring them flour [*daqīq*] from Baṣra and distribute it among them. [One day] I was bringing [flour] to them, as I was accustomed to do, when I passed by him [i.e., the Chief]. At that time he was living in Baranjal, in the Qurashī's palace. His followers arrested me and took me to him and ordered me to greet him, acknowledging his authority, which I did. He asked me about the place whence I came and I told him that I came from Baṣra. He said: 'Have you heard anything about us in Baṣra?' I said: 'No.' He said: 'What about az-Zaynabī?' I said I had never heard of him. He said: 'What about al-Balālīya and as-Sa'dīya?' I said I knew nothing of them either. He asked me about the situation of the slaves of the Shuwarjīyīn: how much flour, meal, and dates each one of them received, and about those who worked the saltpeter, both freedmen and slaves. I told him all about that. He asked me to join his cause, which I did. He then said to me: 'Win as many slaves as you can by artful means and bring them to me.' He promised to make me a leader over those I brought to him, and to be nice to me. He made me swear that I would not tell anyone about his place and that I would come back to him. He then let me go.

"I stayed away from him all day long and then returned to him the next day. [When] I showed up before him, Rafīq, slave of Yaḥyā ibn 'Abd ar-Raḥmān, whom he had sent to Baṣra to run some errands for him, had already returned. Rafīq brought with him Shibl ibn Sālim, one of ad-Dabbasīn's slaves, and a piece of silk he had ordered him to buy so that he could make a banner. He wrote [on the banner], in red and green: 'Lo! Allāh hath bought from the believers their lives and their wealth because the Garden will be theirs: they shall fight in the way of Allāh.' * He wrote his name and his father's [on the banner], and hung it on the top of a pole. He went out, declaring his rebellion, on September 9th, 869.

"When he reached the rear of the palace in which he lived, he met the slaves of one of the Shuwarjīyīn, known as al-'Aṭṭār, who were on their way to work. He ordered that they be arrested, and so they were. Their taskmaster was taken with them, his hands being tied. Then he [i.e., the Chief] headed toward the place where as-Sanā'ī was working, and took away from it five hundred and fifty slaves, among them Abū Ḥudayd. In accordance with his orders their taskmaster was arrested with them. [At that time] they were by the river known as al-Makāthir. He then went to as-Sīrāfī's place and took away from it one hundred and fifty slaves, among whom were Zurayq and Abū al-Khanjar. He then went to Ibn 'Aṭā's place and took away Ṭarīq, Ṣabīḥ al-'Asar, Rāshid al-Maghribī, and Rāshid al-Qarmāṭī, together with eighty slaves. Then he came to the place of Ismā'īl, who was Sahl aṭ-Ṭaḥḥān's slave. He kept acting like that until many of the [slaves of the] Shurwarjīyīn were gathered around him. He assembled them and made a speech. He raised their hopes, and promised to make them leaders and masters and owners of wealth. He swore strong oaths that he would not act treacherously toward them or abandon them, and that he would not deny them anything good. He summoned their masters and said: 'I wanted to behead you because of what you have done to these slaves whom you deemed weak and subjugated and whom you have burdened with what they could not stand. But my followers talked to me on your behalf and I decided to free you.' They said: 'These slaves are runaways; they will run away from you, being loyal neither to you nor to us. So take money and let us have them back.' He ordered the slaves to bring fresh green palm-branches. Then each group threw down its master and taskmaster [upon the ground] and each was given five hundred lashes. He made them swear by all that was holy that they would not tell anyone either where his place was or the number of his followers. He then let them go. They headed toward Baṣra. One of them, called 'Abd Allāh, and known as Karīkhā, kept going until he crossed the [river] Dujayl and warned the Shuwarjīyīn to guard their slaves, who numbered fifteen thousand.

* *Ḳur'ān,* 9: 111–12. Trans.

"After performing the afternoon prayer [the Chief] traveled until he reached the Dujayl. There he found boats loaded with manure and about to set out on the flood tide. He summoned them and boarded them with his followers. [They sailed] until they had crossed the Dujayl and arrived at the river Maymūn. [The Chief] then entered the mosque which was located in the center of the marketplace overlooking the river Maymūn, and stayed there. He kept on like this, that is, collecting blacks around him, until the day of Lesser Bairam.* When he got up on the morning of that day, he summoned his followers to assemble and perform the Bairam prayer. They assembled. He set up the pole on which his banner was and led them in prayer. He delivered a speech in which he referred to the bad condition in which they had been and [to the fact that] God had sent him as their savior; he said that God intended to improve their lot, to make them owners of slaves and wealth and houses, and to help them attain the highest things. He pledged himself to abide by this. When he had finished his prayer and speech, he ordered those who understood him to explain what he had said to the non-Arabs who did not understand, so that they would feel content. They did so. . . ."

Muḥammad ibn al-Ḥasan said: "The Chief of the Zanj told us that when he became aware of the [Baṣran] troops that were marching toward him, whose foremost lines he could see, he dispatched Zurayq and Abū al-Layth al-Iṣbahānī, accompanied by some troops, to lay ambush on the east side of the river Umm Ḥabīb; [he also sent] Shibl and Ḥusayn al-Hamāmī, accompanied by some troops, to lay an ambush on its west side. He ordered 'Alī ibn Abban, together with those forces that were left to him, to hold out against the oncoming [Baṣran] troops; they were to kneel down and conceal themselves with their shields and not rise until the troops reached them and pointed their swords toward them; only then were they to leap up. He instructed the two units in ambush that, when the [Baṣran] troops had gone past them and when they were sure that their friends had begun to engage the [Baṣran] troops, they were to come out from [their places] on the two sides of the river and shout out to terrify the enemy. He also ordered the Zanj women to collect baked bricks and supply the men with them."

* I.e., *küčük-bairam* (Turk.), the "little festival," one of the two great Muslim festivals; it celebrates the breaking of the fast (Ar., *'īd al-fiṭr*). ED.

He [Muḥammad ibn al-Ḥasan] said that later he used to say to his followers: "When I viewed the marching troops that day heading toward me, I saw a dreadful sight; it frightened me and filled my heart with fear and anxiety. I sought the protection [of God]. Only a few of my followers were with me, Muṣliḥ being one of them. Each of us thought death imminent. Muṣliḥ caused me to wonder by [drawing attention to] the number of those troops, and I made a sign to him to stop it. When the troops neared me, I said: 'Oh God! This is the hour of predicament. Help me!' Then I saw white birds engaging the troops. I had hardly finished speaking when I saw a ship [*sumayrīya*] turn over with all its crew, who were drowned; other boats [*shadhā*] followed."

[In the ensuing battle most of the Baṣran troops were killed.]

The heads [of the dead Baṣrans] were gathered for him [i.e., the Chief]. Some of the relatives of the slain men approached him. He exposed the heads before them, and they picked out those they could recognize. As for the rest of the heads, which no relatives claimed, he filled a barge with them. He let the barge float away, drawn by the river Umm Ḥabīb at ebb tide. It reached Baṣra, stopping at the watering-place known as al-Qayyār. People began to come for the heads, picking out those belonging to their relatives. After this day, God's Enemy [i.e., the Chief] was strengthened. Fear took possession of the Baṣrans' hearts and they ceased fighting him. Word reached the Sultan regarding what [the Chief] had done, and the Sultan sent Ju'lān the Turk as a reinforcement to the Baṣrans. He also ordered Abū al-Aḥwās al-Bāhilī to go to Ubulla as governor and supplied him with a Turk called Jurayḥ.

The Wicked One [i.e., the Chief] claimed that his followers, after this battle, said to him: "We have killed the fighting men among the Baṣrans; there remains no one in Baṣra save the weak and those incapable of movement; allow us to invade it!" But he scolded them and denounced their judgment, saying: "Rather, keep away from Baṣra. We have frightened the Baṣrans, and at present you are safe from them. The proper thing to do now is to cease fighting them until they take the offensive again. . . ."

In the year [882 A.D.] Sulaymān ibn Mūsā ash-Sha'rānī, one of the chiefs of the Dissolute One, sent someone to ask of Abū Aḥmad [al-Muwaffaḳ] protection on his behalf. At first Abū Aḥmad refused this because of the wrongdoing [ash-Sha'rānī] had committed and the bloodshed he had caused. Word reached Abū Aḥmad, however, that some of the Wicked One's followers were disappointed at his refusal to grant protection to ash-Sha'rānī. Abū Aḥmad therefore gave the necessary promise of protection, hoping by this to change the hearts of others among the followers of the Dissolute One. He gave orders that the ships [*ash-shadhā*] should be moved to the place indicated by ash-Sha'rānī as a rendezvous. This was done. Ash-Sha'rānī, his brother, and a group of his officers left [their posts], and he * transported them in the ships. The Wicked One had placed ash-Sha'rānī in charge of the rearguard at the river Abū al-Khaṣīb. Abū al-'Abbās led [ash-Sha'rānī] to al-Muwaffaḳ, who was kind to him and granted him protection as he had promised. [Al-Muwaffaḳ] ordered that [ash-Sha'rānī] and his men should be given rewards and robes of honor were bestowed upon them. [Ash-Sha'rānī] was carried about on many horses equipped with perfect saddles and reins. Al-Muwaffaḳ was very generous to [ash-Sha'rānī] and his men and united them with Abū al-'Abbās. He also treated [ash-Sha'rānī] as a friend, and ordered Abū al-'Abbās to expose him on the ships so that the Traitor's men would see him and become more convinced of the possibility of securing amnesty. The ships did not leave their moorings in the river Abū al-Khaṣīb until a large number of the Zanj leaders and others had sought protection. They were brought before Abū Aḥmad [al-Muwaffaḳ], who gave them rewards and bestowed upon them, as he had upon their predecessors, robes of honor and gifts.

When ash-Sha'rānī sought protection, the control of the Wicked One over the rearguard of his army became disrupted and weakened. To perform the duties formerly carried out by ash-Sha'rānī he appointed Shibl ibn Sālim, stationing him at the end of the river Abū al-Khaṣīb. Before the day ended on which al-Muwaffaḳ had exposed ash-Sha'rānī to the sight of the Wicked One, a messenger from Shibl ibn Sālim came to [al-Muwaffaḳ] demanding protection for his master, asking that the ships be anchored near the house of Ibn Sam'ān, toward which he and his officers and men would repair at night. [Shibl] was granted protection, and his messenger was sent back to him. The ships were anchored in the designated place, and he came to them toward dawn, accompanied by his family and chil-

* I.e., Abū al-'Abbās (see two lines down). TRANS.

dren and a number of his officers and men. His men drew their weapons to engage a party of Zanj that the Wicked One had dispatched with the object of preventing Shibl from reaching the ships, for news of the plan had reached him. But Shibl and his men fought against them and killed some of them, and thus reached the ships safely. They were led to al-Muwaffaḳ's palace in al-Muwaffaḳīya, where they arrived at daybreak. Al-Muwaffaḳ ordered that Shibl be rewarded generously, bestowed upon him many robes of honor, and had him carried about on numerous horses equipped with perfect saddles and reins.

This Shibl was a subordinate and long-time follower of the Wicked One and had shown ability and bravery in his service. [He and his men] were put on the ships and exposed to the sight of the Wicked One and his followers. The scene was a distressing one for the Dissolute One and his close associates. . . .

Finding that Shibl was sincere and a man of ability, al-Muwaffaḳ entrusted to him tasks designed to deceive the Wicked One. He ordered him, together with a group of Zanj heroes who had previously sought protection, to attack the Wicked One's army at night. He singled them out for this task because they were familiar with the paths leading to the Wicked One's camp. Shibl did what he was ordered to do, leading his men to a place well known to him. This place he took by surprise in the early morning, and found there a large group of Zanj, together with many of their officers and protectors, whom the Wicked One had stationed at the place to defend the house known as Abū ʿĪsā, where he himself was residing. [Shibl] fell upon the Zanj unawares and inflicted on them a great massacre, capturing numerous Zanj leaders and many weapons. He and his men got away safely; they presented themselves before al-Muwaffaḳ, who rewarded them well, bestowed upon them robes of honor, and decked some of them out with bracelets.

After Shibl and his men had inflicted this blow upon the followers of the Wicked One, they became terrified and could not sleep. They had to keep watch every night. Confusion increased among them because of the fear they felt and because of the despair that found its way into their hearts. The noise they made and the sounds of their watch keepingcould be heard in al-Muwaffaḳīya.

From this time onward al-Muwaffaḳ began to send detachments of troops day and night along both sides of the river Abū al-Khaṣīb to attack the wicked ones. He wore them out with his assaults, made them stay up all night, and prevented them from seeking food. In the meantime his men were familiarizing themselves with the roads and training themselves for the task of penetrating and breaking into the Wicked One's city; the purpose of this training was to make possible an assault on [that part of the city] which before had been considered inaccessible. When al-Muwaffaḳ judged that his men were ready, he decided to cross to the east side of the river Abū al-Khaṣīb and engage the Dissolute One. Calling all his men together, he commanded that the leaders of those who had sought protection, and their best cavalry and infantry, whether black or white, be brought before him. They were paraded so that they could hear his speech. He then addressed them, making them aware of their ignorance and of the errors and sacrilege of which they had been guilty, of their disobedience to God's will (which the Dissolute One had falsely told them was true religion), and of the fact that their heresies had made their death lawful for him to pronounce; nevertheless, he said, he forgave them their sins and was willing to grant them protection, would bestow his grace upon those who had taken refuge with him, and would reward them generously and admit them to his entourage. . . .

They raised their voices, calling God's blessing down upon al-Muwaffaḳ and acknowledging his beneficence. They professed good faith in the matter of obedience and promised to be zealous in fighting his enemy; they would sacrifice their lives [to attain] anything that would bring them closer to him.

SOURCE: Al-Ṭabarī, *Ta'rikh al-Rusul wa 'l-Mulūk* ("The Annals"), 3 (3):1747–51, 1783–86; 3 (4):2068–73 (extracts). Translated for the present volume by Hasan Shuraydi.

26 Aftermath of the Revolt

After 883, in which year the Revolt of the Zanj was finally crushed, the region of lower Mesopotamia came under the control of the Ḳarmaṭīs (Carmathians). The Ḳarmaṭīs were a secret society whose members' attitude toward private property would today be described as communistic. One of the fortress-settlements they built was situated at al-Aḥsā in Baḥrayn.

In 1051 al-Aḥsā was visited by the Persian traveler, Nāṣir-i-Khusraw, whose description of the Ḳarmaṭī form of government is given below. The Ḳarmaṭīs may have been able to create for themselves a kind of welfare state, but it is clear from this account that their high standard of living was dependent on the labor of 30,000 black African slaves.

■

When I was at Lahssa * [the descendants of Abū Sa'īd] owned thirty thousand negro or Abyssinian slaves, bought for silver, and employed in agriculture and gardening. The people pay neither taxes nor the tithe. If a man falls into poverty or debt, he is lent money until his business has recovered; if anyone contracts a debt, his creditor reclaims from him only the capital. Every stranger who knows a trade receives, on arrival at Lahssa, a certain sum of money to use until he has assured himself of a livelihood. He buys the materials and tools needed for his craft and pays back, when he wishes, only the exact sum that was lent to him. If the owner of a house or a mill goes bankrupt, and if he has not the means to repair his property, the governors appoint a certain number of their slaves to repair the damage suffered by the house or mill; nothing is asked of the owner for this service.

There are in Lahssa mills which are owned by the state and in which private persons may grind their wheat and flour free of charge. The upkeep of these mills and the wages of the men who work there are paid by the government.[29]

SOURCE: Nassiri Khosran, *Sefer Nameh: Relation du voyage de Nassiri Khosran en Syrie, en Palestine, en Egypte, en Arabie et en Perse, pendant les années de l'Hégire 437–444 (1035–1040)*, Charles Schéfer, ed. and trans. (Paris: Leroux, 1881), pp. 227–28. (Translated from the French by the editor.)

* I.e., al-Aḥsā. ED.

MUSLIM ATTITUDES TOWARD AFRICA AND AFRICANS

THE ARAB SLAVE TRADE in Africa lasted for at least fifteen hundred years, and probably longer. Like other peoples who through the centuries have exploited the human resources of the African continent, the Arabs felt the need from time to time to justify their actions. They did this in several ways. First, they noted that the African black was a pagan, and, as such, permitted to be enslaved under the law of Islam. Second, they pointed out, once a man was a member of a Muslim society—even though a slave—he had the opportunity to learn the precepts of the true religion and attain Paradise. (A similar argument was used by Christian slavers.) Third, Arab writers portrayed sub-Saharan Africa as so savage a land, so filled with cannibalism and wretchedness, that for an African to be a slave in the "civilized" world was preferable to being free at home.

Nor was the knowledge of Africa any more extensive or accurate elsewhere in the Muslim world. The following brief notice is all that a Persian geographical encyclopedia of the tenth century had to say about "Zangistān," or the east coast of Africa: "It is the largest *(mihtarīn)* country in the south. Some of its eastern regions adjoin Zābaj [Indonesia]; its north adjoins the Great Sea; some of its western parts adjoin Abyssinia; on its south are mountains. Their soil is (full of) gold mines. The country is situated opposite Pārs, Kirmān, and

Sind [the Persian Gulf area]. The people are full-faced, with large bones, and curly hair. Their nature is that of wild animals. They are extremely black. Enmity reigns between them and the Abyssinians and Zābaj." [30]

27 Black Africa according to al-Andalusī

Ṣā'id al-Andalusī (1029–1070) was a Spanish Muslim who held a high government position at Toledo. The following passage is taken from a book on the nations of the world he published in 1068. In it the author draws a distinction between black Africans who have, at least in some degree, been subjected to the beneficial influence of Islam, and those who are still in a state of ignorance. Of the latter he has nothing good to say whatever.

■

All the peoples in this category [that is, those] who have not cultivated the sciences, are more like animals than men. . . . Those among them who . . . live near the equator or below it, as far as the limits of the inhabited world to the south, know a torrid climate and a sky superheated by the sun at its zenith. As a result their temperament has become fiery and their humors ardent; their color has been blackened, their hair has become woolly. Moreover, the rule of virtue and stability of judgment both being lacking in them, choler is dominant among these peoples, foolishness and ignorance general among them. Of such are the populations of the Sudan, who live on the borders of the country of the Abyssinians, and also the Nubians, the Zanj, etc. . . .

All [these nations], indeed, have a common trait: they have never made use of their minds in seeking after wisdom (*ḥikma*) and have not exercised themselves in the study of philosophy (*falsafa*). Nevertheless, the bulk of these populations, who are sedentary and dislike nomads, possess everywhere where we have knowledge of them, to the east, to the west, to the south, and to the north, a monarchical government which controls them, and a divine law to which they are subjected. The only peoples who reject that humane institution and live outside that rational law are some of the inhabitants of the steppe, some of the desert dwellers and . . . the Boga [Beja] rabble, the savages of Gana, the miserable Zanj, and other similar groups.

SOURCE: Ṣā'id al-Andalusī, *Kitāb Tabaḳāt al-Umam* (*Livre des catégories des nations*), Régis Blachère, trans. (Paris: Larose, 1935), pp. 36–38 (extracts; translated from the French by the editor).

28 A Ship's Captain's Tale

Buzurg ibn Shahriyār was a tenth-century Persian ship's captain who collected anecdotes and tall tales about distant lands from merchants and seafaring men like himself. His *Kitāb 'Aja'ib al-Hind* ("Book of the Marvels of India") contains 134 of these tales, one of which is reproduced here. According to tradition, numbers of Persians from Shīrāz and Sīrāf emigrated to East Africa in the ninth and tenth centuries and there was at the time considerable trade between the Persian Gulf and the East African Coast.[31] Thus, although the story as Buzurg tells it is obviously fictitious, it reveals some knowledge of life among the Zanj (more, at least, than was available a century later to al-Andalusī), and, incidentally, conveys a good deal of information about Islamic attitudes to Black Africa in the Middle Ages.

■

Ismaīlouīa tells me, and several mariners have confirmed his story, that, during the year 310 [923 A.D.], he set sail in his ship from Oman to go to Kabila. A storm drove him towards Sofala of the Zindjs.* "Seeing the coast we had reached," said the captain, "and realizing that we had fallen among man-eating negroes, we had no doubt what our fate would be; we performed our ablutions and turned our heart to God, one to another reciting the prayer for the dead. The negroes surrounded us in their canoes and took us into

* I.e., the Zanj. ED.

harbor. There we cast anchor and went ashore. They led us before their king. He was a handsome, well-set-up young negro. He asked us who we were, and whither we were going. We replied that his territory had been our goal.

'You lie,' he said. 'It was by no means here you meant to land. The winds, and they alone, have driven you ashore, willy-nilly.' And when we had admitted that he spoke the truth, 'Bring ashore your merchandise,' he said, 'and buy and sell. You have nothing to fear.'

So ashore we brought our bales, and started to do business; and excellent business for us it was, with no restriction and no duties to pay. We made the king presents, and he replied with others, of an equal or of an even greater value. There we stayed several months. But, at last, the moment of parting came. We asked leave to go, and it was straightway granted. We put on board the goods we had bought, and concluded our transactions. And, as soon as all was settled, the king, hearing of our intention to set sail, bore us company down to the shore with some of his people, and, getting into the boats, they sped us as far as the ship. The king even came on board with seven of his attendants.

But, when I saw them there, I said to myself: 'That young king would fetch at least thirty *dinars,** if he were auctioned in the marketplace at Oman, and his seven attendants a hundred and sixty *dinars* the lot. Their clothes are worth twenty *dinars* at the lowest. Altogether, we should make a profit of not less than three thousand *dirhems,*† without stirring a finger.' Thus reflecting, I gave the crew certain orders; sails were spread, and the anchor was hauled up. Meanwhile the king was behaving in the friendliest possible manner, exhorting us to return presently, and promising us a friendly reception. But, when he saw the sails swelling in the wind and the vessel already under way, his face changed. 'You are going,' he said. 'Well, I will say good-bye.' And he made to climb down into his canoes, which were moored alongside. We cut their painters, and remarked: 'You stay where you are, with us; we are taking you home; and there we'll make it up to you for all your kindness.'

'Strangers,' he said, 'when you happened on our shores, my people wanted to eat you and spoil your goods, as, in their time, they

* The *dīnār,* a gold coin, was the chief unit of currency in early Islamic times. ED.

† The *dirham* was a silver unit of the Arab monetary system, supposedly worth seven-tenths of a *mithkāl* or *dīnār,* but often less. ED.

have done to others. It was I who protected you. I asked nothing of you. As a token of my goodwill, I came on board your ship to see you off. Then treat me as justice demands, and let me go back to my native land.'

But we paid no attention to what he said; little we cared. The wind freshed. Quickly the coastline disappeared. Then night wrapped us in her veils, and we reached the high seas.

Day returned, and the king and his attendants were added to the other slaves, whose number was round about two hundred heads. He received no better treatment than the rest, his companions in captivity. He said no word, and never opened his mouth. He comported himself just as if we were strangers to him, and we knew not who he was. Once arrived at Oman, the slaves were sold and the king with them.

Well, some years later, sailing from Oman towards Kabila, the wind drove us a second time against the seacoast of Sofala of the Zindjs, and we put in at exactly the same place. The negroes saw us, and surrounded us in their canoes, and we recognized one the other. Now we were quite sure of perishing and terror sealed our lips. Silently we performed our ablutions, and recited the prayers for the dead. We said good-bye, every man to his fellow. The negroes took and led us to the king's house. They made us enter. What was our surprise: there was the same king, him whom we had known seated on his throne, as if we had left him there not long ago. Down we flung ourselves in his presence, and, sprawling, had not the strength to rise.

'Aha!' he exclaimed. 'My old friends!' None of us could find tongue to answer. We shook in every limb. 'Come now!' he continued. 'Lift up your heads; I grant you the *aman,** you and your goods.' Some of us raised our heads; but others could not, crushed by shame. And, for his part, he dealt with us kindly and graciously till we had all raised our heads. But even then, we could not pluck up courage to look him in the face, so strongly did remorse and fear affect us. And when, at length, we had come to our senses, reassured by his *aman*, 'Ah, traitors!' he cried, 'how did you treat me, after what I had done for you!' 'Mercy, King, have mercy!' we severally implored. 'I will be merciful,' he said; 'fall to your business of buying

* I.e., *amān* = protection, inviolability; granted to an infidel in Muslim territory. Ed.

and selling as you did before; you have full liberty to traffic.' We could not believe our ears, and feared it might be a ruse to persuade us to unship our merchandise. Nevertheless, unship it we did, offering the king a present of incomparable value. He refused it, remarking: 'You are not worthy I should accept a present from you. I will not soil my fortune with anything coming from your hands.'

Thereupon we went quietly about our business. The time of parting came, and we asked his permission to embark. It was given. When we were actually ready to go, I went to inform him of it. 'Go your way,' he said, 'under the protection of God!' 'O King,' I answered, 'you loaded us with kindness and we requited you like graceless traitors. But how was it you escaped and managed to return home?'

'After you had sold me at Oman,' he replied, 'my buyer took me to a city, called Basra' (and here he described Basra), 'where I learned the usage of prayer and fasting and some parts of the *Koran*. My master sold me to another, who took me into the territory of the king of the Arabs, to a place called Bagdad' (and he described Bagdad). 'In that city, I learned to speak correctly, and completed my education in the *Koran*, praying with the people in mosques. I saw the Caliph, whose name is El-Moqtadir.* A year and longer I stayed in Bagdad, when there came a troop of men of Khorassan, riding camelback. Seeing a great crowd of them, whither were they all going, I asked. To Mecca, they answered me. What was Mecca, I demanded. It was in Mecca, they replied, was the holy House of God, where Musulmans made pilgrimage. And they instructed me, concerning the history of the Temple. I should do well to follow the caravan, I thought within myself. But my master, to whom I communicated the circumstance, was neither willing to go himself nor to let me go of my own accord. So I found a means of eluding his vigilance, and mingling with the crowd of pilgrims on the road, I constituted myself their servant; I was fed and provided with the two garments necessary for the *ihram*.† In fact, under their guidance, I accomplished all the ceremonial observances of the pilgrimage.

'Fearing to return to Bagdad, lest my master should kill me, I

* The 'Abbāsid Caliph Abū 'l-Faḍl Ja'far ibn Aḥmad al-Muḳtadir (ruled 908–932). Ed.

† I.e., *iḥrām*, the state of temporary consecration possessed by a Muslim performing the pilgrimage. Ed.

joined another caravan, going to Cairo. I offered my services to travelers, who, in return, gave me rides upon their camels, and shared with me their food. Arrived at Cairo, I saw the great river, called the Nile. "Where does it flow?" I enquired. "Its source," they replied, "is in the land of the Zindjs." "Whereabouts?" "Near a great city, called Assouan, on the frontier of the territory of the Blacks."

'Hearing this, I followed the banks of the Nile, going from one town to another, and begging alms, which were not refused me. But I fell in with a troop of blacks, who used me ill. They bound me, and laid burdens on me, heavier than I could bear, and put me among the other servants. I escaped, only to fall in with a second troop, who took and sold me. A second time I escaped, and thus traveled on, till, after many adventures of the same kind, at last I found myself in a country, which borders the country of the Zindjs. There I disguised myself; none of the terrors I had experienced, since leaving Cairo, equalled my terror, in approaching my own kingdom. For, said I, a new king has no doubt taken my place on the throne and with the army. To get back one's power is no easy thing. If I declare myself or am discovered, they will take and lead me before the new king, and I shall be slain out of hand. Or, it may be, a partisan of his will lop off my head, to curry favor.

'So, prey to the keenest terror, I traveled at night and hid by day. Reaching the seacoast, I took ship, and, touching at various points, was finally landed one night upon the shore of my native land. I questioned an old woman. "The king who rules here, is he a just king?" I asked. "My son," she answered, "we have no king but God." And the good woman told me how the king had been carried off. I pretended the keenest astonishment, just as if the story did not concern myself and events of which I was so well aware. "The inhabitants of the kingdom," she added, "have agreed not to take another, till they have some definite news of the first. Soothsayers have told them that he is living safe and sound in the country of the Arabs."

'When day dawned, I entered the city and made my way to my palace. There I found my family, as I had left them, but plunged in the greatest affliction. My people listened to my story with surprise and joy. Like me, they adopted the religion of Islam. Thus, a month before your coming, I took up my kingdom once more. I am glad and satisfied with the grace which God has accorded me and mine, instructing us in the precepts of Islam, the true faith, in the usage of prayer, fasting, and pilgrimage, and in the knowledge of what is forbidden and what is allowed; none other in the land of Zindjs has received such favor. And if I pardoned you, it was because you were the first cause of the purity of my faith. But there is still something on my conscience, of which I pray that God will wash away the sin.' 'What is that, O King?' I asked him. 'It is that I left my master, in Bagdad, without his leave, and that I never returned to his service. Could I but find an honest man, I would beg him to take my master the sum necessary to buy me off. If there was among you an upright man, if you were persons of respectability, I would give you the money to hand over to him, a sum ten times the sum he paid, as recompense for the delay. But you are no better than traitors and thieves.'

We bade him good-bye. 'Go,' he said; 'and, if you come back, you shall have no different treatment; you shall have the best possible reception. Musulmans shall know that they may come to us like brothers, since we are Musulmans too. But as for speeding you to your ship, I have my reasons for staying where I am.' And so we parted." [32]

SOURCE: Peter Quennell, trans., *The Book of the Marvels of India* (London: Routledge, 1928), pp. 44–52.

29 The Boast of the Blacks

To a family "probably of Abyssinian origin" there was born in Baṣra in about 776 the remarkable scholar, teacher, theologian, polemicist, and founder of Arabic prose style known as al-Jāḥiẓ.[33] In his youth Jāḥiẓ lived the life of a poor student, wandering the streets of his native city, mingling with the crowds, and joining the groups of listeners in the mosque as the great teachers of the day expounded their doctrines. Baṣra was the chief city of southern 'Irāḳ, a cosmopolitan, free-thinking place, to which sailors, merchants, and intellectuals came from distant parts of the Muslim world, including east and northeast Africa.[34] Jāḥiẓ would thus have had plenty of opportunity to meet and observe Africans,[35] about whom he later wrote at length, and, as will be seen, enigmatically.

The middle part of Jāḥiẓ's life was spend in Baghdād, the capital of the 'Abbāsid Caliphate. There he earned his living as teacher and government servant and gained favor at the Caliph's court, where his patron was the vizier, al-Fatḥ b. Khāqān. "The Commander of the Faithful," al-Fatḥ wrote to him, "has taken a tremendous liking to you and rejoices to hear your name spoken. Were it not that he thinks so highly of you because of your learning and erudition, he would require your constant attendance in his audience chamber to give him your views and tell him your opinion on the questions that occupy your time and thought." [36] But it is as a writer that Jāḥiẓ is chiefly remembered. The catalogues credit him with nearly two hundred works, though only thirty, authentic or apocryphal, have survived.[37] In his old age he returned to his home town of Baṣra. Many legends accumulated around him, one of the better known being that his death in 869 at the age of ninety-three was due to the collapse of a mound of books that he always kept piled around him.[38] The story is no doubt spurious, but it indicates the reputation he acquired for prodigious learning.

A famous essay by Jāḥiẓ is entitled "The Superiority of the Blacks to the Whites" or "The Boast of the Blacks against the Whites." Modern critics point out that this work, which at first sight seems to be a defense of blacks, and especially African blacks, against their detractors, cannot be taken at face value. "The Boast of the Blacks" is, in fact, something of a *jeu d'esprit.* In it, Jāḥiẓ was poking fun at those of his contemporaries who asserted the claims of Persians and other subject peoples living in the Arab Empire to be the equal of the Arabs. Jāḥiẓ himself was a fervent admirer of the Arab cultural tradition and completely identified with it. To him it seemed absurd that Persians could possibly be regarded as "the equal of the Arabs." Using outrageous logic and convoluted argument, he sought in "The Boast of the Blacks" to ridicule his opponents by demonstrating that the equality they demanded could just as appropriately be granted to the Zanj, the most lowly of humanity.[39]

Jāḥiẓ was not, therefore, an early exponent of the doctrine, "Black is beautiful." Elsewhere in his writings he castigated Negroes as "the most wretched creatures, the basest in character." It may not be carrying things too far to assert that he was a ninth-century equivalent of those New World creoles and mulattos of a thousand years later who rejected the African part of their heritage in order the more enthusiastically to praise the "Christian" and "civilized" values of those who had enslaved their ancestors. Jāḥiẓ was himself ridiculed in his lifetime. The traditions about him dwell on his ugliness (*al-jāḥiẓ* means "the goggle-eyed"), and in his writings he often adopted the posture of a buffoon. Perhaps, in selecting the Zanj as his exemplar of baseness, he was trying, under cover of satire, to disassociate himself as much as he could from the inhabitants of a continent where all men were black and to which, ultimately, he owed his dark skin. That he should feel the need to do so is in itself a wry commentary on what it was like to be educated, admired, and famous—and yet part-African—in the medieval Muslim world.

■

1. THE ZANJ

Negroes say: Everybody agrees that there is no people on earth in whom generosity is as universally well developed as the Zanj; and this is a quality found only in those of noble character. These people have a natural talent for dancing to the rhythm of the tambourine, without needing to learn it. There are no better singers anywhere in the world, no people more polished and eloquent, and no people less given to insulting language. All other peoples in the world have their stammerers, those who have difficulty in pronouncing certain sounds, and those who cannot express themselves fluently or are downright tongue-tied, except the Zanj. Sometimes some of them hold forth before their ruler continuously from sunrise to sunset, without needing to turn round or pause in their flow. No other nation can surpass them in bodily strength and physical toughness. One of them will lift huge blocks and carry heavy loads that would be beyond the strength of most Bedouins or members of other races. They are courageous, energetic, and generous, which are the virtues of nobility, and also good-tempered and with little propensity to evil. They are always cheerful, smiling, and devoid of malice, which is a sign of a noble character. Some people say that their generosity is due to their stupidity, shortsightedness, and lack of foresight, but our reply is that this is a scurvy way of commending generosity and altruism. At that rate the wisest and most intelligent man would be the most niggardly and ungenerous. But in fact the Slavs are more niggardly than the Byzantines, and the latter more intelligent and thoughtful; according to our opponents' argument, the Slavs ought to be more generous and open-handed than the Byzantines. . . .

The Zanj say to the Arabs: You are so ignorant that during the *jāhiliyya* * you regarded us as your equals [when it came to marrying] Arab women, but with the advent of the justice of Islam you decided this practice was bad. Yet the desert is full of Negroes married to Arab wives, and they have been princes and kings and have safeguarded your rights and sheltered you against your enemies.

Jāḥiẓ mentions other famous Negroes, and refers to the exploits of the Abyssinians, the things their country produces, etc. He asserts that black is superior to other colors. Negroes are proud of their great numbers; also, the Arabs do not really know them, since all they see is Negro slaves. After some reflections on cross-breeding between races, and on men's tastes for the female slaves commonest in their own countries, he repeats that the blacks outnumber the whites, and gives his views on

2. ORIGIN OF BLACK SKIN

. . . We say that God did not make us black in order to disfigure us; rather that it is our environment that has made us so. The best evidence of this is that there are black tribes among the Arabs, such as the Banū Sulaim b. Manṣūr,† and that all the peoples settled in the Ḥarra ‡ besides the Banū Sulaim are black. These tribes take slaves from among the Ashbān § to mind their flocks and for irrigation work, manual labor, and domestic service, and their wives from among the Byzantines; and yet it takes less than three generations for the Ḥarra to give them all the complexion of the Banū Sulaim. This Ḥarra is such that the gazelles, ostriches, insects, wolves, foxes, sheep, asses, horses, and birds that live there are all black. White and black are the results of environment, the natural properties of water

* The period before the advent of Islam. TRANS.

† Tribe of the Qais, a confederacy of north Arabian tribes. TRANS.

‡ Basalt desert stretching from southern Syria to Medina. TRANS.

§ A people regarded by Muslim writers as of Persian origin. TRANS.

and soil, distance from the sun, and intensity of heat. There is no question of metamorphosis, or of punishment, disfigurement, or favor meted out by God. Besides, the land of the Banū Sulaim has much in common with the land of the Turks, where the camels, beasts of burden, and everything belonging to these people is similar in appearance; everything of theirs has a Turkish look. The soldiers of the frontier garrisons on this side of the 'Awāṣim * sometimes come across Byzantine sheep mixed up with sheep belonging to the local inhabitants, but they have no difficulty in distinguishing the Byzantine flocks from the Syrian by their "Byzantinity." When one comes across the descendants of Bedouin men and women who have ended up in Khurāsān, it is immediately apparent that they are the barbarians of these parts.[40]

SOURCE: Charles Pellat, *The Life and Works of Jāḥiẓ: Translations of Selected Texts* (London: Routledge and Kegan Paul, 1969), pp. 195–97.

30 Race and Color in Islam

"The Mohammedan Negro," wrote Edward Wilmot Blyden in 1875, "has felt nothing of the withering power of caste. There is nothing in his color or race to debar him from the highest privileges, social or political, to which any other Muslim can attain." [41] And a modern authority thus summarizes the teachings of the Islamic religion on matters of race and racial discrimination: "Islam calls on men to pursue knowledge and to employ scientific methods based on observation and experiment, and respects the results obtained by scientific research. Hence its respect for all that science has done to promote the unity of mankind and combat racial discrimination. Islam regards each individual as responsible for his acts, but rejects the notion that any person should be held responsible for something beyond his control, such as color. . . . Mankind, according to Islam, is one large family, created by God from a single soul; from that soul He created a mate for it and then, from both of them, he scattered a multitude of men and women over the face of the earth. The diver-

* Part of the border country between the Byzantine and Arab empires. TRANS.

sity of tongues and colors is simply a manifestation of divine power, and does not imply any notion of preference or privilege. On the contrary, in Islamic thought, privilege is opposed to God's commands of love and brotherhood." [42]

Both these passages are statements of an ideal position. One depicts what ought to have happened in the past; the other, what correct doctrine is today. But many Muslims of medieval and early modern times inevitably fell short of strict adherence to the precepts enunciated by the Prophet in the Ḳur'ān and developed by Muslim jurists and moralists in succeeding centuries. The question is, how far short? To what extent was Muslim principle vitiated by Muslim practice? A recent essay by Bernard Lewis addresses itself to this problem.

■

THE VOICE OF PIETY

. . . During the centuries which followed the death of the Prophet Muḥammad, pious Muslims collected vast numbers of what are known as *Ḥadīths*—that is to say, traditions concerning Muḥammad's actions and utterances. A very large proportion of these are certainly spurious—but this, while it may nullify their value as evidence of the Prophet's own views, still leaves them as important evidence on the development of attitudes during the period in which they were manufactured. A number of these traditions deal with questions of race and color. There are some which specifically condemn one or another race. Thus the Prophet is quoted as saying of the Ethiopian: "When he is hungry he steals, when he is sated he fornicates." This is undoubtedly spurious, but is also well-known in early and modern times as an Arabic proverb about the Zanj.

Such traditions are few, and are not regarded as authoritative. A larger body of traditions survives, the general purport of which is to deplore racial prejudice and to insist on the primacy of piety. One of the commonest is the phrase ascribed to the Prophet, "I was sent to the red and the black"—an expression taken to embrace the whole of mankind. With the passage in the Qur'ān already quoted as point of departure, the manufacturers of tradition—for these too are almost certainly spurious—have as their purpose to insist that true merit is to be found in piety and good deeds, and that these take precedence of gentle, noble, or even of purely Arab birth.

These traditions, and those opposed to them, clearly reflect the great struggles in the early Islamic Empire between the pure Arab *conquistador* aristocracy claiming both ethnic and social superiority, and the converted among the conquered, who could claim neither ethnic nor family advantage and perhaps for that reason insisted on the primacy of religious merit.

Here I may draw attention to a rhetorical device very common in Arabic usage—an argument by the absurd. It is, however, very different from that device which we call the *reductio ad absurdum.* The purpose of the *reductio ad absurdum* is to demonstrate the falsity of an argument by stating it in its most extreme and therefore absurd form. The Arabic rhetorical device to which I refer has the opposite purpose—not to disprove, but to emphasize and reaffirm; it is thus not a *reductio ad absurdum,* but rather a *trajectio ad absurdum,* if I may coin a rhetorical term. A principle is asserted and an extreme, even an absurd example of it is given—but the purpose is to show that the principle still applies even in this extreme and absurd formulation.

One cannot but be struck by the number of times the black man is used to point up this type of argument. Thus, in asserting the duty of obedience, of submission to authority however unlikely the form in which it appears, Muslim jurists cite a dictum attributed to the Prophet: "Obey whoever is put in authority over you, even if he be a crop-nosed Ethiopian slave." This combination of qualities is clearly intended to indicate the ultimate improbability at once in physical, social, and racial terms. On the subject of marriage: "Do not marry women for their beauty, which may destroy them, or for their money, which may corrupt them, but for religion. A slit-nosed black slavewoman, if pious, is preferable." Piety must overcome inclination, though it cannot redirect it.

The same theme occurs in stories about Abū Dharr, an early Muslim hero who is often cited as a model of piety and humility. As examples of his humility it is mentioned that he married a black woman, "for he wanted a wife who would lower him and not exalt him," and that he was willing to pray behind an Ethiopian. The point is most forcibly made by the famous Ibn Ḥazm (994–1064), who observes that "God has decreed that the most devout is the noblest even if he be a Negress's bastard, and that the sinner and unbeliever is at the lowest level even if he be the son of prophets."

The sentiment is impeccably pious and egalitarian—yet somehow does not entirely carry conviction. Significantly, Ibn Ḥazm makes this remark in the introduction to a treatise on Arab genealogy, in which he tries to demonstrate the importance and dignity of this science. In another somewhat equivocal tradition, an Ethiopian says to the Prophet, "You Arabs excel us in all, in build, color, and in the possession of the Prophet. If I believe, will I be with you in Paradise?" The Prophet answers, "Yes, and in Paradise the whiteness of the Ethiopian will be seen over a stretch of a thousand years."

The moral of this and of countless other anecdotes and sayings of the same kind is that piety outweighs blackness and impiety outweighs whiteness. This is not the same as saying that whiteness and blackness do not matter. Indeed the contrary is implied in such tales as that of the pious black who turns white, and the parallel stories of white evildoers who turn black. A vivid example occurs in the *Risālat al-ghufrān,* a vision of heaven and hell by the Syrian poet Abu'l-'Alā al-Ma'arrī (973–1057). In paradise the narrator meets an exceedingly beautiful *houri,* who tells him that in life she was Tawfīq the Negress, who used to fetch books for copyists in the Academy of Baghdad.

"But you were black," he exclaims, "and now you have become whiter than camphor!" To which she replies by quoting a verse: "If there were a mustard-seed of God's light among all the blacks, the blacks would become white." The same association of light with good is shown in the Muslim hagiographic literature, which depicts the Prophet himself as of light or reddish color. Similar descriptions are given of his wife 'Ā'isha, his son-in-law 'Alī and his descendants, and even of his predecessors, the prophets Abraham, Moses, and Jesus.

CONQUEST AND SLAVERY

This great change of attitude, within a few generations, can be attributed in the main to three major developments.

1. The first of these is the fact of conquest—the creation by the advancing Arabs of a vast empire in which the normal distinctions inevitably appeared between the conquerors and the conquered. At first, Arab and Muslim were virtually the same thing and the distinc-

tion could be presented as a religious one. But as conversion to Islam proceeded very rapidly among the different conquered peoples, there came into existence a new class—the non-Arab converts to Islam, whose position rather resembled that of the native Christians in the latter-day European empires. According to the doctrines of Islam—repeatedly reaffirmed by the pious exponents of the Faith—the non-Arab converts were the equals of the Arabs and could even outrank them by superior piety. But the Arabs, like all other conquerors before and since, were reluctant to concede equality to the conquered, and for as long as they could they maintained their privileged position. Non-Arab Muslims were regarded as inferior and subjected to a whole series of fiscal, social, political, military, and other disabilities.

A Spanish-Arab author, Ibn ʿAbd Rabbihi (860–940) describes the attitude of the early Arabs to the non-Arab converts, who were known as *mawlā* (plural *mawālī*)—a term the primary meaning of which was "freedman" or client: "Nāfiʿ ibn Jubayr ibn Mutʿim gave precedence to a *mawlā* to lead him in prayer. People spoke to him about this, and he said: 'I wished to be humble before God in praying behind him.' "

The same Nāfiʿ ibn Jubayr, when a funeral passed by, used to ask who it was. If they said: "A Qurashī," he would say: "Alas for his kinsfolk!" If they said: "An Arab," he would say: "Alas for his countrymen!" If they said: "A *mawlā*," he would say: "He is the property of God, Who takes what He pleases and leaves what He pleases."

They used to say that only three things interrupt prayer—a donkey, a dog, and a *mawlā*. The *mawlā* did not use the *kunya* * but was addressed only by his personal name and by-name. People did not walk side by side with them, nor allow them precedence in processions. If they were present at a meal, they stood while the others sat, and if a *mawlā*, because of his age, his merit, or his learning, was given food, he was seated at the end of the table, lest anyone should fail to see that he was not an Arab. They did not allow a *mawlā* to pray at funerals if an Arab was present, even if the only Arab present was an inexperienced youth. The suitor for a *mawlā* woman did not address himself to her father or brother, but to her patron, who gave her in marriage or refused, as he pleased. If her father or

* In Arab usage, the name a person derives from his or her eldest son, as "Abū . . .". Ed.

brother gave her in marriage without the patron's approval, the marriage was invalid, and if consummated was fornication not wedlock.

It is related that 'Āmir ibn 'Abd al-Qays, known for his piety, asceticism, austerity, and humility, was addressed in the presence of 'Abdallah ibn 'Āmir the governor of Iraq, by Ḥumrān, the *mawlā* of the Caliph 'Uthmān ibn 'Affān. Ḥumrān accused 'Āmir of reviling and abusing the Caliph. 'Āmir denied this, and Ḥumrān said to him: "May God not multiply your kind among us!" To this 'Āmir replied: "But may God multiply your kind among us!"

'Āmir was asked: "Does he curse you and do you bless him?" "Yes," he replied, "for they sweep our roads, sew our boots, and weave our clothes!"

'Abdallah ibn 'Āmir, who was leaning, sat bolt upright, and said: "I didn't think that you, with your virtue and your asceticism, knew about these things." To which 'Āmir replied: "I know more than you think I know!"

The struggle for equal rights of the non-Arab converts was one of the main themes of the first two centuries of Islam. Another theme of comparable importance was the struggle of the half-breeds for equality with the full-breeds. Even among the Arabs in the early empire a clear distinction was maintained between those who were of free Arab parentage on both sides and those who, though their fathers were free Arabs, did not have free Arab mothers. They were the children of concubines and therefore necessarily of persons of other races. Superior to the non-Arab Muslims, they were definitely inferior to those who were of free Arab stock on both sides. As their numbers became greater their demand for equality became more insistent and was eventually realized.

Among these two groups, the non-Arab converts and the half-breed Arabs, color as such does not seem to have been a significant issue. The literature preserves the memory of a bitter struggle in which the three parties are Arabs, half-Arabs, and non-Arabs. The identity of the non-Arab component seems to have been of secondary importance, at least to the Arabs, though it may have meant more among the non-Arabs themselves. The significance of an African origin as distinct from other possible non-Arab origins lay in its visibility. The son of an Arab father and a Persian or Syrian mother would not look very different from the son of two Arab parents.

The difference was in effect social and depended on social knowledge. The son of an African mother, however, was usually recognizable at sight and therefore more exposed to abuse and discrimination. "Son of a black woman" was a not infrequent insult addressed to such persons, and "son of a white woman" was accordingly used in praise or boasting. The half-mythical poet 'Antara was the son of an Arab father, of the tribe of 'Abs, and a black mother. A verse ascribed to him runs:

> I am a man, of whom one half ranks with the best of 'Abs.
> The other half I defend with my sword.

But even he—a manumitted half-breed—is quoted as despising full-breed black slaves.

'Antara is said to have lived in the sixth century, but most of the poems ascribed to him belong to a later period, and reflect a later situation. Some appear to be the work of Suḥaym, Nuṣayb, and other black or half-black poets of the early Islamic period. It is easy to see why they should have made the great pre-Islamic half-breed their hero, and ascribed to him problems which did not exist in his time. The same process no doubt explains the verses ascribed to Khufāf ibn Nadba, a contemporary of the Prophet. The son of an Arab of the Banu Sulaym and a black slave mother, Khufāf was a man of position and a chief in his tribe—something which would have been impossible a century later. It is surely a later poet who composed the verse in which Khufāf remarks that his tribe had made him a chief "despite this dark pedigree."

Incidentally the Caliph 'Umar himself is said to have been the grandson of an Ethiopian woman. An early Arab author, Muḥammad ibn Ḥabīb, tells us that one day, during the lifetime of the Prophet, a man insulted 'Umar and called him "Son of a black woman" whereupon God revealed the Qur'ānic verse "O believers! People should not mock other people who may be better than they are" (chapter xlix, verse 11). The story, which occurs in a rather brief chapter on great men who were the sons of Ethiopian women, is almost certainly a pious invention, but none the less interesting for that. It is probably a reply to Shi'ite propaganda against 'Umar, which made some play with his Ethiopian ancestress in order to discredit him.

2. A factor of importance was the wider range of experience which conquest brought to the Arabs. Before Islam, their acquaintance with Africa was substantially limited to Ethiopia, a country with a relatively high level of moral and material civilization. During the lifetime of the Prophet the good reputation of the Ethiopians was further increased by the kindly welcome afforded to Muslim refugees from Mecca. After the conquests, however, there were changes. Advancing on the one hand into Africa and on the other into southwest Asia, the Arabs encountered fairer-skinned peoples who were more advanced and darker-skinned peoples who were more primitive. No doubt as a result of this they began to equate the two facts.

3. Coupled with this expansion was the third major development of the early Islamic centuries—slavery and the slave trade. The Arab Muslims were not the first to enslave black Africans. Even in Pharaonic times Egyptians had already begun to capture and use black African slaves, and some are indeed depicted on Egyptian monuments. There were black slaves in the Hellenistic and Roman worlds—but they seem to have been few and relatively unimportant. The massive development of the slave trade in black Africa and the large-scale importation of black Africans for use in the Mediterranean and Middle Eastern countries seem to date from the Arab period. Inevitably, it influenced Arab (and therefore Muslim) attitudes to the peoples of darker skin whom most Arabs and Muslims encountered only in this way.

To the Muslims—as to the people of every other civilization known to history—the civilized world meant themselves. They alone possessed enlightenment and the true faith; the outside world was inhabited by barbarians and infidels. However, in this outside world which lay beyond the vast borders of the Islamic oecumene, the Muslims recognized certain distinctions. To the East there were India and China, countries which were pagan but which were nevertheless respected as possessing some civilized attributes. To the West lay Christendom, first Byzantine then European, recognized as a rival faith, a rival culture, and a rival world order. Apart from these there were the northern and the southern barbarians; the white barbarians of the North, Turks, Slavs, and their like, and the dark-skinned barbarians of the South, in Black Africa.

Both were seen primarily as sources of slaves—to be imported into the Islamic world, molded in Islamic ways, and, since they possessed no religion of their own worth the mention, natural recruits for Islam. For these peoples, enslavement was thus a benefaction, and was indeed often accepted as such. This attitude is exemplified in the story of a black pagan king who is tricked and kidnapped by Muslim guests whom he has befriended, and sold into slavery in Arabia. Meeting them again years later, he shows contempt but no resentment, since they had been the means of bringing him to Islam. . . .

BLACK AND WHITE SLAVES

The total identification of blackness with slavery which occurred in North and South America never took place in the Muslim world. There were always white slaves as well as black ones. Nevertheless, the identification of blackness with certain forms of slavery went very far—and in later centuries white slaves grew increasingly rare.

Already in medieval times it became customary to use different words for black and white slaves. White slaves were normally called *mamlūk,* an Arabic word meaning "owned," while black slaves were called *'abd.* In time, the word *'abd* ceased to be used of any slaves but black ones and eventually, in many Arabic dialects, simply came to mean a black man irrespective of whether he was a slave or not. This transition from a social to an ethnic meaning is thus the reverse of the semantic development of our word "slave," which began as the designation of an ethnic group and became a social term. In Western Islam—in North Africa and Spain—the word *khādim,* servant, (dialectal form *khadem*) is often specialized to mean black slave, slave-woman, or concubine.

It is not only in terminology that black and white slaves were distinguished. For one thing, white slaves, especially females, were more expensive; for another, black slaves were far more severely restricted in their social and occupational mobility. In early times black singers were greatly admired, and some of them won fame and fortune—if not for themselves, then for their trainers and owners. Jāḥiẓ, in his essay on singing-girls, mentions an Ethiopian slave-girl who was worth 120,000 dinars, and brought much profit to her master, in the form of gifts and offerings from aspiring and frustrated admirers. Later, the black musicians seem to have been overtaken by whites. The change is ascribed to the great musician Ibrāhīm al-

Mawṣilī (742–804), whose son is quoted as saying: "They used not to train beautiful slave-girls to sing, but they used only to train yellow and black girls. The first to teach valuable girls to sing was my father." The price of these girls, he adds, was very much higher. Ibn Buṭlān, in his handbook, suggests a proper ethnic division of labor for both male and female slaves. For guarding persons and property, he recommends Indians and Nubians; as laborers, servants, and eunuchs, Zanj; as soldiers, Turks and Slavs. In the central Islamic lands, black slaves were most commonly used for domestic and menial purposes, often as eunuchs, sometimes also in economic enterprises, as for example in the gold mines of 'Allāqī in Upper Egypt where (according to Ya'qūbī) "the inhabitants, merchants and others, have black slaves who work the mines," in the salt-mines, and in the copper mines of the Sahara, where both male and female slaves were employed. The most famous were the black slave gangs who toiled in the salt-flats of Basra. Their task was to remove and stack the nitrous topsoil, so as to clear the undersoil for cultivation, probably of sugar, and at the same time to extract the saltpeter. Consisting principally of slaves imported from East Africa, and numbering some tens of thousands, they lived and worked in conditions of extreme misery. They were fed, we are told, on "a few handfuls" of flour, semolina, and dates. They rose in several successive rebellions, the most important of which lasted fifteen years, from 868 to 883, and for a while offered a serious threat to the Baghdad Caliphate. The leader of these black rebels was a white man.

Even religious groups with what some would nowadays call radical and progressive ideals seem to have accepted the slavery of the black man as natural. Thus in the eleventh century we are told that the Carmathians established a kind of republic in Bahrain, abolished many of the prescriptions regarding persons and property which conventional Islam imposed—and had a force of thirty thousand black slaves to do the rough work.

A common explanation of this status, among Muslim authors, is that the ancestor of the dark-skinned peoples was Ham the son of Noah who (according to Muslim legend) was damned black for his sin. The curse of blackness, and with it that of slavery, passed to all the black peoples who are his descendants.

This story, though widespread, was by no means universally accepted. Ibn Khaldūn and many other writers reject it as absurd and attribute blackness to climatic and geographical causes. The idea however that blackness and slavery are associated is clearly expressed in this story. Another sign of this association is the occasional discussion by jurists of the status of black Muslim slaves. Muslim law unequivocally forbids the enslavement of free Muslims of whatever race, and was usually obeyed in this. There is, however, some evidence that the law was not always strictly enforced to protect Muslim captives from black Africa. A legal ruling by a fifteenth-century Moroccan jurist, Aḥmad al-Wansharīsī, is instructive. The question to be decided is whether Ethiopian (i.e., black) slaves professing monotheism and observing religious practices could lawfully be bought and sold. The law is clear. An unbeliever may be enslaved, a Muslim may not; but the adoption of Islam by an unbeliever *after* his enslavement does not automatically set him free. Slavery, says al-Wansharīsī, is a condition arising from current *or previous* unbelief, and persists after conversion, the owner of the slave retaining full property rights. If a group is known to have been converted to Islam, then the taking of slaves from this group should be forbidden. However, the existence of a doubt as to whether conversion took place before or after enslavement does not invalidate the ownership or sale of the slave. It is significant that al-Wansharīsī discusses the question in relation to black slaves; that he is at some pains to insist that Islam does not necessarily involve freedom—and that he gives the benefit of the doubt not to the slave but to the slaveowner. The problem was clearly not academic. Other sources preserve complaints by black Muslim rulers about "holy wars" launched against them to take captives, and by jurists—usually black jurists—at the enslavement of free black Muslims contrary to law.

White slaves were rarely used for rough labor, and filled higher positions in domestic and administrative employment. Both blacks and whites were used as eunuchs, but the blacks soon predominated. The Caliph al-Amīn (r. 809–813), it is said, collected them in large numbers, and formed separate corps of white and black eunuchs, which he called "the locusts" (*jarrādiyya*) and "the ravens" (*ghurābiyya*). An Arabic description of the court of the caliph in Baghdad at the beginning of the tenth century speaks of 7,000 black and 4,000 white eunuchs. Later, white eunuchs became rare and costly.

MILITARY SLAVES

The military slave, so prominent a figure in Islamic history, is overwhelmingly white. In the East he is usually of Turkish origin, in the West of Slavic or other European origin.

Black military slaves are not unknown and indeed at certain periods were of importance. Black soldiers appear occasionally in early Abbasid times, and after the slave rebellion in southern Iraq, in which blacks displayed terrifying military prowess, they were recruited in large numbers into the infantry corps of the caliphs in Baghdad. Aḥmad b. Ṭūlūn (*d.* 884), the first independent ruler of Muslim Egypt, relied very heavily on black slaves, probably Nubians, for his armed forces; at his death he is said to have left, among other possessions, 24,000 white *mamlūks* and 45,000 blacks. These were organized in separate corps, and accommodated in separate quarters at the military cantonments. When Khumārawayh, the son and successor of Aḥmad ibn Ṭūlūn, rode in procession, he was followed, according to a chronicler, by a thousand black guards:

> . . . wearing black cloaks and black turbans, so that a watcher could fancy them to be a black sea spreading over the face of the earth, because of the blackness of their color and of their garments. With the glitter of their shields, of the chasing on their swords, and of the helmets under their turbans, they made a really splendid sight.

The black troops were the most faithful supporters of the dynasty, and shared their fate. When the Tulunids were overthrown at the beginning of 905, the restoration of caliphal authority was followed by a massacre of the black infantry and the burning of their quarters.

> Then the cavalry turned against the cantonments of the Tulunid blacks, seized as many of them as they could, and took them to Muḥammad ibn Sulaymān [the new governor sent by the Caliph]. He was on horseback, amid his escort. He gave orders to slaughter them, and they were slaughtered in his presence like sheep.

A similar fate befell the black infantry in Baghdad in 930, when they were attacked and massacred by the white cavalry, with the help of other troops and of the populace, and their quarters burnt. Thereafter black soldiers virtually disappear from the armies of the eastern caliphate.

In Egypt, the manpower resources of Nubia were too good to neglect, and the traffic down the Nile continued to provide slaves for military as well as other purposes. Black soldiers served the various rulers of medieval Egypt, and under the Fatimid caliphs of Cairo black regiments, known as *'Abīd al-Shirā,* "the slaves by purchase," formed an important part of the military establishment. They were particularly prominent in the mid-eleventh century, during the reign of al-Mustanṣir, when for a while the real ruler of Egypt was the caliph's mother, a Sudanese slave-woman of remarkable strength of character. There were frequent clashes between black regiments and those of other races, and occasional friction with the civil population. One such incident occurred in 1021, when the Caliph al-Ḥākim sent his black troops against the people of Fusṭāṭ (old Cairo, and the white troops joined forces to defend them. A contemporary chronicler of these events describes an orgy of burning, plunder, and rape. In 1062 and again in 1067 the black troops were defeated by their white colleagues in pitched battles and driven out of Cairo to Upper Egypt. Later they returned, and played a role of some importance under the last Fatimid caliphs.

With the fall of the Fatimids, the black troops again paid the price of their loyalty. Among the most faithful supporters of the Fatimid Caliphate, they were also among the last to resist its overthrow by Saladin, ostensibly the caliph's vizier, but in fact the new master of Egypt. By the time of the last Fatimid Caliph, al-'Āḍid, the blacks had achieved a position of power. The black eunuchs wielded great influence in the palace; the black troops formed a major element in the Fatimid army. It was natural that they should resist the vizier's encroachments. In 1169 Saladin learnt of a plot by the caliph's chief black eunuch to remove him, allegedly in collusion with the Crusaders in Palestine. Saladin acted swiftly; the offender was seized and decapitated, and replaced in his office by a white eunuch. The other black eunuchs of the caliph's palace were also dismissed. The black troops in Cairo were infuriated by this summary execution of one whom they regarded as their spokesman and defender. Moved, according to a chronicler, by "racial solidarity" *(jinsiyya)*, they prepared for battle. In two hot August days, an estimated 50,000 blacks fought against Saladin's army in the area between the two palaces, of the caliph and of the vizier.

Two reasons are given for their defeat. One was their betrayal by the Fatimid Caliph al-'Āḍid, whose cause they believed they were defending against the usurping vizier:

> Al-'Āḍid had gone up to his belvedere tower, to watch the battle between the palaces. It is said that he ordered the men in the palace to shoot arrows and throw stones at [Saladin's] troops, and they did so. Others say that this was not done by his choice. Shams al-Dawla [Saladin's brother] sent naphtha-throwers to burn down al-'Āḍid's belvedere. One of them was about to do this when the door of the belvedere tower opened and out came a caliphal aide, who said: "The Commander of the Faithful greets Shams al-Dawla, and says: 'Beware of the [black] slave dogs! Drive them out of the country!' " The blacks were sustained by the belief that al-'Āḍid was pleased with what they did. When they heard this, their strength was sapped, their courage waned, and they fled.

The other reason, it is said, was an attack on their homes. During the battle between the palaces, Saladin sent a detachment to the black quarters, with instructions "to burn them down on their possessions and their children." Learning of this, the blacks tried to break off the battle and return to their families, but were caught in the streets and destroyed. This encounter is variously known in Arabic annals as "the battle of the blacks" and "the battle of the slaves." Though the conflict was not primarily racial, it acquired a racial aspect, which is reflected in some of the verses composed in honor of Saladin's victory. Maqrīzī, in a comment on this episode, complains of the power and arrogance of the blacks: "If they had a grievance against a vizier, they killed him, and they caused much damage by stretching out their hands against the property and families of the people. When their outrages were many and their misdeeds increased, God destroyed them for their sins." Sporadic resistance by groups of black soldiers continued, but was finally crushed after a few years. While the white units of the Fatimid army were incorporated by Saladin in his own forces, the blacks were not. The black regiments were disbanded, and black fighting-men did not reappear in the armies of Egypt for many centuries. Under the Mamlūk Sultans, blacks were employed in the army in a menial role, as servants of the knights. There was a clear distinction between these servants, who were black and slaves, and the knights' orderlies and grooms, who were white and free.

Though black slaves no longer served as soldiers in Egypt, they still fought occasionally—as rebels or rioters. In 1260, during the transition from the Ayyubid to the Mamlūk Sultanate, black stableboys and some others seized horses and weapons, and staged a minor insurrection in Cairo. They proclaimed their allegiance to the Fatimids, and followed a religious leader who "incited them to rise against the people of the state; he granted them fiefs and wrote them deeds of assignment." The end was swift. "When they rebelled during the night, the troops rode in, surrounded them, and shackled them; by morning they were crucified outside the Zuwayla gate." The same desire among the slaves to emulate the forms and trappings of the Mamlūk state is expressed in a more striking form in an incident in 1446, when some five hundred slaves, tending their masters' horses in the pasturages outside Cairo, took arms and set up a miniature state and court of their own. One of them was called Sultan, and installed on a throne in a carpeted pavilion; others were dignified with the titles of chief officers of the Mamlūk court, including the vizier, the commander-in-chief, and even the governors of Damascus and Aleppo. They raided grain caravans and other traffic, and were even willing to buy the freedom of a colleague. They succumbed to internal dissensions. Their "sultan" was challenged by another claimant, and in the ensuing struggles the revolt was suppressed. Many of the slaves were recaptured and the rest fled.

Towards the end of the fifteenth century, black slaves were admitted to units using firearms—a socially despised weapon in the Mamlūk knightly society. When a Sultan tried to show some favor to his black arquebusiers, he provoked violent antagonism from the Mamlūk knights, which he was not able to resist. In 1498 "a great disturbance occurred in Cairo." The Sultan (according to the chronicler) had outraged the Mamlūks by conferring two boons on a black slave called Farajallah, chief of the firearms personnel in the citadel—first, giving him a white Circassian slave-girl from the palace as wife, and second, granting him a short-sleeved tunic, a characteristic garment of the Mamlūks.

> On beholding this spectacle [says the chronicler] the Royal Mamluks expressed their disapproval to the Sultan, and they put on their . . . armor . . . and armed themselves with their full equipment. A battle broke out between them and the black slaves who numbered about five hundred. The black slaves ran away and gathered again in the towers of the citadel and fired at the Royal Mamluks. The royal Mamluks marched on them, killing Farajallah and about fifty of the black slaves; the rest fled; two Royal Mamluks were killed. Then the amirs and the Sultan's maternal uncle, the Great Dawādār, met the Sultan and told him: "We disapprove of these acts of yours [and if you persist in them, it would be better for you to] ride by night in the narrow by-streets and go away together with those black slaves to far-off places!" The Sultan answered: "I shall desist from this, and these black slaves will be sold to the Turkmans. . . ."

In the west of Islam black slave troops were more frequent, and sometimes even included cavalry—something virtually unknown in the east. Black units, probably recruited by purchase via Zawīla in Fezzan (now southern Libya), figure in the armies of the rulers of Tunisia between the ninth and eleventh centuries. They became important from the seventeenth century, after the Moroccan military expansion into the Western Sudan. The Moroccan Sultan Mawlay Ismā'īl (1672–1727) is said to have had a reserve of 150,000 black slaves, from whom he selected and trained his fighting troops. After his death in 1727, a period of anarchic internal struggles followed, which some contemporaries describe as a conflict between blacks and whites. The philosopher David Hume, writing at about the same time, saw such a conflict as absurd and comic, and used it to throw ridicule on all sectarian and factional strife:

> The civil wars which arose some few years ago in Morocco between the *Blacks and Whites,* merely on account of their complexion, are founded on a pleasant difference. We laugh at them; but, I believe, were things rightly examined, we afford much more occasion of ridicule to the Moors. For, what are all the wars of religion, which have prevailed in this polite and knowing part of the world? They are certainly more absurd than the Moorish civil wars. The difference of complexion is a sensible and a real difference; but the controversy about an article of faith, which is utterly absurd and unintelligible, is not a difference in sentiment, but in a few phrases and expressions,

> which one party accepts of without understanding them, and the other refuses in the same manner. . . . Besides, I do not find that the *Whites* in Morocco ever imposed on the Blacks any necessity of altering their complexion . . . nor have the Blacks been more unreasonable in this particular. . . .

Blacks were occasionally recruited into the Mamlūk forces in Egypt at the end of the eighteenth century. "When the supply [of white slaves] proves insufficient," says a contemporary observer, W. G. Browne, "or many have been expended, black slaves from the interior of Africa are substituted, and if found docile, are armed and accoutred like the rest." This is confirmed by Louis Frank, a medical officer with Bonaparte's expedition to Egypt, who wrote an important memoir on the negro slave trade in Cairo.

In the nineteenth century, black military slaves reappeared in Egypt in considerable numbers; their recruitment was indeed one of the main purposes of the Egyptian advance up the Nile under Muḥammad 'Alī Pasha (r. 1805–1849) and his successors. Collected by annual *razzias* from Darfur and Kordofan, they constituted an important part of the Khedivial armies, and incidentally furnished the bulk of the Egyptian expeditionary force which the Khedive Ismā'īl sent to Mexico in 1863, in support of the French. An English traveler writing in 1825 had this to say about black soldiers in the Egyptian army:

> When the negro troops were first brought down to Alexandria, nothing could exceed their insubordination and wild demeanor; but they learned the military evolutions in half the time of the Arabs; and I always observed they went through the maneuvers with ten times the adroitness of the others. It is the fashion here, as well as in our colonies, to consider the negroes as the last link in the chain of humanity, between the monkey tribe and man; but I do not believe the negro is inferior to the white man in intellect; and I do not suffer the eloquence of the slave driver to convince me that the negro is so stultified as to be unfit for freedom.

Between white and black military slaves—even where the latter were numerous and powerful—there was always one crucial distinction. Whereas white slaves could become generals, provincial governors, sovereigns, and founders of dynasties, this hardly every happened with black slaves in the central Islamic lands. In Muslim India, a number of soldiers of African slave origin rose to high office, some even becoming rulers. Elsewhere, their opportunities for advancement were very limited. Only one of them ever became the ruler of a Muslim country, outside the black zone—the famous Nubian eunuch Abu'l-Misk Kāfūr, "Musky Camphor," who in the tenth century became regent of Egypt (and a very capable one).

SOURCE: Bernard Lewis, *Race and Color in Islam* (New York: Harper and Row, 1971), pp. 18–29, 38, 64–78 (footnotes omitted).

AFRICANS IN INDIA

IN INDIA, from medieval times to the present, persons of African origin have been known as "Ḥabshīs" or as "Sīdīs." By the nineteenth century the two terms seem to have become synonymous,[43] but before then they carried slightly different connotations. Writers of the period from the fifteenth to the eighteenth centuries used "Sīdī" when referring to Africans belonging to the seafaring communities of the west coast, while "Ḥabshī" was the preferred term for Africans living in the kingdoms of the interior. There were many exceptions to this practice, however, and sometimes an individual might receive both sobriquets, as in the case of Ḥabash Khān Sīdī Miftāḥ, an official who attained high rank at the court of Delhi under the Mughal emperor, Awrangzīb.[44]

In Arabic, and hence in the usage of Muslim India, a *Ḥabashī* (pl. *Ḥabshī*) was an inhabitant of Abyssinia (Ethiopia). Many, perhaps a majority, of the Africans who went to India before the nineteenth century were of Ethiopian origin, but the term came to signify Africans generally. It is as though, once in India, all Africans were regarded as the same. In any case, the collective term, Ḥabshī, was used indiscriminately for immigrants from Nubia, Somalia, East Africa, Mozambique, and Madagascar, as well as for those who came from Ethiopia itself.

The word *sīdī* is also of Arabic origin, being derived from *sayyid* ("lord"). In the seventeenth and eighteenth centuries the admiral commanding the African seafarers of Janjīra (south of Bombay) was called "the Sīdī," and the title was prefixed to the names of other prominent Africans. But, somewhat confusingly, the sailors on the ships commanded by "the Sīdī" were also called "Sīdīs," as are their descendants who live on the Indian mainland today.[45] In the nineteenth century African coal-trimmers serving in the engine-rooms of ships of the Indian Navy were known as "Seedees," [46] and so were the soldiers who from 1863 onwards formed the famous and distinctive bodyguard belonging to the Nizam of Hyderabad.[47] On the other hand, there is a district in the modern city of Hyderabad which is still known as "Ḥabshī guda" and a mosque called "Ḥabshī masjid." [48] Clearly both terms, Ḥabshī and Sīdī, have survived, and both mean "African," though the official preference of the Indian government—as shown by census listings, for example—seems nowadays to be for "Sīdī."

The number of Africans who emigrated to India in medieval and early modern times is unknown. From such figures as there are, however, it appears that the total may have been considerable. At the time of Ibn Baṭṭūṭa's visit to Sri Lanka in the mid-fourteenth century the *wazīr* of Kalanbū (modern Colombo) employed "about five hundred Abyssinians." [49] In the late fifteenth century there were some 8,000 African slave-soldiers in Bengal (see p. 141), and in the 1530s the west coast settlement of Dāmān was defended against the Portuguese by a Ḥabshī commander, Sayf al-Mulk Miftāḥ, with 4,000 troops under him.[50] In 1553 another Ḥabshī commander, with 400 infantrymen and 300 cavalry, drove the Portuguese away from Diu, and in a campaign near Dāmān in 1562 the chief opponent of the Portuguese was a Ḥabshī at the head of "800 horse and 1,000 foot soldiers." [51] During the reign of sultan Bahādur of Gujarāt (early sixteenth century) there were said to be 5,000 Ḥabshīs in Aḥmadābād, the capital of the sultanate, alone.[52]

Africans began entering India in sizable numbers at least as early as the thirteenth century. They came as adventurers, as soldiers, sailors, and policemen, as traders, bureaucrats, clerics, bodyguards, and concubines, and as servants, both free and slave. Some arrived directly across the ocean from East and Northeast Africa; others came via the Middle East, Persia, Afghanistan, and Southeast Asia, often in the entourages of slaveowners who were themselves seeking their fortunes in India. Many of these African immigrants were descended from families long resident in the Islamic lands to the north and west of the Indian subcontinent, and many were of mixed ancestry (part-Arab, part-Persian, and so on). All, however, were Muslim, except for a tiny fraction of the whole who were brought by the Portuguese to Goa and other ports on the west coast. Perhaps a majority were slaves, though this statement can be misleading unless it is remembered to what positions of high authority a slave in the medieval Islamic world could aspire. In India before the nineteenth century a talented slave often lived a more secure and privileged life than did the majority of free men.

31 Jamāl al-Dīn Yāḳūt, Favorite of the Queen of Delhi

Perhaps the first African to achieve prominence in India was the slave Jamāl al-Dīn Yāḳūt, "Master of the Stables" to Queen Raḍiyya of Delhi in the thirteenth century. Raḍiyya came to the throne of Delhi in 1236. She is described by a contemporary chronicler as "a great sovereign, sagacious, just, beneficient, the patron of the learned. . . . She marched in person against her enemies, set aside female garments, discarded the veil, donned the tunic and assumed the head-dress of a man." [53] Her nobles, however, disliked being ruled by a woman and rose in revolt against her. In the conflict that followed Yāḳūt, her loyal supporter, was killed, and Raḍiyya herself was captured, deposed, and later put to death.

Ibn Baṭṭūṭa, the North African world traveler, heard the story of Raḍiyya and Yāḳūt when he was in Delhi in the early fourteenth century and recorded it in his memoirs. A similar version of the tale appears in the writings of the Persian chronicler, Firishta, who lived at Bījāpur in southern India in the late sixteenth century. Both accounts, extracts from which appear below, suggest that there was something improper in the relationship between Raḍiyya and her stablemaster, and Firishta at least implies that the nobles of the Delhi Sultanate were motivated against Yāḳūt by racial prejudice. Modern historians of India, however, discount such traditions. Raḍiyya was not a romantic Indian queen who lost her throne for love of a black slave. Rather, she appears to have been a hardheaded, competent (and decidedly masculine) ruler, who was opposed by a faction at her court and lost a decisive battle against that faction. In her struggle to survive she sought support where she could find it. One of her most faithful supporters was her stablemaster, who happened to be an Abyssinian (Ḥabshī).

■

When Rukn al-Dīn was put to death the troops determined by general consent to confer the sovereignty on his sister Raḍīya and proclaimed her as queen. She held sovereign rule for four years and used to ride abroad just like the men, carrying bow and quiver . . . and without veiling her face. After that she was suspected of relations with a slave of hers, one of the Abyssinians, so the people agreed to depose her and marry her to a husband.

SOURCE: H. A. R. Gibb, trans., vols. 3 and 4 of *The Travels of Ibn Baṭṭūṭa A. D. 1325–1354* (Cambridge: Cambridge University Press for the Hakluyt Society, 1971), 3:631.

[Jamāl al-Dīn Yāḳūt], an Abyssinian, who was in great favor, was raised from the office of master of the horse, to that of [chief of the nobles]. The nobles, highly offended at this proceeding, were disposed to examine narrowly the cause of so much favor. A very great degree of familiarity was observed to exist between the Abyssinian and the Queen; so much so, that when she rode he always lifted her on her horse by raising her up under the arms. The intimacy, the great favor which he had suddenly attained, and his rapid elevation to the first rank in the realm, might naturally have excited envy had it happened to any individual; but it became the more mortifying when the favorite was merely an Abyssinian slave.

SOURCE: John Briggs, *History of the Rise of the Mahomedan Power in India* [a translation of Firishta's Gulshan-i Ibrāhīmī] (4 vols.; London,1829; repr., Calcutta: Editions Indian, 1966), 1:122–23.

32 The Ḥabshī Sultans of Bengal

In 1352 the Muslim sultanate of Bengal (Bangāla) was founded in northeastern India. During the following century its rulers, the kings of the Ilyās Shāhī dynasty, adopted the practice of importing foreign slaves to act as government functionaries and palace guards. (The use of slave-soldiers was widespread among Muslim states of this period.) Since Bengal had extensive maritime links with the Red Sea, it was convenient for the Ilyās Shāhī kings, using Arab intermediaries, to obtain the slaves they needed from Africa, and by the reign of Bārbak Shāh (1459–74) there were at least 8,000 African, or Ḥabshī, slaves in the kingdom, most of them military men.[54]

Using the power and influence their numbers gave them, the Ḥabshīs of Bengal were soon able to engross the highest offices in the state. They "swarmed in the palace and in the city," and acted in violent and insolent ways.[55] Sultan Fatḥ Shāh, who came to the throne in 1481, decided to curb them, but the repressive measures he adopted provoked a revolt, and in 1486 he was assassinated. Shāhzāda, the Ḥabshī commander of the palace guard and leader of the rebels, then ascended the throne as Bārbak Shāh. Thus began seven years of Ḥabshī rule in Bengal.[56]

Bārbak Shāh had been in power for less than six months when he was assassinated in his turn. His successor was the man who killed him, Andīl (Indīl) Khān, also a Ḥabshī, who had been commander-in-chief of the army under Fatḥ Shāh and at the time of Bārbak Shāh's coup was absent on duty in one of the provinces. On receiving the news of his master's death he had hurried back to the capital with the intention of restoring the dynasty, but, after murdering Bārbak Shāh, decided to take power himself. As Sayf al-Dīn Fīrūz, he ruled for three years, and ruled well. His only fault seems to have been an insistence on disbursing to the poor what his advisers considered were unnecessarily large sums from the public treasury.[57]

After the death of Fīrūz in 1489 the government was seized by his

Ḥabshī *wazīr,* Ḥabash Khān, who ruled as regent on behalf of a boy-king. This boy was perhaps of the legitimate Ilyās Shāhī line, but may have been a son of Fīrūz.[58] The arrangement, in any case, did not last. Before long Ḥabash Khān was assassinated by yet another Ḥabshī, Sīdī Badr Dīwāna, nicknamed "the Madman." Sīdī Badr put the boy-king to death and in 1490 proclaimed himself sultan with the title Shams al-Dīn Muẓaffar Shāh.

The chronicles portray Muẓaffar Shāh as a bloodthirsty monster. He is said to have executed most of the nobility at the capital; he imposed exorbitant taxes on the common people; and he reduced the pay and allowances of his soldiers. By these policies he caused an alliance to be formed against him of three influential segments of the population, and rebellion was inevitable. When it came in 1493, it was led by the chief minister, 'Alā' al-Dīn Ḥusayn. This man was not a Ḥabshī but an Arab; because of his race, he was able to rally around him all who feared and resented the Ḥabshī presence in the kingdom. Declaring war on Muẓaffar Shāh, he besieged him for some months in his citadel at Gaur, and eventually brought about his death. At once the power of the Ḥabshīs collapsed, and they were expelled from Bengal. Many drifted west to Gujarāt and the Deccan where they found employment under other Muslim rulers.[59]

The atmosphere in which the Ḥabshī sultans of late fifteenth-century Bengal lived and exercised their brief authorities is well conveyed by the account of the murder of Bārbak Shāh by Andīl Khān in the *Cambridge History of India,* an extract from which is given below. Another authoritative work describes these sultans as "phantom and tyrannical rulers" who succeeded one another in quick succession while "the people, both Hindu and Muslim, looked upon the palace intrigues and revolutions with complete indifference." [60] This was true so long as Ḥabshī rule did not affect the majority of the population. But when, as happened under Muẓaffar Shāh, that rule became blatantly oppressive, when the foreigners who had taken over the government began to decimate the traditional aristocracy and to show signs of aspiring to become a permanent ruling caste, then the populace aroused itself from its lethargy and threw the Ḥabshīs out.

Another part of India where Ḥabshīs have long been credited with attaining high office is Jaunpur. For most of the fifteenth century this northern Indian state was ruled by a dynasty known as the Sharḳīs, and, until a short time ago, most historians have accepted the view that at least the later members of the dynasty were of African origin. Recent research, however, suggests that this belief is no longer tenable.

The first ruler of Jaunpur (who may have been African) was the eunuch Malik Sarwar, a slave of the Tughluḳ sultan of Delhi, Nāṣir al-Dīn Maḥmūd. In 1394 Nāṣir al-Dīn sent Sarwar to the eastern provinces of the Delhi sultanate to crush a rebellion, granting him the title of Malik (or Sulṭān) al-Sharḳ ("Lord of the East").[61] Having accomplished the purpose for which he was sent, Malik Sarwar died in 1399, leaving to his adopted son, Malik Ḳaranful, a large semi-independent kingdom based on Jaunpur. The word *ḳaranful* means "clove," and in India was often given as a nickname to African slaves. This fact has led many to deduce that Malik Ḳaranful was a Ḥabshī.[62] When he died in 1402, he was succeeded by his brother, Shams al-Dīn Ibrāhīm Shāh, also long assumed to be a Ḥabshī, and it was during the reign of Ibrāhīm (1402–1440) that the kingdom of Jaunpur attained its greatest fame and prosperity. It became a notable center of learning and of artistic and cultural activities, and many imposing monuments were built at the capital, including mosques, palaces, and tombs, some of which still survive. Ibrāhīm "was respected as the wielder of the greatest power in northern India," and contemporaries called his city "the Shirāz of Hind." [63] He was succeeded by a son, Mahmūd Shāh (ruled 1440–57) and then by a nephew, Ḥusayn, under whom Jaunpur was conquered by Bahlōl Lodī in 1479 and reincorporated into the Delhi sultanate.

The hypothesis that the Sharḳīs were a Ḥabshī dynasty rested on only one piece of evidence, namely, that the founder of the line, Malik Ḳaranful, was himself of African origin. Now, however, it has been shown that Ḳaranful was not a Ḥabshī but a Sayyid, and probably a member of the Delhi royal house.[64] The Sharḳīs of Jaunpur, therefore, can no longer be claimed as exemplars of African achievement in India. Yet, in the context of the theme of "Africans

Abroad," their story is not without relevance. It is significant that many of the most respected historians of India have for decades found it reasonable to assume that a Ḥabshī dynasty could have ruled a powerful, cultured, prosperous, and independent Muslim Indian state for eighty years.

■

The malcontents elected as their leader a eunuch named Sultān Shāhzāda, and took advantage of the absence from court, on a distant expedition, of Indīl Khān, who, though an African, was a loyal subject of Fath Shāh and an able military commander, to compass the king's death. The guard over the palace consisted of no less than 5,000 men, and it was the king's custom to appear early in the morning at the relief of the guard and receive the salutes of both guards. The eunuch corrupted the officers of the palace guards, and one morning in 1486, when the king came forth, as usual, to take the salute, caused him to be assassinated and usurped the throne under the title of Bārbak Shāh.

Indīl Khān, at his distant post, heard of the tragedy and was considering on what pretext he could lead his troops to the capital to avenge his master's death when he received a summons from Bārbak. He welcomed the opportunity and hastened with his troops to Gaur, where his influence and the armed force at his command rendered his position secure. He found that the eunuch's rule was already unpopular, and allowed it to be understood that he was a partisan of the old royal house, which was not yet extinct. Bārbak was apprehensive of his designs, and when he appeared at court insisted that he should take an oath not to injure or betray him. A copy of the Koran was produced, and Indīl Khān, who could not refuse the oath, added to it the reservation that he would not injure Bārbak so long as he was on the throne; but he interpreted the reservation literally, and, having bribed the ushers and doorkeepers of the court, awaited an opportunity of avenging the murder of Fath Shāh. This soon presented itself when the eunuch fell into a drunken slumber. Indīl Khān forced his way into the royal apartments, but finding that Bārbak had fallen asleep on the cushions which composed the throne, hesitated to violate the letter of his oath, and was about to withdraw when the drunkard rolled heavily over on to the floor. Indīl Khān at once struck him with his sword, but the blow failed of its effect, and Bārbak, suddenly waking, sprang upon him and grappled with him. His strength and weight enabled him to throw his adversary and sit on his chest, but Indīl Khān called to Yaghrush Khān, a Turkish officer whom he had left without, and who now rushed in with a number of faithful Africans. The lamps had been overturned and extinguished in the struggle, and Indīl's followers hesitated to strike in the darkness, lest they should injure their master, but he encouraged them by shouting that their knives would not reach him through the eunuch's gross body, and they stabbed Bārbak repeatedly in the back. He rolled over and feigned death, and they retired, satisfied that their task was done. After they had left a slave entered to relight the lamps, and Bārbak, fearing the return of Indīl Khān, lay still. The slave cried out that the king was dead, and Bārbak, recognizing his voice, bade him be silent and asked what had become of Indīl Khān. The slave replied that he had gone home, and Bārbak, who believed the man to be faithful to himself, issued an order for the execution of Indīl Khān. The slave left the chamber, but instead of delivering the order to any who might have executed it, went at once to Indīl Khān and told him that his enemy yet lived. Indīl Khān returned to the palace, stabbed Bārbak to death, and, sending for the minister, Khānjahān, consulted him regarding the filling of the vacant throne, the rightful heir to which was a child of two years of age. In the morning the courtiers waited upon Fath Shāh's widow, who urged the avenger of her husband's blood to ascend the throne. Indīl Khān, after a decent display of reluctance, accepted the charge, and was proclaimed a few months after the assassination of Fath Shāh, by the title of Saif-ud-dīn Fīrūz.

SOURCE: *Cambridge History of India* (6 vols.; Cambridge: Cambridge University Press, 1922–27), 3:268–69.

33 The Ḥabshīs of Bīdār

Another Indian state in which Ḥabshīs gained great power was the Bahmanī kingdom of the Deccan. The Bahmanīs, who were by origin northern Muslims, colonized southern India in the fourteenth century. Initially they owed allegiance to the sultans of Delhi but, as they extended their authority over the Deccan tableland and its adjacent coastal plain, they became strong enough to defy the Delhi government and declare their independence. From 1347, when this declaration was made, until the collapse and distintegration of their kingdom in the early sixteenth century, the Bahmanīs were the dominant power in southern India.

In the Deccan the Bahmanīs ruled as a small alien elite, claiming authority over a large and restive indigenous population of Hindus. Although some of the Bahmanī sultans took local wives and made efforts to identify with Hindu culture, the security and effectiveness of their rule ultimately depended on their ability to recruit fellow-Muslims from other lands to fill the ranks of their armies and bureaucraçy. For this reason, particularly from the reign of sultan Fīrūz (1397–1422) onward, foreign adventurers were encouraged to seek their fortunes in the Deccan, "a land where valor was recognized and statesmanship rewarded." [65] Among those who took advantage of the employment opportunities offered by the Bahmanīs were Ḥabshīs from Africa.

The Ḥabshīs who emigrated to the Deccan tended to make common cause with the Dakhnīs, or Deccanīs, as the descendants of the original Muslim invaders came to be called. There were two reasons for this alliance. First, the Ḥabshīs were *sunnī* Muslims, as were the Dakhnīs. The majority of the later immigrants to the Deccan, on the other hand, who were known as Pardesīs (foreigners) or Āfāḳīs (cosmopolitans) and who mostly came from Central Asia and Iran, were *shī'ī*. A common sectarian affiliation therefore drove the Dakhnīs and Ḥabshīs together and set them against the Pardesīs, their religious rivals. Second, a racial factor was involved. Many Dakhnīs were products of intermarriage between their male ancestors, the northern Muslims, and local Hindu women. Darker in hue than the more recently arrived Pardesīs, they were subjected by the latter to discrimination based on skin color, as were the Ḥabshīs. Dakhnīs and Ḥabshīs thus supported one another against the Pardesīs, whom they regarded as interlopers and who were in turn contemptuous of them both.[66]

The Ḥabshī adventurers in the Deccan achieved a degree of power out of all proportion to their numbers, which were always small. Toward the end of the Bahmanī era they seem to have been particularly influential. "At this time," said a contemporary, "the power and authority of the people of Ḥabash and Zangbār in the service of the Sulṭān had increased a thousandfold, and the other State officials no longer had any power except in name. The whole country and the offices and political affairs of the kingdom and government treasuries they divided among themselves, and arrogantly ignoring the sovereign, themselves governed the kingdom." The Pardesīs, however, resenting the great heights to which the Ḥabshīs had reached, united against them. A certain Malik Yusuf, who was a Turk and the future founder of the 'Adil Shāhī dynasty of Bījāpur, wrote in protest to the Bahmanī sultan. His letter provoked the sultan into assembling an army and launching it against the Ḥabshīs. The text of this letter, which has survived, both illustrates the style of correspondence in vogue in those days (and thus the milieu in which the Ḥabshīs operated) and depicts the attitude of a Turkish Pardesī toward his despised African rival:

> Malik Dīnār Dastūrī Mamālik, an Abyssinian eunuch, having placed his foot outside the path of obedience and subjection, has become a traveler on the paths of rebellion and resistance. This slave of the court [i.e., Malik Yusuf himself], in concert with your Majesty, will bring about the punishment of that perfidious unbeliever by placing the lightning-striking sword in his embrace, and so recompense his ingratitude and rebellion. [Also] Malik Khūsh Ḳadam Turk Azīz-ul-Mulk, who was formerly a ruler, having become a fellow-traveler with that black-faced, abandoned one, [the two of them] have scratched the face of fidelity and agreement with the nail of oppression and hypocrisy.

In the ensuing conflict, we are told, "The warriors of . . . the two forces, like two mountains of iron and steel . . . rushed on one another, and drawing the sword of hatred from the scabbard of vengeance, separated the heads of the leaders from their bodies and threw them on the dust of destruction." [67]

This incident was but one among many violent encounters between Ḥabshīs and other seekers after power in the Bahmanī kingdom. Sometimes, as here, the Ḥabshīs lost; at other times, they won. Setbacks, though serious (and often final) for individuals, were never so for powerful groups like the Ḥabshīs, Dakhnīs, and Pardesīs. They were evenly matched, and each seemed capable of throwing up one leader after another in the unending struggle for supremacy. The Ḥabshīs undoubtedly held their own. At one time, of the four major provinces into which the Bahmanī state was divided, two were ruled by Ḥabshī *ṭarafdārs,* or governors, and several Ḥabshīs became chief ministers and ministers of finance of the entire kingdom. Most of the Ḥabshī officials whose names have come down to us were slaves, but, as elsewhere in the Muslim world, their status did not condemn them to remain in the ranks of the underprivileged. "Their condition," one writer has said, "corresponded to that of the middle class." The world they lived in was, after all, one where "slaves could become kings." [68]

The capital of the Bahmanī kingdom was the city of Bīdār. Many Ḥabshīs held office in Bīdār between the fifteenth century, when they served the Bahmanī kings and their successors, the Barīdīs, and the seventeenth, by which time the city had passed under the control of the state of Bījāpur. One "Abyssinian general" named Marjān, who governed Bīdār in the early seventeenth century, placed an inscription in his own memory on the inner entrance of Bīdār fort: "By the grace of the Holy and Almighty God, the buildings of bygone kings, comprising mosques, forts, palaces, and halls, were repaired by the sovereign-like . . . Malik Amarjān, 1027 A.H. (A.D. 1619)." [69] But the majority of the Ḥabshīs of Bīdār left no record behind them. In many cases, their identification with their country of adoption was so complete that the chroniclers do not distinguish between them and notable personages of other nationalities or ethnic origins. Often it is only because of haphazardly applied terms like "Ḥabshī," "Ḥabash," and "Sīdī" that the historian knows that some of the great men of the medieval Deccan had any connection with Africa at all. Nevertheless, "the Abyssinians of Bīdār" were sufficiently well known in their day to have left a clear impression on the folk memory of the people of the area. As the following account shows, this impression has survived into the present century.

■

Ḥabshī Koṭ, or the fortress of the Abyssinians, is a hillock situated close to the town of Bidar towards the east, being separated from the latter by a narrow gorge. The hillock has on its top some tombs of the Abyssinian nobles who were employed at the court of the Baihmanī and Barīdī kings, and who revolted several times against their masters and the Persian and Arab dignitaries in their service. . . .

Some amusing stories regarding buried treasures guarded by genii on this hillock are current in Bidar, and the *Sajjāda Ṣāḥib* of the Dargāh of Ḥaḍrat Shāh Kunj Nishīn told me with great confidence that he knew of a young man who was very fond of resorting to the Koṭ and reciting the holy *Qur'ān* at the tombs there. Suddenly he became very rich, and when people asked him the source of his wealth he told them not to press him on that point. But when the curiosity of the people increased and they forced him to disclose the secret of his wealth, he suddenly became insane. Another story is prevalent that the people of Bidar see occasionally a gigantic Abyssinian rolling and baking cakes of enormous size on the roof of a ruined building, which, owing to the absence of a dome and a parapet, resembles an Indian *chūla* and *tava* (a pan placed on the fire). There is no doubt that the place was at one time occupied by Abyssinians, and as they were severely punished for their misconduct, it is likely that strange stories would have been set afloat about their fabulous wealth and their atrocious character.

SOURCE: G. Yazdani, *Bidar: Its History and Monuments* (London: Oxford University Press, 1947), pp. 180–81.

34 Malik 'Ambar, Ruler of Aḥmadnagar

Of all the Africans who played a role in Indian history the most famous by far was Malik 'Ambar (or 'Anbar), ruler of the state of Aḥmadnagar from 1607 to 1626. He is given an entire chapter in Harris' *The African Presence in Asia,* and some modern Indian writers see him as the greatest man in early seventeenth-century India, a hero and freedom fighter who single-handedly warded off the Mughal conquest of the Deccan for nearly two decades. A military commander of genius, ʻAmbar was also a noted patron of the arts, a brilliant diplomatist, and an innovative and impartial, if somewhat ruthless, administrator. A contemporary said of him: "In charity, piety, justice, and in helping the needy he had a generous hand." [70]

ʻAmbar was born in Ethiopia, probably in 1549. He spent the early part of his life as a slave in Arabia and ʻIrāḳ, but about 1575 a trader brought him to India, where he was purchased by the chief minister (who was himself a Ḥabshī) of the kingdom of Aḥmadnagar in the Deccan. In the service of this official ʻAmbar rose steadily, gaining experience of both civil and military affairs, and eventually attaining the rank of commander of the palace guard. The death of his master led him to seek employment outside Aḥmadnagar, first with the ruler of neighboring Golconda and later with the king of Bījāpur. His fame and reputation for efficiency and enterprise continued to increase. About 1590, following a quarrel about military expenditures, he deserted Bījāpur and decided to strike out on his own. Within a few years he had created a formidable army, whose members owed him personal allegiance. As a result, when in 1596 he was invited to return to Aḥmadnagar to help in defending it against the Mughals, he was able to make his own terms, since the size of his following made him the most powerful military leader in the area. For a while he had to compete with a rival adventurer, Mian Raju, for control of Aḥmadnagar and of its boy-king, Murtaḍā II Niẓām Shāh, but by 1607 he was undisputed master of the state. Despite many vicissitudes he retained this position until his death nineteen years later.[71]

In the Deccan in ʻAmbar's time the politico-military situation was confused and complex. The five kingdoms, of which Aḥmadnagar was one, which had inherited the territories of the medieval Bahmanī sultanate were in a state of semipermanent internecine warfare. To the north the Mughal empire was poised to subdue the entire subcontinent. On those occasions when the Mughal threat seemed especially serious, the kingdoms of the Deccan formed temporary alliances with one another against their common enemy, but such half-hearted efforts at cooperation collapsed as soon as the Mughal pressure was relaxed. Moreover, the Mughals themselves were far from united. After the death of the emperor Akbar in 1605 their generals fell into bickering and mutual recrimination and sought their own personal advantage at the empire's expense. Royal princes sent by Jahangir, the new emperor, to the south to restore order rebelled against him as soon as they were beyond his reach. When it suited their purposes the southern kings readily allied themselves with particular Mughal generals, and as readily broke the promises they had made when these purposes changed. Similarly, Mughal generals tried to form alliances with particular southerners in their efforts to discredit their rivals and secure Delhi's favor. Few kings, ministers, or military commanders on either side held office for long, and few escaped imprisonment, blinding, or unnatural death. If you were a man of consequence in the Deccan of the early seventeenth century, to survive was an achievement. It is against this background that the career of Malik 'Ambar mut be judged.

As a military tactician 'Ambar is credited with devising a new form of guerrilla warfare. Discovering that his troops were no match for the Mughals in open combat, he avoided set-piece battles whenever he could, and relied instead on hit-and-run attacks against his enemy's flanks and rear. The Mughals were used to campaigning over the broad expanse of the north Indian plain. They lacked experience of fighting in hilly terrain like that of the Deccan, and their ponderous armies equipped with long baggage trains proved very vulnerable to the attacks of 'Ambar's disciplined detachments of mobile light cavalry. His guerrilla tactics were later adopted, and used against the Mughals with even more devastating effect, by the Marāthās.[72]

As ruler of Aḥmadnagar 'Ambar established a postal service, encouraged manufactures, and built canals and irrigation channels. He founded schools, awarded pensions to poets and scholars, constructed a mosque and numerous public buildings, and reduced the burden of taxation on the poor. He gave support to his fellow-Africans, the Sīdīs of Janjīra, and helped to establish them as a naval force to be reckoned with in the Indian Ocean. He maintained diplomatic relations with countries as far away as Persia, where, for a time, he had an African, Ḥabash Khān, as his representative.[73]

When news of his death arrived at Delhi, the emperor Jahangir recorded in his journal: "This 'Ambar was a slave, but an able man. In warfare, in command, in sound judgment, and in administration, he had no rival or equal. He well understood that predatory warfare, which in the language of the Deccan is called *bargi-giri.* He kept down the turbulent spirit of that country, and maintained his exalted position to the end of his life, and closed his career in honor. History records no other instance of an Abyssinian slave arriving at such eminence." [74]

When Malik 'Ambar was at the height of his power in Aḥmadnagar, he was visited by Pieter van den Broecke, a factor in the employ of the Netherlands East India Company. An extract from van den Broecke's memoirs is given below. The account includes some details that may not be true: there is no evidence, for example, that 'Ambar married his dead master's widow, though the belief that he had done so was still current in the eighteenth century; [75] and there is no proof that his daughter became one of the wives of the king of Aḥmadnagar.[76] But, as one of the very few firsthand descriptions of Malik 'Ambar that has survived, it is valuable.

■

In the afternoon I went in person to the Melick Ambahaer [Malik 'Ambar], bringing as presents a Japanese saber and an expensive Javanese kris. He liked the Japanese saber but not the kris, because it was decorated with a demon.* He gave it back, gave me also a permit for the rest of our people, was very friendly, and hung two expensive *pomerins* † around my shoulders, one made of gold, the other one of camel's hair; this is the greatest honor one can give a person. He also offered to give me soldiers as a guard and convoy to Golconda.

He had with him an ambassador from King Partabasja, who requested his horse back and compensation for damages done to his people. I told Melick Ambaer that I was now in his land and under

* As a strict Muslim, Malik 'Ambar was not well disposed towards representations of living creatures, as being contrary to his religion.

† *Pomerin,* a corruption of the Marāthī word, *pāmarī,* a colored cloth used as a cloak. Here the sense is "robe of honor."

his authority; that I had come to his land trusting his word, since he is considered in the whole world as a man who scrupulously keeps his word. If it was his wish that I return the horse, then I would give it up, but not of my free will, indeed very much against it. But if this was not his wish, then the . . . soldiers should try to get it by force of arms. He began to laugh and gave the message to the ambassador, who did not like it a bit.

In our company were also some Portuguese *arnegados* * who said, in Portuguese, "Look at that proud dog," *Vede iste suberbe can!* They came to the Melick to request command of 3, 4, or 5,000 horse. They said: "This dog only comes to spy; watch out." With a friendly face he gave me my leave and I rode back to my tent.

This Melick Ambar is a black kaffir from the land of Habessi [Abyssinia] or Prester John's land. He has a cruel Roman † face, and is tall and strong of stature, with white glassy eyes which do not become him. He is a good administrator and was a slave who was sold for 20 ducats in Mocha. After the death of his master, who was a rich nobleman from the Deccan, he married the nobleman's widow, who did not have much property since the kings of those lands generally confiscate the property of the great lords. He therefore had to take to stealing and robbing, in which he was very successful, and attracted many followers, in the end even to the number of 5,000 horse. He began to dominate and with his robbers maintained himself against the king in an unassailable place where King Nisium Sia [Niẓām Shāh] could not harm him at all, because this fox was too smart for him; they were at war for many years. Then, because the king was also at war with the Great Mogul, who was trying to fish in this troubled water and become master of the Deccan, he [i.e., the king] sent for Melick Ambahar and offered him an attractive income if he would return to his obedience and help him against the Great Mogul. The aforementioned Mellick, a cunning man, having noticed the guile and tricks of the king, refused and persisted in his plans, finally having over 8,000 mounted men. He became stronger and got more followers all the time. The king, seeing this, offered peace again. Mellick answered that he would be willing to serve against the Great Mogul and become the king's eternal vassal, on the condition that the king forgot about the past and agreed to marry Mellick's

* *Renegados* (Port.), apostates from the Christian faith.

† In the sense of "strong, martial, courageous." TRANS.

daughter as his queen. The king consented with approval of his council, married Mellick's daughter with great triumph and magnificence, and after that Mellick came with 8,000 well-equipped cavalry to court, where he was welcomed very much and given another 4,000 horse by the king, who thus placed him in direct command over 12,000 cavalry; he was held in high esteem by the king, who gave him considerable income.

At a certain time it happened that the king's first wife, who was a white Persian woman, scolded the daughter of the aforementioned Melick Ambahaer with many bitter words, saying that she was only a kaffir woman and a concubine of the king and that her father had been a rebel against the king. The daughter informed her father of this through someone else, and her father then became so angry that he began to plot the murder of the king. He persuaded Mier Abdel Fatj [Amīr 'Abd al-Fatḥ], the king's secretary, to join him, and the latter poisoned the king a short time later with a potion. The king died immediately, leaving a young son whom Mellick Ambaer captured. He then proceeded to bring the whole country under his command.

The king's son is now already 12 years old; he was only 5 when his father died. The Mellick goes to greet him solemnly twice each week as a token of his obedience. The name of the young king is Nisiam Sia [Niẓām Shāh]. The queen who was the cause of this evil history was also poisoned, shortly after the king her husband.

The aforementioned Melick Ambahaar is now the Governor of the whole country, under the pretext that the king is too young. He carries on a vigorous war against the Great Mogul, and he is supported annually by the kings of Golconda, Visiapour [Bījāpur], and Baligatte, to wit, by the king of Golconda, whose name is Cote Basja [Qutb Shāh], with 6,000 men, by the king of Visiapour [Bījāpur], Ebraham Sia [Ibrāhīm Shāh], with 10,000 men, infantry as well as cavalry, by the king of Baligatte, near Goa, with 12,000 men, infantry and cavalry, plus some more from other little kings; this means that he has every year over 80,000 cavalry in his army, which he must keep continually together because of the Great Mogul, who often launches heavy attacks. If the Gatos * were not so dangerous to cross, he would have lost this land long ago, and that is the reason

* The Ghats, a mountain range. Ed.

why they [i.e., 'Ambar's forces] must be constantly on their guard around this pass through the Gatos.

The aforementioned Melick keeps good order and laws in his country, punishes criminals and thieves severely, and one can travel with gold through his land without any uneasiness. When somebody gets drunk, he has molten lead poured into his throat; nobody is allowed to sell liquor, or even travel with it through the country. The army is very large. . . . At this time of the year it is very cold. In the army camp, called Kerka [Khirki],* one can buy everything one can imagine.

The Mellick wanted very much to keep me in his service. He had an offer made to me of 100 pagodas per month and a nice aldea † or income from a village. There were many Portuguese in his service who had all converted to Islam; some had command over 1000 horse, others over 3,000 and 5,000; one [was] called Mansour Gaen [Manṣūr Khān], a half-caste from India.‡

SOURCE: W. Ph. Coolhaas, ed., *Pieter van den Broecke in Azië* (The Hague: Martinus Nijhoff, 1962), 1:146–51. Translated for the present volume by J. W. Smit.

35 The Sīdīs of Janjīra

Janjīra Island lies in a river estuary on the southern Konkan coast of India, south of Bombay. Because of its excellent position and fortifications, it remained for hundreds of years impregnable against attacks from the land, and its guns dominated one of the best natural harbors on the shores of the Indian Ocean. "The castle [of Janjīra]," wrote an English East India Company official in 1628, "is scituated in the sea upon a little hommock, distant from the shoare a little more then a muskett shot; by nature very strong; wherein are at

* Khirki (or Khadkī), the "rocky town," was the name of the capital city 'Ambar built beneath the fortress of Dawlatābād. Its name was later changed to Awrangābād. (K. A. Kincaid and Rao Bahadur D. B. Parasnis, *A History of the Maratha People* [London: Oxford University Press, 1918], 1: 109.) ED.

† *Aldea* (Port.), a village.

‡ *Indien,* used here in the usual Dutch-language sense of "East Indies," or Indonesia. ED.

least 400 men, six great peeces of ordinance, and some 16 or 18 falconet and ravenet; envyroned with a wall, of 18 or 20 foote towards the land and some 14 foote towards the sea, round about, with battlements and halfe moons; and upon the top and middle of it a great house." [77] From the late fifteenth century to about the mid-eighteenth Janjīra was the headquarters of the powerful community of seafaring Africans known to historians of India as "the Sīdīs." Though no longer possessing any naval forces, the descendants of this community still live on Janjīra and on the mainland close by it.

Exactly when African seamen began settling on the coast of western India is not known. Probably their number was very small until after the development of large-scale commerce between India and eastern Africa, which took place between the twelfth and fourteenth centuries. Then, it may be deduced, some African crewmembers aboard Arab and Persian ships would, on arrival in India, have decided to "jump ship" in order to seek their fortunes in a new land. Others were no doubt sold ashore in India as slaves. By the mid-fourteenth century the African presence in northwestern India and the Persian Gulf was sufficiently noteworthy for Ibn Baṭṭūṭa to comment: "Abyssinian men-at-arms . . . are the guarantors of safety on the Indian Ocean; let there be but one of them on a ship and it will be avoided by the Indian pirates and idolaters." [78]

As the Ḥabshīs who made careers for themselves in the service of the Bahmanīs and their successors discovered, there were plenty of opportunities in the India of those days for enterprising and skilled recruits from overseas. Seafaring men, moreover, must have been especially welcome. The Muslims of India, though accomplished warriors on land, were totally helpless at sea.[79] Unable to compete with their enemies on the Indian Ocean, they sought naval allies, seafarers who could police their maritime trade routes, protect their pilgrim ships on the journey to and from the Red Sea, and combat the pirates of the Malabar Coast, and, later, the fleets of their enemies, the Marāthās. All these tasks the Sīdīs of Janjīra were ready and willing to undertake. Serving a succession of Muslim kings, their commanders eventually rose to the rank of "Admiral of the Mughal Empire," with a stipend (secured on the revenues of the port of Surat) of 300,000 rupees per annum.

The *Gazetteer of the Bombay Presidency,* an official Government of India publication of 1883, contains a long historical description of the exploits of the Sīdīs. Though written so long ago, this account is the most detailed that has yet been attempted on the subject, and all later writers acknowledge their debt to it. The extract from the *Gazetteer* given below carries the story of Janjīra from the establishment of an African colony there to the time when the captains and admirals in charge of it exercised their greatest influence on Indian history, in the late seventeenth and early eighteenth centuries.

■

About the middle of the fifteenth century (1437), when the Bahmani dynasty became independent of Delhi and intercourse with north India ceased, the fashion arose of bringing to western India large numbers of Abyssinians and other East Africans. These men, from the Arab El Habish and the people of northeast Africa, were known as Habshis, or more often as Sidis, which was originally a term of respect, a corrupt form of Syed. Though most Habshis came to India as slaves, their faithfulness, courage, and energy often raised them to positions of high trust in the Bahmani court. According to Orme the successful Abyssinians gathered round them all of their countrymen whom they could procure either by purchase or invitation, including Negroes from other parts of Africa, as well as Abyssinians. From their marriages, first with natives of India and afterwards among their own families, there arose a separate community, distinct from other Musalmāns in figure, color, and character. As soon as they were strong enough they formed themselves into an aristocratic republic, the skill and utility of the lowest orders giving them influence, and influence fostering a pride in their name which made them among the most skillful and daring sailors and soldiers in Western India. . . .

According to a Musalmān history of Ahmadnagar it was Malik Ahmad (1490–1508), the founder of the Ahmadnagar dynasty, who first established Abyssinians as the captains of the island fort of Janjira. During the highest prosperity of the Musalmān kings of Ahmadabad (1450–1530), Danda-Rājpuri is said to have been one of the twenty-five districts or *sarkārs* into which their possessions were divided. . . . About 1490 [Malik] Ahmad . . . took Danda-Rājpuri after a long siege. At this siege, . . . after vainly attacking the island fort of Janjira for six months, Ahmad's troops grew disheartened. Besides his want of success Ahmad's position was very uncertain. He had only lately thrown off his allegiance to Mahmud Bahmani (1482–1518), who was doing his utmost to bribe Ahmad's troops to give up his cause. . . . [But] the siege of Janjira was pressed, the fort taken, and the Koli garrison tied to chains and thrown into the sea. Ahmad rebuilt and strengthened the fort and gave the command to his Abyssinian slave Yākut. . . .

In 1600 Ahmadnagar was taken by the Moghals, and though the great Malik Ambar [see p. 150] soon after recovered most of the territory for his king, local records seem to show that till 1618 the governors of Danda-Rājpuri were Moghal officers. In 1618, an Abyssinian of the name of Sidi Sirul Khān was appointed governor. In 1620 Sidi Sirul was succeeded by Sidi Yākut, and he, in the following year, by Sidi Ambar who was known as Sānak or The Little, to distinguish him from the great Sidi or Malik Ambar who restored and ruled Ahmadnagar till his death in 1626.

In 1636, when Sidi Ambar was governor of Janjira, Ahmadnagar was finally conquered by the Moghals, and the Ahmadnagar Konkan * was handed to Bijāpur.† According to local accounts the importance of the Janjira command was at this time considerably increased, and, on promise of protecting Bijāpur trade and Mecca pilgrims, the country from Nāgothna to the Bānkot river was granted to the leading Abyssinian officer of the Bijāpur fleet, and he was raised to the rank of Wazir. In accordance with the aristocratic constitution of the Sidi community it was arranged that on the death of a Wazir, the first officer of the fleet, not the son of the late governor, was to succeed. Among Bijāpur Wazirs the local records mention Sidi Ambar, who died in 1642, Sidi Yusufa who died in 1655, and Fateh Khān who according to Grant Duff was an Abyssinian, and, according to Khāfi Khān, an Afghān.‡

In 1648, with the help of their Marāthā commandants, Shivāji succeeded in winning from the Sidi the Kolāba forts of Tala, Go-

* I.e., the coastal strip on which both Danda-Rājpuri and Janjīra were situated. Ed.

† Bījāpur, one of the five successor states to the Bahmanī kingdom. Bījāpur was ruled by the 'Adil Shāhī kings. Ed.

‡ An entry in the Surat Factory Records for 1674 makes it clear that Fateh (Fatḥ) Khān was in fact a Sīdī. See Sir Jadunath Sarkar, *Shivaji and His Times* (2 ed.; London: Longmans, Green, 1920), p. 303n. Ed.

sāla, and Rairi or Rāygad. In 1659 . . . Shivāji sent a strong force to invade the Sidi's territory; but the Marāthās were met by Fateh Khān and defeated with great slaughter. Shivāji made every effort to repair this disaster and sent a fresh body of troops. . . . But Fateh Khān maintained his ground and in the following year (1660) gained some important advantages. During the rains of 1661 Shivāji turned his whole strength against Fateh Khān, and, in spite of bad weather, drove back Fateh Khān's troops and captured Danda-Rājpuri before the season was open enough to allow the Bijāpur government to relieve it. He opened batteries against the island fort of Janjira, but, from want of guns and artillerymen failed to make any impression on it. Every season during the next nine years (1661–1670) Shivāji battered Janjira but with little success. Fateh Khān was hard pressed and applied for help to his new neighbors the English. And so great a name for strength had the Janjira rock gained that the English factors at Bombay wrote to Surat, advising the council to give up Bombay and take Janjira instead.

In 1670 Shivāji directed a specially vigorous and determined attack on Janjira, assaulting the place with great force, and, at the same time, attempting to win over Fateh Khān by promises. As the Bijāpur government failed to send help, Fateh Khān determined to surrender the fort to Shivāji and enter his service. Three brave Sidis, Sambal, Kāsim, and Khairiyāt, staunch Musalmāns and deadly foes of Shivāji, prevented this treachery. They told their countrymen that Fateh Khān was planning to give up the island, and, with their approval, threw Fateh Khān into chains. Kāsim and Khairiyāt, who were brothers, waived their claims in favor of Sidi Sambal, who was accordingly appointed governor. Sidi Sambal wrote for help to his master 'Adil Shāh of Bijāpur and to Khān Jahān, the Moghal governor of the Deccan. 'Adil Shāh was little able to help; but the Moghal general, delighted to have so valuable an ally against Shivāji, sent messages of friendship and promises of assistance. Finding that their only chance of support was from the Moghals, the Sidis agreed to transfer their fleet from Bijāpur to the Emperor. Aurangzeb changed Sambal's title from Wazir to Yākut Khān, and gave him an assignment of £30,000 (Rs. 3,00,000) on the revenues of Surat. When Sambal was appointed admiral of the Moghal navy, Sidi Kāsim seems to have received the command of Janjira, and Sidi Khairiyāt of Danda-Rājpuri. Sidi Kāsim took Sambal's place as Moghal admiral in 1677, and Khairiyāt seems then to have succeeded Kāsim in the command of Janjira island, as, according to the state records, he remained governor till his death in 1696.

In 1670, on gaining the help of the Sidis, Khān Jahān, the Moghal governor of the Deccan, gathered ships and sending them down the coast attacked Shivāji's fleet which lay near Danda-Rājpuri, and killed a hundred Marāthā sailors, tying stones to their feet and throwing them into the sea. Shivāji raised a new fleet and there were many fights between the Marāthās and the Abyssinians in which, according to Musalmān accounts, the Abyssinians were often victorious. Sidi Sambal was raised to the dignity of a Commander of Nine Hundred, and, apparently on his becoming admiral of the Moghal fleet, the command of Janjira passed from him to Sidi Kāsim . . . Sidi Kāsim was noted for courage, kindliness, and dignity. He added to his fleet, strengthened his fortress, and defended it against all attacks. He often took Marāthā ships and was constantly planning how he could win back Danda-Rājpuri from Shivāji. In 1671, during the *Holi* feast (March–April) when the Marāthā garrison were drunk or off their guard, Kāsim sent by night four or five hundred men under his brother Sidi Khairiyāt with rope ladders and other apparatus to attack the fort by land, while he with thirty or forty boats approached from the sea. At a given signal Sidi Khairiyāt assaulted the place with loud cries from the land side. The garrison rushed to meet his attack and Kāsim planting his ladders scaled the sea wall. In spite of fierce resistance they pressed on and forced their way into the fort. A powder magazine took fire and exploded with a crash which disturbed Shivāji, asleep forty miles off in Rāygad, who woke with the words, "Something is wrong in Danda-Rājpuri." In the fort a number of men, including ten or twelve of Kāsim's band, were killed. The smoke and noise made it hard to tell friend from foe, but Kāsim raised his war-cry and then two parties of assailants joined and the place was taken. Kāsim followed up his success by gaining six or seven forts in the neighborhood of Danda-Rājpuri. Six forts surrendered after one or two days, but the commandant of the seventh held out for a week. The Abyssinians pushed forward their approaches and kept up so heavy a fire that the commandant was forced to surrender. Kāsim granted quarter to the garrison and seven hundred persons came out. He made the children and pretty women slaves, and forcibly converted them to Islām; the old and ugly he set free, and the men he put to death. . . . Kāsim sent news of his victory to Prince Muhammad Muāzzam, governor of the Deccan, and to Khān Jahān. Both he and his brother Sidi Khairiyāt had their rank raised and were presented with robes of honor.

From 1673, till Sidi Kāsim's death in 1707, as admirals of the Moghal fleet, the Sidis were at constant war with the Marāthās, sometimes laying waste large tracts of Marāthā territory, at other times stripped of their own lands and with difficulty holding the rock of Janjira.

SOURCE: *Gazetteer of the Bombay Presidency.* Vol. 11: *Kolaba and Janjira* (Bombay: Government Central Press, 1883), pp. 433–38 (extracts; footnotes omitted).

36 The Attack on Bombay, 1689–90

In the late seventeenth century the Sīdīs were at the height of their power in northwestern India. Yet compared to other actors on the Indian scene at the time—the Mughal empire, the Marāthās, and the English, Portuguese, and Dutch—they were neither numerous nor wealthy, and at first sight it seems odd that they should have played the considerable role in Indian affairs that they did. The explanation is that the Sīdīs were mercenaries. Their business was protecting convoys and engaging in piracy and raiding, together with a certain amount of agriculture on land when the monsoon made sailing too hazardous. They were not traders and, unlike the Europeans, did not seek commercial privileges in return for the services they offered. They were content with rank, dignity, and an annual stipend. The Mughals, in consequence, found them an extremely useful auxiliary force, and, particularly during the reign of the emperor Awrangzīb (1658–1707), heavily subsidized them, placing as many ships and guns at their disposal as the empire's resources would allow.[80]

By the 1670s, however, the Mughals were beginning to feel the effects of the rising power of the Marāthās, led by their brilliant general, Shivājī. The homeland of the Marāthās lay in the northern

Deccan, inland from the Konkan coast. This happened to be the area where the Sīdīs, based at Janjīra, controlled a considerable section of the mainland, and, because of their command of the sea, were able to carry out hit-and-run raids against Marāthī towns and villages almost at will. Shivājī realized that he would be wise to reduce the power of the Sīdīs before attempting an all-out effort against the Mughals. Yet, despite repeated attacks (see selection 35 above), he failed to dislodge the Sīdīs from Janjīra, and his successor, Sambhājī, who came to the Marāthī throne in 1680, did little better. There was thus every reason why the Mughals should have been satisfied with their alliance with the Sīdīs. By their marauding along the Konkan coast and by attacking Marāthī shipping, the Sīdīs checked for many years the ability of the Marāthās to wage full-scale war against the Mughal empire.

The weakness at sea of both Mughals and Marāthās, the two great land powers of northwestern India, was a major reason why the Sīdīs prospered. The former needed them, and the latter had not the naval strength to suppress them. But the English East India Company, recently established in a new headquarters on Bombay Island, had ample power with which to challenge the Sīdīs if it chose to use it. By bringing its "great ships" into action, it could presumably have defeated them at sea, or bombarded Janjīra Fort into submission, or both. Diplomatic necessity constrained the English company to treat the Sīdīs gently, however. By the 1680s they had two fleets—one, consisting of their own ships and based on Janjīra, and another, based on Surat, and consisting of ships provided by the Mughals. (By the early eighteenth century most of the ships manned by the Sīdīs were in fact Mughal-built and supplied.) The commander of the Surat-based fleet liked to "winter" his ships—that is, provide a refuge for them during the monsoon season—in Bombay Harbor. To this practice the English factors at Bombay objected strongly, partly because the Sīdīs were likely to behave riotously when ashore, but also because they used Bombay as a base from which to launch expeditions against the Marāthās. The Surat Sīdīs paid no attention to the factors' protests, and arrived at Bombay every winter seeking a safe haven for their ships. The English therefore faced a difficult problem. If they denied to the Mughal Admiral shelter in Bombay Harbor, the emperor would be offended and might order reprisals against the Company's factory at Surat. If, on the other hand, the English befriended the Sīdīs too openly, the Marāthās in their turn would be displeased and might attack English factories in their territory.[81]

The result of all this was that for many years the Sīdīs acted towards the English at Bombay more or less as they chose. An example of the lengths to which they were prepared to go was their unprovoked attack on the island in 1689–90. A description of this episode follows.

■

With an unaccountable infatuation, the English Governor had neglected to strengthen the fortifications of Bombay, although the Court of Directors had so urgently reminded him that this was necessary; and on the fourteenth of February, 1689, the Siddee landed at Sewree with twenty or twenty-five thousand men. Although there were several small vessels in the harbor, which might have prevented the disembarkation of his troops, no effort of the sort was made, and the soldiers of a redoubt where he landed, after firing a gun to give the alarm, retired with precipitation. At one o'clock in the morning three guns from the Castle apprised the inhabitants of their danger. Then might be seen European and Native women rushing with their children from their houses, and seeking refuge within the Fort. Next morning the Siddee marched to Mazagon, where was a small fort mounting fourteen guns, which the English abandoned with such haste that they left behind them eight or ten chests of treasure, besides arms and ammunition. Here the Siddee established his headquarters, and despatched a small force to take possession of Mahim Fort, which also was found to be deserted.

The following day the enemy advanced. The General ordered Captain Pean with two companies to drive them back; but he and his little party were defeated. Thus the Siddee became master of the whole island, with the exception of the Castle, and a small tract extending about half a mile to the southward of it. He raised batteries on Dongaree Hill, and placed one within two hundred yards of the Fort. All persons on whom the English authorities could lay hands were pressed into their service. . . . Thus passed the months from April to September.

During the monsoon the Siddee obtained supplies from the interior and from the Jesuits of Bandora, who paid a heavy reckoning for thus assisting the enemy, as at the close of the war their property was seized by the Government of Bombay. Provisions were extremely scarce in the English quarters until the monsoon was over, but then the Company's cruisers being able to put to sea, were so successful in capturing vessels and supplies belonging to the Mogul's subjects that distress was alleviated. Still the danger was imminent; the Siddee's army was increased to forty thousand fighting men, and the English troops, which never amounted to more than two thousand five hundred, dared not venture to meet them in the field. . . .

[The Siddee] did not withdraw his army until the twenty-second of June [1690]. The Company are said to have lost 416,000 pounds by this first throw in the game of war.

SOURCE: Phillip Anderson, *The English in Western India; Being the History of the Factory at Surat, of Bombay, and the Subordinate Factories on the Western Coast* (2d ed.; London: Smith, Elder, 1856), pp. 245–49 (extracts).

37 The Sīdīs in the Nineteenth Century

By the nineteenth century the great days of Sīdī naval power in the Indian Ocean had passed. The chiefs or *nawābs* of the Sīdīs, however, still retained control of Janjīra Island (from 1834 onward under the paramountcy of the British Government of India),[82] and Sīdī rulers had established two other states, both of them in Gujarāt. The manner of life of the nineteenth-century Sīdīs of Janjīra and Gujarāt is described in the two extracts, taken from the 1899 and 1883 editions respectively of the *Gazetteer of the Bombay Presidency*, which are reproduced below.

The daughter states that Sīdīs from Janjīra founded in Gujarāt were Ja'afarābād and Sachin. Ja'afarābād, a small stretch of territory in western Gujarāt, was granted to a Sīdī admiral in 1759. The cession was arranged by the British, who wished to compensate the

Sīdīs for their recent ejection from Surat Castle.[83] Ja'afarābād received a visit in the 1870s from Sir Richard Burton, who described it as "the pleasure-seat of the Sīdī, the African ex-admiral." [84] There were many Sīdīs in those parts, Burton noted, and also in the province of Sind to the west, where a language was spoken which a modern scholar, using Burton's word lists, has recently identified as a form of Swahili. The existence in the 1870s of a Swahili-speaking population in Sind is not, however, to be ascribed to the survival of this language from earlier times, but rather to extensive importation of slaves into the area during the nineteenth century from what is now Tanzania.[85] The second state established by Sīdīs from Janjīra was Sachin, a tract of land near Surat. This acquisition, too, was negotiated by the British, who granted the territory to an unsuccessful claimant to the chieftaincy of Janjīra in return for Janjīra's acceptance—which turned out to be temporary—of Marāthī overlordship.[86]

Today Sīdīs are to be found in many parts of India, though chiefly in Gujarāt. They are poor, and work mainly as servants and unskilled laborers. They no longer speak any African language. But in 1968 a group of them formed a "Siddi Welfare Association" with the object of improving their social and economic condition, and four years later this organization sent a fraternal delegation to East Africa.[87] Some at least among modern Indians of African descent possess an awareness that they are the heirs to a connection with Africa that goes back more than 600 years.

■

Sīdīs, literally Masters, also called Abyssinians *Habashis,* are found in small numbers in all parts of Gujarāt. They are African negroes of different tribes chiefly from the Somālī coast, who have been brought to India as slaves. They form two classes, newcomers *wilāitis* and countryborns *muwallads.* They speak a broken Hindustāni and sometimes among themselves an African dialect, probably the Somālī known as Habashi or Abyssinian.* They generally live like other low-class Musalmāns. In north Gujarāt they sometimes build

* This dialect is not Abyssinian but Somālī.

round hovels about ten feet in circumference, the wall of earth, the roof circular and of grass. The dress both of men and women is that of lower-class Musalmāns. . . .

Except professional players, Sīdīs are the only Gujarāt Musalmāns who are much given to dancing and singing. As a class they are poor. They are Sunnis in faith but are not religious, few of them knowing the Kurāan or being careful to say their prayers. Their chief object of worship is Bāba Ghor, an Abyssinian saint and great merchant, whose tomb stands on a hill just above the Ratanpur * carnelian mines in western Rājpīpla. A point worthy of notice about the Sīdī is his talent for imitation. A band of young Sīdīs taken from a slaveship and brought to Surat have shown themselves equally ready to pick up the ways of their Christian, Musalmān, Hindu, or Pārsi masters.

On marriage and other high days men and women together dance and sing in circles to the sound of the drum *dhol* and a rough rattle *jhunjhuna.* † In begging they go about in bands of ten to fifteen, playing the drum and singing in praise of Bāba Ghor. They marry chiefly among themselves, looking on the newcomers as their betters and fearing that their daughters will not rest contented in a countryborn Sīdī's house, never ask them in marriage. They form a society *jamāat,* but have no headmen and but few rules. . . .

[A]s late as A.D. 1820, Sīdī Ismāil, a native of Cambay, was long powerful in north Gujarāt as minister to the Bābis of Rādhanpur. The Sīdī eunuch nobles of Delhi and Lakhnau up to as late as the 1857 mutinies are well known.

SOURCE: *Gazetteer of the Bombay Presidency.* Vol. 9, Part 2: *Gujarāt Population: Musalmāns and Pārsis* (Bombay: Government Central Press, 1899), pp. 11–12.

* There would seem at one time to have been a considerable colony of Sīdī miners at Ratanpur.

† Their fiddle made of a gourd with a stiff catgut string is surmounted at the end with a bunch of peacock feathers and ornamented with odd glass beads and shells as charms to prevent the evil eye from bursting it. It is played with a bow or stick, one end of it laden with a coconut shell in which stones rattle. The Sīdīs hold their musical instruments in great veneration, never touching them unless they are ceremonially pure. They call the *jhunjhuna* or rattle the instrument of Māma or Mother Misrah, and their big drum that of a leading male saint. If he is careless in touching the instruments when sexually impure Mother Misrah or Father Ghor is sure to punish the offender.

Sidis, the representatives of Habshi or Abyssinian slaves and soldiers of fortune, are found . . . in Janjira island. They number 258 and rank next in importance to Konkanis. Most of them are relations of the Nawāb or head of the state, and have inherited state land grants or allowances. They speak Hindustāni and Konkani both at home and abroad. They are tall, strong, and well made, with good features and brown or wheat skins. The men shave the head and wear the beard though their faces have generally little hair. The women, who are like the men in appearance, never appear in public and add nothing to the family income. Indoors the men wear a waistcloth or *lungi,* a jacket, and a skullcap, and out of doors a turban or head scarf, a long coat, and loose trousers. The women wear the Hindu robe over a petticoat, which is also used as a night dress, and a bodice. When they go out in the evening to pay visits they shroud themselves in a large white sheet which hides the whole face except the eyes. They are fond of ornaments and have a good store of earrings and noserings, bracelets, anklets, and necklaces. As among Konkani women, the glass and gold-bead necklace is put on the first day after marriage and is worn constantly and kept with care. Both men and women are neat and clean in their habits. Rich Sidis generally deck their houses with swords, shields, lances, muskets, knives, and daggers hung on the walls from wooden pegs. As a class they are luxurious, hot-tempered, and dishonest, but sober and thrifty. They are either landholders or state servants, and, except a few who are poor, are generally well-to-do and able to meet special charges. They are Sunnis of the Hanafi school, and, except a few of the younger men, are religious and careful to say the daily prayers. They obey the Kāzi and employ him to arbitrate in family and other disputes. They have no special class organization and no special religious head. They teach their boys some Urdu and Marāthi and to read the Korān. A few learn English.

SOURCE: *Gazetter of the Bombay Presidency.* Vol. 11: *Kolaba and Janjira* (Bombay: Governmental Central Press, 1883), pp. 420–21.

AFRICANS IN CHINA

FOR MORE than a thousand years, from about the fourth century A.D. to the eighteenth, African slaves were imported into China. Most were supplied by professional Arab traders, who established an entrepôt for the purpose at Canton as early as 300 A.D., and most arrived by sea, either directly from the Middle East and the East African coast, or via mainland Southeast Asia and the islands. In 1382, for example, "101 male and female Negroes," who presumably had been transported from Africa to Indonesia at some earlier time, were sent to an emperor of the Ming dynasty as tribute from Java.[88] In the medieval period a few African slaves also entered China overland. Traded eastward along the Central Asian caravan routes, they can have formed only a small fraction of the hordes of slaves—Turkic, Tibetan, and Iranian—being imported into China from inner Asia at that time.[89]

It is impossible to estimate how many Africans were enslaved in China in historic times, since no statistics, of even the most approximate kind, are available. The total number, in any case, cannot have been large. Unlike India (to say nothing of the Middle East or the Americas), China today does not possess even a remnant population of Africans or persons of African descent to bear witness to past influxes of blacks. Yet, if the number of Africans who entered China over the centuries was not large, neither was it insignificant. The literature of the T'ang (618–907) and Sung (960–1279) dynasties contains many references to black slaves, and it is clear that even at that remote period the physical appearance of Africans was well known to the ordinary Chinese. By Mongol times (1260–1368) important men in north China "were said not to be perfect gentlemen" unless they had in their households Korean maidservants and Negro manservants.[90] And from the sixteenth century onward, with the start of direct trade between China and the West, African slaves in small numbers began to enter the country in the entourages of European merchants. Some of these Africans are known to have escaped from servitude to become sailors on Chinese ships in the Canton area, while others acted as official executioners to the Portuguese government at Macao.[91] Most, however, were employed as domestics, typically as doorkeepers.

In Chinese, black slaves were called *k'un-lun-nu,* that is, *k'un-lun* slaves. They were also known as "devil-slaves," "wild men," "black servants," "barbarian servants," and "barbarian slaves," but *k'un-lun* seems to have been the epithet the Chinese most commonly used. The term has a curious history. Originally employed to describe the vault of heaven, it gradually became a place name, applied first to a chain of mountains in Tibet and then to parts of India. Next it was used to denote the inhabitants of any distant and exotic land, but especially those with dark skins living in countries lying to the south of China, and, by extension, anyone with a dark skin. The northern Chinese priest Tao-an, for example, who lived in the fourth century A.D., was known as "the K'un-lun" (the black one) or "the lacquered monk" because he was so swarthy, and a dark-complexioned consort of a Chinese emperor of the same era was also nicknamed "K'un-lun".[92] Then, as Chinese knowledge of world geography increased, the term came to be applied to the dark-skinned peoples who inhabited the westernmost region to which (from a Chinese point of view) one could go, namely, the east coast of Africa. What had been a generic term, used for any and all peoples of whom the Chinese had knowledge and who had skins darker than their own, gradually became a specific one.[93] By the Ming period, and in many instances before that time, when the expression *k'un-lun-nu* appears in the Chinese records, it may often be deduced that African slaves are being referred to. In the year 977, for example, the official history of the Sung dynasty states that a party of Arab ambassadors arrived at the imperial Chinese court. These ambassadors were accompanied by attendants who "had sunken eyes and black skin and . . . were called K'un-lun-nu." [94] In the tenth century A.D. it seems very likely that black-skinned attendants accompanying Arab ambassadors to China would have been slaves from Africa.

The meaning of the term *k'un-lun* has been discussed at length because before the modern era the Chinese do not appear to have coined a term for Africans as such—one, that is, that they could use to distinguish the inhabitants of Africa from other dark-skinned peoples with whom they had contact. In consequence, a man or a woman described in a medieval Chinese account as a *k'un-lun* cannot be assumed to be African unless other evidence supports that conclusion. The term can equally be applied to a Papuan or Melanesian, [95] and, to make matters worse, Indonesian negritos were—at times and apparently by analogy—referred to by the Chinese as Zangī—a word which unequivocally indicates an African origin—without being Africans.[96] The researcher seeking examples of the African presence in early China therefore needs to be on his guard.

38 The "Devil-Slaves" of Canton

The *P'ing-chou k'o-t'an* (*Notes on P'ing-chou*), which was compiled by Chu yü in 1119, contains a description of "devil-slaves" living in Kuang-chou (Canton). That the "devil-slaves" of this passage were Africans may be argued as follows. First, the locale is Canton, where the Arab slave trade from the Middle East and East Africa had its terminus. There would certainly have been African slaves in Canton in the twelfth century. Second, the slaves are portrayed as "very strong." This could hardly have been said of most *k'un-lun-nu* in China, such as negritos imported from mainland Southeast Asia, who were and are small men, shorter indeed than the Chinese themselves. Third, elsewhere in his book Chu Yü notes that if a Chinese ship sprang a leak and the crew could not mend it from inside the vessel, they ordered their "devil-slaves" to caulk the seams with oakum from the outside. The slaves were easily able to do this because of their ability to see under water. A knack of this kind is to be associated with seafarers like the East African *Zanj,* and not with the darker-skinned peoples of Southeast Asia, who are mostly mountain dwellers. (It may be argued that the description could apply to certain populations of India, who are both seafarers and black, but there is no evidence that any of these people were ever taken to China as slaves.)

■

In Kuang-chou rich people keep many "devil-slaves," who are very strong, being able to carry several hundred catties.* In their language and tastes they are strange. Their disposition is gentle, and they do not run away. They are also called "wild people." They are black in color, as black as ink. Their lips are red, their hair curly and yellow.† Both sexes are found among them; they are natives of the islands beyond the sea. They live (in their native land) on raw food; when caught and fed on food cooked with fire, it purges them daily and this is called "changing the bowels." Many during this treatment sicken and die, but if they do not they may be reared and become able to understand human speech [i.e., Chinese], though they themselves cannot [learn to] speak it. There is a variety of wild men from near the sea which can dive in water without closing the eyes; these are called "K'un-lun slaves."

SOURCE: Friedrich Hirth and W. W. Rockhill, eds., *Chau Ju-kua* (St. Petersburg: Imperial Academy of Sciences, 1911), p. 31n.

* One catty (*chin*) was equal to about 1⅓ lbs. ED.

† Since no race in the world has both black skin and yellow hair, this is probably a textual corruption. ED.

39 Mo-leh, the Faithful Servant

K'un-lun-nu often appear in Chinese romances and fables of the T'ang period, and many of them are recognizably African. The black heroes of these stories are described as cunning, resourceful, and brave men of powerful physique, who are able to support huge weights, dive to the bottom of lakes and rivers to recover valuables lost by their masters, and filch treasures from between the paws of sleeping dragons. They are strikingly larger than life.

An example of this genre is given below. In T'ang times the story of Mo-leh was popular and appeared in several works, including one called *K'un-lun Nu Ch'uan* (Record of K'un-lun Slaves). His exploits are wholly fanciful, but the account given of his life and circumstances provides at least an impression of what being an African slave in medieval China may have been like.

■

During the Ta Li period (A.D. 766–779) of the T'ang dynasty there was a young man named Ts'ui whose father was a famous mandarin and a personal friend of the Chief Imperial Astronomer Yi P'in. When Ts'ui was a Ch'ien-niu mandarin, he visited Yi P'in who was sick. Now Ts'ui had a complexion like unto jade. He was of a calm and retiring disposition; his demeanor was placid and courteous and his accent was distinct and cultured. When he reached his destination, Yi P'in ordered a singing-girl to lift the door-curtain and bid him enter. After Ts'ui had communicated the greetings of his father and paid the customary homage to his host, Yi P'in, who became charmed with the young man's appearance, invited him to sit down for a chat. In a little while three singing-girls of extraordinary beauty entered the room, the foremost carrying a golden bowl full of pink peaches, which she peeled and sprinkled with sweet milk. Yi P'in then ordered one of the girls, who was dressed in a robe of red silk, to serve the peaches to his guest in a small bowl. Ts'ui, who by reason of his youth was exceedingly bashful in the presence of the girls, declined to partake of the proffered fruit. Thereupon Yi P'in ordered the girl in red to feed him with a spoon. Ts'ui was forced to yield to such insistence and the girl smiled at him on taking her departure. When Ts'ui finally took leave of his host, the latter said: "If you can bear with the company of an old man like myself, you must by all means come again whenever you are at leisure." The girl in red was again ordered to attend on Ts'ui's departure. As he was leaving he looked back for another glimpse of the girl and saw that she held up three fingers, and that turning her hand three times she pointed to the small mirror on her breast saying: "Remember!" Thereupon she withdrew without further ado. Having reported the result of the visit, Ts'ui retired to his study. During the ensuing days he was absent-minded and listless, his words were few, and his face assumed a far-off expression. . . .

All the servants were alarmed at the condition of their young master. At that time there was in the household a K'un-lun slave named Mo-leh, who observed him closely and said: "What have you on your mind? Why do you act like one distraught with some great sorrow? Why not give your confidence to me, your old slave?" Ts'ui made answer: "How could an uncouth fellow like you appreciate that which is in my heart?" "But tell me anyway," said Mo-leh, "and I shall find a remedy for your troubles, be they present or future." Ts'ui, greatly impressed by the assurance of the slave, made a full confession. Whereupon the latter declared: "That is an easy matter. Why did you not tell me sooner and save yourself much worry?" When Ts'ui asked him to explain the signs made by the girl, Mo-leh replied: "Why should they be hard to interpret? When she held up three fingers, she meant that she dwells in the third of the ten courtyards that Yi P'in assigns to the singing-girls. When she turned her hand thrice, she meant *fifteen,* that is, the fifteenth of the moon. By pointing to the small mirror, she meant a night when the moon is full. In other words, she wanted to make an appointment with you."

On hearing this Ts'ui was overcome with joy and ecstasy. "What plan," he asked, "would you suggest of attaining my heart's desire?" With a smile, Mo-leh answered: "The night after next will be the fifteenth night. Pray dye two pieces of silk to a dark hue to make a vesture for yourself. In the house of Yi P'in there is a ferocious hound that guards the entrance to the courtyards of the singing-girls and is sure to kill anyone who attempts to enter. This dog is clever as a demon and as fierce as a tiger; it was bred at Meng-hai in the district of Tsao-chow. None in the world save myself is capable of killing this dog, and I shall kill it tonight."

After Ts'ui had feasted the slave on meat and wine, the latter departed taking with him a chain and a hammer. After the space of a meal time he returned and said: "The dog is now dead, and we shall meet with no obstacle." At midnight on the appointed date, Mo-leh bade Ts'ui don his dark attire and lifted his master over the wall, which was ten *li* in circumference. Thence the two made their way to the courtyards of the singing-girls and stopped at the third gate, which they observed to be ajar and revealing a dim light within. When they entered they heard the singing-girl sigh and noticed that she sat as though waiting for someone's arrival. Her lustrous hair was somewhat dishevelled, her countenance slightly flushed, and she looked very sad and forlorn. . . .

Ts'ui lifted the curtain and entered her room. The girl remained motionless gazing at him for a long time. At last she sprang up from her couch and seized Ts'ui by the hand saying: "I knew that your wit was keen and that you would interpret aright the signs which I made to you. But I never anticipated that you would respond with such alacrity." Whereupon Ts'ui told her all about Mo-leh's cunning and how he had made it possible for his master to scale the wall. "Where is he?" she asked, and he replied: "Standing outside." Thereupon the girl bade Mo-leh enter and gave him wine in a golden goblet. Turning to Ts'ui the girl said: "My home is in So-fang. I was the ward of a general who compelled me to become a singing-girl. I have often wished I were dead but have never had the courage to take my own life. Though my face may seem fair and radiant, yet my heart is oppressed with heavy sorrow. Though I eat with chopsticks of jade and drink from golden goblets; though I am surrounded with magnificent screens and clothed in the finest cloth; though I sleep on a silken couch inlaid with pearls and precious stones: yet all these things, far from giving me happiness, make me feel as if I were a prisoner. Since your noble body-servant is endowed with such extraordinary prowess, will you not essay to rescue me from this captivity? If you but harken to my prayer, I will rejoice to become your humble handmaiden and will die so without regret. Pray suffer me to bask in the light of your countenance. Lo, I am eagerly awaiting your reply!"

As Ts'ui stood silent and irresolute, Mo-leh spoke up. "Since the lady," said he, "has made up her mind, it will not be hard to fulfill her wish." The maiden was overjoyed at this reassurance. Mo-leh requested her to pack up her clothing and other gear, which he carried out in three trips. Returning from the third trip, he warned them of the approach of dawn. Then picking up both Ts'ui and the girl, he vaulted with them over the wall and ran off carrying them on his shoulders for a distance of ten *li.* As none of the watchmen noticed what was going on, the trio reached Ts'ui's home in safety and there they concealed the girl.

Yi P'in's household did not become aware either of the girl's absence or of the death of the dog until the following morning. Yi P'in was then greatly alarmed and exclaimed: "The seclusion of my gates and walls has been hitherto inviolate, every means of ingress being barred by bolts and locks. The intruder would seem to have been a winged being, for he has not left behind a single trace. He must forsooth be a knight of stupendous prowess. Do not noise the matter abroad, lest perchance we incur some further misfortune."

After the girl had lived in seclusion with Ts'ui for the space of two years, she ventured forth in blossom-time riding on a cart to Ch'u-chiang. There she was recognized by one of Yi P'in's servants who duly reported the matter to his master. Yi P'in in his surprise summoned Ts'ui and questioned him closely. Ts'ui in his fright made a full confession, describing Mo-leh's part in the affair. Yi P'in said: "The girl has indeed been guilty of a great offense. Inasmuch, however, as she has lived with you for more than a year, I will overlook the matter. But touching the complicity of Mo-leh, I must needs put an end to him; for he is a public menace."

Whereupon Yi P'in ordered fifty mail-clad soldiers, all armed to the teeth, to surround Ts'ui's house for the purpose of capturing Mo-leh. Whereat the latter, snatching up a dagger, vaulted over the wall, seeming to his pursuers like some winged being endowed with the speed of an eagle. They let fly at him a veritable shower of arrows but none of these could reach him. An instant later he completely vanished from view. This feat not only astounded Ts'ui but terrified Yi P'in as well, causing the latter to rue bitterly the rash step he had taken. Thenceforth Yi P'in was wont, when he retired at night, to surround himself with a guard of servants armed with swords and spears. And he continued this practice for a whole year before he finally gave it up.

After an interval of more than ten years one of Ts'ui's servants, on a visit to Loyang, saw Mo-leh selling medicinal herbs in the market-place. Time had not availed to change his appearance in the least.

SOURCE: Chang Hsiang-lang, "The Importation of Negro Slaves to China under the T'ang Dynasty (A.D. 618–907)," *Bulletin of the Catholic University of Peking* (1930), 7:46–49.

Part Two

AFRICANS IN LATIN AMERICA AND THE CARIBBEAN

THE BLACK AFRICAN EXPERIENCE in classical times and in the Middle East, India, and China has been little studied by historians, and the materials for such study are sparse. By contrast, the literature on blacks in the Americas is enormous. The subject has engaged the attention of some of the most distinguished historians—as well as sociologists, anthropologists, political scientists, linguists, musicologists, and theologians—of recent generations.

The selections in this part are therefore different in kind from those in the Introduction and in Part One. Emphasis has been placed on primary materials, on out-of-print secondary ones, and on translations from works in foreign languages. It seemed to the compiler that there was little point in excerpting from books like Freyre's *The Masters and the Slaves* or Tannenbaum's *Slave and Citizen;* the student should read the whole of these works, not attempted distillations or summaries. Thus Part Two contains a sample (which has been made as representative as possible) of the kinds of primary materials that are available for the study of Africans in Latin America and the Caribbean. For texts, syntheses, and comparative and analytical treatments of the subject, see the books listed under "For Further Reading" at the end of the volume.

In what follows the effective presence of Africans in the New World is assumed to date from the late fifteenth century, and all authorities from which excerpts have been taken are exclusively concerned with the period of Latin American and Caribbean slavery. No attempt has been made to include materials that illustrate, or claim to illustrate, the existence of contacts between Africa and the Americas before the time of Columbus. This omission is deliberate. However, in view of the long-standing controversy on the subject, which goes back more than a hundred years and is still active, a brief explanation of why the "pre-Columbian evidence" has not been adduced is in order.

The material in question is of two main kinds, historical and cultural. Perhaps the most cogent piece of purely historical evidence on African links with pre-Columbian America is contained in the writings of the fourteenth-century Arabic chronicler, al-'Umarī. Quoting what had been told him by one of those present, al-'Umarī describes a statement made in Cairo in 1323–24 by the *mansa* Mūsā I of Mali to the effect that, during the reign of Mūsā's predecessor on the Malian throne (i.e., before c.1312), two large fleets left the shores of western Africa in order to explore the "Circumambient [Atlantic] Ocean." Of the 400 vessels that constituted the first of these fleets only one returned, and none at all came back from the second fleet, which consisted of no fewer than 2,000 vessels.[1] Some scholars regard this anecdote as simply a tall story told by Mūsā to enhance his prestige in Cairo. But others take it more seriously, and point out that since so many ships—always assuming they existed in the first place—could hardly have disappeared without trace, some at least of their crews must have finished up in the New World, probably at or near the mouth of the Amazon River.[2] Another line of historical argument derives from the writings of the earliest European explorers of America. It is claimed that the reports of—for example—Columbus and Vespucci show, first, that African traders from Guinea were present on the coasts of the New World when the first Europeans arrived there and, second, that settlements of blacks, presumably Africans, existed in many places in the Americas at the beginning of the sixteenth century and thus before the trans-Atlantic slave trade began. These pieces of evidence support a hypothesis that there was not merely commercial contact with the New World but actual colonization of it by Africans before the arrival of the Spaniards and Portuguese.[3]

Cultural evidence for the existence of pre-Columbian African influence in the Americas is diverse and voluminous. The traditions of certain Amerindian ethnic groups, it has been suggested, assert that black men came from overseas in ages past and that originally black gods were worshipped in America. Skeletal remains excavated by archaeologists and antique sculptures and figures, notably the "Olmec heads" of Mexico, show marked Negroid characteristics. African languages, religious concepts and rites, games, styles of picture writing, clothing, regalia, dances, calendrical systems, and agricultural techniques are all to be observed, though often much modified by local adaptation, in pre-Columbian America. The nonbarking dogs of Cuba came from Africa, as did the cowrie shells found in at least one American archaeological site.[4] Most of the writers who argue in favor of early African influences in the New World attempt to show the impact of West Africa, but some see major cultural diffusions across the Atlantic from ancient Egypt and North Africa as well.[5]

The search for evidence of external influences on the New World before Columbus has occupied numerous researchers for centuries. This has been particularly true of the United States, where members of ethnic minorities have sought to prove that it was *their* ancestors who first crossed the ocean to America, not parvenus like Columbus and John Cabot, who have had undeserved greatness thrust upon them. Over the Atlantic ocean to the New World, such investigators have maintained, there came at various times Phoenicians, ancient Gauls, Visigoths, Irish, Welsh, Venetians, Poles, and Portuguese [6]—all predecessors of that Italian navigator who, sailing under the banner of Castile, chanced upon San Salvador island in the Bahamas in 1492. As for the Pacific, "there is not a race of eastern Asia—Siberian, Tartar, Chinese, Japanese, Malay, with the Polynesians—which has not been claimed as discoverers, intending or accidental, of American shores." [7]

Should, therefore, Africa's claim to have had links with the New World before the end of the fifteenth century be set aside? Is it on a par with similar assertions about the Irish, the Welsh, and the rest—all of them based on hypotheses never proved true, and, in the opinion of many, unprovable? The African claim is certainly more plausible than most. The west coast of Africa is much closer to the

Americas than is Europe. Moreover, the navigational and logistical problems of sailors striking west from Guinea are comparatively simple. A sailing canoe running at five knots before the northeast trade winds could have made the journey from Cape Verde to Brazil, a distance of only 1,600 miles, in three weeks or less. And the canoes known to have been in use on the West African coast in the fifteenth century were large enough to have made the passage safely, and capacious enough to have carried adequate provisions for their crews.[8] It cannot thus be said that Africans were incapable of anticipating Columbus; but we lack incontrovertible evidence that they did so.

However, we have not excluded source materials on this subject because of doubt about their validity. Such materials are plentiful, have great interest in themselves, and can easily be illustrated. We have omitted them because even if pre-Columbian Afro-American contacts did take place, the record of relations between the Old and New Worlds, taken as a whole, shows that such contacts cannot have been either extensive or persistent. To establish this point it is necessary to look at what happened in tropical America immediately after the start of the age of European exploration, setting aside, for the moment, speculation about what may have happened before.

When the Spaniards and Portuguese landed on the shores of Central and South America and the Caribbean islands and began to penetrate the interior, they encountered a physical environment that was, in significant respects, alien to them. Many of the most commonplace items of material life that they had left behind them, including their domesticated animals and their basic vegetable foods, were unknown in the New World. They found there no horses, cattle, sheep, pigs, goats, or chickens. Neither barley nor wheat grew in the Americas. Instead the newcomers found a large number of entirely new crops—potatoes, maize, manioc, cacao, peanuts, pineapples, and tobacco—unknown in temperate Europe as well as in tropical Africa. Before Columbus there had apparently been no exchange of useful animals and plants between the Old World and the New. Yet when this exchange began in the late fifteenth and early sixteenth centuries, each region put what the other had to offer to immediate and profitable use. Africa imported all the tropical American crops; many years had to pass before some of them became important commercially, but all could be grown in Africa from the beginning. A few—tobacco is the best example—spread throughout the western part of the continent like wildfire. Similarly, Old World cultivated plants like bananas and sugar cane flourished in the Americas from the moment they were introduced, and Old World animals, notably cattle and pigs, found an equally favorable environment.[9]

We may draw an obvious conclusion from the rapid and permanent invasion of the New World by African and European crops and livestock. If the invasion was so successful immediately post-Columbus, it could have occurred just as easily in earlier centuries; yet it did not. Therefore any contacts that Africans (and Europeans) may have had with the Americas prior to the late fifteenth century must have been ephemeral. It cannot be supposed that African colonists of tropical America would have taken none of their animals and food plants with them; of these, however, there is no trace. In Africa, moreover, there are no local traditions recalling pre-Columbian contact with the New World, and no American crops were known there before the sixteenth century.[10]

Proof of the effective separation of the Old and New Worlds in pre-Columbian times may also be derived from the evidence of human biology and of the history of epidemic diseases. Among the indigenous population of the Americas blood distribution by type is extremely uniform, being almost entirely of the O type. Throughout the Old World, on the other hand, including Africa, there is a marked disuniformity of distribution.[11] The absence among American indigenes of African blood types argues against the idea that a significant influx of African settlers occurred in the New World before Columbus. Finally, there is the well-known fact that the Americas, when brought into contact with Europe and Africa as a result of the Spanish and Portuguese conquests, possessed no immunity to any of the Old World's epidemic diseases. The American disease environment was entirely different, and must have developed in isolation from Europe, Africa, and, for that matter, Asia, for a very long time.[12] Otherwise, the spectacular and tragic mortality that after the arrival of the Conquistadores afflicted the New World, particularly its tropical areas, would never have occurred.

If Africans had migrated to the Americas before the end of the fifteenth century, they would be likely to have taken with them some of their domestic animals—not horses or camels, to be sure, but probably goats and chickens, and perhaps pigs. They would also have introduced into the New World their most useful root crops, such as yam and taro, which would have been able to survive a trans-Atlantic crossing without difficulty. And they quite certainly could not have colonized the Americas without carrying with them, however unwillingly, the epidemic diseases of tropical Africa in their blood and on their breath.

THE EXPERIENCE OF SLAVERY

BETWEEN THE sixteenth and the nineteenth centuries three main types of society evolved in the New World. There was the society of the highlands of Central and South America, found typically in Mexico and Peru, which consisted of a small number of whites engaged in pastoralism, agriculture, and mining, and controlling a largely Amerindian laboring population. There was the white settler society of the temperate zones, that is, most of North America, and Argentina and Chile; here the few indigenous inhabitants were quickly killed off or driven away, enabling an Old World society to be re-created in the New. Finally, there was the society of the tropical and subtropical regions of the West Indies and lowland Central and northern South America. In these areas almost all the work was done by Africans and the descendants of Africans under a system of slave labor. Although, as the records show, the slaves filled every conceivable type of role from classical musician to ranchhand to placer miner to storekeeper and stevedore, the predominant unit of economic production was the plantation, and it was on the plantations and in the industries associated with them that the majority of slaves lived, worked, and died.

The selections that follow (40 to 44) describe the institution of slavery as it existed in the British West Indies. They range in time from an account of Barbados in 1657, when the "sugar revolution" made possible by the importation of Africans was under way, to one of Jamaica in 1823, by which time the British slave trade had been declared illegal and the institution of slavery itself was coming under increasingly powerful attack.

40 A Sugar Plantation in Barbados, 1657

It were somewhat difficult, to give you an exact account, of the number of persons upon the Iland; there being such store of shipping that brings passengers dayly to the place, but it has been conjectur'd, by those that are long acquainted, and best seen in the knowledge of the Iland, that there are not lesse than 50 thousand soules, besides *Negroes;* and some of them who began upon small fortunes are now risen to very great and vast estates.

The Iland is divided into three sorts of men, viz. Masters, Servants, and slaves. The slaves and their posterity, being subject to their Masters for ever, are kept and preserv'd with greater care than the servants, who are theirs but for five yeers, according to the law of the Iland. So that for the time, the servants have the worser lives, for they are put to very hard labour, ill lodging, and their dyet very sleight. When we came first on the Iland, some Planters themselves did not eate bone meat, above twice a weeke: the rest of the seven days, Potatoes, Loblolly, and Bonavist. But the servants no bone meat at all, unlesse an Oxe dyed: and then they were feasted, as long as that lasted, And till they had planted good store of Plantines, the *Negroes* were fed with this kind of food; but most of it Bonavist, and Loblolly, with some eares of Mayes toasted, which food (especially Loblolly) gave them much discontent: But when they had Plantines enough to serve them, they were heard no more to complaine; for 'tis a food they take great delight in, and their manner of dressing and eating it, is this: 'tis gathered for them (somewhat before it be ripe, for so they desire to have it,) upon Saturday, by the keeper of the Plantine groves who is an able *Negro,* and knowes well the number of those that are to be fed with this fruite; and as he gathers, layes them all together, till they fetch them away, which is about five a clock in the afternoon, for that day they breake off worke sooner by an houre: partly for this purpose, and partly for that the fire in the furnaces is to be put out, and the Ingenio and the roomes made cleane; besides they are to wash, shave and trim themselves against Sunday. But 'tis a lovely sight to see a hundred handsome *Negroes,* men and women, with every one a grasse-green bunch of these fruits on their heads, every bunch twice as big as their heads, all comming in a train one after another, the black and green so well becomming one another. Having brought this fruit home to their own houses, and pilling off the skin of so much as they will use, they boyl it in water, making it into balls, and so they eat it. One bunch a week is a *Negroes* allowance. To this, no bread nor drink, but water. Their lodging at night a board, with nothing under, nor any thing a top of them. They are happy people, whom so little contents. Very good servants, if they be not spoyled by the English. . . .

It has been accounted a strange thing, that the Negres, being more than double the numbers of the Christians that are there, and they accounted a bloody people, where they think they have power or advantages; and the more bloody, by how much they are more fearfull than others: that these should not commit some horrid massacre upon the Christians, thereby to enfranchise themselves, and become Masters of the Iland. But there are three reasons that take away this wonder; the one is, They are not suffered to touch or handle any weapons: The other, That they are held in such awe and slavery, as they are fearfull to appear in any daring act; and seeing the mustering of our men, and hearing their Gun-shot, (than which nothing is more terrible to them) their spirits are subjugated to so low a condition, as they dare not look up to any bold attempt. Besides these, there is a third reason, which stops all designs of that kind, and that is, They are fetch'd from severall parts of *Africa,* who speake severall languages, and by that means, one of them understands not another: For, some of them are fetch'd from *Guinny* and *Binny,* some from *Cutchew,* some from *Angola,* and some from the River of *Gambra.* And in some of these places where petty Kingdomes are, they sell their Subjects, and such as they take in Battle, whom they make slaves; and some mean men sell their Servants, their Children, and sometimes their Wives; and think all good traffick, for such commodities as our Merchants sends them.

When they are brought to us, the Planters buy them out of the Ship, where they find them stark naked, and therefore cannot be deceived in any outward infirmity. They choose them as they do Horses in a market; the strongest, youthfullest, and most beautifull, yield the greatest prices. Thirty pound sterling is a price for the best man Negre; and twenty five, twenty six, or twenty seven pound for a Woman; the Children are at easier rates. And we buy them so, as the sexes may be equall; for, if they have more men than women, the men who are unmarried will come to their Masters, and complain, that they cannot live without Wives, and desire him, they may have Wives. And he tells them, that the next ship that comes, he will buy them Wives, which satisfies them for the present; and so they expect the good time: which the Master performing with them, the bravest fellow is to choose first, and so in order, as they are in place; and every one of them knowes his better, and gives him the precedence, as Cowes do one another, in passing through a narrow gate; for, the most of them are as neer beasts as may be, setting their souls aside. Religion they know none; yet most of them acknowledge a God, as appears by their motions and gestures: For, if one of them do another wrong, and he cannot revenge himselfe, he looks up to Heaven for vengeance, and holds up both his hands, as if the power must come from thence, that must do him right. . . .

On Sunday they rest, and have the whole day at their pleasure; and the most of them use it as a day of rest and pleasure; but some of them who will make benefit of that dayes liberty, goe where the Mangrave trees grow, and gather the barke of which they make ropes, which they trucke away for other Commoditie, as shirts and drawers.

In the afternoons on Sundayes, they have their musicke, which is of kettle drums, and those of several sises; upon the smallest the best musitian playes, and the other come in as Chorasses: the drum all men know, has but one tone; and therefore varietie of tunes have little to doe in this musick; and yet so strangely they varie their time, as 'tis a pleasure to the most curious eares, and it was to me one of the strangest noyses that ever I heard made of one tone; and if they had the varietie of tune, which gives the greater scope in musick, as they have of time, they would doe wonders in that Art. And if I had not faln sicke before my comming away, at least seven months in one sickness, I had given them some hints of tunes, which being understood, would have serv'd as a great addition to their harmonie; for time without tune, is not an eighth part of the science of Musick.

I found *Macow* very apt for it of himselfe, and one day comming into the house, (which none of the Negroes use to doe, unlesse an Officer, as he was,) he found me playing on a Theorbo, and singing to it which he hearkened very attentively to; and when I had done took the Theorbo in his hand, and strooke one string, stopping it by degrees upon every fret, and finding the notes to varie, till it came to the body of the instrument; and that the neerer the body of the instrument he stopt, the smaller or higher the sound was, which he found was by the shortning of the string, considered with himselfe, how he might make some triall of this experiment upon such an instrument as he could come by; having no hope ever to have any instrument of this kind to practise on. In a day or two after, walking in the Plantine grove, to refresh me in that cool shade, and to delight my selfe with the sight of those plants, which are so beautifull, as though they left a fresh impression in me when I parted with them, yet upon a review, something is discern'd in their beautie more than I remembred at parting: which caused me to make often repair thither; I found this *Negro* (whose office it was to attend there) being the keeper of that grove, sitting on the ground, and before him a piece of large timber, upon which he had laide crosse, sixe Billets, and having a handsaw and a hatchet by him, would cut the billets by little and little, till he had brought them to the tunes, he would fit them to; for the shorter they were, the higher the Notes which he tryed by knocking upon the ends of them with a sticke, which he had in his hand. When I found him at it, I took the stick out of his hand, and tried the sound, finding the sixe billets to have sixe distinct notes, one above another, which put me in a wonder, how he of himselfe, should without teaching doe so much. I then shewed him the difference between flats and sharpes, which he presently apprehended, as between *Fa* and *Mi:* and he would have cut two more billets to those tunes, but I had then no time to see it done, and so left him to his own enquiries. I say this much to let you see that some of these people are capable of learning Arts.

Another, of another kinde of speculation I found; but more ingenious than he: and this man with three or foure more, were to attend mee into the woods, to cut Church wayes, for I was imployed sometimes upon publique works; and those men were excellent Axe-men, and because there were many gullies in the way, which were impassable, and by that means I was compell'd to make traverses, up and down in the wood; and was by that in danger to misse of the poynt, to which I was to make my passage to the Church, and therefore was faine to take a Compasse with me, which as a Circumferenter, to make my traverses the more exact, and indeed without which, it could not be done, setting up the Circumferenter, and observing the Needle: This *Negre Sambo* comes to me, and seeing the needle wag, desired to know the reason of its stirring, and whether it were alive: I told him no, but it stood upon a poynt, and for a while it would stir, but by and by stand still, which he observ'd and found it to be true.

The next question was, why it stood one way, & would not remove to any other poynt, I told him that it would stand no way but North and South, and upon that shew'd him the foure Cardinall poynts of the compass, East, West, North, South, which he presently learnt by heart, and promis'd me never to forget it. His last question was, why it would stand North, I gave this reason, because of the huge Rocks of Loadstone that were in the North part of the world, which had a quality to draw Iron to it; and this Needle being of Iron, and toucht with a Loadstone, it would alwaies stand that way.

This point of Philosophy was a little too hard for him, and so he stood in a strange muse; which to put him out of, I bad him reach his ax, and put it neer to the Compasse, and remove it about; and as he did so, the Needle turned with it, which put him in the greatest admiration that ever I saw a man, and so quite gave over his questions, and desired me, that he might be made a Christian; for, he thought to be a Christian, was to be endued with all those knowledges he wanted.

I promised to do my best endeavour; and when I came home, spoke to the Master of the Plantation, and told him, that poor *Sambo* desired much to be a Christian. His answer was, That the people of that Iland were governed by the Lawes of *England,* and by those Lawes, we could not make a Christian a Slave. I told him, my request was far different from that, for I desired him to make a Slave a Christian. His answer was, That it was true, there was a great difference in that: But, being once a Christian, he could no more account him a Slave, and so lose the hold they had of them as Slaves, by making them Christians; and by that means should open such a gap, as all the Planters in the Iland would curse him. So I was struck mute, and poor *Sambo* kept out of the Church; as ingenious, as honest, and as good a natur'd poor soul, as ever wore black, or eat green.

On Sundaies in the afternoon, their Musick plaies, and to dancing they go, the men by themselves, and the women by themselves, no mixt dancing. Their motions are rather what they aim at, than what they do; and by that means, transgresse the lesse upon the Sunday, their hands having more of motion than their feet, & their heads more than their hands. They may dance a whole day, and neer heat themselves; yet, now and then, one of the activest amongst them will leap bolt upright, and fall in his place again, but without cutting a capre. When they have danc'd an houre or two, the men fall to wrastle, (the Musick playing all the while) and their manner of wrastling is, to stand like two Cocks, with heads one against another, hoping to catch one another by the leg, which sometimes they do: But if both parties be weary, and that they cannot get that advantage, then they raise their heads, by pressing hard one against another, and so having nothing to take hold of but their bare flesh, they close, and grasp one another about the middle, and have one another in the hug, and then a fair fall is given on the back. And thus two or three couples of them are engaged at once, for an houre together, the women looking on: for when the men begin to wrastle, the women leave of their dancing, and come to be spectatours of the sport.

When any of them die, they dig a grave, and at evening they bury him, clapping and wringing their hands, and making a dolefull sound with their voyces. They are a people of a timerous and fearfull disposition, and consequently bloody, when they finde advantages. If any of them commit a fault, give him present punishment, but do not threaten him; for if you do, it is an even lay, he will go and hang himselfe, to avoid the punishment. . . .

I can name a Planter there, that feeds daily two hundred mouths, and keeps them in such order, as there are no mutinies amongst them; and yet of severall nations. All these are to be employed in their severall abilities, so as no one be idle. The first work to be considered, is Weeding, for unlesse that be done, all else (and the Planter too) will be undone; and if that be neglected but a little time, it will be a hard matter to recover it again, so fast will the weeds grow there. But the ground being kept clean, 'tis fit to bear any thing that Country will afford. After weeding comes Planting, and they account two seasons in the year best, and that is, *May* and *November;* but Canes are to be planted at all times, that they may come in, one field after another; otherwise, the work will stand still. And commonly they have in a field that is planted together, at one time ten or a dozen acres. This work of planting and weeding, the Master himselfe is to see done; unlesse he have a very trusty and able Overseer; and without such a one, he will have too much to do. The next thing he is to consider, is the Ingenio, and what belongs to that; as, the Ingenio it selfe, which is the *Primum Mobile* of the whole work, the Boyling house, with the Coppers and Furnaces, the Filling room, the Still-house, and Cureing-house; and in all these, there are great casualties. If any thing in the Rollers, as the Goudges, Sockets, Sweeps, Cogs, or Braytrees, be at fault, the whole work stands still; or in the Boylinghouse, if the Frame which holds the Coppers, (and is made of Clinkers, fastned with plaister of *Paris*) if by the violence of the heat from the Furnaces, these Frames crack or break, there is a stop in the work, till that be mended. Or if any of the Coppers have a mischance, and be burnt, a new one must presently be had, or there is a stay in the work. Or if the mouths of the Furnaces, (which are made of a sort of stone, which we have from *England,* and we call it there, high gate stone) if that, by the violence of the fire, be softened, that it moulder away, there must new be provided, and laid in with much art, or it will not be. Or if the barrs of Iron, which are in the flowre of the Furnace, when they are red hot, (as continually they are) the fire-man, throw great shides of wood in the mouths of the Furnaces, hard and carelesly, the weight of those logs, will bend or break those barrs, (though strongly made) and there is no repairing them, without the work stand still; for all these depend upon one another, as wheels in a Clock. Or if the Stills be at fault, the *kill-devill* cannot be made. But the main impediment and stop of all, is the losse of our Cattle, and amongst them, there are such diseases, as I have known in one Plantation, thirty that had died in two daies. And I have heard, that a Planter, an eminent man there, that clear'd a dozen acres of ground, and rail'd it about for pasture, with intention, as soon as the grasse was growne to a great height, to put in his working Oxen; which accordingly he did, and in one night fifty of them dyed; so that such a losse as this, is able to undo a Planter, that is not very well grounded. What it is that breeds these diseases, we cannot finde, unless some of the Plants have a poysonous quality; nor have we yet found out cures for these diseases; Chickens guts being the best remedy was then known, and those being chopt or minc't, and given them in a horn, with some liquor mixt to moisten it, was thought the best remedy; yet it recovered very few. Our Horses too have killing diseases amongst them, and some of them have been recovered by Glisters, which we give them in pipes, or large seringes made of wood, for the same purpose. For, the common diseases, both of Cattle and Horses, are obstructions and bindings in their bowells; and so lingring a disease it is, to those that recover, as they are almost worn to nothing before they get well. So that if any of these stops continue long, or the Cattle cannot be recruited in a reasonable time, the work is at a stand; and by that means, the Canes grow over ripe, and will in a very short time have their juice dried up, and will not be worth the grinding.

SOURCE: Richard Ligon, *A True & Exact History of the Island of Barbadoes* (London: Moseley, 1657), pp. 43–56 (extracts).

41 The "Negros" of Jamaica, 1707

The Inhabitants of *Jamaica* are for the most part *Europeans,* some *Creolians,* born and bred in the Island *Barbados,* the Windward Islands, or *Surinam,* who are the Masters, and *Indians, Negros, Mulatos, Alcatrazes, Mestises, Quarterons, &c.,* who are Slaves. . . .

The *Negros* are of several sorts, from the several places of *Guinea,* which are reckoned the best Slaves, those from the *East-Indies* or *Madagascins,* are reckoned good enough, but too choice in the Diet, being accustomed in their own Countries to Flesh Meat, *&c.* and do not well here, but very often die. Those who are *Creolians,* born in the Island, or taken from the *Spaniards,* are reckoned more worth than others in that they are season'd to the Island. . . .

The *Negros* from some Countries think they return to their own Country when they die in *Jamaica,* and therefore regard death but little, imagining they shall change their condition, by that means from servile to free, and so for this reason often cut their own

Throats. Whether they die thus, or naturally, their Country people make great lamentations, mournings, and howlings about them expiring, and at their Funeral throw in Rum and Victuals into their Graves, to serve them in the other world. Sometimes they bury it in gourds, at other times spill it on the Graves. . . .

They are fruitful, and go after the birth of their children to work in the Field, with their little ones Ty'd to their Backs, in a Cloth on purpose one Leg on one side, and the other on the other of their Mother, whence their Noses are a little flatted against the Mothers Back, which amongst them is a Beauty. The same is the reason of the broadness of their and *Indians* Faces. . . .

Their unskilful cutting the Navel String, does occasion that swelling which usually appears in their Navels, and makes their Bellies prominent. Their Children called *Piganinnies* or rather *Pequenos Ninnos,* go naked till they are fit to be put to clean the paths, bring Firewood to the Kitchen, *&c.* when a Boy Overseer, with his Wand or white Rod, is set over them as their Task-Master.

They are rais'd to work as soon as the day is light, or someties [sic] two hours before by the sound of a *Conche*-Shell, and their Overseers noise, or in better Plantations by a Bell. They are suffered to go to Dinner at Twelve, when they bring Wood, *&c.* one burden lest they should come idle out of the Field home, return to the Field at One, and come home at night. . . .

They have *Saturdays* in the Afternoon, and *Sundays,* with *Christmas* Holidays, Easter called little or *Pigganinny, Christmas* and some other great Feasts allow'd them for the Culture of their own Plantations to feed themselves from Potatos, Yams, and Plantaines, *&c.* which they Plant in Ground allow'd them by their Masters, besides a small Plantain-Walk they have by themselves.

They formerly on their Festivals were allowed the use of Trumpets after their Fashion, and Drums made of a piece of a hollow Tree, covered on one end with any green Skin, and stretched with Thouls or Pins. But making use of these in their Wars at home in *Africa,* it was thought too much inciting them to Rebellion, and so they were prohibited by the Customs of the Island. . . .

Their Physick consists for the most part in Cupping with *Calabashes* on the pain'd place. They first apply the *Calabash* with some Chips or Combustible matter burning in it, when that is pull'd off they cut the place with Scarifications, and then apply the Cuping glasses or *Calabashes* again. Their Lancet is a sharp Knife with which they cut through the Flesh held between their Fingers.

This, instead of relieving, sometimes seems rather to add more pain to the place, by making a Flux of Blood that way. There are few *Negros* on whom one may not see a great many Cicatrices or Scars, the remains of these Scarifications, for Diseases or Ornament, on all their Faces and Bodies, and these Scarifications are common to them in their own Countries, and the *Cicatrices* thought to add beauty to them. The *Negros* called *Papas* have most of these Scarifications. Other *Negros* take great pleasure in having their woolly curled Hair, cut into Lanes or Walks as the *Parterre* of a Garden, and this I have seen them do, for want of a better Instrument, with a broken piece of a Glass bottle. . . .

Bathing is very much used by them. They boil Bay-leaves, Wild Sage, *&c.* in water, in one of their Pots, when boil'd they tye a *Fasciculus* of these Plants up together, and by putting that into the Decoction sprinkle their Bodies all over with it as fast as they can, they being naked.

The *Negros* and *Indians* use to Bath themselves in fair water every day, as often as conveniently they can. . . .

The *Indians* and *Negros* have no manner of Religion by what I could observe of them. 'Tis true they have several Ceremonies, as Dances, Playing, *&c.* but these for the most part are so far from being Acts of Adoration of a God, that they are for the most part mixt with a great deal of Bawdry and Lewdness.

The *Negros* are usually thought to be haters of their own Children, and therefore 'tis believ'd that they sell and dispose of them to Strangers for Money, but this is not true, for the *Negros* of *Guinea* being divided into several Captainships, as well as the *Indians* of *America,* have Wars, and besides those slain in Battles many Prisoners are taken, who are Sold for Slaves, and brought hither. But the Parents here, altho their Children are Slaves for ever, yet have so great a love for them, that no Master dare sell or give away one of their little ones, unless they care not whether their Parents hang themselves or no. . . .

The Punishment for Crimes of Slaves, are usually for Rebellions burning them, by nailing them down on the ground with crooked sticks on every Limb, and then applying the Fire by degrees from the Feet and Hands, burning them gradually up to the Head, whereby their pains are extravagant. For Crimes of a lesser nature Gelding, or chopping off half of the Foot with an Ax. These Punishments are suffered by them with the greatest Constancy.

For running away they put Iron Rings of great weight on their Ankles, or Pottocks about their Necks, which are Iron Rings with long Necks rivetted to them, or a Spur in the Mouth.

For Negligence, they are usually whipt by the Overseers with Lance-wood Switches, till they be bloody, and several of the Switches broken, being first tied up by the Hands in the Mill-Houses. Beating with *Manati* straps is thought too cruel, and therefore prohibited by the Customs of the Country. The Cicatrices are visible on their Skins for ever after; and a Slave, the more he have of those, is the less valu'd.

After they are whip'd till they are Raw, some put on their Skins Pepper and Salt to make them smart; at other times their Masters will drop melted Wax on their Skins, and use several very exquisite Torments. These Punishments are sometimes merited by the Blacks, who are a very perverse Generation of People, and though they appear harsh, yet are scarce equal to some of their Crimes, and inferior to what Punishments other *European* Nations inflict on their Slaves in the *East-Indies.*

SOURCE: Hans Sloane, *A Voyage to the Islands Madera, Barbados, Nieves, S. Christophers and Jamaica* (2 vols.; London: Printed for the Author, 1707, 1725, 1: xlvi–lvii (extracts).

42 Social Structure of a Slave Society, 1789

Tho' the inhabitants of this Island [Jamaica] may be naturally enough distinguished by their parent countries into *English, Irish, Scotch,* and natives the descendants of all, I shall for the present deem them but one united people, whom I shall class into planters, settlers, merchants, and dependents; the most natural distinctions to communicate a satisfactory idea of the colony.

Many of the planters are men of very extraordinary fortunes, but the major part, though rich, and in easy circumstances, are seldom out of debt; for the charges attending a sugar settlement, are very considerable, and constant; the interest of money very high, and their natural propensity to increase their possessions, constantly engaging them in new disbursements and contracts. They are generally men of a free and open disposition, friendly where they take, honest in their dealings, and punctual, when the demands does [sic] not exceed their ability, or a new purchase engage the produce of the year; they are observed to be remarkably fond of grandeur and distinction, which, doubtless, proceeds from the general obsequiousness of their numerous slaves and dependents, as well as from the necessity of keeping them at a distance; which in time gains into a habit.

Among these you frequently meet with men of as good a taste, as much learning, and as well acquainted with the world, as may be met with in any part of *Europe;* nor is it uncommon to find those who (though never out of the Island) shine in many parts of life, with as much delicacy and judgment, as if they had been bred in the most polished courts. How soon these gentlemen might make the Island a wealthy and valuable settlement by becoming guardians to the public happiness, subjecting the lands to the due payment of moneys at an easy interest in *Europe,* and becoming the sureties of the industrious and careful, may be easily observed; but alas! many of them seem to think it not their interest to have the Island better settled in their own days. As to the more amiable sex, there are but few of them besides the natives here, who are generally great lovers of decency, and cleanliness, always sprightly and good humored, naturally modest, genteel, and lovers of mirth; nor does any people excel them in the labors of the needle, or economy, when they take to those useful occupations; but many of them have been remarked both for their indolence, and the want of consideration; which too often deters the gentlemen in these colonies from entering into the matrimonial state, wherein the most engaging behavior would be requisite to break them of those vicious habits, which they seldom fail of acquiring in the more early state of manhood.*

The settlers form another rank of people, that differs from the former only in degree; they are generally such as have some foundation, though seldom enough to complete a settlement; and for this reason commonly above one-half of their estates in debt, which they find no easy matter to discharge, as the produce seldom answers ei-

* What I mean by vicious habits, are their great attachment to Negroe-women; there being but few gentlemen but what have several of those ladies very early in keeping.

ther in quantity or quality at the beginning; though constantly attended with exorbitant charges and expenses; for the lender of monies in those parts, is seldom satisfied with interest alone; he must be factor for the estate, and supply every thing that may be wanted at his own price; he must dispose of the produce, and draw the usual commissions, however inconvenient it may be to the owner to send it so far to market, who frequently meets with an opportunity of disposing of his effects at the next shipping place; or would willingly ship them for some *European* market, and draw bills in favor of his creditor for the neat proceeds thereof; but an attempt of this kind would expose him to the immediate rigor of the laws, and likely prove the ruin of his growing hopes: his goods must be shipped on board of some drover, where they seldom fail paying the usual tributes of pilferage and wastage, besides the common expense of freight; they must be landed at a certain wharf, where they pay double centage; they must be coopered afresh at a certain expense, and sold, when a convenient opportunity offers, to pay the charges and interest; for they seldom reach the capital, until the produce becomes very considerable.

The trading part of the people is not at this time so numerous, and may be naturally distinguished into factors, merchants, and pedlars: the former transact business chiefly for *European* merchants, and others that supply this market with different sorts of commodities at their own risk; as well as for the different planters, for whom they may be occasionally concerned; and have a regular commission on the sale and purchase of every thing that passes through their hands: these people are generally industrious, and seldom fail making considerable fortunes when well befriended, or furnished with money; which many of them do with a very fair character, while others, and indeed, the great numbers, are observed to lay hold of every opportunity of serving themselves. The merchants import their own goods, and run the risk of the markets; but generally turn pedlars in the disposal of them: the business was, indeed, beneficial while they could supply the neighboring markets, and export to advantage what would not answer so well within the colony; but every opportunity of this kind is now gone, and very few of them are observed to rise; for the principal planters are now supplied with every conveniency at their own risk; and the next class is entirely engrossed by the factors, who generally import such commodities as are commonly wanted at a plantation. But goods of all sort have been imported there in such abundance of late years, in expectation of some foreign trade, that they have been frequently sold under the prime cost.

The dependents form a fourth class, and not the least useful to the community; it is constituted of mechanics, clerks, and servants of all sorts, whose useful industry deserves encouragement, and adds to the public welfare in every soil; and most of these that follow the more useful mechanical branches, as carpenters, coopers, brick-layers, millwrights, coppersmiths, and tailors, acquire very decent, if not ample fortunes; and are frequently raised by an honest industry, so far as to be considered among the first rank of people: clerks, when they behave with a proper attention to the interest of their employers, are generally promoted, and interested in the business, in proportion as these grow less active, and more fond of indulging themselves; nor does the vigilant servant ever fail of gaining his master's esteem, who generally rewards his care with some decent gratuity at the expiration of his time.

To these we may add the Negroes, as a fifth and more numerous class, who are now computed to be more than 120,000 in number; and by whose labors and industry almost alone, the colony flourisheth, and its productions are cultivated and manufactured.

But although the methods of living in this colony, vary among the different classes of its inhabitants; there are but few in the general run of mankind that live with more satisfaction. The planters, and others whom affluence has supplied with conveniences above the rest, are decent, and often magnificent in their buildings; neat and rich in their furniture and dresses; and plentiful, with order and delicacy at their tables: they have great quantities of poultry and all sorts of stock raised at their plantations; *North America* supplies them with flower; and the fields almost without culture, with a variety of greens, roots, and fruit: the general produce of their estates, affords them wholesome diluting drinks; and, from *England,* and *Madeira,* they are supplied with those various wines and other liquors generally used at their tables: of late they give more than usual into the use of soups which they find more agreeable to their weakened stomachs; but in the general dispositions of their tables, and methods of cookery, the *English* customs are observed.

The settlers and middling sort of people in every other station of life, are not far short of those in the essential and necessary conveniences; their habitations are generally commodious and decent, their dresses neat and simple, and their tables well supplied with all sorts of fresh provisions, as well as necessary liquors: but the inconvenience of carriage, and frequent scarcity of flour among those that cannot purchase a considerable quantity at a time, often oblige them to substitute plantains, cassada, or yams, in the room of bread; which, though not so elegant, or agreeable to strangers, is not much inferior in wholesomeness or degree of nourishment.

The servants in this colony are mostly *Europeans,* and indented for a certain number of years; at the expiration of which, they are not only capable of providing decently for themselves, but generally receive some gratuity that enables them to enter more easily into life: These people generally live in smaller houses built about the sugar works, that they may be in, or out, with greater conveniency in the crop time: By the laws and customs of the country they are allowed a certain quantity of salt, beef, and flour, every month or quarter; and a proportionate quantity of sugar, and rum, to supply them with drink; but in no way restrained in the use of the more natural productions of the plantation, as plantains, yams, potatoes, cassada, and greens, which they have in great abundance everywhere: they are obliged to be active and vigilant by day, and much exposed to the sun when their station is in the field; but at nights their occupations vary with the employments of the season, for in planting and weeding times, they can rest to the dawn of day; but when the labors of the years are to be collected in a short space, time becomes more precious, and they, like the industrious slaves, frequently undressed, are obliged to watch by spells every night, and to engage with equal vigor in the toils of the day; while the planter and the overseer pass the midnight hours in uninterrupted slumbers, anxious to secure the reward of their annual labors; which, an unseasonable gust of wind, or heavier rains, would undoubtedly destroy, or a trifling accident retard: and happy is he, who at this season can have servants, on whose activity and inclinations he may depend; or whom health and vigor will allow to attend in person.

The Negroes who constitute the last class of the inhabitants of this country are, for the most part, the property of the Whites; and bought and sold like every other commodity in the country, being always reckoned a part of their estates, either real or personal: they live in huts or small thatched cabins, sustained by crotchets, whose interspaces are latticed, and plastered or daubed with clay; these are disposed in the form of villages, in proper places; and generally divided into two rooms, for the greater conveniency of the inhabitants. They are commonly allowed a few yards of blanket, or coarse linens every year, which serves to protect them a little from the cold in the more inclement seasons; and keep them warm, and secure from the open air, when sick: they generally provide themselves with food in the country parts, and for this purpose every planter supplies his slaves with a rich and convenient piece of ground, where they are obliged to employ the Lord's day, as well as the few other hours allowed them,* both to stock the ground and provide provisions for the following week; and yet the produce of these few hours' labor, is not only sufficient to supply them with plenty in a seasonable year, but affords enough to furnish the neighboring markets also. Every plantation, however, is provided with a plantain-walk, and quantities of yams and corn, to supply the new, and the infirm; and to relieve the others in an unseasonable year, or when their own provisions fail.

When we consider the inconveniences under which these creatures labor, the toils they are obliged to undergo, and vicissitudes of heat and cold to which they are exposed, and the grossness of their food in general; we ought not to be surprised if they had been still more slothful and sickly than they are commonly observed to be; or if the diseases to which they are obnoxious, had differed more apparently from our own: these are indeed frequently of a peculiar nature, and require a consummate knowledge of symptoms and disorders, to discover the real sources of them; yet the owners, whose interest depends chiefly on their welfare, will commit them to the care of some raw youth, or ignorant assumer, that is hardly skilled enough to breath a vein, or dispense a dose of physic: but this pro-

* In the country parts of this Island, every Negroe is allowed a *Saturday* afternoon, or some other afternoon in the week, to stock and manure his particular patch of ground, which he generally plants in cassada, yams, potatoes, *Indian* and *Guinea* corn; and on Sunday they provide provisions for the ensuing week, and send some to market, to supply themselves with a little salt beef, pork, or fish, and a little rum, which are the greatest delicacies they can come at, unless a cat, a rat, or dog fall in their way. It is true, many of them raise a few poultry, and other stock; but these they generally sell to enable them to purchase some decent as well as necessary cloathes for their wives and themselves.

ceeds more from ignorance and vanity, than any real want of humanity; for few of them are judges of physic, and each would be thought to have a doctor of his own; and these have in the course of time, introduced such methods of practice in those colonies, that you may now frequently observe gentlemen of the first consequence, to be vomited and blistered to death in a yellow fever, and the ladies, poisoned with bark in verminous inflammations; while others lie neglected in the easy beginning of an undistinguished remittent, until the disorder gains beyond relief.

SOURCE: Patrick Browne, *The Civil and Natural History of Jamaica* (London: White, 1789), pp. 22–26.

43 Population of the British West Indies, 1791

The present state [1791] of the population in the British West Indies appears, on a summary of the several accounts given in former parts of this work, to be as follows, viz.

	Whites	*Blacks*
Jamaica	30,000	250,000
Barbadoes	16,167	62,115
Grenada	1,000	23,926
St. Vincent	1,450	11,853
Dominica	1,236	14,967
Antigua	2,590	37,808
Montserat	1,300	10,000
Nevis	1,000	8,420
St. Christopher's	1,900	20,437
Virgin Isles	1,200	9,000
Bahamas	2,000	2,241
Bermudas	5,462	4,919
Total	65,305	455,684

There is, likewise, in each of the Islands, a considerable number of persons, of mixed blood, and Native Blacks, of free condition. In Jamaica they are reckoned, as we have shown, at ten thousand; and I have reason to believe they do not fall short of the same number in all the other Islands collectively taken. The whole inhabitants therefore may properly be divided into four great classes. 1. European Whites; 2. Creole or Native Whites; 3. Creoles of mixed blood, and free Native Blacks; 4. Negroes in a state of slavery.

SOURCE: Bryan Edwards, *The History, Civil and Commercial, of the British Colonies of the West Indies* (3d ed.; 3 vols.; London: Stockdale, 1801), 2:1–2.

44 Plantation Slavery in Early Nineteenth-Century Jamaica

[We] are anxious to avoid the imputation of unfair dealing towards the holders of slaves in the British colonies. We might have brought forward, in abundance, proofs of the excessive rigor of the slave code in the colonies of the French and Dutch. We might have shown, by an induction of particulars, resting on the best authority, with what terrible ferocity that code is often administered in practice; how it serves to divest the female character of its most amiable attributes, rendering not the masters only, but the mistresses of slaves, dead alike to the feelings of tenderness and delicacy; and how it converts even the most sacred functions of criminal justice into the means of indulging the worst passions of the human heart, and of gratifying a barbarous and sanguinary thirst of vengeance. It might be said, however, that, in doing this, we were exciting unjust prejudices against our own West India planters; that our own colonial institutions bear in themselves a much milder aspect than those of the French and Dutch, and are besides administered by Englishmen, in the spirit, and according to the maxims, of English jurisprudence. We will not now stop to controvert the correctness of this statement; we will give our countrymen the benefit of the plea, so far at least as to abstain, for the present, from illustrating our general position by facts drawn from the foreign colonies of the West Indies. The proofs already exhibited, in confirmation of it, have been drawn from the nature and effects of the slave system in the United States, the general spirit of whose legislation and jurisprudence is, to say no more, as liberal as our own; and we mean, in what follows, to confine the examination to the British islands.

Here again, we propose to take a view of the state of slavery, which must be admitted, by West Indians themselves, to be the least unfavorable to the character of their system. We shall not now have recourse to the writings of that able and faithful delineator of Negro slavery in our own islands, the Rev. James Ramsay, because the scenes he witnessed, however they may serve to mark the genius of that institution, it might be alleged, are now upwards of forty years old. Neither shall we have recourse to any part of the evidence taken before the Privy Council, or before Parliament, when the question of the Slave Trade was first agitated in this country. We shall not even cite, in support of our general views, the testimony of Dr. Pinckard; nor the recorded atrocities communicated by Lord Seaforth in 1803, as illustrative of the state of slavery in the oldest of our colonies, Barbadoes; lest it should be argued, that these authorities do not apply to the actually existing state of things. We shall abstain even from laying any stress on the still more recent exemplifications of the spirit and tendency of colonial slavery, which are furnished to us in the cases of Huggins of Nevis, Hodge of Tortola, and Rawlins of St. Kitts, lest we should be charged with too much confining our view to small and insulated communities, where individuals are less influenced by public opinion than in larger societies.* We recollect, indeed, to have heard West Indians, when these cases are alluded to in Parliament, challenge the opponents of the slave system to look, for a just appreciation of its character, not to our smaller islands, but to Jamaica, which exceeds them all in extent of population, and the liberal nature of whose institutions they did not hesitate to set up as a model for general imitation. We accept the challenge; and we propose, therefore, for the present, to confine our view to a consideration of the slave system as it exists in Jamaica, the colony in which we are told that it may be seen under the most favorable circumstances, and where we are also told that the slaves are under the protection of a humane code of laws, humanely and equitably administered.

In this delineation, also, of slavery, as it exists in Jamaica, we shall abstain from selecting particular instances of cruelty, and shall farther abstain from specifying such cases of general treatment, in the

* Let it not be supposed, that we admit the validity of the objections to which, in the present instance, we think proper to defer. We may have other opportunities of showing that they have no real force whatever.

management of plantations, as might be deemed to be peculiarly harsh and rigorous. On the contrary, we shall select, for our most prominent example, the case of an estate, the owner of which is distinguished even in this country for gentlemanly and kindly feeling; and (which is perhaps of still more importance) is possessed of wealth which relieves him from the necessity, to which many by their circumstances are unhappily driven, of exacting from their slaves an undue portion of labor, or of denying them the requisite supplies for their sustentation and comfort. In short, the proprietor in question, it is well known, is himself an excellent master to his slaves, and does all in his power to render their situation comfortable. But he lives in this country, and is therefore obliged to trust to the agency of others; and in point of fact his best efforts appear to have been employed in vain to mitigate the intrinsic oppressiveness of the system.

The Rev. Thomas Cooper published, in the course of the last year, in a periodical work called the *Monthly Repository,* several papers, with his name affixed to them, on the subject of Negro Slavery in the West Indies. These papers attracted considerable notice, being evidently the production of an able, intelligent, and upright man; and naturally induced persons taking an interest in the question to communicate with him upon it. The following statement is the result of these communications; and it is now given to the public with the permission of Mr. Cooper himself, who, we are most happy to announce to our readers, is engaged in preparing for the press a more complete detail of his observations on Negro Slavery during his residence in the West Indies, as well as a fuller development of his views on the subject.

1. EVIDENCE OF THE REV. THOMAS COOPER

In the year 1817, Robert Hibbert, Esq., of East Hide, near Luton, Bedfordshire, engaged the Rev. Thomas Cooper to go over to Jamaica, for the express purpose of ascertaining the practicability of improving, by means of religious instruction, the condition of the Negroes on his estate of Georgia, in the parish of Hanover, in that island. With a view to render his task as agreeable as possible, Mr. Cooper was authorized to adopt his own plans of tuition, "provided they should in no respect be found incompatible with the order and management of the plantation." A house was provided for him, pleasantly situated about a mile from the Negro village, and he was made quite independent of the other White people connected with the slaves. He reached the estate on Christmas day, 1817, and continued upon it for upwards of three years, after which he returned to England, where he now resides.

The owner of this estate, who himself resides in England, is, as may be inferred from his proceedings in this very instance, a man of great benevolence. He was at the entire expense of Mr. Cooper's mission, and he seemed disposed to spare no outlay which he thought likely to contribute to the comfort of his slaves, of whom there were about 400 attached to the estate. The estate had formerly been made to produce 400 hogsheads of sugar; but Mr. Hibbert, considering that the labor required for the production of so large a quantity pressed too heavily upon his slaves, directed that only 300 hogsheads should be made, and it is to this moderated scale of employment, and to a gang of Negroes thus favorably circumstanced, in relation to their proprietor, that Mr. Cooper's information refers.

One great obstacle to his success as a religious instructor, which Mr. Cooper had to encounter at the very outset of his undertaking, was this, that the slaves had no time to attend upon him. This will require a somewhat lengthened explanation, which will serve, at the same time, to throw light incidentally on several material features of the slave system.

The season of crop, in other words, the sugar harvest, commenced about the time of Mr. Cooper's arrival in Jamaica, and continued for about five months. During that period, the general plan is, and that plan was followed on Georgia estate, to begin the manufacture of sugar on Sunday evening, and to continue it generally, without intermission, either day or night, till about midnight of the following Saturday, when the work stops for about eighteen or twenty hours, to commence again on the Sunday evening.* In order to prevent any interruption of this process during the week, the slaves capable of labor, are, with some necessary exceptions, divided into two gangs or spells, which, besides being both fully occupied in the various occupations of the plantation during the day, are engaged the whole of

* By an act of the Jamaica legislature of Dec. 1816, it is forbidden to set the sugar mills to work before five on Monday morning. But this regulation appears to have been practically disregarded in this instance.

the night, on alternate nights, in the business of sugar making.* Their labor, during crop time, is thus equal to six days and three nights in the week. And in the exaction of this labor, no distinction is made between men and women: both are subjected to the same unvarying rule.

The canes are carried on the backs of mules, or in carts, from the field to the mill. The men employed in this part of the work have no regular time of rest, either night or day. Their task is to keep the mill regularly supplied with canes, and it is only when they have been able, by exertion, to accumulate a quantity there, that they can venture to take rest. It seldom happens that they get a whole night's rest at one time. Besides the alternate night of rest allowed to the other slaves, that portion of them who were not attending the sugar works had half an hour allowed them to sit down in the field to eat their breakfast, and two hours further interval of labor allowed them in the middle of the day, generally from one to three. The same allowance of time for breakfast and dinner was continued to the laboring slaves the whole year round.†

During the five months of crop, therefore, it is pretty evident, that it would have been found "incompatible with the order and management of the plantation" to allot any portion of time for religious instruction, unless it were on Sunday.

But here it will be said, that Sunday was the very day on which that instruction might most conveniently and appropriately have been given; and that it could hardly be alleged, with any fairness, that the Negroes had no time to attend to religious instruction, when the middle of that day might have been set apart for the purpose. To this arrangement, however, Mr. Cooper found there were insuperable objections: it was wholly "incompatible with the order and management of the plantation." In the first place, the persons who had been toiling for six days and three nights in the preceding week, many of whom had continued that toil till past midnight on Satur-

* On many estates the two gangs or spells, instead of alternating the whole of the night, labor half of each night, the one being replaced by the other at midnight.

† The law referred to above specifies these periods of half an hour and two hours as the proper intervals of labor during the day; and it adds that, except in crop time, the slaves are not to be obliged to work before five in the morning, or after seven in the evening.

day, could not be expected voluntarily to assemble, at a very early hour, to listen to lessons which they had not learned to appreciate. In the next place, Sunday was the *only* day which was allowed them, during the five months of crop, for cultivating their provision-grounds; for bringing thence the food requisite for their sustenance during the week; and for going to market.

It may not be generally understood, that not only is Sunday a market day in Jamaica, but that, for the Negroes, whether as vendors of the fruit or vegetables or poultry or other articles of food they may have to dispose of, or as purchasers of the little necessaries or comforts they may wish to buy in return, *Sunday is the only market day.* Such, however, is the fact.

The distance of the place of market, varying from one to five, ten, and even more miles, and which must be twice traversed by such slaves as go to it, and who have generally heavy loads to carry thither, tends further, independently of the time required for their sales and purchases, to abridge the hours which could, by any possibility, be given to religious worship on the Sunday.

It is sound labor even to fetch on that day from their provision-grounds the plantains, or yams, or eddoes, or other food which they may require, to feed themselves and any children they may have, during the succeeding week; a labor which is often aggravated by the distance of those provision-grounds from the homestall of the plantation; a distance often extending to six, and sometimes even to ten miles. The distance of the provision-grounds on Georgia estate was about three miles from the Negro village, which was thought moderate. Still the very walk thither and back was sufficient to diminish, by two hours, the brief respite from plantation-labor which Sunday afforded to the slaves.

But besides these different uses to which the Sunday was necessarily appropriated, there remained another of a still more engrossing nature. Sunday was *the only day which was allowed to the slaves, during crop, for cultivating and keeping in order their provision-grounds, from which provision-grounds they derived their sole means of subsistence,* if we except a weekly allowance of seven or eight herrings to each adult, and half that number to each child, and a small present of a pound or two of salt fish at Christmas. If, therefore, they neglected to employ in their provision-grounds a sufficient portion of the Sunday, to secure to them an adequate supply of food, they might be reduced to absolute want; and although the want might be supplied, yet the neglect would not fail to be punished.

When all these circumstances are weighed, we shall have no difficulty in comprehending how it was that Mr. Cooper, during the first five or six months of his residence on Georgia estate, could find no time, for the religious instruction of the slaves, which was *compatible with its order and management.*

The Sunday shone no Sabbath day to them.

Nor was their case, in this respect, on Mr. Hibbert's estate, at all peculiar. It was the common lot of the plantation slaves generally throughout the island.

Crop time, however, lasted only for five, or, at most, six months of the year. How did Mr. Cooper succeed during the remaining six or seven months? During those months, as well as during crop time, the Sunday was wholly and exclusively applied, in the case of the slaves, to the various secular objects already mentioned; but chiefly and above all, Sunday being the day especially appropriated for the cultivation of their provision-grounds, which were the allotted source of subsistence for themselves and their families while engaged in the weekly labors of the plantation, it was felt to be impossible to require that a portion of it should be given to attendance on religious instruction, at least unless an equivalent portion of time had been given them, during the week, for the purpose of cultivating their grounds. But, even then, to have enforced such attendance on the Sunday would have proved a grievous imposition. It would have operated as an interdict from attending market, on the only day on which there was any market to attend. Under these circumstances, even Mr. Cooper was forced to admit that it would have been the greatest cruelty to compel the slaves to attend Divine worship on Sundays.

But it may be asked whether no time, except Sunday, is given to the slaves for the raising of food. The law of the island requires that one day in a fortnight, except during the time of crop, should be allowed to the slaves, exclusive of Sunday, for cultivating their provision-grounds.* This would amount to from fourteen to sixteen days in the year. The proprietor of Georgia was, however, more liberal

* See the amended Slave Act of Jamaica, presented to the House of Commons, along with various other papers respecting the West Indies, on the 10th June, 1813.

than the law. There the slaves were allowed for this purpose (and other proprietors in that quarter, Mr. Cooper thinks, may have been equally liberal) every Saturday after crop, until they began to dig the land into holes for the fall-plant, when they are allowed only every second Saturday. By this arrangement, the Negroes belonging to Georgia had about twenty-eight days in the year allowed them for the cultivation of their grounds, besides Sundays.

As this time, however, had been given them for the express purpose of raising their food, it would have been unjust to the slaves, and would have placed both religion and its minister in an odious light, had any part of it been authoritatively diverted from its original destination, with a view to attendance upon him. Accordingly it was agreed that, out of crop, an afternoon every fortnight should be allowed for religious worship and instruction. Mr. Cooper had thus an opportunity of preaching to the slaves about eleven or twelve times in the year. But the moment crop began, there was an entire cessation for five or six months of all meetings of the kind.

After remaining in this unsatisfactory state for upwards of three years, Mr. Cooper, as has been already remarked, quitted Jamaica and returned to Great Britain. He justly observes, that it could perhaps hardly be expected that he should have consented to consume his time amongst a people to whom he could preach only twelve times in the year.

Having thus made our readers in some measure acquainted with the respectable witness to whose testimony we mean in the first instance to refer them, we shall now proceed to adduce his further evidence, both as it respects the particular estate on which he resided, and the condition of the slaves generally in the island. When the statements are general, they are to be considered as comprehending Georgia, unless that estate be particularly excepted. . . .

2. GENERAL TREATMENT

The gangs always work before the whip, which is a very weighty and powerful instrument. The driver has it always in his hand, and drives the Negroes, men and women, without distinction, as he would drive horses or cattle in a team. Mr. Cooper does not say that he is always using the whip, but it is known to be always present, and ready to be applied to the back or shoulders of any who flag at their work, or lag behind in the line.* The driver, who is generally a black man, has the power not only of thus stimulating the slaves under him to exertion, by the application of the whip to their bodies while they are proceeding with their work, but, when he considers any of them to have committed a fault deserving of a more serious notice, he has the power also of prostrating them (women as well as men) on the ground, causing them to be held firmly down, by other Negroes, who grasp the hands and legs of their prostrate companion, when he may inflict upon the bare posteriors such a number of lashes as he may deem the fault to have merited; the whole number which he may inflict at one time, without the presence of the overseer, being, by the Slave Act of 1816, limited to ten. One of the faults which the driver most frequently punishes in this way, is that of coming too late to the field, either in the morning or after dinner. Those who arrive after the fixed time are pretty sure to get a few, perhaps, five or six lashes. Mr. Cooper, on one occasion, saw three or four old women come too late: they knew they were to be whipped, and as soon as they came up, threw themselves down on the ground to receive the lashes: some of them received four, others six lashes. These minor punishments, Mr. Cooper says, are very frequent. He believes that seldom a day passes without some occurring; and he has heard of as many as sixty Negroes being flogged in one morning, for being late.

More serious punishments are only inflicted by the authority of the overseer; and the mode of their infliction is usually the same as has been already described. Whether the offender be male or female, precisely the same course is pursued. The posteriors are made bare, and the offender is extended prone on the ground, the hands and feet being firmly held and extended by other slaves; when the driver, with his long and heavy whip, inflicts, under the eye of the overseer, the number of lashes which he may order; each lash, when the skin is tender and not rendered callous by repeated punishments, making an incision on the buttocks, and thirty or forty such lashes leaving them in a dreadfully lacerated and bleeding state. Even those that have become the most callous cannot long resist the

* In one of his printed letters, in which he is replying to an objection, Mr. Cooper incidentally, but very significantly remarks, that "to a Jamaican man" it would be "truly astonishing" to learn that the whip was not needed, or that its sound was rarely heard.

force of this terrible instrument, when applied by a skillful hand, but become also raw and bloody; indeed, no strength of skin can withstand its reiterated application.

These punishments are inflicted by the overseer, whenever he thinks them to have been deserved. He has no written rules to guide his conduct, nor are the occasions at all defined on which he may exercise the power of punishment. Its exercise is regulated wholly and solely by his own discretion. An act of neglect or disobedience, or even a look or a word supposed to imply insolence, no less than desertion or theft or contumacy, may be thus punished; and they may be thus punished, without trial and without appeal, at the mere pleasure and fiat of the overseer. Doubtless, any slave may, *after having been punished,* complain of his overseer to the attorney of the estate, or to a magistrate; but such complaint often does him more harm than good.

The law professes to limit the number of lashes which shall be given at one time to thirty-nine: but neither this law, nor any other which professes to protect the slave, can be of much practical benefit to him: it cannot, under existing circumstances, be enforced; and its existence in the statute-book, therefore, is but a mockery. A Negro, especially one who is the slave of an absentee proprietor, may be considered as entirely in the power of the overseer, who is his absolute master, and may be at the same instant his lawgiver, accuser, and judge; and may not only award sentence, but order its execution. And supposing him to act unjustly, or even cruelly, he has it in his power to prevent any redress from the law. The evidence of a thousand slaves would avail nothing to his conviction; and, even if there were any disposition in the inferior Whites to inform or to bear testimony against him, he has only to take care that the infliction does not take place in their presence.

In point of fact, Mr. Cooper believes that the limitation of the number of lashes to thirty-nine is practically disregarded, whenever the overseer thinks the offense deserving of a larger measure of punishment. The information he received on this subject all went to show that the law was not attended to. One overseer told him, that a woman had disobeyed his orders, and he put her in the stocks by way of punishment. She complained to the attorney of this proceeding. He ordered her to be thrown down on the ground, in the customary manner, and thirty-nine lashes were inflicted on her naked posteriors; after which she was raised up and immediately thrown down again, and received thirty-nine lashes more, applied in the same manner.

The law permits the Negroes to make their complaints to magistrates. In one case several Negroes went to complain to a magistrate of their want of houses, or proper accommodation. Mr. Cooper saw them, on that occasion, at the magistrate's door. The magistrate, however, told him it would never do to interfere in such matters, for, if they did, there would be no getting on between masters or overseers and magistrates; and, with respect to these complainants, what he did was to desire them to return home and trust to their master's kindness: and Mr. Cooper thought that, all things considered, he could not well have done otherwise.

Two women, who were pregnant, desired to quit the field during rain, on account of their pregnancy. The overseer refused them permission. They went to complain of this refusal to a magistrate, but were stopped in their way by a neighboring overseer, and by him thrown into the stocks until he sent them back to their own overseer, who put them again into the stocks on their own estate, and had them flogged. Of this proceeding they complained to the attorney. The attorney was of opinion that the overseer had acted with undue severity; but he considered the women to have been highly to blame for attempting to complain to the magistrate; whereas, he said, they ought in the first instance to have complained to him.

It is common for Negroes, who have been guilty of what is deemed a serious offense, to be worked all day in the field, and during the intervals of labor, as well as during the whole night, to be confined, with their feet fast in the stocks. In the case of one Negro, who was so confined for some weeks, Mr. Cooper begged hard to obtain a remission of his punishment, but did not succeed. Another Negro, belonging to the estate, was a notorious runaway. Being taken, he was flogged in the usual manner, as severely as he well could bear, and then made to work in the field. During the interval of dinner-time he was regularly placed in the stocks, and in them also he was confined the whole night. When the lacerations, produced by the flogging he had received, were sufficiently healed, he was flogged a second time. While the sores were still unhealed, one of the bookkeepers told Mr. Cooper that maggots had bred in the lacerated flesh. Mr. Cooper mentioned the circumstances to the attorney, who did not manifest surprise on hearing it.

An old African Negro, well known to Mr. Cooper, who appeared to possess a sound and superior mind, and was reckoned the best watchman on the estate, was placed to watch the provision-grounds for the use of the overseer's house. These were robbed, and the robbery being imputed to his neglect, he received a very severe flogging. The old man declared (Mr. Cooper does not vouch for the truth of the excuse) that he could not help what had happened, the grounds being too extensive for him to guard them effectually, so that while he was on one side of them, the Negroes could easily steal on the other. This flogging made a great alteration in the old man, and he never seemed well after it. In two or three weeks another robbery occurring, he received a still more severe flogging than before. One morning, while Mr. and Mrs. Cooper were at breakfast, they heard a groaning, and going to the window, saw this poor man passing along in a state which made Mrs. Cooper shrink back with horror. Mr. Cooper went out to him, and found his posteriors, which were completely exposed, much lacerated, and bleeding dreadfully. He seemed much exhausted. He attempted to explain the case, but was incapable from fatigue and suffering. A Negro boy was standing by; the old man pointed to him, and said, "Massa, him tell you." The poor old man from this time was never well or cheerful, and he soon afterwards died.

Mr. Cooper never saw a Negro, who, when uncovered, did not exhibit marks of violence, that is to say, traces of the whip on his body.

It has been already mentioned that the Negroes on this estate, and the same is the case generally throughout the island, have no food beyond a small allowance of salted fish, except what they raise on their own grounds; Sundays, and a certain number of days beside, being allotted for their cultivation.

The Negroes have in general too few houses; but the having a house to themselves, be it ever so bad, gives some feeling of importance. On Georgia there are many houses built in rather a superior style, which have cost the proprietor a heavy sum of money; but in general their huts are like sheds. They are made with posts put into the ground. The sides are wattled, some being plastered with mortar, and some not. They are thatched, sometimes shingled. They often have one room to sit in, with one or two for sleeping. They lie on boards, or on a door covered with a mat of their own making, and sometimes a blanket for covering; but they have not all blankets. A woman with children has a blanket, and also the aged men; but many men have none.

SOURCE: *Negro Slavery; or, a View of Some of the More Prominent Features of that State of Society, as It Exists in the United States of America and in the Colonies of the West Indies, especially in Jamaica* (London: Hatchard, 1823), pp. 43–53, 60–65.

■

The next two selections (45 and 46) describe the system of slavery as practiced in the French West Indies (Saint-Domingue) and in Dutch Surinam. In the eighteenth century these two colonies were the most valuable that the French and Dutch possessed in the region.

45 Saint-Domingue, 1731

I will finish my account with a discussion of the Negroes, who today make up the largest number of subjects of this colony. Nothing is more miserable than the condition in which this people lives. It seems they are the disgraced of man and the outcasts of nature. Exiled from their country and deprived of that which all other nations guard jealously, namely liberty, they see themselves almost reduced to beasts of burden. A few roots make up their entire source of food. Their clothing is two wretched rags that protect them neither from the heat of the day nor from the excessive coolness of the nights. Their homes resemble pits made for keeping bears. Their beds are mattresses of interwoven twigs more suitable, it would seem, for breaking their backs than for providing repose. Their belongings consist of several gourds and a few trays of wood or clay. Their work almost never ends; their time for sleep is quite short; they receive no wages but get twenty lashes of the whip for the slightest infraction. This is how these men, who do not lack spirit and cannot be unaware that they are absolutely necessary to those who treat them with force, have been degraded.

In spite of all this they enjoy perfect health, while their masters, who have everything in abundance and lack none of the comforts of life, are subject to an infinite number of illnesses. Exposed bareheaded to the sun every day, which, it seems, would give them brain fever, they never complain except about the cold; hence they enjoy the most precious of all blessings and appear insensible to the loss of others. It is said that it is not even a good deed to take them out of their painful and very humiliating state because they would take advantage. It is true that those who speak thus have an interest in so doing and are at the same time their judge and their adversary. After all, it must be admitted that if there is no service that flatters human pride more than that of these slaves, there is no other that is so subject to more vexatious reverses; and there is no one in our colonies who does not consider himself unfortunate in having no other kind of servants. Would that there were only this feeling—so natural in man and in which we even partake of the nature of God—to count for nothing what is done for us through fear, if the heart has no part in it. But here it is a necessary evil; at least one sees little remedy for it. In the colonies, unfortunate is he who has many slaves; they are the source of so many worries for him and a continual occasion for exercising patience. Unfortunate is he who has no slaves at all; he can do absolutely nothing. Unfortunate is he, finally, who has but a few slaves; he must suffer everything from fear of losing them and all his goods along with them. Properly speaking, only the Africans between the White Cape and the Negro Cape can be said to be born to servitude. These wretches admit unabashedly that an inner feeling tells them they are accursed. The most intelligent, like the Senegalese, have learned from a tradition which perpetuates itself among them that this misfortune is a consequence of their *Papa Tam,* who mocked his father. These Senegalese are the most handsome of all the Negroes, the easiest to discipline, and the best suited to domestic service. The Bambaras are the biggest, but they are thieves; the Aradas best understand the cultivation of the land, but they are the proudest; the Congos are the smallest and the best fishermen, but they desert easily; the Nagos are the most humane; the Mondingos are the cruelest; the Minas are the most resolute, the most capricious, and the most subject to despair. Lastly, the Negro Creoles, from whatever nation they originate, retain from their forefathers only the spirit of slavery, and their color. Although born in slavery, they have somewhat more love of freedom; they are also the cleverest, the most reasonable, the most adroit, but they are lazier, more swaggering, and more dissolute than the Dandas—that is the term for all those who have come from Africa.

One has seen Negroes at Saint-Domingue that were carried away from Monomotopa; one has seen those in other colonies that came from the island of Madagascar. Neither have profited their masters. The latter are practically unmanageable; the former perish quickly through various causes. As for intelligence, all the Negroes of Guinea are endowed with it in the most limited fashion; several even appear stupid and dazed. There are some who can never count above three nor learn the Lord's Prayer. They never think anything for themselves, and the past is as unknown to them as the future. They are machines whose springs must be rewound every time one wants to set them in motion. Some people have believed that there is more malice in them than lack of memory, but they are mistaken; to be convinced of this it is only necessary to consider their lack of foresight in things that concern them personally.

It is, however, rather difficult to agree with what everyone generally believes, that they are skillful and shrewd in their dealings, that they are extremely zealous, and that they often make dupes of their masters. It is also said that they jest rather ingeniously and that they know marvelously well how to take ridicule; that they are very adept at the art of dissimulating; and that, whereas they are the most stupid Negroes in everyday affairs and for their master an impenetrable mystery, they penetrate him with a surprising facility. What is certain is that it seems their secret is their treasure and that they would rather die than reveal it. Nothing is more amusing than to see their expression when one wants to extract this secret from them. They feign surprise so naturally that it takes much experience not to believe that they are sincere. They burst out laughing in such a way as to baffle the most confident. They are never disconcerted, and if one were to catch them lying, blows would not make them admit what they had resolved to deny. They are as a rule quite gentle; they are humane, docile, simple; but credulous and excessively superstitious. They do not know how to bear hate, and they do not know envy, dishonesty, or slander. One can say that when they have learned about God religion is what they value most: It is the fruit of reason, and no passion dominates. Certain examples to the contrary prove nothing against general experience; except that usually these examples have no other basis than the irreligion of their masters, who would like to justify by them the small care that they take in the education of these unfortunates.

One winds up correcting a good many of their faults with the whip when one uses this means effectively, but it is necessary to keep at it. However, although severity, or at least a certain severe manner, should predominate in one's behavior toward them, gentleness should not be entirely dispensed with. The English consider it right never to temper punishments, which they always administer in a cruel fashion. And there is much likelihood that if we had them as neighbors at Saint-Domingue in place of the Spaniards, it would be up to us to lead their slaves astray. The Negro is not disloyal, but one must not always count too much on his fidelity or his blind attachment. He would be a rather good soldier if he were well disciplined and led. He is brave, but this is often because he does not recognize danger, or because his vanity conceals it from him. If he were in combat next to his master and if he had not been mistreated without reason, he would do his duty quite well; but one should not be in the position of having punished him unjustly, because he distinguishes perfectly well whether one behaves toward him with passion and harshness, or whether one punishes him with necessary severity; he knows how to judge justice. Bands of Negroes in revolt ought to be disbanded immediately; they will normally do so when threatened with the stick and the lash. If one hesitates at first, and then seeks to fight them, they defend themselves well. As soon as they realize it is necessary to die, it matters little to them how, and their least success makes them almost invincible. The most effective means of assuring oneself of their faithfulness is to take an interest in them and make good Christians of them.

Among these people song is a rather ambiguous sign either of gaiety or of sadness. They sing in adversity to while away their troubles, and they sing when they are happy to give vent to their joy. It is true that they have mournful songs and joyous songs, but it takes some experience to be able to distinguish the ones from the others. . . . Many masters do not feed their slaves, and are content to give them a chance to obtain or earn their living. But, despite the inquiries that have been made, it has not yet been discovered how they survive. It is known, moreover, that what is sufficient to nourish a white man for one meal can nourish a Negro for three days. They do not fail to eat well when they have something, but however little they eat and sleep they are always strong and ready for work. It must be added that, despite the little they have, they share it willingly with those who are indigent, even if they are strangers.

As for religion, it should be noted that the different kinds of Negroes that are brought to our colonies from Africa can be divided into three principal nations—the Congos, the Aradas, and the Senegalese. Strictly speaking, none has any religion. Nevertheless, the Congos were converted to Christianity by the Portuguese 200 years ago; their kings have always been Christians since that time, and many of these Negroes are baptized. But one scarcely finds in some of them even a slight knowledge of our mysteries. Some Senegalese, neighbors of Morocco, are Mohammedans and are circumcised. The Aradas are sunk in the thickest gloom of idolatry to the point of making a divine cult of the grass snakes of their country.

SOURCE: Fr. Pierre François Xavier de Charlevoix, *Histoire de l'Isle Espagnole ou de S. Domingue* (2 vols.; Paris: Guerin, 1730–31), 2:496–506 (extracts). Translated for the present volume by Edward B. Cone.

46 Surinam, 1770

[The Negroes] love to sing, but their music is unpleasant and the sound of it by no means gratifying. They have few musical instruments, and these few very simple. One is a sort of guitar called a *banja,* which is made of half a calabash to which a neck two feet long is attached. This neck is covered with leather. It has a comb over which four strings are strung, and the Negroes play on these with their fingers. They also have drums of two sizes: the larger one is 3 or 4 feet long and 15 or 16 thumb-breadths across; the smaller, which they call *baboula,* is of the same length but only half as wide. These instruments are made of two strips of wood formed into a hoop [at each end]. Over one hoop is stretched a goat- or sheep-skin from which the hair or wool has been scraped. They play on this with four fingers. The small drum is used to make a roaring noise without a beat; the larger provides the beat in the bass. In their country they have at least twenty or more kinds of drums and are very proud of them. They can communicate on these drums and sometimes say untoward things, which often causes disagreements and leads to hand-to-hand fighting; quite a few of them are killed [in these struggles].

They are great lovers of dancing, but their dances usually contain postures and motions which are contrary to all modesty. . . .

Each slave is given a wife by his master. If the couple do not agree, the master will dismiss the wife and then marry her to someone else. Weddings are celebrated without much formality except that bottles of *kilthum* are provided; this is a kind of brandy mulled with sugar.

The Negro women have a great deal of respect for their husbands and will seldom eat at the same time as they do, particularly during holidays. They serve their husbands standing up and will not eat until given permission to do so.

The women both carry their babies and are delivered of them with ease. They do not cohabit with their husbands during the nursing period; for a woman to do so is considered improper. During this period a husband is free to go with another woman. . . .

Immediately after the birth of a child a woman goes to the river or other body of water and washes herself and her baby. Afterwards she carries the child on her back in a piece of *Osnabrug* * linen which has been presented to her by her master. . . .

When one of these Negroes dies, his fellow-slaves make a great deal of commotion and beat the drum as a sign that death has taken place. Some set about making a grave. The dead person is put into a coffin dressed in his newest or best clothes (the women wear their bloodstones and beads) and is carried to the grave on the shoulders of eight men who are followed by the close friends of the deceased; these lament and yell mightily. After the body has been put into the ground the coffin is covered with white linen or with Salempouri † if they have it. Then the *bomba* or head slave pours for all those present from a *wieda,* which is a cup made from a calabash, or from a glass of *kilthum,* and each person pours a few drops on the coffin, saying: "Winje mooij," i.e., 'good-bye,' "you have gone to a happy place; rest quietly; others have gone before you and you will find

* Osnabrück, in what is now West Germany. The town gave its name to a kind of coarse linen cloth that was extensively imported into the West Indian plantations in the eighteenth century. Ed.

† A type of cotton cloth imported via Europe from western India. Ed.

them there." After that the old calabashes and pots and pans of the deceased are broken in pieces on the grave. Then the close relatives take a cock, hold it over the grave, and cut off its head. They take the body of the bird and return with it to the deceased's home, where they cook it with rice and put it in front of the door. Then one of the oldest relatives comes and throws some of the cooked meats in front of the door and distributes the remainder to poor people or to the children. . . .

The slaves, both male and female, go practically naked, except that the men wear a pair of *musquite* pants or a loin cloth and the women a short skirt of *Osnabrug* linen. During the major holidays, such as Easter, Whitsuntide, and Christmas (when their masters treat them on the second or third day with *kilthum,* tobacco, and pipes), the women dress up in flowered cotton or Salempouri skirts, and with a silk scarf hanging on their right side, and the men wear colorful skirts or striped *musquite* pants. Some planters give their slaves hats to wear against the burning of the sun. The slaves paint their faces and half of their bodies with *laan,* a bluish paint which lasts for nine days and protects against both the sun's rays and the bites of insects. . . .

On the plantations the slave huts are made of wood and usually have a door but no windows. They are about thirty feet long and fifteen feet wide and are roofed with straw thatch. In the middle of each hut is a fireplace. The smoke from the fire has to find its way through the door. Around this fireplace [the slaves] lie down on two or three planks raised somewhat above the floor. A woven rush mat, spread over the planks, serves as a mattress. Bolsters or pillows are not known, except that a wooden block may be used for that purpose. Furniture does not impede the slaves much, since all they have are some iron and earthernware pots and pans, a few calabashes, benches, and other small things. They possess wooden containers, too, which they use when they work their garden plots.

The living quarters stand in rows. Each family has its own quarters and a vegetable garden to go with it. In these gardens they plant the crops they need to support themselves—yams, potatoes, manioc, corn, bananas, cassava, tobacco, and Spanish peppers; their masters give them only a pound or a pound and a half of meat, some barley, peas, or horse-beans on Saturday evenings, and once in a while a dram or two of *kilthum,* and some short pipes and tobacco. At one time, on some of the plantations, the slaves tried to raise pigs. This, however, is not being done any more, because these animals are very destructive of produce, and, if they run loose, spoil everything. It is, however, the custom to allow the slaves to keep poultry and ducks; they take good care of these, and, by selling them, make money with which to buy something for themselves or for their wives. On Saturday afternoons and Sundays, which the slaves have off, they work in their gardens, and the rest of the time they spend in gaiety. On most plantations the *bomba,* or supervisor, closes the doors of the Negro huts at night to prevent the slaves' wandering around.

If the slaves run away or misbehave in some other way, the *bomba* beats them severely with a pita-whip. Afterwards the raw flesh is rubbed with a mixture of brine, lemon juice, and pimento. This causes pain, but the purpose is not to be cruel but to prevent the flesh from corrupting. The slaves are also punished frequently with the so called "Spanish *bok*"—the hands are bound together, the knees are put through the knot so made, and then a stick is driven firmly into the ground through the opening of the knees and the tied hands. The slaves lie curled round the stick and are beaten on the buttocks with rods cut from the guava or tamarind; when they have been thoroughly beaten on one side, they are turned over and beaten on the other. Sometimes hoop sticks are used for these floggings, but the method is dangerous, as the slaves often die of it. In Paramaribo, on complaint by a master, this punishment is inflicted publicly at the corners of the streets but, before it can take place, the master has to make a written report to the fiscal about his slave's misbehavior. . . . The masters are not allowed to inflict the death penalty; if such is required, the slaves have to be handed over to the courts. . . .

As the majority of the inhabitants of Surinam are slaves and as too much permissiveness toward them could turn out badly for the masters, strict regulations have been issued to keep them in check. Among other things they are not allowed to sail up or down the rivers without written permission; they cannot carry sticks, swords, or clubs on the street; they cannot possess knives with hollow iron handles and these are confiscated if found; they cannot travel the streets at night without a lighted candle in a lantern, and they cannot talk to each other after nine o'clock. At no time may they enter private residences, or break into them, or steal or plunder from them. After sunset they cannot go into the savannas outside Paramaribo whether for a funeral, recreation, or otherwise; if they do, the patrols may shoot at them if they fail to stand still when ordered to do so. No citizen may sell powder or shot to a slave without written permission from his master.

SOURCE: Jan Jacob Hartsinck, *Beschryving van Guiana, of de Wildekust, in Zuid-America* . . . (2 vols.; Amsterdam: Tielenburg, 1770), 2:907–17 (extracts). Translated for the present volume by Elise P. Wright.

■

Slavery was abolished in the British West Indies in 1833, in the French West Indies in 1848, and in the Dutch West Indies in 1863. (In 1794 the Revolutionary Government of France had declared slavery illegal in Saint-Domingue, but Napoleon rescinded the order; the Saint-Domingue slaves did not become unequivocally free until, as Haiti, the former French colony achieved full independence in 1804.) By the 1860s all the Spanish-American republics had freed their slaves.

In Cuba, however, slavery remained legal until 1886 and in Brazil until 1888. Moreover, it was to these two areas that most of the slaves brought from Africa during the nineteenth century came. In consequence both attracted foreign travelers and observers in large numbers, and there is a rich literature on nineteenth-century Cuban and Brazilian slavery. Descriptive passages typical of this literature are reproduced below.

47 The Life of a Slave, 1828

It is a matter of serious inquiry with me, how slaves are treated by different nations, who compose the population of this island, and in the different species of culture [of] sugar and coffee. There is a marked difference in the methods in Carolina * and Cuba, of employing their slaves; in Carolina, all work on land is done in tasks, and the task is the same on all plantations, and for all hands, male

* South Carolina.

and female;—one hundred and five feet square, which is duly staked out for every negro, is his task for the day, which performed, his master has no claim upon him for further service for that day. The vigorous and active perform the task by three or four o'clock, sometimes by one or two; the strong are seen to help out the weak, the husband the wife, the parent the child, and good feeling is promoted among the gang. In Cuba, they have no measured task on coffee or sugar estates. With the exception of part of Saturday, and a part of Sunday, the whole time of the slave is his master's. They rise at daybreak, and commence their toil; and with short intervals to take their food, they labor till the light is gone, and renew it on some plantations, by the light of the moon or stars, or a blazing fire. As they move to the field in Indian file, the driver brings up the rear with a word and a harmless snap of his whip, to quicken their pace; and in the field they work near together, and occasionally the driver rouses the gang to a quicker movement by an inspiriting call, like a carter speaking to his oxen. But I believe the lash is seldom applied; I have never seen it. Nor have I seen occasion for it. The step of the slaves is quick as they walk, their persons erect, the back commonly hollowing in, and the arms hanging a little back; and a cheerful, vigorous movement, and often a lofty and graceful air, strike the stranger's eye.

It astonishes one to see with what rapidity they pass over a field of weeds and bushes with their machet, an instrument like a butcher's cleaver, leaving neither root nor branch behind. This, as I should esteem it, *uncouth* instrument, is wielded with a rapidity and effect, which imply sleight of hand, and strength of wrist, even in females of fourteen or sixteen. Some planters give them the common hoe of our country, in weeding ground not stony; and esteem it a more efficient instrument, and it is certainly a more humane one, as the machet requires the laborer to bend his body low, to work with effect, which must be fatiguing and exhausting under a tropical sun.

It is certain that they work more hours than the farmers in the north of our own country, and I verily believe in each hour accomplish as much and more. There is no conversation among them, no lounging or leaning on the hoe, no slouch in their gait, and every stroke seems to tell. I should not think the opinion extravagant, that the slaves in Cuba accomplish one-third more labor than the tasked slaves of Carolina.

So far as I have been able to observe, they have wholesome, and even delicious food, and as much as they desire. It is not generally measured to them, as in Carolina, nor left to their own cooking. They come to the cookroom with their gourd and take as much as they choose of the delicious plantain; they have rations of fish, indeed, of jerk beef, and of hearts and skirts, to make a variety. A pretty good sized codfish is cut into three parts, and one of them given to a laborer for the day. A pound of jerk beef also, is a ration. In addition to the common fare, they have their own favorite dishes, cooked in their private kettles, in which they put melanga, ochra, and anything they please, raised in their own gardens. They cook their own suppers; and on Saturday evening, they make entertainments, and invite guests with as much form and ceremony as their hospitable masters.

The simplicity and wholesomeness of their food, and constancy of their exercise, commonly secure to them the blessing of health. . . .

It is generally agreed that the labor on sugar estates is most exhausting to the negroes, and it is confidently said, that on many estates there is a loss of from 10 to 15 percent of their laborers each year. This, however, does not take place on well-conducted estates. The severity of the toil on sugar plantations seems acknowledged by the circumstance, that some estates purchase males only, and where both sexes are employed there is often little or no increase of population. As difficulties are thrown more and more in the way of importation of slaves from Africa, a greater attention is paid to pregnant females, to preserve the stock of the plantation. I trust there is with many, I know there is with some, a commiseration of female slaves in that delicate situation. They are exempt from labor for a month before and after the birth, to nurse themselves and the child, and have hours of the day for months after for the same purpose, during which others are at work.

It is said, that on many Spanish sugar estates in the grinding season, they have but two watches, from twelve at noon to twelve at night, and from twelve at night to twelve at noon. On Mr. W.'s, three watches, which plan gives the negroes four whole nights' rest in the week, and three half nights. Mr C. remarks that in French sugar estates on other islands, they work in turn four hours at a time, which makes the fatigue comparatively light. He remarks further, that mills going by steam must prevent much of the expense of grinding;

and that there is no danger, but there will be fuel to raise the steam and boil the sugar, in the cane itself. In St. Croix there is not a tree for fuel on the island, and their mills go by steam. . . .

In 1825 the smallpox broke out on this estate, and ninety slaves had it the natural way, of which only *one* died. [The proprietor] had at the same time forty sick of other diseases.

The proprietor carefully avoids overworking his negroes, as tending to fill his infirmary. In the winter he gives them a recess from labor at noon of an hour and a half, and in summer of three hours, and no night work is permitted on the estate. The best comment on these humane arrangements is that a more healthy, muscular, active set of negroes, as many have remarked, is not to be found on the island.

The bohea, or square of negro huts, is judiciously arranged on a hill, fifteen or twenty rods east from the principal building of the batey. Two families are accommodated under one roof, and a space of a few yards is left between each two buildings, fenced by a high open picket. In this manner the negro huts enclose a large square, which is entered by an iron gate. When the plantation becomes as populous as the proprietor hopes it will, this square will be a little negro city, with streets running at right angles.

The valley between the mansion and the bohea is to be an extensive garden; and at the head of this valley are forming immense tanks, to be filled with water from the well-arranged coffee driers, from which every rod of the garden can almost without trouble be irrigated.

Other parts of his plan, less original, are omitted. I only add, that the 1st of January is the negro's red-letter day on this estate. On this day no work whatever is done; it is entirely given up to mirth and festivity. All liberties, except crimes, are permitted. At three in the morning, they make a general rush upon their master, and wish him a happy new year. Each receives a handkerchief as a present. Pardons are distributed in all cases, except of crimes which the laws of the land proscribe; and for one day in the year the slaves are everything but master.

Mr. S. has a peculiarity in sending his coffee to market, to which he may be indebted for getting the highest price. Coffee he remarks, often suffers by rain, on its way to Havana, though covered with hides,—and afterwards by dampness in stores and at sea. To prevent this he packs his coffee in large casks, neatly made by his own coopers, of atage wood, and iron bound. By this means it arrives at Havana and the most distant market perfectly *dry.* In cleaning his coffee, he highly approves of Chartrand's divider, and has a half dozen of them in use.

His crop of corn this year was 3,750 bushels. I saw in his loft many bags of dried plantain, saved in the abundant season for his negroes in that season when it yields less abundantly. A new species of corn, I saw also in sacks, which he called melio.

Mr. S. has prepared his last bed, or tomb, at the northern entrance into his estate; and the coffin, he remarked, was to be soon made of incorruptible wood.

He intends soon to hire a musician, to be employed in selecting and instructing a band of forty of his negroes, that they may amuse him in his declining years, and attend him with mournful airs to his grave.

SOURCE: Abiel Abbot, *Letters written in the Interior of Cuba . . . 1828* (Boston: Bowles and Dearborn, 1829), pp. 39–42, 144–45.

48 The Interior of Cuba, 1840

Between the planters of Cuba and those of the British colonies, there is this remarkable difference, than when an Englishman does not reside on his estate, he is an absentee from the island altogether, and is willing to remain in England, or at least in Europe, until he has run so far ahead of his resources, that he is compelled to return to the tropics for the sake of retrenchment. This state of things has given rise to the race of planting attorneys so admirably described in the work of my friend, Dr. Madden, and has also made it necessary to employ a superior class of overseers to those who enjoy the corresponding station of *Mayoral* in the island of Cuba. Unlike the British planter, the Cuba proprietor has no desire to return to the mother country, between which and the colony the ties of affection are becoming daily more relaxed, leaving nothing in their stead but the iron grasp of power, which some unforeseen accident may burst suddenly, at once and for ever.

The Spanish planter, although he does not leave the island, scarcely ever resides on his estate; where there is rarely any mansion house fit for his reception. The great majority of them live constantly at the Havana, and a few have taken up their residence at Santiago and Matanzas, and the minor cities of the island. They may possibly be separated from their estates by a distance of hundreds of miles, without the advantage of any thing in the shape of roads that are either safe or practicable. Finding nothing on his plantation to repay the fatigue of his journey, or supply the place of the luxuries of the colonial capital, he visits it so seldom that he may be considered quite as much an absentee from his estate as the Jamaica planter who has taken up his residence at Rome or Naples.

As the experience of years had taught me to believe that the Spaniards are a kind and warm-hearted race, and as I had frequently been told that the slaveowners of the Havana were the most indulgent masters in the world, I was not a little surprised to find, as the result of personal inquiry and minute observation, that in this last particular I had been most miserably deceived, and that in no quarter, unless, perhaps, in the Brazils, which I have not visited, is the state of slavery so desperately wretched as it is at this moment on the sugar plantations of the queen of the Indies, the far-famed island of Cuba.

The error I had fallen into is so universal among people who have never visited the island, and so common even with those who have made some stay at the Havana but have never proceeded into the interior that when I discovered it, I felt that it deserved some little investigation. When a stranger visits the town residence of a Cuba proprietor, he finds the family surrounded by a little colony of slaves of every variety of complexion from ebony to alabaster. Most of them have been born in the house, have grown with the growth of the family, and are, perhaps, the foster brothers or foster sisters of the master or his children. In such circumstances, it would be surprising if an uncivilized barbarian were to treat them harshly; and for a Spanish, and much more for a Creole, master to do so, imbued as he is with all the warmth of the social affections, is totally out of the question. These long retinues of domestics are kept up by some from an idle love of pageantry, but, by others, from the more honorable desire of not parting with those born under their roof, and for that reason, bearing their name; as it is the practice in Cuba, and in other slave countries into which Africans are imported, for the first proprietor, whether his title be acquired by purchase or inheritance, to bestow his own patronymic, together with a Christian name, on his slave, whether an imported Bozal or an infant Creole, at the time when the indispensable ceremony of baptism is performed.

The distinction of ranks among the various classes of society is as carefully kept up in Cuba as in the most aristocratical countries of the Old World. The first includes the resident grandees of Spain, of whom there are about thirty, the Titulos of Castile, resembling as nearly as possible the anomalous rank of Baronet in England, and the Hacendados, or landed gentry, of the island. Next after them come the Empleados, or civil functionaries in the public offices, of whom, at the Havana alone, there are said to be 1,000; and on the same level with these gentlemen may be placed the officers of the army and navy. The merchants, Spanish, Creole, or foreign, hold only the third place in the order of precedency. After them come their clerks, French, English, North American, or German; such of them as come from Spain being chiefly *Gaditanos.* Retail merchants and shopkeepers hold a still lower station; they come in general from the Canaries, Catalonia, Biscay, or North America. The Gallegos, like our own Irish laborers, occupy the lowest place in the social scale; the colored and negro race being tabooed altogether. The emigrants from Old Spain and the Canaries, but especially the Catalans and Gallegos, with their descendants, may be considered a permanent addition to the population; but foreigners, who generally come as clerks and depart as merchants, take root but rarely.

It has often been remarked that even hired servants have an interest directly opposed to that of their masters. How much more true is the old Latin proverb, "*Quot servi, tot hostes,*" when applied to the owner of a long retinue of slaves? In the course of time the numbers of the domestic colony increase so much, that it becomes necessary to employ them in other than household duties; so that, in one of the great houses of the Havana, you may generally find a tailor and a shoemaker, and perhaps a mantua-maker or a milliner, attached to the establishment. When in the course of years the number of the domestic slaves has increased beyond all bounds, the surplus are allowed to hire themselves out as tradesmen or household servants, on the condition of their bringing home to their owner a fixed sum weekly or monthly from the amount of their earnings; and in justice to the slavemasters of the Havana, it is but fair to add that the exaction thus made is, in general, not so exorbitant but that a prudent and industrious slave might be able in a few years from his surplus earnings to purchase his entire emancipation from bondage, step by step, according to the gradual system prescribed by the Spanish colonial code.

When we get into the country and visit the coffee, and especially the sugar plantations, where I propose by and by to carry the reader, if he has the patience or the heart to accompany me through the revolting details, we shall see how very differently the unhappy field negro is treated. It is there we verify the words of the poet:—

Sunt lachrymae rerum, et mentem mortalia tangunt.

In fact, the most dreadful of all threats with which one of the wealthy inhabitants of the Havana contrives to terrify a delinquent domestic from the errors to which he is prone, is to hint at the necessity of sending him to rusticate for a season, under the charge of the Mayoral, on his master's estate in the country.

In our own sugar colonies, during the prevalence of slavery, there was the same tendency to an unreasonable increase of the planter's domestic establishment, but as "the great house" was probably situated within sight of the sugar mill, so that the master became acquainted with the persons and characters of his field negroes and their families, by daily observation and intercourse, it was not unusual to make exchanges from the house to the field, or vice versa. These changes, although still a punishment sufficiently severe for the one party, had nothing so terrible in their aspect, as the banishment from a life of pampered luxury and ease in the Havana, to that worst of penal settlements, a Cuba sugar plantation. Under the tender mercies of the Mayoral, he knows well before leaving the Havana that he has nothing to expect in the plantation but a wretched existence of overlabor and starvation, accompanied by the application, or at least the constant terror, of the lash as an incentive, relieved only by the hope of that dissolution, which sleepless nights and incessant toils are so speedily and so surely to accomplish.

The change from the apprenticeship to perfect freedom in the British colonies will not be immediately favorable to the supernumerary class of domestics, as the planter can never afford to pay wages to so many servants even in his own family, as he has heretofore been accustomed to allow to his overseer. I have seen, for instance, in the house of an English overseer, whose salary might not, perhaps, exceed some three hundred pounds sterling a year, a most disproportionate array of attendants, butlers, footmen, grooms, stable boys, cooks, housemaids, and washerwomen, amounting altogether to, perhaps, twenty in number, yet not equal, after all, to the third of a great Havana establishment. The state of things in the British colonies to which we have referred, must now of course be altered, and the overseer must be content with an addition to his salary to compensate him for the defalcation in his household arrangements.

To those who are not wilfully blindfold, there are not wanting even at the Havana, not to speak of the sugar or even of the coffee plantations, a thousand palpable indications of the misery which attends the curse of slavery, independent altogether of the superior horrors of the Slave Trade.

On the public Alameda, just outside the gates of the fortified portion of the city, and therefore within the limits of a dense population, there may be seen a modest-looking building protected from public gaze by lofty wooden parapets, in the interior of which are a series of whipping posts, to which unwilling or disobedient slaves are sent to receive their allotted quota of punishment, as a saving of time or labor, or perhaps to spare the too tender feelings of their masters or mistresses. But, although by means of the parapets, the authorities have succeeded in shutting out the inquisitive glances of the passers-by, excluding from public view the streaming blood and lacerated flesh of the sufferers, they have totally failed in shutting in their piercing screams and piteous shrieks for mercy.

Those visitors at the Havana who are accustomed to speak in terms of inconsiderate satisfaction of the comforts and indulgences of the slaves, sometimes sneeringly comparing them with the privations to which an English or an Irish laborer is exposed, have probably never heard of those family arrangements by which the spirit of a slave, who has first been spoiled by overindulgence, is to be systematically and periodically broken. The mistress of many a great family in the Havana will not scruple to tell you that such is the proneness of her people to vice and idleness, she finds it necessary to send one or more of them once a month to the whipping post, not so much on account of any positive delinquency, as because without these periodical advertisements the whole family would become unmanageable, and the master and mistress would lose their authority.

SOURCE: David Turnbull, *Travels in the West: Cuba, with Notes on Porto Rico, and the Slave Trade* (London: Longman, 1840), pp. 47–54.

49 The Cuban Slave Trade, 1841

The question of the slave trade having been of late so frequently a topic of discussion, it may not be disagreeable to your readers to know something of the enormous profit made by West Indian and North American slave dealers; I shall, therefore, hand you for publication a letter addressed to me when I was in America, in 1841, proposing to me to take a share in a speculation of the kind.

The original was written in French, and was addressed to me by Captain Auguste L., one of the most notorious slave dealers, and was delivered to me by his own hand.

The calculations of Captain L., it will be seen, are not quite accurately summed up; still I have sent them as they are, a nearly literal translation, without altering any part of the original.

Heinrich Flindt

Conto Finto of the Probable Result of a Cargo of 250 Negros

Preliminary Expenses

	Dollars
Purchase of a suitable vessel	4,000
Equipment and advance to the crew	2,000
300 muskets, of the usual quality	700
600 machetas, or negro knives	300
1,500 pieces of calico, gingham, &c.	3,000
1,000 pieces of cloth	1,000
1,000 lbs. of tobacco	200
1,500 lbs. of gunpowder	400
800 casks of tafia	200
Bullets, flints, knives, and looking-glasses	400
Fittings up between the decks, chains, 300 small demi-feannes, water casks, and medicine chests	800
	13,000

The captain's wages are 150 dollars a month, besides 12 per-cent. on gross produce of the slaves. The first mate's wages are 80 dollars a month, and four dollars a head on each negro; the second mate 60 dollars, and two dollars a head. The cook receives monthly 50 dollars, the carpenter 50 dollars, and each sailor 35 dollars.

Expenses after landing the negroes

To be paid to the captain and crew, say	16,000
To the consignee	4,000
To the governor, one ounce per head	4,000
	24,000

The value of the ship remains to the owners, say 2500 dollars, and might be sold to cover the cost of lodging and feeding the cargo till the sale.

The gross proceeds of the sale, estimating the 250 negroes to bring the very low price of 22 Spanish ounces, or 374 dollars a head (they seldom bring less than 400 dollars),

would be	dollars 93,500
Deduct expenses	37,000
There will remain a net profit of	56,000

Every thousand-dollar share will, therefore, produce 4,345 dollars netto.

The equipment may take place either at Havana or in the United States. In the latter case, however, the muskets and machetas must be bought at Havana, as these articles would not be easily obtained in an American harbor.

It will be well to let the equipment begin immediately, as about four months are required to complete the affair, namely, between the departure from Havana and the return thither. It would be possible, therefore, to be back in August, and at this season there are few or no cruisers to be apprehended, most of them taking shelter for the winter in the harbors. The moment of landing the slaves is, perhaps, the only one of real danger.

It would be better, in many respects, that this affair should be undertaken in shares.

(From the *Hamburger Nachrichten*)

SOURCE: "The Slave Trade," *The British and Foreign Anti-Slavery Reporter* (December 28, 1842), 79 (3,26):212.

50 A Sugar Plantation in Cuba, 1844

A sugar plantation, during the manufacture of sugar, presents a picture not only of active industry but of unremitting labor. The oxen are reduced towards the end of the season to mere skeletons, many of them dying from overlabor; the negroes are allowed but five hours sleep, but although subjected to this inordinate tasking of their physical powers, in general, preserve their good looks. Before the introduction of the steam-engine, and the example of a milder treatment of the negro by foreign residents in Cuba, the annual loss by death was fully 10 percent, including, however, new slaves, many of whom died from the change of climate. At present the annual loss in Limonar, I was informed by an intelligent English physician, does not exceed 2.5 percent, even including the old. On some plantations, on the south side of the island, the custom still prevails of excluding all female slaves, and even on those where the two sexes are well proportioned in number they do not increase. On a sugar estate employing two hundred slaves, I have seen only three or four children. That this arises from mismanagement is proved by the rapid increase on a few estates where the negroes are well cared for. The Saratoga sugar estate, which with the Carlotta belongs to a highly intelligent merchant of Havana, is noted for the great number of children born on it; while several coffee estates, where the slaves are deprived of sufficient rest, are also unproductive.

It cannot be denied that the slave's life, while employed in the manufacture of sugar, is a very laborious one; from November until the end of May his physical powers are tasked to the utmost, still his peculiar frame of mind, that dwells only on the present, sustains him under it. The weightiest cares cannot drive sleep from his eyelids, or deprive him of his appetite; and so well do the negroes appear even at the end of the grinding season, that one would be tempted to doubt the amount of labor they have performed. During the rest of the year their daily tasks are comparatively light, consisting chiefly in removing the weeds from the fields, and cutting fuel for the next winter.

The greater portion, during the grinding season, are employed in cutting the cane. This is done by a short, swordlike cleaver, one stroke sufficing to cut the stalk close to the ground, and another to remove the unripe tops, which with their leaves are thrown in one long heap, while the rest, divided into two or more sticks, are thrown in another. The latter are removed in carts to the mill, and the tops are left for the cattle to feed on. In the best constructed mills a revolving platform conveys the canes to the rollers, through which they pass, and which express from them all the juice. The crushed stalks fall on another revolving way, and are carried off to a spot where a number of negroes are waiting with baskets to convey them into the yard. They are there exposed to the sun until quite dry, when they are packed under large sheds, and used as fuel for boiling the cane-juice.

The juice flows from the rollers through a gutter into a large reservoir, in which it is gently heated, and where it deposits the dirt and portions of cane that have escaped with it from the rollers. From this it is drawn off into a large cauldron, where it undergoes a rapid boiling, and has its acidity corrected by the admixture of more or less lime. When reduced to a certain degree, it is dipped out by ladles into another cauldron, where it is suffered to boil until it reaches the granulating point. It is now removed by large ladles into a long wooden trough, and stirred by long paddles until cold.

The mass now consists of the granulated sugar and its molasses, and when it is intended simply to remove the latter and make the quality called muscovado, it is conveyed into wooden cisterns twelve feet square and two deep, and thence into the hogsheads, where it undergoes its final draining, the molasses escaping through a hole into gutters, which carry it to a general reservoir.

To make the white Havana quality, it is removed from the trough into earthern or tin conical pans, each capable of holding about 80 lbs. of the mass, having at their apices openings closed with a few dried cane leaves, through which the molasses percolates, and falls into gutters below. Clay, made into a soft paste by being well mixed with water, is next spread over the sugar about three inches thick. The water, separating slowly from it, passes through the brown sugar below, and washes off the molasses from each grain, converting it into the quality known by the name of Havana white. After a certain time the mass becomes consolidated, and the loaf is removed from the pan, and carried to the driers, large wooden frames fixed on railways, on which they can be readily rolled under cover of the shed when it rains. The base of the conical loaf is the whitest, while the apex is of a dirty-brown hue, and the intervening portion of a light brown. It is divided into these three kinds by the negroes, who with their cleavers walk over the sugar with their bare feet, cutting the masses into small lumps. To a stranger the sight of two or three dozen half-naked negroes thus employed under a broiling sun, and sweating over their task, is far from being pleasant; and I have known more than one who have been afterwards very sparing in the use of clayed sugar. A machine has, however, been lately invented for crushing the loaves, and the present unclean method will probably be generally abandoned.

In well constructed furnaces the dried cane stalks called *bagassa,* are found sufficient for boiling the juice, but wood is required to produce steam for the engine. This is brought to the mill at the expense of great labor; and in consequence of its great consumption, large tracts of land are now bare of forests, and the difficulty of procuring fuel increases every year. Much labor is also expended in raising water from the deep wells to supply the engine boiler, the amount of which may be imagined by the reader, when he learns that they are from one to four hundred feet deep, and that the water is generally drawn up by single buckets. During the dry season the sugar planter is also in constant dread of his fields being fired by some malicious neighbor, when in a few hours his whole crop and perhaps all his buildings might be destroyed. The canes are so thickly planted, and their numerous dead leaves form such a closely interwoven mass, that when ignited while the wind is fresh, the flames spread with inconceivable rapidity over the whole field. Although the prince of agriculturists, the sugar planter is now at the mercy of any of the canaille he may have offended, and an opportunity is not unfrequently taken at this season to revenge some past slight or injury.

As soon as the fire is discovered the large bell of the estate, which can be heard several miles, is rapidly tolled, and the neighboring estates at the summons disgorge their troops of slaves, who hasten to the spot. Alleys are cut through the field to the leeward of the burning portion and counterfires ignited, and a large quantity of cane is often thus saved. In some cases the alley is cut too close to the fire, which sweeping across it surrounds the workers, some of whom are not unfrequently suffocated by the dense clouds of smoke. I was present on one occasion, and the scene was most exciting. The roaring of the flames, the sharp cracking of the burning cane, the volumes of smoke that now and then swept along the ground, enveloping everything in its dark cloud, the gang of half-naked negroes, numbering more than five hundred, with their swordlike *machets,* hewing down the canes, while others with torches were setting fire to the windward edge of the road, the mounted mayorals with long swords and holsters galloping about, and shouting out orders and counterorders, and a certain vague sense of danger, combined to render the whole a most animating sight.

It was near midnight when it occurred; and deceived in the distance by the light, I had left the estate, on which I was residing, on foot, and soon learned, to my cost, that I had to walk more than a mile. On my return I lost my way, and had to scramble through briars and over rocks to reach the public road, which I had no sooner done, than I was stopped by a sudden challenge from a man, who stepping from the hedge intercepted me. As he paid no attention to my answers to his demand *quien es?* and kept advancing, I hastily opened a dirk-knife as he came close to me, and prepared for my defense. He was an athletic fellow, the gloom may have made him appear more so, and had I not been completely exhausted by fatigue, it is very probable that I would have retreated, perhaps ran. No other thoughts, however, passed through my mind than of selling my life as dearly as I could when the sharp click of the knife's spring struck his ear, and he stopped suddenly within two feet of me with his hand on his weapon. His bravado instantly ceased, and I found my highway-robber to be only a watch, that had been secreted on the road to arrest any suspicious person he might see lurking about the cane field. He had believed from the click of my knife that it was a pistol, and not knowing me, had been, as he confessed, as heartily frightened as I was. He was the closest approach to a true robber that I had met in three years on the island, and our rencontre ended in our walking together towards our homes, which were close to each other.

To encourage the cultivation of the cane, the Spanish government has granted many privileges to the sugar planter, some of which are at the expense of justice. The island government has, however, never been remarkably overscrupulous in the choice of means to increase its revenue. His slaves cannot be seized for debt, nor can his plantation be sold for less than its value adjudged by arbitration; he pays no tithes on his sugar, and late laws have so well protected him, that the creditor is literally compelled to wait until it suits him to pay his debt. All that he can do, is to place an agent on the estate, who secures the crops, from which, however, the planter can deduct sufficient to support himself and workmen, and to pay all the other necessary expenses of the estate.

The picture I have given of the labor exacted from the slaves on a sugar estate does not apply to all. On some, so well are the tasks regulated, that they do not work more than the English peasant, while on others much cruelty is exercised. This is often the case when the proprietor does not oversee his concerns, but leaves the whole to an administrador, who is expected to make as many boxes of sugar as his predecessor, and if possible a few more. If he fail he is dismissed, so that to secure his place he tries to accomplish the task, regardless of the comfort and lives of those under his authority. A cruel taskmaster is, however, as much detested in Cuba by his brother planters, as a distraining landlord is in England; and it is very doubtful if of the two the latter is not generally the less humane. . . .

No work on Cuba, how limited soever may be its pretensions, would be complete without a review of her system of slavery. The first people enslaved by the Spaniards on the island were the aborigines; but these were soon so much thinned by overlabor, that the race was in danger of becoming at once exterminated. It was to supply their place that, in 1523, three hundred negroes were imported from Africa to till the soil and work in the rich copper mines, and those of gold, that were then eagerly sought after. "Thus," exclaims the pious Arrati, "began that gathering of an infinite number of gentiles to the bosom of our holy religion, who would otherwise have perished in the darkness of paganism." Would that the laws of Spain on the subject of the religious instruction of slaves, than which none could be more liberal, had been enforced; and his countrymen had performed faithfully those duties incumbent on every Christian slaveowner, who, like the head of a family, is accountable for the moral instruction of those under him.

"It is impossible," the same historian continues, "to compute how much the purchase of slaves has cost the island, but the royal company, who were permitted to import only 4,986, paid for them $717,561 and seven rials." The importation of them has continued to this day, but feebly checked by the efforts of Europe and the United States to stop the trade. From the number introduced into the island during the three winters I have spent there, it is probable that nearly two thousand are now annually imported. In 1841 three hundred were openly carried on the deck of a steamboat from Havana to Matanzas; their owner, an Italian, was my fellow-passenger, and I learned that he had made eight hundred thousand dollars by the trade, and intended to continue it until he had accumulated a million. In the spring of 1843 two thousand were congregated in and near Havana for sale, or had been sold at its marts, and much anxiety was felt by the slavers lest the English should notice it; these had been imported within a few months. The whole island is in favor of continuing the trade and consequently no one interferes.

It is related of the British ex-Consul, Mr. Turnbull, that having discovered a thousand of the negroes exposed in the Havana mart to have been just imported, he hastened to the Captain-General with the news, affirming that he knew also the owners and the vessels that had brought them. The latter, with feigned surprise that the laws should be thus openly broken in the very capital, ordered a company of horse to attend Mr. Turnbull to the spot, and capture both the slaves and sellers. On the way thither the commanding officer became suddenly indisposed, and getting rapidly worse, was compelled to stop at his house, where several physicians were soon in attendance on him, and his case was pronounced to be very dangerous. In about three hours, however, he was sufficiently relieved to accompany the consul in a volante at the head of his troop, but when they reached the mart, only a few *ladinos* were found there. The next day a bill of two thousand doubloons was sent to the owners of the slaves; one half as hush-money for the Captain-General, and the other half a remuneration for the physicking the officer of the troop had undergone on their behalf, during which a timely notice had caused them to remove all the *bozales* from the mart. This anecdote, for the truth of which I do not vouch, was circulated in 1841, and is related to show the feelings of the people on the subject.

When brought by the slaver, they are either landed on the coast near the plantations, for which the living cargoes are purchased in advance; or are sent overland to Havana, where they are divided into their different tribes, the value of which differs according to their physical or mental capacities. Thus the Lucomees are fine, athletic men, and when not worried by their overseers, excellent laborers, surpassing in intelligence all the other negroes. They are, however, bold and stubborn if injudiciously treated; and having been in their country at the head of the warlike tribes, if already arrived at manhood when brought from the coast, are much disposed to resist undue oppression from their masters. They are very prone to commit suicide, believing with all Africans that after death they become retransported to their native country.

One of my friends, who had purchased eight newly arrived from the coast, found occasion soon after to chastise slightly one of them. The punishment of the whip is applied to the delinquent lying on his face, and when he was ordered to place himself in that position, the other seven lay down with him, and insisted on being also punished. Their request, however, was not granted, but they were told that if at any time they required it, punishment would be inflicted. I continue the narrative in the words of my friend, although I cannot give his graphic description of the scene that ensued. "The boy was punished," he said, "before breakfast, and I had not been long seated to that meal, when the contra-mayoral (a negro overseer) came to the door, and advised me to go to the negroes, for they were greatly excited, and were singing and dancing. I immediately seized my pistols, and getting on my horse rode with him to the spot. The eight negroes, each one with a rope tied around his neck, on seeing us, scattered in different directions in search of trees on which to hang themselves. Assisted by the other slaves we made all haste to secure them, but two succeeded in killing themselves; the rest, having been cut down before life was extinct, recovered. The captain of partido was summoned to hold his inquest over the dead bodies, which he examined minutely to see if any marks of the whip could be discovered, but fortunately for me there was not a single one, or I should have had to pay a heavy bill.

"The rest refused to work, and I asked the captain if I punished them, and they then committed suicide, would I be chargeable with the result; he answered that I certainly would be, if he found the smallest sign of injury on their bodies. My neighbors then offered each to take one home, but they would not consent to be separated, and I was quite at a loss what to do; when I determined to run the risk of the law, and punished all the six. They went to work immediately, they are now in the gang, and are the best behaved of all my negroes."

The Caraballis are like the Lucomees, quick-tempered, and require to be watched; their neighbors, the Lalas, are similar to them, and both generally come intermingled with the first. In consequence of the warlike propensities of these three tribes, not as many of them are made prisoners in Africa and sold to the slavers as of the other tribes. The Gangas and Mandigoes are the most tractable and trustworthy. The Congos are stupid, great drunkards and sensualists; the Longos are hard to learn, but are lively; the Maguas are as brutal as the Congos; the Queesees are like the Mandigoes, and are as much sought after for their honesty; the Breechees and Minas resemble somewhat the Lucomees but are differently marked, while the Neebees are remarkable for their lively disposition. These different tribes are distinguished either by peculiar cuts and tattooing on their faces and bodies, or by their stature and habits, some being quite free from marks.

They bring with them from Africa all their original animosity against each other, having themselves in many cases been made prisoners by each other's tribe, and thus been transported to Cuba; and it is often a difficult task for the mayoral to decide correctly in the mutual accusations made to him, and distinguish between the true and false. This mutual jealousy, also, will ever prevent the combination of any large number for the purposes of insurrection to remain long secret, and with her present slave population Cuba need never fear a simultaneous rising.

With so many different dispositions to curb or direct, it will readily be seen that the treatment of the slaves must vary much. They are, indeed, governed more by the fear of punishment than are the slaves in our Southern States; but then the Spaniard has a wild, untutored man to deal with, while we have one greatly superior to his parent stock in intelligence and morality. I do not think they accomplish much more than our tasked slaves, especially those on coffee estates, but they are worked more constantly. The chief object in Cuba seems to be never to let them remain idle; and I have excited the astonishment of many a Creole, by stating the quantity of leisure our slaves enjoy after their daily tasks are over; they could not believe they would remain disciplined. Nor was their astonishment lessened when I told them that in my native State, South Carolina, some planters paid missionaries to preach to their slaves, had chapels erected on their estates, and sometimes exhorted them in the absence of clergymen.

The laws in Cuba regulating slavery are, however, very liberal to the slave. Thus by them every owner is bound to instruct his slaves in the principles of the Catholic religion, after the labor of the day has been finished, to the end that they may be baptized and partake of the sacrament. On Sundays and feast-days they are not to be employed longer than two hours, for the necessary labor of the estate, the feeding the animals, etc., except when the gathering of the crop admits of no delay. They are required to have daily six or eight plantains, or an equivalent in potatoes, yams, yucas, or other edible roots, eight ounces of meat or fish, and four ounces of rice or flour. The quantity of clothes is also prescribed, and the treatment of women who are *enciente* or nursing, with respect to the amount of their labor, diet, and lodgings.

Except during the harvest of the canes on sugar estates, when they may be employed sixteen hours daily, they are not to be worked longer than nine or ten hours; and on Sundays and other holidays they must be allowed to attend to their own gardens and private occupations. Those only between sixteen and sixty years can be employed in tasks, nor shall any who are disabled by injuries or old age be liberated, without granting them sufficient funds for a permanent subsistence.

Illicit intercourse shall be prohibited by their owners, and matrimonial alliances encouraged; nor shall the slaves of different masters be forbid to intermarry. When this takes place, and neither master will sell his respective slave for a reasonable price, that they might live together under one roof, both slaves united in marriage shall be sold to a third person. Owners who maltreat their slaves shall be compelled by a magistrate to sell them, and if a slave desire to buy his freedom, he shall obtain it for the actual valuation decided by arbitration. By paying not less than fifty dollars of his value he may purchase a smaller or larger portion of his liberty; and if sold to another owner, that sum must be deducted from his purchase money, so that he may accomplish his liberation whenever the balance of his first valuation shall have been paid. Three arbiters are chosen to decide the value of a slave; one by the master, and two by the *Sindico Procurador general.*

Liberty and fifty dollars shall be bestowed on any slave who shall have given information respecting a conspiracy of his fellow-slaves or of free persons; the purchase of his freedom and the reward to be paid out of the public funds from fines inflicted on slaveowners. No owner is allowed to give more than twenty-five lashes to a slave, and for offenses calling for a severe punishment, the latter must be tried before a magistrate. Criminal processes shall be instituted against those who maim or otherwise seriously injure their slaves, whom they shall then, moreover, be compelled to sell. Other penalties, in fines of twenty to two hundred dollars, shall be inflicted on the owners who disobey the laws relating to slavery.

No slave shall leave the estate of his master with arms, unless accompanied by the latter, when he may carry his machete, nor when alone, without a license. At night they shall all be enclosed within the boheas, the general gate of which shall be secured by a lock; and the two guards placed to watch at night, shall inform the mayoral of any disturbance among them. After nine o'clock they must all retire to their rooms, and only on Sundays and feast days shall they be permitted to play on their drums, or indulge in their national dances and other amusements.

The local laws of Cuba, from which the preceding has been condensed, also oblige the public officers of justice to attend personally to the observance of these regulations, holding them responsible for all omissions of duty. But this article caused so much dissatisfaction to the planters, that the Captain-General, Valdes, issued a circular absolving them from this duty, and limited their obligations to the hearing complaints made before them.

These laws are not all observed, but so many are, that the slave in Cuba is in some respects better off than the European peasant. With respect to the religious and moral government of them, baptism and burial in consecrated ground are alone enforced. On a few Spanish estates prayers are repeated to them before going to work in the morning, and before retiring to their dormitories; but no attention is paid to the matrimonial compact, some being polygamists, and others making mutual exchanges of their wives when tired of them. In the country the slaves do not often compel their masters to sell them to other owners more to their liking, but this not unfrequently is done in cities; and both on plantations and in towns many annually purchase their freedom against the will of their owners.

The Creoles have an excellent custom respecting a runaway slave.

The delinquent gives himself up to a neighbor of his master, who becomes his *padrino,* and intercedes for him. Unless his offense is very grievous he is forgiven, and returns to his work unpunished. On an adjoining sugar estate, through the negligence of the guards at night, several hogs were stolen. The four negroes on duty discovered the loss, and to avoid the punishment of their carelessness ran away. The owner was very vexed at this double crime, and threatened condign punishment on all four, but he was outwitted by his absconded slaves. Daily was one presented to him by the physician of the estate, Dr. H., a kind-hearted Yankee, who acted as their *padrino;* and three, through his intercessions, were pardoned. But the fourth remained in the woods several weeks, and on him the owner declared all the merited punishment should fall. At length one morning he saw him trotting by the horse of the doctor, who had once more been applied to as padrino. "You need not intercede for him," he exclaimed when he approached, "you well know that I have determined to punish him, and that he richly deserves it." The doctor made no reply, but dismounting from his horse, fell on his knees with mock humility before the master, and implored the pardon of his slave. It was too much for the gravity of the Spaniard, and the prayer was granted.

During the winter, when the labor on the sugar estates is very great, many of the slaves abscond, and lead a roving life in the woods. They often make extensive depredations on the hogs and plantains of the coffee planters, and are sometimes hunted by bloodhounds. The greatest number are captured by the slaves on the different estates, who obtain from the captain of partido four dollars for each prisoner; and they are as active in the chase, as they would be in their native forests to collect a supply for the slavers. On a single estate, where I resided, ten runaways were caught in a few months by three or four of the negroes, who at their own request were permitted to patrol about the grounds after the last curfew. Notwithstanding all these means, some contrive to lead a wandering life for several years; and the mountains about the Pan of Matanzas, and several of the savannas, have ever been favorite hiding-places for them. Armed with spears, made of the hard woods of the island, and the machetes they had stolen from their masters, they are often very formidable to those who with bloodhounds make it a business to ferret them out of their retreats.

I have already noted the mortality of the slaves, and the propensity of some tribes to commit suicide; the following summary of the interments in the cemetery of Limonar from the 1st of July, 1842, to the 5th of July, 1843, which was kindly furnished by the worthy padre of that district, will give the relative mortality of the white and colored population: Whites,—27 men, 4 boys, 7 women, 4 girls; total, 42; Slaves,—92 men, 20 boys, 34 women, 21 girls; total, 167; Free colored,—5 men, 1 woman; total, 6. Of these, one white man and nine negroes committed suicide, two negroes were accidently drowned, and one of the free blacks was murdered by his own slave. This would reduce the mortality by sickness, among the whites, to 41, and among the slaves to 156. I could not ascertain the exact population of the curacy, the dead of which were buried in the cemetery of Limonar; but that of the partido Guamacaro, in which it is situated, is 1,196 whites, and 11,813 slaves. By this it will be seen that the relative mortality of the whites was more than twice as great as that of the slave population, completely refuting the absurd tales told of the numbers of the latter killed by overlabor.

SOURCE: J. G. F. Wurdeman, *Notes on Cuba* (Boston: Munroe, 1844), pp. 152–59, 253–63.

51 The Life of a Slave, 1851

The "bujios" or huts of the negroes . . . formed quite a little village of themselves. A day's proceedings on this estate is soon described, as things went on beneath the strict yet merciful sway of my good friend. Bitterly, I make no doubt, do the negroes, poor creatures, feel his loss! The head overseer's berth, on an estate like this, is verily no sinecure. He must be watchful and wakeful as a cat; for if *he* slept, who would think himself called on to wake? Accordingly, when the morning star indicates the near approach of dawn, he rises and generally rings the great bell himself. This is called the "Ave Maria," and it is pleasant to hear the hour struck by a number of bells, when many estates join. That no one may mistake the exact moment, they publish it in the journals, and overseers near Habana make a point of being exact to a second. The negroes, who are however already up, are allowed some little time to get ready, and, in effect, *they* chiefly make good use of their minutes by warming a cup of coffee for themselves, and a cake of maize, or roasting a plantain or two, before encountering the hard morning's work. When now the dawn is plainly declared, two or three taps more are given on the bell and the whole sally forth. In crop time, however, those who are engaged in the boiling are exempt from this rule, they being divided into *watches* of twelve hours turn generally, and in the same way hands are retained to feed the mill. Sometimes, when hard-pressed for time, they retain the same hands to feed the mill, which work has not to be continued always; but four rests of two hours each are allowed in the twenty-four hours, which it must be confessed is certainly a full proportion of *work.* All arrived at the overseer's quarter, he reads the names, to which all must answer. They are generally fully informed of their work for the day, on the preceding evening; of course in crop time the only work is cutting and carting canes. Before the last name on the roll is called, they all file off down the hill; the second overseer, already mounted on his pony, brings up the rear. In a few minutes more, the oxen are taken out of the pens and stalls, and yoked, and soon a long string of carts rattle down after the negroes. When certain descriptions of work are going on, they are done by task work; cane cutting is one. According to the growth of the canes, four or five cartloads may be cut by a slave, and they generally finish their task by two o'clock, and spend the rest of the day in their "cunucus." But who is the negro that is not blessed with a sweetheart or a wife? Alas for him, the lady sometimes lags; and as they are the pink of gallantry, he must finish her task for her also, that they may spend the evening together.

The bell again sounds at twelve, and generally an hour and a half's recess is allowed for dinner. This is cooked for some by the owner (for as many as so ask it), or else is served out raw once a week to men with wives, to cook as they please. They are not all bound to present themselves at noon, for most prefer to hold out till they finish the task. In weeding also, and work of that kind, the overseer leaves it optional with them whether they will take a certain piece of work as a task, or "stick it out" the whole day. They generally prefer the former, and it is surprising to see how hard they will labor. The overseer watches them as does a cat a mouse; he is "up to" every "dodge" in the negro calendar of schemes, and detects in a second the quickest possibly executed movement, of covering a tough root with a weed or by a little earth, with the *toe* or the *hoe.*

After the sun has set about a quarter of an hour, the bell is again sounded; this is called "La Oracion," or the hour of prayer. The negroes may now go where they please for the next two hours. At the end of that time the bell is smartly struck three or four times, and all repair to the front of the mill house. They are now expected to work an hour by the light of a large fire of cane trash, which is kept burning in the middle of the yard, when there is no moon. This work is called "La fagina," because performed at the light of a faggot. The negroes, so far from making any objection to this, would not miss it on any account. During the *fagina,* the overseers never get angry, and the negroes take many liberties they would not dare to do at other times. In crop time the *fagina* is taken advantage of, to get into the house the "magass" (dried squeezed canes) used for fuel, and which have not all been stored up during the day, after which every one seizes a broom, and sweeps the whole yard as clean as possible. All loose canes are collected and piled near the mill. If masons are at work, bricks are placed ready for the next day, and large logs are rolled for the carpenters or the sawmill. At nine, the bell sounds a stroke, and the *fagina* being over, all come together; the roll is called, and the people file off one by one repeating "Buenas noches, mi amo" (good night, my master). At half past nine, two very light strokes of the bell are heard, the signal for silence and sleep.

People will think this a very agreeable picture perhaps of the life of a slave? Maybe a day's experience would undeceive them. The overseer's is bad enough, as I can tell. During the kind administration of my friend, indeed, these negroes had little to complain of, but afterwards I greatly doubt they did not fare so well, since I heard of *fifty* hogsheads of sugar hinted at, in place of thirty! Speaking of the "fagina," that is also the time when the negroes are punished, if it is necessary. By the laws of Cuba, no negro can be punished on the spot. If his offense is something very heinous, he is handcuffed or put in the stocks till night; the case is regularly heard, and the full number of lashes (twenty-five) permitted by law are given *in the evening,* or a less number, as the owner or head overseer may order. I do not deny that sometimes the number twenty-five is exceeded, but very seldom, to my knowledge. It is against the law however, and the owner or manager could be fined if *his* gold was not more powerful than the negro's complaint to the "protegidor," a government official.

SOURCE: J. G. Taylor, *The United States and Cuba* (London: Bentley, 1851), pp. 185–88.

52 The Rights of a Slave, 1859

It is difficult to come to a satisfactory conclusion as to the number of slaves in Cuba. The census of 1857 puts it at 375,000; but neither this census nor that of 1853 is to be relied upon, on this point. The Cubans are taxed for their slaves, and the government find it difficult, as I have said, to get correct returns. No person of intelligence in Cuba, however desirous to put the number at the lowest, has stated it to me at less than 500,000. Many set it at 700,000. I am inclined to think that 600,000 is the nearest to the truth.

The census makes the free blacks, in 1857, 125,000. It is thought to be 200,000, by the best authorities. The whites are about 700,000. The only point in which the census seems to agree with public opinion, is in the proportion. Both make the proportion of blacks to be about one free black to three slaves; and make the whites not quite equal to the entire number of blacks, free and slave together.

To ascertain the condition of slaves in Cuba, two things are to be considered: first, the laws, and secondly, the execution of the laws. The written laws, there is no great difficulty in ascertaining. As to their execution, there is room for opinion. At this point, one general remark should be made, which I deem to be of considerable importance. The laws relating to slavery do not emanate from the slave-holding mind; nor are they interpreted or executed by the slave-holding class. The slave benefits by the division of power and property between the two rival and even hostile races of whites, the Creoles and the Spaniards. Spain is not slave-holding, at home; and so long as the laws are made in Spain, and the civil offices are held by Spaniards only, the slave has at least the advantage of a conflict of interests and principles, between the two classes that are concerned in his bondage.

The fact that one Negro in every four is free, indicates that the laws favor emancipation. They do both favor emancipation, and favor the free blacks after emancipation. The stranger visiting Havana will see a regiment of one thousand free black volunteers, parading with the troops of the line and the white volunteers, and keeping guard in the Obra Pia. When it is remembered that the bearing arms and performing military duty as volunteers is esteemed an honor and privilege, and is not allowed to the whites of Creole birth, except to a few who are favored by the government, the significance of this fact may be appreciated. The Cuban slaveholders are more impatient under this favoring of the free blacks than under almost any other act of the government. They see in it an attempt, on the part of the authorities, to secure the sympathy and cooperation of the free blacks, in case of a revolutionary movement—to set race against race, and to make the free blacks familiar with military duty, while the whites are growing up in ignorance of it. In point of civil privileges, the free blacks are the equals of the whites. In course of law, as witnesses or parties, no difference is known; and they have the same rights as to the holding of lands and other property. As to their social position, I have not the means of speaking. I should think it quite as good as it is in New England, if not better.

So far as to the position of the blacks, when free. The laws also directly favor emancipation. Every slave has a right to go to a magistrate and have himself valued, and on paying the valuation, to receive his free papers. The valuation is made by three assessors, of whom the master nominates one and the magistrate the other two. The slave is not obliged to pay the entire valuation at once; but may pay it in installments, of not less than fifty dollars each. These payments are not made as mere advances of money, on the security of the master's receipt, but are part purchases. Each payment makes the slave an owner of such a portion of himself, *pro parte indivisa,* or as the common law would say, in tenancy-in-common, with his master. If the valuation be one thousand dollars, and he pays one hundred dollars, he is owned, one-tenth by himself and nine-tenths by his master. It has been said, in nearly all the American books on Cuba, that, on paying a share, he becomes entitled to a corresponding share of his time and labor; but, from the best information I can get, I think this is a mistake. The payment affects the proprietary title, but not the usufruct. Until all is paid, the master's dominion over the slave is not reduced, as respects either discipline, or labor, or right of transfer; but if the slave is sold, or goes by operation of law to heirs or legatees or creditors, they take only the interest not paid for, subject to the right of future payment under the valuation.

There is another provision, which, at first sight, may not appear very important, but which is, I am inclined to think, the best practical protection the slave has against ill-treatment by his master: that is, the right to a compulsory sale. A slave may, on the same process of valuation compel his master to transfer him to any person who will pay the money. For this purpose, he need establish no cause of complaint. It is enough if he desires to be transferred, and some one is willing to buy him. This operates as a check upon the master, and an inducement to him to remove special causes of dissatisfaction; and it enables the better class of slaveholders in a neighborhood, if cases of ill-usage are known, to relieve the slave, without contention or pecuniary loss.

In making the valuation, whether for emancipation or compulsory transfer, the slave is to be estimated at his value as a common laborer, according to his strength, age, and health. If he knows an art or trade, however much that may add to his value, only one hundred dollars can be added to the estimate for this trade or art. Thus the skill, industry, and character of the slave do not furnish an obstacle to his emancipation or transfer. On the contrary, all that his trade or art adds to his value, above one hundred dollars, is, in fact, a capital for his benefit.

There are other provisions for the relief of the slave, which, although they make even a better show on paper, are of less practical value. On complaint and proof of cruel treatment, the law will dissolve the relations between master and slave. No slave can be flogged with more than twenty-five lashes, by the master's authority. If his offense is thought greater than that punishment will suffice for, the public authorities must be called in. A slave mother may buy the freedom of her infant, for twenty-five dollars. If slaves have been married by the Church they cannot be separated against their will; and the mother has the right to keep her nursing child. Each slave is entitled to his time on Sundays and all other holidays, beyond two hours allowed for necessary labor, except on sugar estates during the grinding season. Every slave born on the island is to be baptized and instructed in the Catholic faith, and to receive Christian burial. Formerly, there were provisions requiring religious services and instruction on each plantation, according to its size; but I believe these are either repealed, or become a dead letter. There are also provisions respecting the food, clothing, and treatment of slaves in other respects, and the providing of a sick room and medicines, etc.; and the goverment has appointed magistrates, styled síndicos, numerous enough, and living in all localities, whose duty it is to attend to the petitions and the complaints of slaves, and to the measures relating to their sale, transfer, or emancipation.

As to the enforcement of these laws, I have little or no personal knowledge to offer; but some things, I think, I may treat as reasonably sure, from my own observation, and from the concurrent testimony of books, and of persons of all classes with whom I have conversed.

The rule respecting religion is so far observed as this, the infants are baptized, and all receive Christian burial. But there is no enforcement of the obligation to give the slaves religious instruction, or to allow them to attend public religious service. Most of those in the rural districts see no church and no priest, from baptism to burial. If they do receive religious instruction, or have religious services provided for them, it is the free gift of the master.

Marriage by the Church is seldom celebrated. As in the Roman Church marriage is a sacrament and indissoluble, it entails great inconvenience upon the master, as regards sales or mortgages, and is a restraint on the Negroes themselves, to which it is not always easy to reconcile them. Consequently, marriages are usually performed by the master only, and of course, carry with them no legal rights or duties. Even this imperfect and dissoluble connection has been but little attended to. While the slave trade was allowed, the planters supplied their stock with bozales (native Africans) and paid little attention, even on economic principles, to the improvement, or, speaking after the fashion of cattle-farms, to the increase of stock on the plantation. Now that importation is more difficult, and labor is in demand, their attention is more turned to their own stock, and they are beginning to learn, in the physiology of increase, that canon which the Everlasting has fixed against promiscuous intercourse.

The laws respecting valuation, the purchase of freedom at once or by installments, and the compulsory transfer, I know to be in active operation in the towns, and on plantations affording easy access to towns or magistrates. I heard frequent complaints from slaveholders and those who sympathized with them, as to the operation of these provisions. A lady in Havana had a slave who was an excellent cook; and she had been offered $1,700 for him, and refused it. He applied for valuation for the purpose of transfer, and was valued at $1,000 as a laborer, which, with the $100 for his trade, made a loss to the owner of $600, and, as no slave can be subsequently sold for a larger sum than his valuation, this provision gave the slave a capital of $600. Another instance was of a planter near Matanzas, who had a slave taught as a carpenter; but after learning his trade, the slave got himself transferred to a master in the city, for the opportunity of working out his freedom, on holidays and in extra hours. So general is the enforcement of these provisions that it is said to have resulted in a refusal of many masters to teach their slaves any art or trade, and in the hiring of the labor of artisans of all sorts, and the confining of the slaves to mere manual labor. I heard of complaints of the conduct of individuals who were charged with attempting to influence the credulous and too ready slaves to agree to be transferred to them, either to gratify some ill-will against the owner, or for some supposed selfish interest. From the frequency of this tone of complaint and anecdote, as well as from positive assertions on good authority, I believe these provisions to have considerable efficacy.

As to the practical advantage the slaves can get from these provisions in remote places; and as to the amount of protection they get anywhere from the special provisions respecting punishment, food, clothing, and treatment generally, almost everything lies in the region of opinion. There is no end to statement and anecdote on each side. If one cannot get a full and lengthened personal experience, not only as the guest of the slaveholder, but as the companion of the local magistrates, of the lower officers on the plantation, of slave dealers and slave hunters, and of the emancipated slaves, I advise him to shut his ears to mere anecdotes and general statements and to trust to reasonable deductions from established facts. The established facts are, that one race, having all power in its hands, holds an inferior race in slavery; that this bondage exists in cities, in populous neighborhoods, and in remote districts; that the owners are human beings, of tropical races, and the slaves are human beings just emerging from barbarism, and that no small part of this power is exercised by a low-lived and low-minded class of intermediate agents. What is likely to be the effect on all the parties to this system, judging from all we know of human nature?

If persons coming from the North are credulous enough to suppose that they will see chains and stripes and tracks of blood; and if, taking letters to the best class of slaveholders, seeing their way of life, and hearing their dinner-table anecdotes, and the breakfast-table talk of the ladies, they find no outward signs of violence or corruption, they will probably, also, be credulous enough to suppose they have seen the whole of slavery. They do not know that that large plantation, with its smoking chimneys, about which they hear nothing, and which their host does not visit, has passed to the creditors of the late owner, who is a bankrupt, and is in charge of a manager, who is to get all he can from it in the shortest time, and to sell off the slaves as he can, having no interest, moral or pecuniary, in their future. They do not know that the barking last night was a pursuit and capture, in which all the white men on the place took part; and that, for the week past, the men of the plantation have been a committee of detective and protective police. They do not know that the ill-looking man who was there yesterday, and whom the ladies did not like, and all treated with ill-disguised aversion, is a professed hunter of slaves. They have never seen or heard of the Sierra del Cristal, the mountain range at the eastern end of Cuba, inhabited by runaways, where white men hardly dare to go. Nor do they know that those young ladies, when little children, were taken to the city in the time of the insurrection in the Vuelta de Arriba. They have not heard the story of that downcast-looking girl, the now incorrigibly malignant Negro, and the lying mayoral. In the cities, they are amused by the flashy dresses, indolence, and good humor of the slaves, and pleased with the respectfulness of their manners, and hear anecdotes of their attachment to their masters, and how they so dote upon slavery that nothing but bad advice can entice them into freedom; and are told, too, of the worse condition of the free blacks. They have not visited the slave jails, or the whipping-posts in the house outside the walls, where low whites do the flogging of the city house servants, men and women, at so many reals a head.

But the reflecting mind soon tires of the anecdotes of injustice, cruelty, and licentiousness on the one hand, and of justice, kindness, and mutual attachment, on the other. You know that all coexist; but in what proportion you can only conjecture. You know what slavery must be, in its effect on both the parties to it. You seek to grapple with the problem itself. And, stating it fairly, it is this—Shall the industry of Cuba go on, or shall the island be abandoned to a state of nature? If the former, and if the whites cannot do the hard labor in that climate, and the blacks can, will the seven hundred thousand whites, who own all the land and improvements, surrender them to the blacks and leave the island, or will they remain? If they must be expected to remain, what is to be the relation of the two races? The blacks must do the hard work, or it will not be done. Shall it be the enforced labor of slavery, or shall the experiment of free labor be tried? Will the goverment try the experiment, and if so, on what terms and in what manner? If something is not done by the government, slavery will continue; for a successful insurrection of slaves in Cuba is impossible, and manumissions do not gain upon the births and importations.

SOURCE: Richard Henry Dana, Jr., *To Cuba and Back: A Vacation Voyage* (Boston: Ticknor and Fields, 1859), pp. 120–28.

53 Chinese Slave Labor in Cuba, 1862: A Comparison

The manual labor on these plantations is performed almost entirely by slaves—"Congoes" as they are called here, and "Coolies" from the Celestial Empire. These two classes of operatives, though intimately associated, are by no means alike in appearance or disposition. The former are natives of Africa, jet black, with short crispy hair, and are slaves *for life.* The latter are of Asiatic origin, copper-colored, with long, straight, black hair, and are slaves for a *term of years.* They are less stubborn and intractable than the negro, but more crafty, unprincipled, and revengeful; and if thwarted in any of their designs, or punished, however slightly, for any offense, they frequently commit suicide, knowing that the loss of their services would be a serious inconvenience, if not a great pecuniary misfortune to their masters. It appears that these Coolies go into servitude voluntarily. They enter into contract with the importer or his agent in China, to serve them or their assigns during a term of eight years from the date of the agreement, for the nominal sum of four dollars a month. At the expiration of that time they are to be sent back to their own country—if they are alive and desire to return—free of charge or expense to themselves. A bond to that effect is required by the Chinese authorities before they will allow their subjects to be taken away. So great is the demand on this island for the labor of these orientals, that the importer frequently receives a bonus of three or four hundred dollars per head for their services during eight years, notwithstanding their ignorance of the Spanish language, liability to disease, and well-known propensity to commit suicide upon the slightest provocation. Cargoes of these oriental productions are of frequent arrival, and their importation has become an important item in the commerce of Cuba.

During the manufacturing season—a period of about four months—the *ingénio* presents a scene of unceasing labor and activity. The engine is kept at work night and day, and the slaves are allowed but four or five hours' sleep out of the twenty-four; although at other times they can, if they choose, sleep from the setting to the rising of the sun. Notwithstanding this increase of labor, the slaves do not appear to dread the sugar season, for they are better fed during that period, and are allowed many privileges and indulgences that they do not have at other times, and which, to them, are more than equivalent to any excess of labor that may be imposed on them.

SOURCE: Carlton H. Rogers, *Incidents of Travel in the Southern States and Cuba* (New York: Craigshead, 1862), pp. 119–21.

54 A Diamond Mine in Brazil, 1812

This rich river, formed by the junction of a number of streams which will be hereafter noted, is as wide as the Thames at Windsor, and in general from three to nine feet deep. The part now in working is a curve or elbow, from which the current is diverted into a canal cut across the tongue of land, round which it winds, the river being stopped just below the head of the canal by an embankment, formed of several thousand bags of sand. This is a work of considerable magnitude, and requires the cooperation of all the negroes to complete it; for, the river being wide and not very shallow, and also occasionally subject to overflows, they have to make the embankment so strong as to resist the pressure of the water, admitting it to rise four or five feet.

The deeper parts of the channel of the river are laid dry by means of large *caissons* or chain-pumps, worked by a water-wheel. The mud is then carried off, and the *cascalho* is dug up and removed to a convenient place for washing. This labor was, until lately, performed by the negroes, who carried the *cascalho* in *gamellas* on their heads, but Dr. Camara has formed two inclined planes about one hundred yards in length, along which carts are drawn by a large water-wheel, divided into two parts, the ladles or buckets of which are so constructed that the rotatory motion may be altered by changing the current of water from one side to the other; this wheel, by means of a rope made of untanned hides, works two carts, one of which descends empty on one inclined plane, while the other, loaded with *cascalho,* is drawn to the top of the other inclined plane, where it falls into a cradle, empties itself, and descends in its turn. At a work, called Cangica, formerly of great importance, about a mile up the river on the opposite side, there are three cylindrical engines (*wims*) for drawing the *cascalho,* like those used in the mining country of Derbyshire, and also railways over some uneven ground. This was the first and only machinery of consequence which I saw in the Diamond District, and there appear many obstacles to the general introduction of it. Timber, when wanted of large size, has to be fetched a distance of one hundred miles at a very heavy expense; there are few persons competent to the construction of machines, and the workmen dislike to make them, fearing that this is only part of a general plan for superseding manual labor.

The stratum of *cascalho* consists of the same materials with that in the gold district. On many parts, by the edge of the river, are large conglomerated masses of rounded pebbles cemented by oxide of iron, which sometimes envelop gold and diamonds. They calculate on getting as much *cascalho* in the dry season as will occupy all their hands during the months which are more subject to rain. When carried from the bed of the river whence it is dug, it is laid in heaps containing apparently from five to fifteen tons each.

Water is conveyed from a distance, and is distributed to the various parts of the works by means of aqueducts, constructed with great ingenuity and skill. The method of washing for diamonds at this place is as follows: A shed is erected in the form of a parallelogram, twenty-five or thirty yards long, and about fifteen wide, consisting of upright posts which support a roof thatched with long grass. Down the middle of the area of this shed a current of water is conveyed through a canal covered with strong planks, on which the *cascalho* is laid two or three feet thick. On the other side of the area is a flooring of planks, from four to five yards long, embedded in clay, extending the whole length of the shed, and having a slope from the canal, of three or four inches to a yard. This flooring is divided into about twenty compartments or troughs, each about three feet wide, by means of planks placed on their edge. The upper ends of all these troughs (here called canoes) communicate with the canal, and are so formed that water is admitted into them between two planks that are about an inch separate. Through this opening the current falls about six inches into the trough, and may be directed to any part of it, or stopped at pleasure by means of a small quantity of clay. For instance, sometimes water is required only from one corner of the aperture, then the remaining part is stopped; sometimes it is wanted from the center, then the extremes are stopped; and sometimes only a gentle rill is wanted, then the clay is applied accordingly. Along the lower ends of the troughs a small channel is dug to carry off the water.

On the heap of *cascalho,* at equal distances, are placed three high chairs * for the officers or overseers. After they are seated, the negroes † enter the troughs, each provided with a rake of a peculiar form and short handle, with which he rakes into the trough about fifty or eighty pounds of weight of *cascalho.* The water being then let in upon it, the *cascalho* is spread abroad and continually raked up to the head of the trough, so as to be kept in constant motion. This operation is performed for the space of a quarter of an hour; the water then begins to run clearer, having washed the earthy particles away, the gravel-like matter is raked up to the end of the trough; after the current flows away quite clear, the largest stones are thrown out, and afterwards those of inferior size, then the whole is examined with great care for diamonds.‡ When a negro finds one, he immediately stands upright and claps his hands, then extends them, holding the gem between his forefinger and thumb; an

* In order to insure the vigilance of the overseers, these chairs are constructed without backs or any other support on which a person can recline.

† The negroes employed in these works are the property of individuals, who let them to hire at the daily rate of three *vintens* of gold, equal to about eightpence, Government supplying them with victuals. Every officer of the establishment is allowed the privilege of having a certain number of negroes employed.

‡ The negroes are constantly attending to the *cascalho* from the very commencement of the washings, and frequently find diamonds before this last operation.

overseer receives it from him, and deposits it in a *gamella* or bowl, suspended from the center of the structure, half full of water. In this vessel all the diamonds found in the course of the day are placed, and at the close of the work are taken out and delivered to the principal officer, who, after they have been weighed, registers the particulars in a book kept for that purpose.

When a negro is so fortunate as to find a diamond of the weight of an *octavo* (17½ carats), much ceremony takes place; he is crowned with a wreath of flowers and carried in procession to the administrator, who gives him his freedom, by paying his owner for it. He also receives a present of new clothes, and is permitted to work on his own account. When a stone of eight or ten carats is found, the negro receives two new shirts, a complete new suit, with a hat and a handsome knife. For smaller stones of trivial amount proportionate premiums are given. During my stay at Tejuco a stone of 16 ½ carats was found: it was pleasing to see the anxious desire manifested by the officers, that it might prove heavy enough to entitle the poor negro to his freedom; and when, on being delivered and weighed, it proved only a carat short of the requisite weight, all seemed to sympathize in his disappointment.

Many precautions are taken to prevent the negroes from embezzling diamonds. Although they work in a bent position, and consequently never know whether the overseers are watching them or not, yet it is easy for them to omit gathering any which they see, and to place them in a corner of the trough for the purpose of secreting them at leisure hours, to prevent which they are frequently changed while the operation is going on. A word of command being given by the overseers, they instantly move into each other's troughs, so that no opportunity of collusion can take place. If a negro be suspected of having swallowed a diamond, he is confined in a strong room until the fact can be ascertained. Formerly the punishment inflicted on a negro for smuggling diamonds was confiscation of his person to the state; but it being thought too hard for the owner to suffer for the offense of his servant, the penalty has been commuted for personal imprisonment and chastisement. This is a much lighter punishment than that which their owners or any white man would suffer for a similar offense.

There is no particular regulation respecting the dress of the negroes: they work in the clothes most suitable to the nature of their employment, generally in a waistcoat and a pair of drawers, and not naked, as some travelers have stated. Their hours of labor are from a little before sunrise until sunset, half an hour being allowed for breakfast, and two hours at noon. While washing they change their posture as often as they please, which is very necessary, as the work requires them to place their feet on the edges of the trough, and to stoop considerably. This posture is particularly prejudicial to young growing negroes, as it renders them in-kneed. Four or five times during the day they all rest, when snuff, of which they are very fond, is given to them.

The negroes are formed into working parties, called troops, containing two hundred each, under the direction of an administrator and inferior officers. Each troop has a clergyman and a surgeon to attend it. With respect to the subsistence of the negroes, although the present governor has in some degree improved it by allowing a daily portion of fresh beef, which was not allowed by his predecessors, yet I am sorry to observe that it is still poor and scanty: and in other respects they are more hardly dealt with than those of any other establishment which I visited: notwithstanding this, the owners are all anxious to get their negroes into the service.

SOURCE: John Mawe, *Travels in the Interior of Brazil* (London: Longman, 1812), pp. 314–20.

55 Brazilian Sugar Plantations, 1815

THE BUILDINGS

The buildings which are usually to be seen upon the plantations are the following:

The mill; which is either turned by water or by cattle. Some of the plantations possess both of these, owing to the failure of the water in the dry season; and indeed there are few estates upon which the crops are so large as to require that there should be both.

The boiling-house; which is usually attached to the mill, and is the most costly part of the apparatus; for the coppers, &c. must be obtained from Europe.

The claying-house, or *caza de purgar;* which is oftentimes connected with the boiling-house. It is also generally made use of as the still house or distillery.

The chapel; which is usually of considerable dimensions. This building, and all the foregoing, are almost universally constructed of brick.

The dwelling-house for the owner or manager; to this is usually attached a stable for the saddle horses. The dwelling-houses are frequently made of timber and mud.

The row of negro dwellings; which I have described in another place as looking like neglected almshouses in England, and are made of the same materials as the house of the owner. From the appearance of the negro huts, an idea may usually be formed of the disposition of the owner of a plantation. All these buildings are covered with tiles.

The estates have no regular hospital for the sick negroes; but one of the houses of the row is oftentimes set apart for this purpose. The stocks in which disorderly slaves are placed, stand in the claying-house.

STOCK

Of those estates which I have seen, I think that the average number of negroes sent to daily labor in the field does not reach forty for each; for although there may be upon a plantation this number of males and females of a proper age for working, still some of them will always be sick or employed upon errands, not directly conducive to the advancement of the regular work. An estate which possesses forty able negroes, males and females, an equal number of oxen, and the same of horses, can be very well worked: and if the lands are good, that is, if there is a fair proportion of low and high lands fit for the culture of the sugar cane, such an estate ought to produce a number of chests of sugar of fifteen hundred weight each, equal to that of the able slaves. I speak of forty slaves being sufficient, because some descriptions of work are oftentimes performed by freemen; thus, for instance, the sugar-boilers, the person who clays the sugar, the distiller, the cartmen, and even some others are very frequently free. Only a very small proportion of the sugar will be muscavado, if the business is conducted with any degree of management. I have heard it said by many planters, that the molasses will pay almost every expense; and that if rum is made, the proceeds of the molasses are rendered fully equal to the usual yearly expenditure.

The negroes may be valued at 32£ each; oxen at 31£ each; and horses at the same; but by management the two last may be obtained at lower prices. A sugar plantation of the first class, with suitable buildings, may be reckoned as being worth from 7,000£ to 8,000£, and some few are valued as high as 10,000£; but an advance of one-sixth of the price would probably be accepted, the remainder to be paid by yearly installments. The inland plantations may be reckoned at from 3,000£ to 5,000£ and a few are rather higher. But a smaller advance would be required than upon the purchase of prime plantations: and the installments would be more moderate. Plantations of the first class ought to have eighty negroes at least, and an increased number of animals, owing to their capability of employing more hands.

The only carts which are used upon the plantations are very clumsily made. A flat surface or table (*meza*) made of thick and heavy timber, of about two feet and a half broad, and six feet in length, is fixed upon two wheels of solid timber, with a moveable axle-tree; a pole is likewise fixed to the cart. These vehicles are always drawn by four oxen or more: and as they are narrow, and the roads upon which they must travel are bad, they are continually overturning. The negroes who drive the carts have generally some indulgencies, with which their fellow-slaves are not favored, from the greater labor which this business requires, and from the continual difficulty and danger to which they are exposed, owing to the overturning of the carts and the unruliness of the oxen. In the whole management of the concerns of a plantation, the want of mechanical assistance to decrease the labor of the workmen, must strike every person who is in the habit of seeing them, and of paying any attention to the subject. I will mention one instance; when bricks or tiles are to be removed from one place to another, the whole gang of negroes belonging to the estate is employed in carrying them: each man takes three or perhaps four bricks or tiles upon his head, and marches off gently and quietly. He lays them down where he is desired so to do, and again returns for three or four more. Thus thirty persons sometimes pass the whole day in doing the same quantity of work that two men with wheelbarrows would have performed with equal ease in the same space of time.

SOURCE: Henry Koster, *Travels in Brazil, 1809 to 1815* (2 vols.; Philadelphia: Carey, 1817), 2:137–40 (footnotes omitted).

56 A Spectrum of Occupations, 1830

The whole labor of bearing and moving burdens is performed by these [Negroes], and the state in which they appear is revolting to humanity. Here was a number of beings entirely naked, with the exception of a covering of dirty rags tied about their waists. Their skins, from constant exposure to the weather, had become hard, crusty, and seamed, resembling the coarse black covering of some beast, or like that of an elephant, a wrinkled hide scattered with scanty hairs. On contemplating their persons, you saw them with a physical organization, resembling beings of a grade below the rank of man; long projecting heels, the gastronomic muscle wanting, and no calves to their legs; their mouths and chins protruded, their noses flat, their foreheads retiring, having exactly the head and legs of the baboon tribe. Some of these beings were yoked to drays, on which they dragged heavy burdens. Some were chained by the necks and legs, and moved with loads thus encumbered. Some followed each other in ranks, with heavy weights on their heads, chattering the most inarticulate and dismal cadence as they moved along. Some were munching young sugar canes, like beasts of burden eating green provender, and some were seen near the water, lying on the bare ground among filth and offal, coiled up like dogs, and seeming to expect or require no more comfort or accommodation, exhibiting a state and conformation so unhuman, that they not only seemed, but actually were, far below the inferior animals around them. Horses and mules were not employed in this way; they were used only for pleasure, and not for labor. They were seen in the same streets, pampered, spirited, and richly caparisoned, enjoying a state far superior to the negroes, and appearing to look down on the fettered and burdened wretches they were passing, as on beings of an inferior rank in the creation to themselves. Some of the negroes actually seemed to envy the caparisons of their fellow brutes, and eyed with jealousy their glittering harness. In imitation of this finery, they were fond of thrums of many-colored threads; and I saw one creature, who supported the squalid rag that wrapped his waist by a suspender of gaudy worsted, which he turned every moment to look at, on his naked shoulder. The greater number, however, were as unconscious of any covering for use or ornament, as a pig or an ass.

The first impression of all this on my mind, was to shake the conviction I had always felt, of the wrong and hardship inflicted on our black fellow-creatures, and that they were only in that state which God and nature had assigned them; that they were the lowest grade of human existence, and the link that connected it with the brute, and that the gradation was so insensible, and their natures so intermingled, that it was impossible to tell where one had terminated and the other commenced; and that it was not surprising that people who contemplated them every day, so formed, so employed, and so degraded, should forget their claims to that rank in the scale of beings in which modern philanthropists are so anxious to place them. I did not at the moment myself recollect, that the white man, made a slave on the coast of Africa, suffers not only a similar mental but physical deterioration from hardships and emaciation, and becomes in time the dull and deformed beast I now saw yoked to a burden.

A few hours only were necessary to correct my first impressions of the negro population, by seeing them under a different aspect. We were attracted by the sound of military music, and found it proceeded from a regiment drawn up in one of the streets. Their colonel had just died, and they attended to form a procession to celebrate his obsequies. They were all of different shades of black, but the majority were negroes. Their equipment was excellent; they wore dark jackets, white pantaloons, and black leather caps and belts, all which, with their arms, were in high order. Their band produced sweet and agreeable music, of the leader's own composition, and the men went through some evolutions with regularity and dexterity. They were only a militia regiment, yet were as well appointed and disciplined as one of our regiments of the line. Here then was the first step in that gradation by which the black population of this country ascend in the scale of humanity; he advances from the state below that of a beast of burden into a military rank, and he shows himself as capable of discipline and improvement as a human being of any other color.

Our attention was next attracted by negro men and women bearing about a variety of articles for sale; some in baskets, some on boards and cases carried on their heads. They belonged to a class of small shopkeepers, many of whom vend their wares at home, but the greater number send them about in this way, as in itinerant shops. A few of these people were still in a state of bondage, and brought a certain sum every evening to their owners, as the produce of their daily labor. But a large proportion, I was informed, were free, and exercised this little calling on their own account. They were all very neat and clean in their persons, and had a decorum and sense of respectability about them, superior to whites of the same class and calling. All their articles were good in their kind, and neatly kept, and they sold them with simplicity and confidence, neither wishing to take advantage of others, nor suspecting that it would be taken of themselves. I bought some confectionery from one of the females, and I was struck with the modesty and propriety of her manner; she was a young mother, and had with her a neatly dressed child, of which she seemed very fond. I gave it a little comfit, and it turned up its dusky countenance to her and then to me, taking my sweetmeat, and at the same time kissing my hand. As yet unacquainted with the coin of the country, I had none that was current about me, and was leaving the articles; but the poor young woman pressed them on me with a ready confidence, repeating in broken Portuguese, *outo tempo.* I am sorry to say, the "other time" never came, for I could not recognize her person afterwards to discharge her little debt, though I went to the same place for the purpose.

It soon began to grow dark, and I was attracted by a number of persons bearing large lighted wax tapers, like torches, gathering before a house. As I passed by, one was put into my hand by a man who seemed in some authority, and I was requested to fall into a procession that was forming. It was the preparation for a funeral, and on such occasions, I learned that they always request the attendance of a passing stranger, and feel hurt if they are refused. I joined the party, and proceeded with them to a neighboring church. When we entered we ranged ourselves on each side of a platform which stood near the choir, on which was laid an open coffin, covered with pink silk and gold borders. The funeral service was chanted by a choir of priests, one of whom was a negro, a large comely man, whose jet black visage formed a strong and striking contrast to his white vestments. He seemed to perform his part with a decorum and sense of solemnity, which I did not observe in his brethren. After scattering flowers on the coffin, and fumigating it with incense, they retired, the procession dispersed, and we returned on board.

I had been but a few hours on shore, for the first time, and I saw an African negro under four aspects of society; and it appeared to me, that in every one his character depended on the state in which he was placed, and the estimation in which he was held. As a despised slave, he was far lower than other animals of burthen that surrounded him; more miserable in his look, more revolting in his nakedness, more distorted in his person, and apparently more deficient in intellect than the horses and mules that passed him by. Advanced to the grade of a soldier, he was clean and neat in his person, amenable to discipline, expert at his exercises, and showed the port and being of a white man similarly placed. As a citizen, he was remarkable for the respectability of his appearance, and the decorum of his manners in the rank assigned him; and as a priest, standing in the house of God, appointed to instruct society on their most important interests, and in a grade in which moral and intellectual fitness is required, and a certain degree of superiority is expected, he seemed even more devout in his impressions, and more correct in his manners, than his white associates. I came, therefore, to the irresistible conclusion in my mind, that color was an accident affecting the surface of a man, and having no more to do with his qualities than his clothes—that God had equally created an African in the image of his person, and equally given him an immortal soul; and that an European had no pretext but his own cupidity, for impiously thrusting his fellowman from that rank in the creation which the Almighty had assigned him, and degrading him below the lot of the brute beasts that perish. . . .

The night of Holy Thursday is the time devoted to female slaves, during which they are permitted and encouraged to make up amendoas, and dispose of them for their own profit; and at the door or passage leading to every church is a market established, where they are sold. Here the poor girls, dressed in their best clothes, and decked out in their simple ornaments, display their confectionery, sometimes on tables covered with napkins, sometimes on the ground with lighted candles. It consists of almond comfits in conical bags, or in paper baskets neatly cut and painted, and sometimes of little figures of frosted sugar, of different characters and costumes, having their insides filled with a variety of good things. These figures generally sell for two patacs, or about 2s. 6d. each, and I never purchased anything with more pleasure, than at this "holy fair," so humanely instituted to promote the industry and profit of poor female slaves. It is one of the many little institutions which mark the good and kindly traits of the Brazilian character; and it almost smoothed the rough and hideous aspect of slavery, to see so many in a state of bondage on this night so neatly dressed, so cheerful, and apparently so happy.

SOURCE: Robert Walsh, *Notices of Brazil* (2 vols.; London: Westley and Davis, 1830), 1:134–41; 391–92.

57 Slavery in Bahia, 1845

Around the landing places cluster hundreds of canoes, launches, and various other small craft, discharging their loads of fruit and produce. On one part of the Praya is a wide opening, which is used as a marketplace. Near this a modern building has been constructed for an exchange. The merchants, however, make but little use of it, preferring a very indifferent room in which they have long been accustomed to meet.

This lower town is not calculated to make a favorable impression upon the stranger. The buildings are old, although generally of a cheerful exterior. The street is very narrow, uneven, and wretchedly paved. Besides, the gutter passes directly through the middle, rendering it unavoidably filthy. At the same time it is crowded with peddlers and carriers of every description. You here learn one peculiarity of the city of Bahia. Owing to the irregularities of its surface, and the steepness of the ascent which separates the upper town from the lower, it does not admit of the use of wheel carriages. Not even a cart or truck is to be seen, for the purpose of removing burdens from one place to another. Whatever requires change of place in all the commerce and ordinary business of this seaport, and it is second in size and importance to but one other in South America, must pass on the heads and shoulders of men. Burdens are here more frequently carried upon the shoulders, since the principal exports of the city being sugar in cases, and cotton in bales, it is impossible that they should be borne on the head like bags of coffee.

Immense numbers of tall, athletic negroes are seen moving in pairs or gangs of four, six, or eight, with their loads suspended between them on heavy poles. Numbers more of their fellows are seen setting upon their poles, braiding straw, or lying about the alleys and corners of the streets, asleep, reminding one of black snakes coiled up in the sunshine. The sleepers generally have some sentinel ready to call them when they are wanted for business, and at the given signal they rouse up like the elephant to his burden. Like the coffee-carrie[r]s of Rio, they often sing and shout as they go, but their gait is necessarily slow and measured, resembling a dead march rather than the double-quick step of their Fluminensian colleagues. Another class of negroes are devoted to carrying passengers in a species of sedan chair, called cadeiras.

It is indeed a toilsome, and often a dangerous task, for white persons to ascend on foot the bluffs on which stands the *cidade alta,* particularly when the powerful rays of the sun are pouring, without mitigation, upon their heads. No omnibus or cab, or even *sege,* can be found to do him service. Suited to this state of things, he finds near every corner or place of public resort, a long row of curtained cadeiras, the bearers of which, with hat in hand, crowd around him with all the eagerness, though not with the impudence, of carriage drivers in New York, saying, *"Quer cadeira, Senhor?"* "Will you have a chair, sir?" When he has made his selection and seated himself to his liking, the bearers elevate their load and march along, apparently as much pleased with the opportunity of carrying a passenger, as he is with the chance of being carried. To keep a cadeira or two, and negroes to bear them, is as necessary for a family in Bahia, as the keeping of carriages and horses elsewhere. The livery of the carriers, and the expensiveness of the curtaining and ornaments of the cadeira, indicate the rank and style which the family maintains.

SOURCE: Daniel Kidder, *Sketches of Brazil* (Philadelphia: Sorin and Ball, 1845), pp. 19–21.

58 Slavery in Rio de Janeiro, 1856

This morning a slave came along with a load on his head and both hands in a large gourd, out of which he drew a fashionable waltzing tune. I took the opportunity of examining the popular *Marimba.* Every African nation has its own, so that a Congo, Angola, Minas, Ashantee, or Mozambique instrument is recognizable, but the differences are not great. A series of thin steel rods, from ten to fifteen, are fixed on a thin board, five or six inches square, in the manner of flute-keys, which they resemble. A long and a short one alternate: sometimes they diminish like Pan-pipes. The board is secured in the larger half of a dry calabash. Grasping it with his fingers beneath, and his thumbs on the keys, he produces, by pushing them down at one end and letting them fly back, a soft humming sound allied to that of the Jews'-harp. The city is an Ethiopian theater, and this the favorite instrument of the orchestra. Slaves are daily met playing African airs on it, and groups returning to the country have commonly one or two among them. . . .

As this is Ash-Wednesday, there is to be a procession, toward evening, from the Church of "St. Francis of the Penitence." Fourteen images, and among them "Black Benedict," are to come down the hill and parade the streets. *Angels,* too—real, living, winged spirits—will, it is said, join the pageant.

The lime of Rio is made of shells scooped out of the Bay, and, of course, is in powder. See that falua—a light boat of one mast—riding at anchor some fifty feet from the Gloria Beach. She is charged with lime, and, dancing on the swell, is unloading her cargo. The slave on her bows, keeping her head to the shore with a long bamboo, is captain; the other, on the gunwale, raising the dust on the blade of a hoe, is her deckhand. Observe those four blacks, with empty tea chests on their heads, wading toward her, and as many coming from her with their boxes filled. How steadily they move, where the waves would take a stranger off his feet! The water is at the armpits of him who is lifting his load from the edge of the vessel; and see, as he turns and breasts that retiring swell, it swashes over his eyes. Now he comes dripping out, ascends the bank, and, crossing the street, empties his chest on the floor of an establishment for the sale of building materials. As he does, so do eight or ten more, keeping the hoe (used in place of a shovel) in constant motion.

Their dresses are too primitive for laborers on our wharves. Some are, like the skippers on the craft, in shirts minus both sleeves and skirts; others wear a petticoat that neither reaches the knees nor meets behind; and two have aprons not one whit wider than aprons usually are. White as their contents, the boxes contrast strongly with their moving pedestals, while these increase in height as they near the beach, and all but disappear at the falua. One, while his box was being filled, plunged over head and washed himself; then tore off a part of his pinafore, and fastened it over his shoulders, to protect them from the caustic dust. The scene altogether is a novel one, though common enough here. One old man's head is so whitened with the dust as to remind one of a cauliflower on a coal-sack. . . .

I emerged from the long avenue in Dereita Street, not far from the Custom-house, where street passengers have to run a muck through piles of bales, barrels, packages, crates, trucks, and bustling and sweating negroes. Here are no carts drawn by quadrupeds for the transportaion of merchandise. Slaves are the beasts of draught as well as of burden. The loads they drag, and the roads they drag them over, are enough to kill both mules and horses. Formerly, few contrivances on wheels were used at the Custom-house. Every thing was moved over the ground by simply dragging it. A good deal of this kind of work is still done. See! there are two slaves moving off with a cask of hardware on a plank of wood, with a rope passed through a hole at one end, and the bottom greased or wetted! Such things were a few years ago very common.

Trucks in every variety are now numerous. Some recent ones are as heavily built and ironed as brewers' drays, which they resemble, furnished with winches in front to raise heavy goods. Each is of itself sufficient for any animal below an elephant to draw; and yet loads varying from half a ton to a ton are dragged on them by negroes. Two strain at the shafts and one or two push behind, or, what is quite as common, walk by the wheels and pull down the spokes. It is surprising how their naked feet and legs escape being crushed, the more so as those in front can not prevent the wheels every now and then sinking into the gutters, and whirling the shafts violently one way or the other. One acts as foreman, and the way he gives his orders is a caution to the timid. From a settled calm he in a moment rages like a maniac, and seems ready to tear his associates to pieces.

A slave was chained to one heavy truck. He had been absent when it was wanted, and his enraged owner took this method of preventing him from losing another job. The links of the chain were three-quarter-inch round iron.

Neither age nor sex is free from iron shackles. I met this morning a very handsome Mozambique girl with a double-pronged collar on; she could not have been over sixteen. And a few evenings ago, while standing on the balcony of a house in Custom-house Street, a little old negress, four-fifths naked, toddled past, in the middle of the street, with an enormous tub of swill on her head, and secured by a lock and chain to her neck. "Explain that, Mr. C——," I said. "Oh, she is going to empty slops on the beach, and being probably in the habit of visiting vendas, she is thus prevented, as the offensive vessel would not be admitted. Some slaves have been known to sell their slops for rum, and, such are sent to the fountains and to the Praya accoutred as that old woman is."

With a friend I went to the Consulado, a department of the Customs having charge over exports. Gangs of slaves came in continually with coffee for shipment. Every bag is pierced and a sample withdrawn while on the carrier's head, to determine the quality and duty. The tariff, based on the market price, is regulated every Saturday. At present the duty amounts to 11 percent on coffee and 7 on sugars. The instrument used to withdraw samples of coffee is a brass tube, cut precisely like a pen. The point is pushed in at the underside of the bag, and the berries pass through the tube. A handful is abstracted. On withdrawing the instrument, its point is drawn over, and closes the opening. The operation occupies but a few seconds. The samples amount to some tons in a year. They, with those of exported sugars, are given to the Lazaretto.

Every gang of coffee-carriers has a leader, who commonly shakes a rattle, to the music of which his associates behind him chant. The load, weighing 160 lbs., rests on the head and shoulders, the body is inclined forward, and the pace is a trot or half-run. Most are stout and athletic, but a few are so small and slightly made that one wonders how they manage to keep up with the rest. The average life of a coffee-carrier does not exceed ten years. In that time the work ruptures and kills them. They have so much a bag, and what they earn over the sum daily required by their owners they keep. Except four or five, whose sole dress was short canvas shirts, without sleeves, all were naked from the waist upward and from the knees below; a few had on nothing but a towel round the loins. Their rich chocolate skins shone in the sun. On returning, some kept up their previous chant, and ran as if enjoying the toil; others went more leisurely, and among them some noble-looking fellows stepped with much natural grace.

A gang of fourteen slaves came past with enormously wide but shallow baskets on their heads. They were unloading a barge of *sea-coal,* and conveying it to a foundry or forge. The weight each bore appeared equal to that of a bag of coffee (160 lbs.). This mode of transporting coal has one advantage over ours, since the material is taken directly from the vessel to the place where it is to be consumed. As with coal, so with every thing; when an article is once mounted on the head of a negro, it is only removed at the place where it is to remain.

A couple of slaves followed the coal-carriers, each perspiring under a pair of the largest-sized blacksmith bellows—a load for a horse and cart with us. A week ago I stood to observe eight oxen drag an ordinary wagonload of building stone for the Capuchins up the steep Castle hill; it was straining work for them to ascend a few rods at a time; today I noticed similar loads of stone discharged at the foot of the ascent, and borne up on negroes' heads.

No wonder that slaves shockingly crippled in their lower limbs are so numerous. There waddled before me, in a manner distressing to behold, a man whose thighs and legs curved so far outward that his trunk was not over fifteen inches from the ground. It appeared sufficiently heavy, without the loaded basket on his head, to snap the osseous stem and drop between his feet. I observed another whose knees crossed each other, and his feet preternaturally apart, as if superincumbent loads had pushed his knees in instead of out. The lamplighter of the Catholic district exhibits another variety. His body is settled low down, his feet are drawn both to one side, so that his legs are parallel at an angle of thirty degrees. The heads of Africans are hard, their necks strong, and both, being perpendicular to the loads they are called to support, are seldom injured. It is the lower parts of the moving columns, where the weights are alternately thrown on and off the jointed thighs and legs, that are the weakest.

These necessarily are the first to give way under excessive burdens; and here are examples of their having yielded and broken down in every direction.

Among lithographic scenes of life in Rio, designed and published by native artists, those relating to the slaves are not the least conspicuous. There is no more fastidiousness, that I observed, about portraying them in shackles than in their labors and their pastimes. . . .

It is said slaves in masks are not so often encountered in the streets as formerly, because of a growing public feeling against them. I met but three or four, and in each case the sufferer was a female. The mask is the reputed ordinary punishment and preventative of drunkenness. As the barrel is often chained to the slave that bears it, to prevent him from selling it for rum, so the mask is to hinder him or her from conveying the liquor to the mouth, below which the metal is continued, and opposite to which there is no opening.

Observing one day masks hanging out for sale at a tin and sheet iron store, I stopped to examine them, and subsequently borrowed one. . . . Except a projecting piece for the nose, the metal is simply bent cylinder-wise. Minute holes are punched to admit air to the nostrils, and similar ones in front of the eyes. A jointed strap (of metal) on each side goes round below the ears (sometimes two), and meets one that passes over the crown of the head. A staple unites and a padlock secures them.

At most of the smith's shops collars are exposed, as horseshoes are with our blacksmiths; at one shop in Rua das Violas there was quite a variety, with gyves, chains, etc. Most of the collars were of five-eighths-inch round iron, some with one prong, others with two, and some with none except a short upright tubular lock.

Here, too, were the heaviest and cruelest instruments of torture—shackles for binding the ankles and wrists close together, and consequently doubling the bodies of the victims into the most painful and unnatural positions. Had I not seen them, I could hardly have thought such things were. While making a memorandum of their form and dimensions, the proprietor or his adjutant, a black man, in his shirt sleeves, came from the rear, and handling them, spoke by way of recommending them, supposing I was a customer. They were made of bar iron, *three-inches wide and three-eights of an inch thick!* Each consisted of three pieces, bent, jointed, and fastened. . . . The large openings were for the legs, the smaller for the wrists. A screw-bolt drew the straight parts close together. . . . The distance from joint to joint was two feet.

Such are the tortures which slaves privately endure in the cellars, garrets, and outhouses of their masters. T——, a native merchant, says another common punishment is to inclose the legs in wooden shackles or stocks. Some owners fasten their hands in similar devices, and some, again, retain relics of the old thumbscrews to lock those members together. In the northern provinces, he says, the slaves are much worse used than in Rio; that it is no uncommon thing to tie their hands and feet together, hoist them off the ground, and then "beat them as near to death as possible." A heavy log fastened by a chain to the neck or leg of a slave who has absconded, or who is supposed to be inclined to run away, is a usual punishment and precaution. He is compelled to labor with it, laying it on the ground when at work, and bearing it under his arm or on his shoulder when he moves.

I observed one day a slave wearing a collar, the largest and roughest of hundreds I have seen. . . . Of inch round iron, with a hinge in the middle, made by bending the metal of its full size into loops, the open ends flattened and connected by a half-inch rivet. The upright bar terminated in a *death's head,* which reached above that of the wearer, and to it another piece, in the form of the letter S, was welded. The joint galled him, for he kept gathering portions of his canvas shirt under it. Rest or sleep would seem impossible.

A Bahian planter, the brother of an ex-councilor, dined with us one day, and spoke with much freedom on slavery. With most men, he thinks the land can never be cultivated in the northern provinces by whites. The city slaves of Bahia, he said, are principally Minas. Shrewd and intelligent, they preserve their own language, and by that means organize clubs and mature schemes of revolution which their brethren of Pernambuco have repeatedly attempted to carry out. Some write Arabic fluently, and are vastly superior to most of their masters. In the interior, he remarked, the slaves are badly fed, worse clothed, and worked so hard that the average duration of their lives does not exceed six years. In some districts it reaches to eight, while the number that see ten years after leaving Africa is small indeed. Deceptions are played off on foreign agents of the Slavery Commissions. These visit the Engenhos once or twice a year.

The planters, informed when they set out, have their slaves decently garbed and *well oiled,* to make them look supple and in good condition. On a late visit, the examiners were so highly gratified that one left, and wrote home a flattering account of the treatment of the helots. The other continued his inquiries, came to a fazenda where he was not looked for, and there beheld what he did not expect—a negro about to be *boiled to death* for some act of insubordination. His owner had invited, according to custom in such cases, neighboring proprietors to witness the tragedy.

From the little I have seen, I should suppose the country slaves are the worst off. Every morning, while nature was enshrouded in blackness of darkness, did I hear them driving wagons through the thick mist, and as late as ten at night were they shouting at the oxen as the jolting and groaning wheels rolled by. (This was, however, in the busiest season.) I often wondered how they found their way over the horrid roads, how their naked feet and limbs escaped unharmed, and how they then worked in the fields, unless their pupils had the expansile and contractile powers of night animals.

On large estates, a few days' rest are given them every three or four weeks during the sugar season, but on smaller ones, where owners commonly have difficulty to keep out of debt, they fare badly, and are worked to death. Staggering into their huts, or dropping where their labors close, hardly do their aching bones allow the Angel of Sleep to drive away the memory of their sorrows, than two demons, lurking in the bell and lash, awaken them to fresh tortures. To say these poor creatures are better off than when ranging their native lands is an assertion that language lacks the power justly to describe. It may be true, if the life of an omnibus hack is better than that of a wild horse of Texas. I would rather, a thousand times, be a sheep, pig, or ox, have freedom, food, and rest for a season, and then be knocked on the head, than be a serf on some plantations. I say *some,* because there are in Brazil, as in other lands, humane planters.

Suicides continually occur, and owners wonder. The high-souled Minas, both men and women, are given to self-destruction. Rather than endure life on the terms it is offered, many of them end it. Then they that bought them grind their teeth and curse them, hurl imprecations after their flying spirits, and execrate the saints that let them go. If individuals are ever justified in using the power Heaven has placed in their hands to terminate at once their earthly existence, it must be these. Those who blame them for putting the only barrier between them and oppression could not endure half their woes. And how characteristic of human frailties! Here are slave-dealers who weep over the legendary sufferings of a saint, and laugh at worse tortures they themselves inflict; who shudder at the names of old persecutors, and dream not of the armies of martyrs they make yearly; who cry over Protestants as sinners doomed to perdition, and smile in anticipation of their own reception in the realms above by Anthony and Loyala, Benedict and Becket.

Rich people who lose a slave by suicide or flight scarcely feel the loss, but to many families the loss is ruinous. There are not a few that live on the earnings of one or two helots. The papers are constantly noticing the flight of slaves who have manumitted themselves by escaping across a river their oppressors dare not attempt, since they there become denizens of a country in which Brazilian process can not be served. They unsheath their spirits, and leave the scabbards for their masters.

It is only suicides reported by the police that become publicly known. Were all recorded, every issue of the daily press would, I am told, contain more or less. Instances that have occurred within the last few weeks are taken from the *Diario.*

June 22–24. "In the parish of Sta. Anna, an inquest was held on the body of the black, Justo, who killed himself by hanging. He was the slave of Major José de Paiva e Silva. Also on the body of the slave Rita, who destroyed herself by drowning. The body of a black, in a state of putrefaction, was found, thrown ashore by the tide, on the beach near the Public Garden."

July 1. The body of one was found near the Carioco Fountain; another, a female, in another parish, had released her spirit with a rope—"suicidou-se com um baraço." *July 5.* Another, in a fit of despair, precipitated himself from an upper window upon a mass of granite. *23d.* The slave Luiz Pharoux killed himself with a rope. *24th.* The slaves Pedro and Camillo by strangulation. *August 1.* Another drowned himself on the Praya Manoel. On the 4th, my last day in Brazil, one was lying on the rocks at the city end of the Gloria Beach, washed up by the tide. He was apparently under thirty years of age. As I stood looking down on him, a Mozambique girl came along, put her basket on the low wall near me, dropped a tear on the corpse, and passed on.

When the means of suspension are not at hand, it is no unusual thing for high-minded Africans, of both sexes, to expire under circumstances surpassing aught that history records. Some draw ligatures tight round their throats, lie down, and deliberately die. Others, I am told, have the art of folding back their tongues so as to prevent respiration, and thus resolutely perish.

I dined one Sunday with a party at the beautiful and hospitable retreat of Messrs. M—— and M'G——, at Boto-Fogo. Strolling alone up an adjacent mount, I was very much startled by two of the most frightful-looking and importunate of human beings rushing suddenly out of the bushes in front of me. Negroes of middle age, and wholly naked, except filthy rags round their loins, each had an iron ring about his neck connected by an ox-chain to shackles at his ankles. By another chain one hand of each were locked together. They bent forward, kneeled, held out their arms, sobbed, cried, screamed, and made such frightfully agonizing supplications, that I have often thought neither criminals condemned to die, nor even souls in Purgatory, could make more moving appeals. Poor fellows! I did not make out what they asked for—money, victuals, or intercession with their master, the owner of the hill and of a neighboring quarry, in which he employed over 200 slaves. These two had attempted to escape, and, when not at work, were ordered to this sequestered spot and forbidden to leave it.

SOURCE: Thomas Ewbank, *Life in Brazil* (New York: Harper, 1856), pp. 111–13, 115–19, 436–42.

59 A Gold Mine in Brazil, 1869

I proceed now to give my account of the black miner as I found him at Morro Velho.

Without including 130 children of hired blacks, and who are not under contract, the establishment consists of 1,450 head, thus distributed:

Company's blacks, 254 (109 men, 93 women, and 52 children); Cata Branca blacks, 245 (96 men, 87 women and 62 children); blacks hired under contract, 951.

In these numbers we may see a modification of Saint Hilaire's statement, "le service des mines ne convient pas aux femmes"; this might have been true under the old system, it is not so now. Generally in the Brazil men are preferred upon the sugar plantations, women on those that grow coffee, and as they are wanted for domestic purposes it is not so easy to hire them.

The "Company's Blacks" consider themselves the aristocracy, and look down upon all their brethren. Both they and the Cata Brancas are known by the numbers on their clothing; the hired negroes wear also M.V. marked on their shirts. The establishment expends per mens. £1,400 upon contracts: I need hardly remark what a benefit this must be to the large proprietors of the neighborhood. Thus the Commendador Francisco de Paula Santos lets under contract a total of 269 (including 173 children), his son-in-law Sr. Dumont 145 (97 adults and 48 children), and the Cocaes or National Brazilian Mining Association contributes 142 negroes and 13 children.

The figures given below will show the average of hire: * clothing, food, and medical treatment are at the Company's expense. Usually the agreement is for three to five years, during which period the slave cannot be manumitted. As a rule the Superintendent employs only robust men who have passed a medical examination, but he will take in doubtful lives under annual contract. The slave is insured by a deduction of 10$000 to 20$000 per annum for a fixed period; and if he dies before the lease has expired the owner still receives his money—there are actually eighty-nine cases of this kind. Pay ceases only if the negro runs away: it is issued every third or sixth month, and the contractors can obtain one year's advance, at a discount of 10 percent.

As regards labor, all are classified according to their strength into first-, second-, and third-rate blacks. In 1847 permission to work overtime, that is to say, beyond nine hours forty-five minutes, was given to the first-rates. There is another division into surface and underground blacks. The former are smiths and mechanics, especially carpenters and masons, who work between 6 A.M. and 5 P.M., with one hour forty-five minutes of intermission for meals. The oldest and least robust are turned into gardeners, wood fetchers, and

* Annual hire of first-class slaves . . . men 220$000 women 100$000; not paying in case of death or flight . . . men 230$000 women 110$000; annual hire of second-class slaves . . . men 150$000 women 75$000; not paying in case of death or flight . . . men 160$000 women 75$000.

grass cutters. The regular working day at Morro Velho is as follows—

5 A.M. Reveille sounded by the gong, and half an hour afterwards the Review.

6 A.M. Work.

8.15 A.M. Breakfast.

9 A.M. Work.

12.30 P.M. Dinner.

1.15 P.M. Work.

2 P.M. Change guard. Blasting in the mine.

5.30 P.M. Mechanics' work ended.

8.30 P.M. Return to quarters. The slaves cook their own meals and eat supper at home. Saturday is a half-holiday: they leave off work at 2.30 P.M., and retire at 9 P.M.

The underground laborers are borers, stope cleaners, trammers who push the wagons, kibble fillers, and timbermen: they are divided into three corps, who enter the mine at 6 A.M., 2 P.M., and 10 P.M. On Sunday the gangs shift places, so that only one week in three is night work. A rough estimate makes the number of the gang in the mine at the same time 620, including all hands. When work is over they proceed to the changing-house, and find a tepid bath at all hours. They put on their surface clothes, and leave the mine suits either to be dried in the open air, or by flues during the rains. The precaution is absolutely necessary, though very difficult and troublesome to be enforced: the English miners shirk it, and the free Brazilians are the most restive, though they are well aware how fatal are wet garments.

The blacks lodge in the two villages situated halfway between the bottom of the river valley and the Morro Velho hill. Thus, while they escape malaria they are saved fatigue when going to, or coming from, work. They begin the day with coffee or Congonhas tea. Their weekly allowance, besides salt and vegetables, comprises 9 lb. of maize meal, 4½–5 lb. of beans, 13½ oz. of lard, and 2 lb. of fresh beef. Meat of the best quality here averages 3$000 per arroba, or twopence a pound, and the laborers purchase, at cost prices, the heads and hoofs, the livers and internals of the bullocks killed for the use of the establishment. The industrious have their gardens and clearings: they keep poultry and pigs fattened with bran, which they receive gratis. Part they eat, the rest they sell to procure finery and small luxuries. "Carne Seca" and farina are issued when the doctor orders. Nursing women have something added to the six-tenths of a plate of meal, one-quarter of beans, and two ounces of lard, and children when weaned claim half rations. All the articles are of good quality, and if not a report is made to the Manager of Blacks.

Drink is not issued every day, nor may it be brought into the establishment. A well-conducted negro can obtain a dram once per diem with permission of the chief feitor or overseer. Each head of a department has a supply of "restilio," which he can distribute at discretion, and the mine captain can give a "tot" to any negro coming wet from duty. It is, however, difficult to correct the African's extreme fondness for distilled liquors, which in this light and exciting air readily affect his head, and soon prove fatal to him. He delights also in "Pángo," here called Arirí, the well-known Bhang (Cannabis sativa) of India, and of the east and west coast of Africa. He will readily pay as much as 1$000 for a handful of this poison.

I never saw negroes so well dressed. The men have two suits per annum—shirt, and overalls of cotton for the hot, and of woollen for the cold season; the "undergrounds" receive, besides these, a stout woollen shirt, and a strong hat to protect the head. Each has a cotton blanket, renewed yearly, and if his dress be worn or torn, the manager supplies another. The women work in shifts of thin woollen stuff, and petticoats of stronger material; they usually wear kerchiefs round their neck, thus covering the bosom, and one shoulder, after the fashion of African "Minas," is left bare. In winter capes of red broadcloth are added to the Review costume.

The slave laborer is rewarded with gifts of money; he is allowed leave out of bounds, even to Sabará; he is promoted to offices of trust and of increased pay; he is made an overseer or a captain over his own people; at the Review he wears stripes and badges of distinction, and he looks forward to liberty.

The chief punishments are fines, which negroes, like Hindus, especially hate; the penalties, which now amount to 400$000, have been transferred to charitable purposes, and swell a small reserved trust fund, intended to support the old and infirm. Other pains are, not being allowed to sell pigs, poultry, and vegetables; arrest within the establishment or confinement in a dry cell, with boards like a soldier's guardroom; fugitives are put in irons. Formerly the manager and the head captain, who required implicit obedience from the 500 hands of the underground department, could order a flogging. This was abolished, not, I believe, with good effect. Every head of a department can still prescribe the "Palmatorio," * but he must note and report the punishment to the Superintendent. Only the latter can administer a flogging with the Brazilian cat of split hide; and this is reserved for confirmed drunkenness, disobedience of orders, mutiny, or robbing fellow-workmen. The punishment list is sent in every fortnight, and as a rule is small. . . .

Briefly to sum up the statistics of Morro Velho, in these its greatest golden days. The Company has outlived the thirty-seventh year, and during the last six it has paid upwards of £10,000 income tax to the British Exchequer. The present outlay of the establishment is, in round numbers, £146,000 per annum, and the income £230,000. As a mine it has no parallel in the Brazil; the excavation has descended to zones unreached by other works, and, as has been seen, its breadth is without a parallel. It directly employs 2,521 souls; indirectly double that number.

Besides the 343 English at Morro Velho there are at least 500 of our own countrymen scattered about the Province of Minas. All are destitute of protection; their marriages are to be contested in civil courts, the nearest consulate for registration is that of Rio de Janeiro, and the cost of a journey to the coast and back would not be less than £50. There is the same difficulty touching wills and inheritances, especially in the case of the Company's officers, and the English medical men who live in the remoter parts of the Province. The French, Spanish, and Portuguese Governments have vice-consuls or consular agents at Barbacena and Ouro Preto, although none save the latter have many constituents. We shall probably see fit to follow their example.

And now adieu to Morro Velho, a place where I found, wonderful to relate, work carried on by night and by day in the heat of the Tropics, and in the heart of the Brazil.

SOURCE: Richard F. Burton, *Explorations of the Highlands of the Brazil* (2 vols.; London: Tinsley, 1869), 1:273–78 (extracts; some footnotes omitted).

* A "paddle," for inflicting punishment on the hand. ED.

60 A Brazilian Sugar Plantation, 1880

A large plantation, like that of Sr. S., is a little world in itself. There are smithies and workshops; machines for preparing mandioca, a sawmill, and a cornmill, and a sugar-cane mill, and a still where the canejuice is made into rum. At one end of the enclosure there is a brick kiln, and near by a pottery, where most of the pots in the viveiro were prepared. The machinery is moved, partly by a turbine wheel, but principally by a large steam engine, which Sr. S. shows with pardonable pride. From the machine house, he takes us to his stockyard, which, though entirely a subsidiary affair, is by no means insignificant; there are eighty fine oxen, and nearly thirty mules, a hundred swine, and fifty sheep, with turkeys, fowls, guinea-hens, and pigeons—a feathered host. To crown all, there is a zebu ox from India, which Sr. S. bought in Paris, and imported for experiment.

Picturesque groups of washerwomen gather about the great stone basin, where their work is done. Every morning we hear the clatter of a chopping machine, cutting up sweet cane-tops for the cattle. In the kitchen the slave rations are prepared in great kettles and ovens. Here a blacksmith is busy at his forge; there a carpenter is hammering or sawing. Among all we do not see an idle negro, for even the white-haired octogenarians are employed in basket weaving or other light work, and all children, except the merest babies, must go to the fields with the rest. Only on Sundays, a few of the weaker ones gather about the quarters and indulge in something like recreation.

The negroes are kept under a rigid surveillance, and the work is regulated as by machinery. At four o'clock in the morning all hands are called out to sing prayers, after which they file off to work. At six coffee is given to them; at nine they breakfast on jerked beef, mandioca-meal, beans and corn-cake; at noon they receive a small dram of rum; at four o'clock they get their dinner, precisely like the breakfast, and, like that, served in the field, with the slightest possible intermission from work. At seven the files move wearily back to the house, where they are drawn up to the sound of a bugle. From the tripod at one side a bright fire half illumines, half conceals, the dark figures, sending flashes over the walls beyond, and casting long shadows on the ground. The tools are deposited in a storehouse, and locked up; two or three of the crowd, perhaps, advance timidly to make requests of the master; after that all are dispersed to household and mill work until nine o'clock; then the men and women are locked up in separate quarters, and left to sleep seven hours, to prepare for the seventeen hours of almost uninterrupted labor on the succeeding day. On Sunday there is a nominal holiday, which, practically, amounts to but three or four hours; none of the Catholic holidays are celebrated here, and even Christmas is passed unnoticed.

The Brazilian system of gradual emancipation, however wise it may be in some respects, brings with it an inevitable evil. If a man has unrestrained control of his slave as long as the latter may live, he treats him well, as he would treat his horse well; he does not wish to diminish the value of his property. But if the slave is to be freed in ten or fifteen or twenty years, the policy of the master is to get as much service as possible out of him. A young, able-bodied negro, even if he is overworked and cruelly treated, may reasonably be expected to last twenty years. Humane masters look beyond that, and treat their slaves well; but the majority see the matter simply in a business light. If a man is foolish enough to lend his horse for five years, he must expect to get back a poor, broken-down animal. Yet he who overdrives the horse or the slave may be rather blinded than naturally cruel; blinded by that thickest of all bandages, business.

SOURCE: Herbert H. Smith, *Brazil, the Amazons and the Coast* (London: Sampson, Low, 1880), pp. 524–27.

MAROONS

AT ALL TIMES the black slave in the Americas sought deliverance from a system that denied him the right to live as a man. The range of his response ran from suicide or self-mutilation through passive resistance, malingering, and sabotage, to flight and violent revolt. Which response a slave chose depended more on what opportunities were open to him at a particular time and place than on the degree of oppression he lived under. A slave did not, for example, flee or rebel because he was subjected to especially inhuman treatment. Usually, the worse the masters treated their slaves, the more efficient were the methods of surveillance and control they employed and, as a result, running away (except temporarily, in desperation, and in the expectation of early recapture) was not often attempted unless the chances of a permanent break were thought to be favorable. Such chances rarely existed in small islands, in cities, or in heavily settled rural areas with large white populations. But opportunities for successful and permanent escape from slavery were much greater in the larger islands, like Jamaica and Cuba, and in mainland territories like Brazil and the Guianas, where the whites were mostly confined to the river estuaries and coastal plains and where the hinterland provided almost unlimited concealment.

The five passages that follow are taken from descriptions of permanent or semipermanent settlements of runaway slaves in the Caribbean and Latin America. Selection 61 comes from a history of Brazil written in the early eighteenth century (though not published until 1880) and provides a Portuguese view of the famous *quilombo* of Palmares, which lasted for almost a century, from 1605–6 to 1694.[13] Selections 62 to 64 are eighteenth-century descriptions of the "Maroons" of Jamaica, the "Bush Negroes" of Surinam, and the "Black Caribs" of St. Vincent, and 65 is a nineteenth-century account of the *palenques* of Cuba. The word "maroon" comes from the Spanish, *cimarron,* which meant, originally, an escaped domestic animal and, by extension, a runaway slave.

61 The Quilombo of Palmares

When the province of Pernambuco was possessed and tyrannized by the Dutch, some forty Negroes of the Guiné tribe who came from various sugar mills from the town of Porto do Calvo, gathered together and united, intending to flee from their masters, not because of any cruelties which were practiced on them, but because they yearned for a life of freedom. In secret (rarely seen among this race and amongst such a number of persons) they planned their flight and carried it out, taking with them some slaves, wives and concubines, who were also accomplices in their criminal escape. They also took many different arms, some which they had acquired and others which they had robbed from their owners at the time of their flight. They penetrated the vast backlands of that town, which they discovered were uninhabited, and found that they were surrounded only by beasts which served them as both food and company, in all of which they judged themselves fortunate, preferring liberty among wild animals to subjection among men.

During the first years following their flight, this fire which was smoldering and which would later grow into a great conflagration, did not cause public damage, but only the loss of slaves whose owners were unable to find them, since they did not know in what part of that huge and impenetrable jungle they dwelt. Until that time the fugitives supported themselves only with the game and wild fruits of that unknown land, and did not leave it except to steal manioc plants and other seedlings from the less remote plantations. They did this in order to start their own tillage, taking these plants by force if they found any resistance, and without it if they found no opposition. However, by then the fugitive hideout was already notorious in that vicinity. Many Negroes and some mulattoes who were guilty of domestic and public crimes, went there to seek shelter from the punishment of their owners or of the law, and the Negroes of Palmares received them, welcoming them as citizens of their new republic.

Thus, with this aid from fugitives who continuously joined them, the power of the Negroes grew, so that they could cause the same damages to the people of Pernambuco as those practiced on Rome in the time of the slave war, when a few gladiators, joining together with many ruthless men, caused so much havoc to that noble republic. Since the Negroes understood that in order to increase and multiply they needed, besides the children who were being born to them, to have more women, they took steps to obtain them. They did this without the forethought with which the Romans carried away the Sabine women, but only with sheer strength, breaking into the plantations and houses of the inhabitants of those regions, settlements and districts, and taking Negroes and mulattoes who were either in domestic service or who worked in the fields. They stole from the masters of these slaves, dresses, clothing, and arms which they found, threatening also to violate their wives and daughters if they did not ransom them with money or other gifts. This ransom was promptly offered to them, because, despite the fact that privileges of money and nobility were so important to the Portuguese that they took advantage of the opportunity to exploit the riches surrounding them, so that they could return rich to their own country, they always held honor above material possessions.

As time went by, the number of people in the rebel state multiplied. They penetrated the forest and discovered vast lands. These they divided up among families who put them under cultivation and thus made the community richer and more expansive. Hence, without the philosophy with which Plato and Aristotle created their republics, and without written laws such as those published in Athens by Solon, or in Lacedemonia or Sparta by Lycurgus, or in Crete or Candia by Minos, or in Rome, Carthage, and Egypt by Numa, Charondas, and Trimegistus, they formed a rustic republic in Palmares which was in its own way well ordered.

They elected for their Zombi (which would henceforth be the

name of their prince and which means "devil" in their dialect) a young man who was one of the most just and brave among them. Although he was to be elected to this high office, he would have life tenure. Negroes, mulattoes, and mestizos (that is, the children of a mulatto and a Negro) who conducted themselves properly and who were proven in experience and bravery, were eligible for this office. It is not told, nor is it known, if there was favoritism in the choice made, either toward those who qualified because of their competence or toward those who coveted the position through ambition to rule, nor if they ever killed anyone in order to enthrone another, nor if all took part in the election with obedience and unity, all of which are pillars on which empires are supported.

There were other officers of the justice and of the militia who were named according to the lands they governed. Crimes they invariably made punishable by death were homicide, adultery, and theft, because the same acts which were licit among strangers, were prohibited among their own citizens. The slaves who came to them of their own will were allowed to live in liberty; those whom they had coerced remained captive and might even be sold. There was also capital punishment for those who had put themselves under their power voluntarily and then tried to return to their owners. Those who had the same impulse to return but who had been taken by force were treated less severely. At the time in which we made war upon them, the grandchildren and great-grandchildren of those first rebels were living and the founders' statutes and laws had been learned by heart and passed down by word of mouth from father to son. In this way both law and order were maintained.

They dressed as they had in their native land, without covering more than modesty required, with the exception of a few of the more important people, who dressed themselves with clothes which had either been robbed or were made of materials taken from their executed prisoners. They kept only the outward signs of the Catholic religion, such as the sign of the holy cross and some poorly remembered prayers. These were mixed with other words and ceremonies which had been invented or introduced from their African superstitions. On the one hand, if they could not be called heathen since they conserved remnants of Christianity, on the other hand they might be called heretics, as they had neither sacraments nor ministers of the Church. These last they could not obtain both because of their state of rebellion and because of their free customs which were repugnant to the precepts of our Catholic Church and which excluded them from marriage, guilds, and from being counted among the faithful.

Some inhabitants of those regions, through fear of the damages they might receive and to safeguard their houses, families, and crops from the evils which the Palmares Negroes could cause them, made with them a secret agreement, giving them arms, powder, and bullets, clothing, materials from Europe, and keepsakes from Portugal, in exchange for gold, silver, and money which the rebels had stolen, along with some provisions which they had gathered from their fields. These planters, finding themselves implicated in various inquiries, and knowing that they were guilty and that they would be punished unless they warned one another, kept this secret pact at all costs, in spite of the extremely serious risks which they incurred, because the present danger made them forget future punishment. Thus, their houses remained secure, and also their slaves could go where they were sent with the safe-conducts, consisting of certain pass signs and figures, they had received from the enemy. The rebel captains and soldiers respected these signs and let them pass freely.

Despite the fact that the governors of Pernambuco saw the affliction under which the inhabitants lived, they could do nothing to remedy the situation since they lacked the power to assault and extinguish the enemy who, by now, was reputed to be very large. This was at least what they gathered from the reports given by certain slaves who, having been taken violently and having been forced to live with the rebels, had the good fortune to return to their owners. These returned slaves made much of the large number of people under the rebels' rule, the valiant warriors which they found in their midst, the skill with which they used all types of weapons, the great strength of the wall which served as their rampart, the abundance of the crops they harvested; things which showed that those enemies could resist a long siege, and thwart the thrust of our arms. All this made us lose hope of taking them by storm, and was the very reason that the only steps the governors of the province took were to redouble the penalties of those who communicated with the foe, and to put on certain plantations, way stations with people who could resist the enemies' passage, measures which were woefully inadequate to deal with the force of their great power.

However, Governor Caetano de Mello de Castro, nobly judging that it is the most hazardous enterprises which receive the greatest acclaim, took up this challenge with such zeal that he was able to carry it to a glorious end. He wrote to the governor and captain general, D. João de Lencastro, telling him of his determination, and asking him to order Domingos Jorge, quartermaster of the Paulistas (it was thus that those from the region surrounding São Paulo were commonly called) to march with his troops who were stationed in the backlands of Bahia, on Porto do Calvo, where he would encounter both the men sent from Olinda and Recife, and those from the towns most endangered by and closest to Palmares. D. João de Lencastro, who was pleased only with great undertakings, gave his approval, and ordered the quartermaster, Domingos Jorge, to proceed with the greatest speed possible toward that enterprise at Porto do Calvo. This Domingos Jorge did with great dispatch, setting forth with his Indians, captains, and officers toward that city.

From Pinhancó, where he had his headquarters, Domingos Jorge journeyed, accompanied by his soldiers who numbered about a thousand men. Crossing the Urubá River, as he marched he wanted to take a first look at Palmares, in order to size up the rebel fortification, and to succeed in engaging the enemy, thus winning the first glory by initiating that war. But the very opposite to what he had imagined happened, because three days after they had bivouacked in Garanhuns in front of the enemy walls, while his soldiers were entertaining themselves gathering fruits from the Negro banana plantations, they were attacked by a huge squadron of rebels. The rebels sallied forth from the fort, and attacking the Paulistas who arrayed themselves as well as they could in such a surprise assault, engaged them in a battle in which more than four hundred persons on both sides were killed, and a great number more were wounded. Moreover, the losses the Paulistas suffered would have been even greater if they had not, recognizing how greatly they were outnumbered by the enemy, begun their retreat, a retreat carried out with great valor and high morale, to Porto do Calvo where they found the army which the governor had sent to that town.

The army consisted of three thousand men, which Caetano de Mello de Castro had gathered together from Olinda, Recife, and from neighboring villages and settlements, from many wealthy people who wished to join that expedition, driven on by their own valor and by the vengeance which they hoped to wreak upon those enemies for the injuries they had received, and from some of the more renowned companies which existed in the two-thirds of Pernambuco's paid infantry. Finally, from all the army, the Governor appointed to the post of militia chief, Bernardo Vieira de Mello, who led many armed men from his plantation of Pindobas, and who had offered his services to the Governor for that campaign and conquest. He was both noble and valiant, as well as being a veteran in the war against the Negroes, having emerged successfully from a previous encounter in which he either beheaded or took captive a large number of their troops, in one of the fortified camps which had been set up to repel their invasions. These were the reasons for which Caetano de Mello chose him to command this campaign.

There assembled one thousand five hundred men from the settlements of Alagôas, São Francisco do Penedo, and villages of São Miguel and Alagôas do Norte, under the leadership of the master sargeant, Sebastião Dias. These men arrived in Porto do Calvo, where awaiting them were the chief alcaide, Christovam Lins de Vasconcellos, the militia chief, Rodrigo de Barros Pimentel, coronel, Christovam da Rocha Barbosa, with all the leading citizens and troops of that illustrious city. Thus the army, composed from all this infantry, numbering close to six thousand men, marched toward Palmares amidst military pomp, festive commotion, and all the provisions necessary to the maintenance of a prolonged siege.

Palmares is situated nine degrees to the north, on the terrestrial continent surrounding the towns of Porto do Calvo and Alagôas and at almost equal distance from both, though slightly nearer the first. This name came into use after the Negroes took possession of the land, because of the many palm trees they planted. More than a league encompassed the settlement, the walls of which were made up of two rows of tall stakes, hewed into four facets, tough, unassailable, and thick such as can be found in those great jungles which abound in colossal trunks. The ramparts had three gates of the same strong wood, with platforms along the top, all equidistant. In time of peace, each gateway was guarded by one of the militia chiefs of highest reputation, and more than two hundred soldiers. However, in this time of war, it was garrisoned by the maximum number of troops.

In various parts of those regions, there were stockades of the same strong construction. The palace of their Zombi was crudely sumptuous both in its form and its size; the houses of its citizens were, in their way, magnificent, and lodged more than twenty thousand souls of both sexes, ten thousand of them men capable of carrying arms. The weapons they used were of all types, firearms as well as swords, cutlasses, arrows, darts, and other missiles. Within their settlement there was a very high elevation which served them as a suicide cliff; from it they could sight distant villages and places of Pernambuco which lay far into the horizon. There was a small lake which gave them plentiful fish, and many streams and wells, which they call "cacimbas" (water holes), from which they drew sparkling water. Outside the fortifications they had large orchards and tilled fields, and to guard them they made other small settlements, called "mocambos" (hideaway huts) in which they were aided by their most faithful and experienced soldiers.

Our army arrived. Journeying in the direction of those fields and plantations in order to enjoy them, they found them stripped of both fruits and vegetables, because the enemy, foreseeing the siege with soldierly astuteness, had harvested all that were ripe, and destroyed those which might ripen in the course of it and thus serve our men; and abandoning their outlying huts, they had assembled within their ramparts, uniting all their power, with high hopes of triumphing over our forces which had tolerated them for so many years, and, since they were in firm possession of the fort, hopeful of not being assaulted.

Once our army was divided into various camps, the militia chief, Bernardo Vieira de Mello, posted himself at the middle gateway; the quartermaster of the Paulistas, Domingos Jorge, took charge of the right one; and the left one was assigned to the sargeant major, Sebastião Dias; the other officers took up their stations around the ramparts. On many sides of the walls they raised ladders which they had cannily brought with them, but they were soon repulsed by their enemies, both with firearms and arrows shot from the bulwarks, as well as with boiling water and live coals hurled from the stockades. In this way we received many of our deaths and casualties. Our forces repaid this treatment in kind, on any of the enemy whom they could discover in the vicinity, repeatedly assaulting them to bring them to the point of exhaustion and anxiety in order to weaken their resolve and lower their morale.

As the battle days dragged on, the Negroes began to lack powder which was in short supply to begin with, since they only had what their allies were able to obtain before the war began. And since they were not sufficiently forewarned, in order to gather all the provisions necessary for a prolonged siege, they also began to suffer from a shortage of these foodstuffs, although this did not affect their perseverance, which merely increased with the persistence of our army. Over them, they shot such a cloud of arrows, and hurled such a shower of missiles that bullets seemed unnecessary. All this our men resisted to their utmost. However, having hacked the walls and gates continuously with an abundance of strong axes and other implements, all to no effect except to lose a great many men, they asked Governor Caetano de Mello de Castro to be reinforced with both soldiers and artillery, knowing that without them it would be impossible to break through the enemy fortifications.

To this plea our Governor answered that he would begin to call up men and arrange artillery wagons in order to reinforce them personally; but this news did not stop our army's attacks even at the cost of undergoing great risks and discomforts. They craved victory, knowing that the more difficult the endeavor, the more glorious their success. Nevertheless they recognized that they needed more troops, and that cannon would be necessary to break down the ramparts. They also began to take precautions since the provisions which they had brought were running low and were already less than they needed; in this their officers led the way by surrendering the privileged extra portions which they received because of their posts, in favor of their soldiers.

The Negroes began to weaken. They already lacked the weapons which they had thrown and the food which they had consumed, and they were unable to go to the fields, which were their granaries, to gather there what usually nourished them. They only kept up their spirits by hoping that our army could not continue long in the siege, because the number of our own men was diminishing. Since the war with the Dutch was the last one our men had engaged in, the rebels also felt that our army would be little accustomed to the discomforts which they now suffered and unable to resist the inclement weather of the campaign. Moreover, because of our distance from our stores of foodstuffs, they realized that we were already suffering short rations. All these were reasons on which they founded the supposition that the siege would shortly be lifted. However, soon afterwards our success, which they had not foreseen, demonstrated how wrong they were in their presuppositions.

Looking out from their height or watch tower they saw the fields beginning to swarm with large and small cattle, and with carts and horsedrawn wagons, which proceeded from the towns of Penedo, Alagôas, and from the settlement of São Miguel. They journeyed toward our army in a great convoy, from which the Negroes began to infer our persistence and their ruin. So completely were they discouraged that they busied themselves more with their own terror than with their defense when our troops, aided by the new supplies and by some men who accompanied them, commenced to ram the fort gateways with such renewed vigor and such success that the one attacked by the sargeant major Sebastião Dias, began to sway beneath the arms and hatchets his men wielded. At the same time Bernardo Vieira, militia chief, burst through the one at which he was stationed, at which news the quartermaster of the Paulistas, who was posted at a distant point, rushed with incredible speed to aid his comrade in his moment of danger and glory.

They burst through the walls together, encountering less resistance than they had suspected. This was because the rebel prince Zombi, together with his bravest warriors and most loyal subjects, wishing to avoid being captured by our men, and scorning death by our swords, mounted their great watch tower and hurled themselves from it of their own free will. It was in this manner that they showed us that they did not love a life of enslavement, and that they disdained death at our hands.

All the others who survived, along with a great number of women and children who wept and wailed inconsolably, surrendered themselves. Our men spent many days combing the settlement for some very poor spoils, the most important being their rich and varied arms, which they had used so heroically and which they treated with such polish and care. The officers immediately sent word to the Governor, Caetano de Mello de Castro, whom the messengers found ready to depart the following day with a great number of reinforcements he had assembled in Recife, consisting of two thousand men and six artillery pieces. He received the news with public rejoicing, throwing money from the palace to the people, and afterwards making a solemn procession in thanksgiving, although he would have valued even more the chance to take part in the glory of battle, the end for which he had readied the relief troops with the greatest possible speed.

The Negroes were removed to Recife, and taking from them the levies which belonged to the King, the remainder were given to the officers and soldiers, divided according to the amount of prisoners they had captured upon entering the fortifications. All those who were capable of escaping or rebelling were transported to other Brazilian provinces, and others were sent to Portugal. The women and children, who because of their sex or age were not suspect, remained in Pernambuco.

Thus the war which we waged against the Negroes of Palmares ended in a manner as useful as it was glorious, owing not only the vigor of its undertaking, but also the means of its prosecution, to the valor and zeal with which Caetano de Mello de Castro governed the province of Pernambuco. For this, and for other services rendered in Ethiopia, where he was General of the Sena Rivers, he emerged with such credit and acclaim, that they earned for him the high office of Viceroy of India, a position which he administered with great wisdom, always leaving behind him a distinguished reputation.

SOURCE: Sebastião da Rocha Pitta, *Historia da America portugueza* (Lisbon: F. A. daSilva, 1880), pp. 234–42. Translated for the present volume by Marion Berdecio.

62 The Maroons of Jamaica

When Jamaica was conquered by the English in the year 1655, most of the Spanish inhabitants retired to the island of Cuba; but the troops not being sufficiently numerous to do more than occupy the principal places on the south side, many Spaniards, with the few negroes they possessed, continued to inhabit remote parts of the island on the north side. Their chief residence was in the neighborhood of a town called Sevilla Neuva that had risen to some consequence, and of which the remains are still to be seen about half a mile from St. Ann's Bay, in the fields of a plantation called Seville; where the ruins of a church, convent, and other buildings are plainly traced. In this situation they kept up an intercourse with their countrymen, who, on abandoning Jamaica, had fixed themselves on the south side of Cuba, a distance of about twenty-four hours sail. In a short time these were prevailed upon to make a descent on the island, with the hope of regaining the possession of it; and accordingly Don Arnoldo de Sasi, the old governor, with 500 of the former inhabitants, and 1000 troops from old Spain, landed at Rio Nuevo to the east of Seville, and built a fort. The attempt however was rendered abortive by the vigorous measures pursued by Colonel Doyley, the English Governor, who, with a body of 500 men, marched from the south side, attacked the Spaniards, forced them, after a warm contest, to abandon their settlements, and finally compelled all of them to seek refuge in Cuba.

It may be imagined that at their departure many of the slaves would be disinclined to follow the fortunes of their masters, and still less disposed to submit to the conquerors. Almost every part of the island, particularly the mountains on the north and east sides of it, afforded them secure retreats. To these they fled, and it is supposed that for some time they were instigated by their former masters to commit hostilities against the new possessors of the country; a supposition by no means improbable, as the Spaniards, being so close at hand, and so well acquainted with the sea coasts, might purposely have kept up a communication.

Previous to the final embarkation of the Spaniards, large bodies of the Spanish slaves had fled to the woods in different parts of the island; and a very formidable number had collected in the mountains of Clarendon, under a chief named Juan de Bolas, whose name is still given to the spot which he occupied. The negroes under him were fugitives from the Spanish Planters of the south side, but, though acting upon the same system of plunder and massacre as the fugitives on the north side, it is doubtful whether they ever had any communication with them. This body the Governor soon found means to conciliate, and they surrendered on an acknowledgment of their freedom, and an amnesty for all offenses. They could not indeed be well considered as slaves by the conquerors; and their crimes, though horrid, were better regarded as the effects of a barbarous warfare than made the grounds of endless hostility. At first they readily engaged to act against the other fugitives in the island; but being defeated, and their leader slain, their ardor cooled, and their numbers greatly decreasing, they sought quiet and protection in the vicinity of towns and settlements; nor were any of them ever known to return to their former haunts in the mountains of Clarendon.

The rest of the fugitive negroes, now designated by the appellation of Maroons, or hog-hunters, continuing for many years to wage a desultory war against the inhabitants, were confined chiefly to the eastern and northern parts of the island: but in the year 1690 there was an insurrection of the slaves in the parish of Clarendon, who found a secure retreat in the interior of the country, where they occasionally recruited their numbers from among the plantation negroes, with whom they kept up a communication, and from whose grounds they were often supplied with provisions. By degrees they became very formidable, and in their predatory excursions greatly distressed the back settlers, by plundering their houses, destroying their cattle, and carrying off their slaves by force. This party for many years retarded the settlement of that side of the country, and obliged the Planters, who had made some progress in their estates, to live in a continual state of alarm and preparation for defense, and to build their houses accordingly. These were so placed as to command the plantation works, buildings, and negro houses, and were frequently constructed with flankers and loopholes, for the purpose of firing upon the assailants when they approached so near.

This body of Clarendon rebels were unconnected with the original fugitives, and were not included in the general distinction of Maroons, who, as I have said, continued in the north and east of the island. At first their depredations had been carried on in small parties, and they were satisfied with killing cattle now and then; but in the course of time they habituated themselves to such excesses that frequent complaints were made to the legislature, who at length listened to the representations made, and resolved to reduce the rebels by an armed force that should penetrate the recesses of the woods and discover them if possible. They were in the outset surprised by some parties, dispersed, and many of them killed. Previous to this they had no general leader or chief of the body, but wandered in gangs under the direction of different leaders; but now finding that the colonists had determined to suffer themselves to be annoyed no longer by a lawless band of plunderers, and that parties were fitted out to attack them wherever they could be found, they concentered their force, and elected a chief, whose name was Cudjoe, a bold, skillful, and enterprising man, who, on assuming the command, appointed his brothers Accompong and Johnny leaders under him, and Cuffee and Quao subordinate Captains.

While the Clarendon rebels were carrying on their depredations on the south side of the island, the Maroons in the east continued theirs, and for a long series of years rendered every attempt to settle near them impracticable. Ineffectual efforts were made to subdue them, and, although they suffered greatly in several surprises and well-projected attacks, they remained a rallying point for all who were disposed to quit a state of labor, and to increase their body. They were joined from time to time by a number of slaves, principally those imported from the Coromantee country, a people inured to war on the coast of Africa.

Whether it was that this body of Maroons had to sustain more vigorous and frequent assaults than suited the dispositions of many of the people, or that dissensions had taken place among them, or that both these causes cooperated, which is probable, certain it is, that previous to the year 1730 a party of them separated from the others, and distinguished themselves by the name of the Cottawoods; having, it is supposed, originally come from a place so called, near the present Maroon Charlestown, in the parish of St. George's. On learning that a considerable body of slaves had quitted the upper Settlements in Clarendon, and were carrying on a war against the White inhabitants, under a negroe called Cudjoe; that these people were Coromantees, and their leader a brave and enterprising man; and having probably had some previous communication with him by means of emissaries, about a hundred of them, consisting of men, women, and children, contrived, by long marches through a wild and unexplored country, to join the Clarendon rebels, and put themselves under the command of Cudjoe. At subsequent periods, smaller bodies of the Cottawood party attached themselves to this chief, and by degrees the whole party were united under him: but though consolidated into one body for all the purposes and projects of a community of freebooters, the distinction of their origin was always kept up. The name of Cottawood was preserved among the descendants of that tribe, and the original body of negroes under Cudjoe were distinguished by the appellation of Kencuffees, in which line the succession of their chiefs continued. . . .

At length, in the year 1733, the administration began to tire of the ineffectual system that had been so long pursued. Cudjoe's party had been greatly augmented; and, besides being joined by the Cottawoods and Madagascars, he had now established a general interest with the windward Maroons, who had persisted in hostilities against the eastern planters, and on hearing of Cudjoe's activity and success, had become bolder and more enterprising. The Government, therefore, determined to establish several advanced posts near the usual resorts of each party, in order to check their incursions, and protect the neighboring settlers: accordingly some were formed in the east, in the vicinity of the windward Maroons, and one in the center of the island; that being supposed nearest to the general rendezvous of Cudjoe's party, which was become by far the most formidable. The spot chosen for this post was on Cave River, at the western extremity of a very singular flat about seven miles long and three wide, surrounded on all sides by very high mountains, and nearly half a mile perpendicular above the level of the sea. Here a large range of barracks was built within a high wall, flanked with four regular bastions. Other posts, on a smaller scale, were raised in different parts of the island. By thus advancing forces and supplies closer to the Maroons, long marches were avoided, and a communication being kept up between different posts by small footpaths purposely opened, the operations of the parties employed to wage a constant and harassing war upon them, were facilitated.

The island at this time had but few regular troops, which were sufficiently occupied by the windward Maroons, and to have called out the militia would have been injurious to the prosperity of the colony. It was therefore thought best that independent companies and rangers should be raised; which was done, and these companies, commanded by men chosen for their vigor and activity, were stationed at the barracks on Cave River, the militia being only occasionally called out to assist. To this force was attached a number of confidential negroes, called Black-shot, Mulattoes, and Indians; for the last of whom, several vessels had been dispatched to the Mosquito shore. From the frequent excursions of these forces in the interior of the country, under very active officers, among whom Captain James of the Rangers particularly distinguished himself, Cudjoe and his party found themselves extremely harassed, and much disappointed in the hope they had placed on the difficulty of access to their retreats, where they had begun to cultivate provision-grounds. The Black-shot and Musquito Indians proved of great service in tracing the haunts of the Maroons, and of course Cudjoe's settlements and provisions were successively discovered and destroyed: not, however, without frequent skirmishes, which, though terminating in the defeat of the Maroons, were always attended on the side of the assailants with the greater loss.

It is not clear that the Maroons were always to be considered as defeated when they retired and left the ground of action to their enemy; for surprise and ambush were the chief principles of their warfare; they had not confidence in themselves in open fields, and therefore seldom risked a regular battle. The grand object of a Maroon chief in war was to take a station in some glen, or, as it is called in the West Indies, Cockpit, enclosed by rocks and mountains nearly perpendicular, and to which the only practicable entrance is by a very narrow defile. From the first Cockpit there is a succession of them, running from east to west, on a line in which they are passable from one to the other, though with more or less difficulty. There are also parallel lines of Cockpits, but as their sides are often perpendicular, from fifty to eighty feet, a passage from one line to another is scarcely to be found practicable to any but a Maroon. The northern aspect is commonly the steepest and often a solid perpendicular rock, so that if the opposite ascent were practicable, to descend into the parallel line would be impossible. This is the general character of these recesses, though they may in some degree differ in their direction. They have probably been formed along the large mountains of the island by violent earthquakes. On the difficult ascents there are either no trees, or such as have not strong roots: there are trees in the glens, and the entrance of the defiles is woody. In some, water is found near the passages on either end, but not in the center.

Such are the natural fortifications in which the Maroons secured themselves in times of danger, and from which it has been ever found so difficult to dislodge them. Having but one common entrance, the way to it was so trodden by the frequent egress and ingress of their parties who go in quest of provisions and plunder, that when a distant track was observed by a sharp-sighted guide, it hardly ever failed to lead to the mouth of the defile. At this mouth, which looks like a great fissure made through a rock by some extraordinary convulsion of Nature, from two hundred yards to half a mile in length, and through which men can pass only in a single file, the Maroons, whenever they expected an attack, disposed of themselves on the ledges of the rocks on both sides. Sometimes they advanced a party beyond the entrance of the defile, frequently in a line on each side, if the ground would admit; and lay covered by the underwood, and behind rocks and the roots of trees, waiting in silent ambush for their pursuers, of whose approach they had always information from their out-scouts. These, after a long march, oppressed by fatigue and thirst, advance towards the mouth of the defile, through the track obscured by trees and underwood, in an approach of many windings, which are either occasioned by the irregularity of the ground, or designedly made for the purpose of exposing the assailants to the attacks of the different parties in ambush. A favorable opportunity is taken when the enemy is within a few paces to fire upon them from one side. If the party surprised return the fire on the spot where they see the smoke of the discharge, and prepare to rush on towards it, they receive a volley in another direction. Stopped by this, and undecided which party to pursue, they are staggered by the discharge of a third volley from the entrance of the defile. In the meantime the concealed Maroons, fresh, and thoroughly acquainted with their ground, vanish almost unseen before their enemies have reloaded. The troops, after losing more men, are under the necessity of retreating; and return to their posts, frequently without shoes to their feet, lame, and for some time unfit for service. Such was the nature of the Maroon-war; though it is reasonable to suppose that the people under Cudjoe had not arrived to the perfection of tactics displayed by his successors in the late contest. Indeed, it is known that for a considerable time his operations were carried on about Mouth River, Hector's River, the black grounds, and tracts to the eastward of the greater cockpits, where, though the country was rugged and difficult, it was easy in comparison with the feat of war in the year 1795.

Cudjoe, finding his haunts accessible to the rangers, who were stationed at the barracks to the east of him, and the communication of his foraging parties with his old friends in the back parts of Clarendon cut off, resolved to change his position, and to seek a situation of greater security for his quarters, as well as a more extensive field for his operations. He accordingly removed to a place in Trelawney, near the entrance of the great cockpits to the Northwest, the first of which, called Petty River Bottom, now well known, was accessible by a very narrow defile. This cockpit was considered as a very large one, containing about seven acres of land, and a spring of water. Cudjoe displayed great judgment in choosing this position, as in case of alarm he could throw himself into the cockpit, whence no valor or force could drive him; and at the same time he placed the great range of cockpits between him and his former annoyers. The choice of the position was equally judicious in respect to predatory incursions, as the parishes of St. James's, Hanover, Westmoreland, and St. Elizabeth's lay open to him; and presenting more extensive and less defensible frontiers, afforded him opportunities of acting with smaller detachments, and of obtaining abundant supplies from different quarters. He sent out parties in various directions to a great distance, in order to deceive the Government, and even kept up an alarm in the neighborhood of his old position. Cudjoe now augmented the body he had placed under the command of his brother Accompong, and established them on the northern borders of St. Elizabeth, where the country afforded more cattle, but where also his men had to act against a greater number of inhabitants, prepared to defend their property. This station was above the mountains of Naussau, a place where there is still a town called Accompong after his name.

In this situation did these people maintain themselves in a state of savage freedom for several years, living in indolence while their provisions lasted, and ravaging the country when excited by their wants. In their inroads they exercised the most horrid barbarities. The weak and defenseless, whenever surprised by them, fell victims to their thirst of blood; and, though some were more humane than others, all paid implicit obedience to the command of a leader, when that was given to imbrue their hands in blood: but, murder once commenced, no chief ever had power to stay the hand of his meanest follower; and there is hardly an instance of a prisoner having been saved by them. The Maroons have been accused of torturing their prisoners; but there is no grounds for this charge, as their eagerness to dispatch a wounded enemy falling into their hands was such that he was soon released from his misery by one of the many cutlasses which on the sight of him were raised to strike off his head.

Eight or nine years had now elapsed, since Cudjoe's renown had united all the fugitive negroes in the island, of whatever origin they were, in a general interest; and since the appellation of Maroons had been given indiscriminately to all the tribes of them. Force after force had been employed to subdue them in vain; their hostile operations against the inhabitants were carried on with unremitted vigor. At length the colonists resolved to make every sacrifice, and use every exertion, to put an end to so harassing a war. All who could carry arms volunteered their service, and a large body of the people were assembled under the command of Colonel Guthrie of the militia, and Captain Sadler of the regulars. Amidst these formidable preparations, there were great apprehensions entertained of the uncertainty of the most vigorous measures; the failure of which would not only encourage the enemy, and entail a perpetual war upon the island, but might operate on the minds of the slaves, who would be convinced of the power of the Maroons to maintain a successful opposition against the Government. The governor, Edward Trelawney, was therefore urged by the principal persons of the country to offer them terms of peace.

This being resolved upon, it was necessary that it should be done with the utmost expedition; for a treaty, the purport of which was to establish the freedom and independence of a body of negroes, could not be suffered to remain long pending in the contemplation of slaves, numbers of whom might be tempted to aim at obtaining the like advantage: Guthrie and Sadler were accordingly directed to communicate the offers to Cudjoe as speedily as possible. They could not but be acceptable to the Maroons, who were equally tired of war, and to whom the objects of their hostilities were conceded. On receiving intelligence of the offers to be made, Cudjoe called in his detachments, which had already fallen back, hearing of the preparations made against them. The formidable state of these threw a great difficulty in the way of negotiation, for the distrust of the Maroons would not allow them to reconcile it with the offering of peace; and the sincerity of the Government was doubted.

Governed by this motive, the cautious Cudjoe collected his force, and waited the approach of the peacemakers, on a spot the most favorable to action in his mode of war, and on which his people might defend themselves, were treachery intended on the part of the Government. His men were placed on the ledges of rocks that rose almost perpendicularly to a great height, on a ground which, compared to those precipices, might be called a plain, the extremity being narrowed into a passage, upon which the fire of the whole body might bear. This passage contracted itself into a defile of nearly half a mile long, and so narrow that only one man could pass along it at a time. Had it been entered by a line of men, it would not have been difficult for the Maroons from the heights to have blocked them up in the front and in the rear, by rolling down large rocks at both ends, and afterwards to have crushed them to death by the same means. This Defile, which has ever since retained the name of Colonel Guthrie, was one of the passages to the large cockpit called Petit River, already mentioned. The entrance was impregnable, the continuation of the line of smaller cockpits rendered the rear inaccessible, and Nature had secured the flanks of her own fortification. In this dell were secured the Maroon women and children, and all their valuable things deposited. On the open ground before the defile the men had erected their huts, which were called Maroon town, or Cudjoe's town, whence, in case of an alarm, the people could fly in a minute to the ledges of the rocks at the mouth of the cockpit; nor would their town have been a great loss had it been burnt. They did not, however, confide solely to the security afforded them by the cockpit, and the ease with which they made themselves masters of the defile; every approach to their mountains was, for a mile or two, at other difficult passes, well guarded by small advanced parties, who on the appearance of an enemy might alarm their straggling bodies by means of their horns, which were heard at a considerable distance, and gave timely notice for every one to repair to his post. Thus situated, Cudjoe patiently waited the arrival of the olive branch, and clearly manifested his intentions, and his wishes for an accommodation, by ordering his advanced posts not to fire a shot. His parties therefore merely sounded their horns, and retired to the main body.

At this solemn juncture Colonel Guthrie advanced unmolested with his troops, through situations in which the Maroons might have greatly annoyed him, even with the large force he then had under him. Making, however, the best disposition of his troops that the nature of the ground would admit, he marched on with confidence, and judging of the distance he was from the Maroons by the sound of their horns, he continued advancing till he thought he could make them hear his voice: he then halted, and observing the smoke of their huts within a few hundred yards, though he could not see one of them, called in a loud tone that he was come by the Governor's order, to make them an offer of terms and treat for peace, which the white people sincerely desired. An answer was returned, declaring that the Maroons wished the same, and requesting that the troops might be kept back. This request being apparently dictated by suspicion, Colonel Guthrie proposed to them to show the confidence he had in their sincerity by sending a person to them to assure them that the white people were sincere on their part, and to inform them of the particulars relative to their freedom and security, which the Government had authorized him to propose to them.

This being readily consented to, Dr. Russell was selected for that purpose. He advanced very confidently towards their huts, near which he was met by two Maroons, whom he informed of the purport of his message, and asked if either of them were Cudjoe. They replied in the negative, but said that if he would stay a little while and no men followed him, he would see Cudjoe. They then called out in the Coromantee language to their people; on which several bodies of them, who were before invisible, appeared on the rocks above. Being within the reach of the voice, Dr. Russell addressed himself to them, and begged particularly to have a conversation with Cudjoe, of whom he spoke in high terms; saying, that if he were with them, he was sure, that as a brave and good man he would come down, and show a disposition to live in peace and friendship with the white people.

Several Maroons now descended, and among them it was not difficult to discover the Chief himself. Cudjoe was rather a short man, uncommonly stout, with very strong African features, and a peculiar wildness in his manners. He had a very large lump of flesh upon his back, which was partly covered by the tattered remains of an old blue coat, of which the skirts and the sleeves below the elbows were wanting. Round his head was tied a scanty piece of white cloth, so very dirty, that its original use might have been doubted. He had on a pair of loose drawers that did not reach his knees, and a small round hat with the rims pared so close to the crown, that it might have been taken for a calibash, being worn exactly to the rotundity of his head. On his right side hung a cow's horn with some powder, and a bag of large cut slugs; on the left side he wore a mushet, or couteau, three inches broad, in a leather sheath, suspended under his arm by a narrow strap that went round his shoulder. He had no shirt on, and his clothes, such as they were, as well as the part of his skin that was exposed, were covered with the red dirt of the Cockpits, resembling oker. Such was the Chief; and his men were as ragged and dirty as himself: all had guns and cutlasses. Cudjoe constantly cast his eyes towards the troops with Col. Guthrie, appeared very suspicious, and asked Dr. Russell many questions before he ventured within his reach. At last Russell offered to change hats with him as a token of friendship; to which he consented, and was beginning to converse more freely when Col. Guthrie called aloud to him, assuring him of a faithful compliance with whatever Dr. Russell promised. He said that he wished to come unarmed to him with a few of the principal gentlemen of the island, who should witness the oath he would solemnly make to them of peace on his part, with liberty and security to the Maroons on their acceding to it.

Cudjoe, after some hesitation, consented to their coming forward, and persuaded his people to come down from the rocks, which a few did, but not without their arms. As the gentlemen approached Cudjoe, he appeared to be in great trepidation, but whether caused by joy or fear was doubtful; though he was certainly under the protecting fire of his own men, and the negotiators were unarmed. Colonel Guthrie advanced to him holding out his hand, which Cudjoe seized and kissed. He then threw himself on the ground, embracing Guthrie's legs, kissing his feet, and asking his pardon. He seemed to have lost all his ferocity, and to have become humble, penitent, and abject. The rest of the Maroons, following the example of their chief, prostrated themselves, and expressed the most unbounded joy at the sincerity shown on the side of the white people. Colonel Guthrie and Captain Sadler repeated the offers that had been communicated by Dr. Russell, which was accepted with joy; and confidence being established on both sides, the parties intermixed, exchanged hats, and other tokens of congratulation, and reciprocally testified their satisfaction.

If relief from the fatigues of a vexatious and uncertain war was agreeable to the white inhabitants of the island, it was no less so to the Maroons, who had for some time before been kept in a continual state of alarm, and had begun to feel that want of means to continue hostilities, or even to support a defensive war. How long Cudjoe might have protracted it, is uncertain; but he acknowledged that he had for some time been in a state of want and despondency. Had any of his men been bold enough to propose returning to the masters to whom they originally belonged merely on an assurance of pardon, many, if not the greater part of the Maroons, would have supported the proposal; but all were deterred from expressing such a sentiment, by shame and the dread of punishment. At length, the treaty was concluded with Cudjoe by Colonel Guthrie and Captain Sadler, and all the solemnities attending it were executed under a large cotton-tree growing in the middle of the town at the entrance of Guthrie's Defile. The tree was ever after called Cudjoe's tree, and held in great veneration. I shall here subjoin the treaty.

ARTICLES OF PACIFICATION WITH THE MAROONS OF TRELAWNY TOWN, CONCLUDED MARCH 1, 1738.

IN the name of God, amen. Whereas Captain Cudjoe, Captain Acompong, Captain Johnny, Captain Cufee, Captain Quaco, and several other negroes, their dependants and adherents, have been in a state of war and hostility, for several years past, against our sovereign Lord the King, and the inhabitants of this island; and whereas peace and friendship among mankind, and the preventing the effusion of blood, is agreeable to God, consonant to reason, and desired by every good man; and whereas his majesty George the Second, king of Great Britain, France, and Ireland, and of Jamaica, Lord, Defender of the Faith, &c. has, by his letters patent, dated February the twenty-fourth, one thousand seven hundred and thirty-eight, in the twelfth year of his reign, granted full power and authority to John Guthrie and Francis Sadler, esquires, to negotiate and finally conclude a treaty of peace and friendship with the aforesaid Captain Cudjoe, and the rest of his captains, adherents, and others his men; they mutually, sincerely and amicably, have agreed to the following articles:

First, That all hostilities shall cease on both sides for ever.

Second, That the said Captain Cudjoe, the rest of his captains, adherents, and men, shall be forever hereafter in a perfect state of freedom and liberty, excepting those who have been taken by them, within two years last past, if such are willing to return to their said masters and owners, with full pardon and indemnity from their said masters or owners for what is past; provided always, that, if they are not willing to return, they shall remain in subjection to Captain Cudjoe and in friendship with us, according to the form and tenor of this treaty.

Third, That they shall enjoy and possess, for themselves and posterity for ever, all the lands situate and lying between Trelawny Town and the Cockpits, to the amount of fifteen hundred acres, bearing northwest from the said Trelawny Town.

Fourth, That they shall have liberty to plant the said lands with coffee, cocoa, ginger, tobacco, and cotton, and to breed cattle, hogs, goats, or any other stock, and dispose of the produce or increase of the said commodities to the inhabitants of this island; provided always, that when they bring the said commodities to market, they shall apply first to the custos, or any other magistrate of the respective parishes where they expose their goods to sale, for a licence to vend the same.

Fifth, That Captain Cudjoe, and all the Captain's adherents, and people now in subjection to him, shall all live together within the bounds of Trelawny town, and that they have liberty to hunt where they shall think fit, except within three miles of any settlement, crawl, or pen; provided always, that in case the hunters of Captain Cudjoe, and those of other settlements meet, then the hogs to be equally divided between both parties.

Sixth, That the said Captain Cudjoe, and his successors, do use their best endeavors to take, kill, suppress, or destroy, either by themselves, or jointly with any other number of men, commanded on that service by his excellency the Governor, or commander in chief for the time being, all rebels wheresoever they be, throughout this island, unless they submit to the same terms of accommodation granted to Captain Cudjoe, and his successors.

Seventh, That in case this island be invaded by any foreign enemy, the said Captain Cudjoe, and his successors hereinafter named or to be appointed, shall then, upon notice given, immediately repair to any place the Governor for the time being shall appoint, in order to repel the said invaders with his or their utmost force, and to submit to the orders of the commander in chief on that occasion.

Eighth, That if any white man shall do any manner of injury to Captain Cudjoe, his successors, or any of his or their people, they shall apply to any commanding officer or magistrate in the neighborhood for justice; *and in case Captain Cudjoe, or any of his people, shall do any injury to any white person he shall submit himself, or deliver up such offender to justice.*

Ninth, That if any negroes shall hereafter run away from their masters or owners, and fall into Captain Cudjoe's hands, they shall immediately be sent back to the chief magistrate of the next parish where they are taken; and those that bring them are to be satisfied for their trouble, as the legislature shall appoint.

Tenth, That all negroes taken, since the raising of this party by Captain Cudjoe's people, shall immediately be returned.

Eleventh, That Captain Cudjoe, and his successors, shall wait on his Excellency, or the commander in chief for the time being, every year, if thereunto required.

Twelfth, That Captain Cudjoe, during his life, and the Captains succeeding him, shall have full power to inflict any punishment they think proper for crimes committed by their men among themselves, death only excepted; in which case, if the Captain thinks they deserve death, he shall be obliged to bring them before any justice of the peace, who shall order proceedings on their trial equal to those of other free negroes.

Thirteenth, That Captain Cudjoe with his people, shall cut, clear, and keep open, large and convenient roads from Trelawny town to Westmorland and St. James's, and, if possible, to St. Elizabeth's.

Fourteenth, That two white men, to be nominated by his Excellency, or the commander in chief for the time being, shall constantly live and reside with Captain Cudjoe, and his successors, in order to maintain a friendly correspondence with the inhabitants of this island.

Fifteenth, That Captain Cudjoe shall, during his life, be chief commander in Trelawny town; after his decease the command to devolve on his brother Captain Accompong; and in case of his decease, on his next brother Captain Johnny; and, failing him, Captain Cuffee shall succeed; who is to be succeeded by Captain Quaco; and after all their demises, the Governor, or Commander in Chief for the time being, shall appoint, from time to time, whom he thinks fit for that command.

In testimony, &c. &c.

SOURCE: Robert Charles Dallas, *The History of the Maroons, from their Origin to the Establishment of their Chief Tribe at Sierra Leone* (2 vols.; London: Longman and Rees, 1803), 1:22–31, 35–65 (footnotes omitted).

63 The "Bush Negroes" of Surinam

From the earliest remembrance some fugitive negroes have taken refuge in the woods of Surinam, but these were of very small consideration till about the year 1726, or 1728, when their hostile numbers were much increased, and they had acquired lances and firelocks, which they had pillaged from the estates. By the accession of these arms, in addition to their usual weapons, bows and arrows, they were enabled to commit continual outrages and depredations upon the coffee and sugar plantations, as well from a spirit of revenge for the inhuman treatment which they had formerly received from their masters, as with a view of carrying away plunder, and principally gunpowder and ball, hatchets, &c. in order to provide for their future subsistence and defense.

These negroes were in general settled in the upper parts of the rivers Copename and Seramica, from the latter of which they take the name of the Seramica rebels, in distinction from the other gangs which have since revolted.

Several detachments of military and plantation people were sent against them, but were of very small effect in reducing them to obedience by promises, or extirpating them by force of arms.

In 1730 a most shocking and barbarous execution of eleven of the unhappy negro captives was resolved upon, in the expectation that it might terrify their companions, and induce them to submit. One man was hanged alive upon a gibbet, by an iron hook stuck through his ribs; two others were chained to stakes, and burned to death by a slow fire. Six women were broken alive upon the rack, and two girls were decapitated. Such was their resolution under these tortures, that they endured them without even uttering a sigh. . . .

[This] inhuman massacre produced an effect very contrary to what had been expected. Indeed it so much enraged the Seramica rebels, that for several years they became dreadful to the colonists; who no longer being able to support the expenses and fatigues of sallying out against them in the woods, in addition to the great losses which they so frequently sustained by their invasions, of which they lived in continual terror, at last resolved to treat for peace with their sable enemies.

Governor Mauricius, who was at this period at the head of the colony, now sent out a strong detachment to the rebel settlement at the Seramica river, for the purpose of effecting, if possible, a peace so ardently desired. This detachment, after some skirmishing with the straggling rebel parties, at last arrived at their headquarters, where they demanded and obtained a parley. A treaty of peace, consisting of ten or twelve articles, was actually concluded between the different parties in the year 1749, similar to that which had been made by the English in the year 1739, with the rebels in the island of Jamaica. The chief of the Seramica rebels was a Creole negro, called Captain Adoe, who upon this occasion, received from the governor, as a present, a fine large cane, with a silver pummel, on which were engraven the arms of Surinam, as a mark of their independence, and a preliminary to the other presents that were to be sent out the year following as stipulated by treaty, particularly arms and ammunition, on the performance of which the peace was to be finally concluded. Adoe presented in return a handsome bow with a complete case of arrows, which had been manufactured by his own hands, as a token that during that time all enmity should cease on his side.

This affair gave great satisfaction to many and indeed to most of the inhabitants of Surinam, who now flattered themselves that their effects were perfectly secure; while others regarded this treaty as a very hazardous resource, and even as a step to the inevitable ruin of the colony.

I must confess, indeed, that, notwithstanding the good intentions of Governor Mauricius, nothing appears to be more dangerous than making a forced friendship with people, who by the most abject slavery and ill usage are provoked to break their chains, and shake off their yoke in pursuit of revenge and liberty, and who by the trust which is placed in them have it in their power to become from day to day more formidable.

The insurrection having risen to such height, the colonists ought perhaps to have continued to oppose it, while they were possessed of the power of opposition, not indeed from a motive of cruelty, but for the political good of so fine a settlement.

If it appeared that cruelty and ill treatment had driven these poor creatures to these extremities, policy, not less than humanity, ought to have dictated to the colonists a different conduct in future; but it may be asked, Whether it is possible to keep the African negroes in habits of obedience and industry without the strictest and often the severest discipline?—No. But I ask again, Why is it necessary to inflict such inhuman tortures, according to the humor and caprice of an unfeeling master, or a still more unprincipled overseer? Why should their reasonable complaints be never heard by a magistrate who has it in his power to redress them? Is it because this magistrate is a planter, and that he is interested in the arbitrary government of this unhappy race?—This is too evident.—It would, however, be great injustice if I were not to bear witness that I have not unfrequently seen the plantation slaves treated with the utmost humanity, where the hand of the master was seldom lifted, but to caress them; and where the eye of the slave sparkled with gratitude and affection.

Let us now proceed, and see what were the fruits of making peace with the Seramica rebels.

In 1750, which was the year after, the promised presents were dispatched to Captain Adoe; but the detachment that carried them were attacked on their march, and the whole of the corps murdered on the spot, by a desperate negro, called Zam Zam, who not having been consulted concerning the treaty of peace, had afterwards put himself at the head of a strong party, and now carried off the whole stock of the detachment, consisting of arms, ammunition, checked linens, canvas cloth, hatchets, saws, and other carpenter's tools; besides salt beef, port, spirits, &c. and kept them as his own private property. Adoe, on the other hand, not receiving the presents at the time he expected, too hastily concluding he was only to be amused with expectation till a reinforcement of troops should arrive from Europe to subdue him, renewed his incursions: by this accident therefore the peace was immediately broken; cruelties and ravages increased more than before, and death and destruction once more raged throughout the colony.

In 1751 this settlement was in the utmost distress and confusion; when, in compliance with a request from the inhabitants, presented to the States General, Baron Spoke was sent to Surinam, with 600 fresh troops, drafted from the different regiments in the Dutch service, and on their arrival the members of the court were ordered to send Governor Mauricius to Europe, to account for his proceedings;

who never returned to the colony, having in 1753 asked and obtained his dismission, after having been honorably acquitted. Baron Spoke, who during the absence of Mauricius was appointed to officiate as Governor, found every thing in the greatest disorder, disunion having even arisen between the inhabitants and their rulers, to which it was highly necessary to apply the speediest means of redress. This application was indeed made by the Baron, but he died the year after, and a general distraction again took place.

In 1757, the aspect of affairs daily becoming worse (during the administration of a Mr. Cromelyn, who now was Governor of this colony), a new revolt broke out in the Tempaty Creek amongst the negroes, owing to the treatment which they received from their masters. This fresh insurrection indeed soon became of the most serious consequence. The new rebels joined themselves to sixteen hundred of the old fugitive negroes already settled in eight different villages near Tempaty Creek, and after repeated battles and skirmishes the enemy being mostly well armed, and in their resistance generally successful, the colonists saw themselves once more reduced to sue for peace with their own slaves, near Tempaty Creek, as they had done in the year 1749 with the rebels of Seramica. . . .

To evince the absurdity of that prejudice which considers human creatures as brutes merely because they differ from ourselves in color, I must beg leave to mention a few of the principal ceremonies that attended the ratification of this peace.

The first thing proposed by the colonists was a parley, which was agreed to by the rebels; when the last not only desired, but absolutely insisted, that the Dutch should send them yearly, among a great variety of other articles, a quantity of good firearms and ammunition, as specified in a long list, expressed in broken English, by a negro whose name was Boston, and who was one of their Captains.

Govern Cromelyn next sent two commissioners, Mr. Sober and Mr. Abercrombie, who marched through the woods, escorted by a few military, etc., to carry some presents to the rebels, previous to the ratification of the peace, for which they now were commissioned finally to treat.

At the arrival of the above gentlemen in the rebel camp, at the Jocka Creek, about fifteen miles east of Tempaty Creek, they were introduced to a very handome negro, called *Araby,* who was their chief, and born in the forests amongst the last sixteen hundred that

I have just mentioned. He received them very politely, and taking them by the hand, desired they would sit down by his side upon the green; at the same time assuring them that they need not be under any apprehensions of evil, since from their coming in so good a cause, not one intended or even dared to hurt them.

When the above-mentioned Captain Boston, however, perceived that they had brought a parcel of trinkets, such as knives, scissors, combs, and small looking-glasses, and forgotten the principal articles in question, viz. gunpowder, firearms, and ammunition, he resolutely approached the commissioners, and demanded, in a thundering voice, whether the Europeans imagined that the negroes could live on combs and looking-glasses; adding, that one of each was quite sufficient to let them all see their faces, while a single gallon of *man sanny,* viz. gunpowder, would have been accepted as a proof of their confidence; but since that had been omitted, he should never consent to their countrymen, till every article of the list should be dispatched to them, and consequently the treaty fulfilled.

This expostulation occasioned the interference of a negro captain, called Quaco, who declared that these gentlemen were only the messengers of their Governor and court; and as they could not be answerable for their master's proceedings, they should certainly return to the settlement without injury or insult, and no person, not even he, Captain Boston, should dare to oppose them.

The Chief of the rebels then ordered silence, and desired Mr. Abercrombie to make up a list himself of such articles as he, Araby, should specify; which that gentleman having done, and promised to deliver, the rebels not only gave him and his companions leave peaceably to return with it to town, but allowed the Governor and court a whole year to deliberate whether they were to choose peace or war, unanimously swearing that during that interval all animosity should cease on their side; after which, having entertained them in the best manner their situation in the woods afforded, they wished them a happy journey to Paramaribo.

One of the rebel officers, on this occasion, represented to the commisioners how deplorable it was that the Europeans, who pretended to be a civilized nation, should be so much the occasion of their own ruin by their inhuman cruelties towards their slaves. "We desire you," continued the negro, "to tell your Governor and your court, that in case they want to raise no new gangs of rebels, they ought to take care that the planters keep a more watchful eye over their own property, and not to trust them so frequently in the hands of drunken managers and overseers, who by wrongfully and severely chastising the negroes, debauching their wives and children, neglecting the sick, &c. are the ruin of the colony, and willfully drive to the woods such numbers of stout active people, who by their sweat earn your subsistence, without ever giving the Christians the smallest trouble."

After this, the commissioners left the rebels, and the whole detachment arrived safe at Paramaribo.

The year of deliberation being ended, the Governor and court sent out two fresh commissioners to the negro camp, to bring the so much wished-for peace to a thorough conclusion; which, after much debate, and many ceremonies on both sides, was at last finally agreed upon. Presents were promised to be sent by the Christians, agreeably to the wishes of the negroes; while these last, as a proof of their affection to the Europeans, insisted that each of the commissioners should, during their remaining stay in the rebel camp, take for his constant companion one of their handsomest young women.—They treated them also liberally with game, fish, fruit, and the choicest productions of the forest, and entertained them, without intermission, with music, dancing, and repeated volleys.

At the return of the commissioners, the stipulated presents were sent to the negroes at the Jocka Creek, and, what is remarkable, under the care of the identical Mr. Mayer, who had formerly not dared to fight against them, and escorted by six hundred men, soldiers and slaves. The pusillanimity of this gentleman, however, appeared again on this occasion, and he had nearly undone the whole business by departing from his orders, delivering all the presents to the rebels without receiving the hostages in return. Fortunately Araby kept his word, and sent down four of his best officers as pledges to Paramaribo. By this the peace was perfectly accomplished, and a treaty of twelve or fourteen articles was signed by the white commissioners, and sixteen of Araby's black captains, in 1761; which ceremony took place on the plantation *Ouca,* in the river Surinam, where all the parties met, this being the spot of rendezvous appointed for the purpose, after four different embassies had been sent from the Europeans to the negroes.

Signing this treaty alone, however, was still not considered as sufficient by the rebel chief Araby and his people. They immediately bound themselves by an oath, and insisted on the commissioners doing the same, after the manner which is practiced by themselves, not trusting entirely, they alleged, to that made use of by the Christians, which they had seen them to frequently violate. It must indeed be confessed, that the negroes themselves are uncommonly tenacious of these solemn engagements, as I never heard of an instance, during all the time I resided in the colony, of one of them violating his oath.

The solemnity made use of on this day consisted in each party's letting a few drops of blood with a lancet or penknife from the arms, into a callibash or cup of clear spring water, in which were also mixed a few particles of dry earth, and of this all present were obliged to drink, without exception, which they call drinking each other's blood, having first shed a few drops upon the ground by way of libation; when their gadoman, or priest, with upcast eyes and outstretched arms, took heaven and earth to witness, and with a most audible voice and in a most awful manner, invoked the curse of the Almighty on those who should first break through this sacred treaty made between them, from that moment forward to all eternity. To this solemn imprecation the multitude answered *Da so!* which signifies in their language *Amen.* . . .

The solemnity being ended, the chief Araby and each of his captains (to be distinguished from the inferior negroes, as the Seramican chief Adoe had been before in 1749) was presented with a fine large cane and silver pummel, on which was also engraven the arms of the colony.

The above-mentioned negroes are called *Oucas,* after the name of the plantation where the peace articles were signed; and by that name they are since distinguished from those of Seramica, whom I have already described.

At this time the charter was renewed to the West India Company, by their High Mightinesses, for the term of thirty years longer (as it had been before in 1670, 1700, and 1730), in consideration of a loan of about 5 million sterling, at the rate of 6 percent.

This same year peace was also a second time concluded with the Seramica rebels, who were at that time commanded by a negro called *Wille,* instead of their former chief Adoe, who was dead. But this second peace was unfortunately broken by a rebel captain, called

Muzinga, who had received none of the presents, which had in fact been again intercepted and captured on their way to the chief Adoe, by the very same enterprising and rapacious plunderer Zam Zam, with this difference only, that none of the detachment that were sent with them were now murdered, as on the preceding occasion, nor even one single person injured.

Upon this supposed breach of faith, Captain Muzinga fought most desperately against the colonists; he gave battle face to face, and beat back, at close quarters, above one hundred and fifty of their best troops, killing numbers, and carrying off all their baggage and ammunition.

Soon after this, however, when the real cause of Muzinga's discontent was known, means were found and adopted to pacify this gallant warrior, by making him receive and share the presents sent out by the colonists, on an equal footing with his brother heroes, when peace was a third and last time concluded in 1762, between the Seramica rebels and the colony, which has providentially been kept sacred and inviolable, as well as that with the Ouca negroes, to this day. By their exertions in the field they thus obtained their freedom. . . .

The hostages and chief officers of both the above-mentioned negro cohorts, on their arrival at Paramaribo, were entertained at the Governor's own table, having previously paraded in state through the town, accompanied by His Excellency in his own private carriage.

By their capitulation with the Dutch, the above Ouca and Seramica rebels must yearly receive, as I have mentioned, a quantity of arms and ammunition from the colony, for which the Europeans have received in return the negroes' promises of being their faithful allies, to deliver up all their deserters, for which they are to receive proper premiums, never to appear armed at Paramaribo above five or six at a time, and also to keep their settlement at a proper distance from the town and plantations: the Seramica negroes at the river Seramica and those of the Ouca negroes at the Jocka Creek, near the river Marawina, where one or two white men, called postholders, were to reside among them, in the quality of envoys.

Both these tribes were supposed, at the period I speak of, to amount in all to three thousand, and but a few years after by those that were sent to visit their settlements (including wives and children) they were computed to be not less than fifteen or twenty thousand. They are already becoming overbearing and even insolent, brandishing their silver-headed canes in defiance of the inhabitants, and forcing from them liquors, and very often money, and reminding them how cruelly their ancestors had murdered their parents and their husbands.

SOURCE: Captain J. G. Stedman, *Narrative of a Five Years' Expedition, against the Revolted Negroes of Surinam, in Guiana, on the Wild Coast of South America; from the Year 1772, to 1779* (2d ed.; 2 vols.; London: Johnson and Payne, 1806), 1:58–75 (extracts).

64 The "Black Caribs" of St. Vincent

TREATY OF PEACE, FEBRUARY 27, 1773

Art. I. All hostile proceedings are to cease, and a firm and lasting friendship to succeed.

II. The Caribs shall acknowledge His Majesty to be the rightful Sovereign of the Island, and Domain of St. Vincent, take an oath of fidelity to him as their King, promise absolute submission to his will, and lay down their arms.

III. They shall submit themselves to the laws and obedience of His Majesty's Government, and the Governor shall have power to enact such further regulations for the public advantage as shall be convenient. (This Article only respects their transactions with His Majesty's Subjects, not being Indians, their intercourse and customs with each other in the Quarter allotted them, not being affected by it.) And all new regulations are to receive the approbation of His Majesty's Governor, before carried into execution.

IV. A portion of the lands hereafter mentioned, shall be allotted for the residence of the Caribs, from the River Byera to point Espagnole on the one side, and from the River Auilabou to Espagnole on the other side, according to lines to be drawn by His Majesty's Surveyors from the sources of the rivers to the tops of the mountains. The rest of the land formerly inhabited by the Caribs, for the future to belong entirely to His Majesty.

V. Those lands not to be alienated either by sale, lease, or otherwise, but by persons properly authorized by His Majesty to receive them.

VI. Roads, ports, batteries, and communications shall be made as His Majesty pleases.

VII. No undue intercourse with the French Islands shall be allowed.

VIII. Runaway Slaves in the possessions of the Caribs, shall be given up, and endeavors used to discover and apprehend all others, and an engagement shall be entered into, not to encourage, receive, or harbor in future any Slaves whatever, a forfeiture of lands shall be the penalty for harboring them, and carrying them off the Island shall be considered a capital crime.

IX. All persons guilty of capital crimes against the English, are to be delivered up.

X. In time of danger, the Caribs are to be aiding and assisting His Majesty's Subjects against their enemies.

XI. The Three Chains to belong, and remain to His Majesty.

XII. All conspiracies and plots against His Majesty, or His Government, are to be made known to the Governor, or other civil Magistrate.

XIII. Leave, if required, to be given to the Caribs to depart this Island with their families and properties, with assistance in their transportation.

XIV. Free access to the Quarter to be allowed to the Caribs, to be given to persons properly empowered to go in pursuit of runaway Slaves, and safe conduct allowed them.

XV. Deserters from His Majesty's service, if any, and runaway Slaves from the French, to be delivered up, in order that they may be returned to their Masters.

XVI. The Chiefs of the different Quarters are to render an account of the names and numbers of the inhabitants of the several districts.

XVII. The Chiefs and other Carib inhabitants are to attend the Governor, when required for His Majesty's service.

XVIII. All possible facility consistent with the Laws of Great Britain, is to be afforded the Caribs in the sale of their produce, and in their Trade to the different British Islands.

XIX. Entire liberty of fishing, as well on the coast of Saint Vincent, as at the neighboring Quays to be allowed them.

XX. In all cases where the Caribs conceive themselves injured by His Majesty's Subjects, or other persons, and are desirous of having reference to the Laws, or to the Civil Magistrates, an agent, being one of His Majesty's natural born Subjects, may be employed by themselves, or if more agreeable at His Majesty's cost.

XXI. No Strangers or white persons are to be permitted to settle among the Caribs, without permission obtained in writing from the Governor.

XXII. These Articles subscribed to, and observed, the Caribs are to be pardoned, secured, and fixed in their property, according to His Majesty's directions given, and all past offenses are to be forgotten.

XXIII. After the signing of this Treaty, should any of the Caribs refuse to observe the conditions of it, they are to be considered and treated as enemies by both parties, and the most effectual means are to be used to reduce them.

XXIV. The Caribs shall take the following Oath: viz. We A. B. do swear in the name of the immortal God and Christ Jesus, that we will bear true allegiance to His Majesty George III. of Great Britain, France, and Ireland, King, Defender of the Faith, and that we will pay due obedience to the Laws of Great Britain, and the Island of Saint Vincent, and will well and truly observe every Article of the Treaty concluded between His said Majesty and the Caribs, and we do acknowledge that His said Majesty is rightful Lord and Sovereign of all the Island of Saint Vincent, and that the lands held by us the Caribs, are granted through His Majesty's clemency.

(On the part of His Majesty) W. DALRYMPLE
(On the part of the Caribs) JEAN BAPTISTE, DUFONT, &C.

SOURCE: Charles Shephard, *A Historical Account of the Island of Saint Vincent* (London: Nicol, 1831), pp. 30–35.

65 The Palenques of Cuba

Now, at the very eastern end of Cuba, within the triangle between the cities of St. Jago and Baracoa, and Point Mäysi, a wild and rugged tract of country exists, and in the center of all, an immense mountain, called the Sierra del Cristál, which I have often seen from the sea. Hither no adventurous topographer has yet directed his steps, but were proper measurements made, I am almost certain, the Cristál would be found the highest eminence in Cuba. On this mountain range everyone unites in declaring that the runaway negroes, stopped by its inaccessible summits, have established a large settlement. Collections of wild Indians, or negroes, so established, are called *Palenques,* and the people, "Apalencadoes." For the capture of what is called a "cimarrón simple," a mere runaway, that is, any slave found wandering more than twelve miles from his master's house without a passport, a reward of four dollars is recoverable from the owner, and many poor Spaniards turn a penny by looking out for such chances. The Palenques come under a different regulation. Sometimes they form themselves in more accessible districts, and a settlement of runaways is termed a palenque when there are more than seven congregated. The business is superintended by an official, called a Contador del Consulado, and the court a Consulate.

Expeditions for the reduction of Palenques must be undertaken under the auspices of this tribunal. If the expedition be considered one of extreme danger, special rates of reward are offered. In that case, *extirpation* is probably determined on; but such cases have rarely happened. Otherwise they are governed by the following rules:—If the number, killed, wounded, and prisoners, amounts to twenty, eighteen dollars a head are paid to the captors; if they exceed twelve, sixteen dollars; and if six, ten dollars; but nothing is paid for those, who either die or are so badly wounded that their masters will not have them; and they may refuse them if the expenses of the capture amount to more than the value, which might easily happen, as about one shilling sterling per diem is exacted for costs of maintenance, and one shilling and sixpence for every league they are brought back. The rewards are equally divided among the party, only one-sixth part more is awarded to the captain.

The great Palenque of the Cristál, however, remains as much a mystery as ever, and some even doubt if the Spanish Government does not leave it purposely as a kind of safety valve for the discontented, for no expedition of importance enough to reduce it has ever been undertaken, although small parties are annually formed in Baracoa, who hover about it, and capture a great many negroes. Common report says, that the settlement is high up on an elevated plateau, only approachable by one pass, which is fortified by overhanging rocks, kept ready to hurl on the invaders, and strictly guarded by wary sentinels; and that on this plateau, whose inhabitants are said to amount to many hundreds, grain, tobacco, &c., are grown sufficient for their wants. It is further hinted, that some whites have more dealings with the Apalencados than they would wish generally known, and supply them with clothes, and necessaries unattainable in the Palenque. While I was at Gibara, a negro was brought in belonging to an estate there, who had received eighteen or twenty sword cuts, having made a desperate resistance. I have often been seized with an intense longing to visit this Palenque, but was deterred by two good reasons. If I had attempted it singly, I should assuredly have been murdered, and if with the connivance of any other individual, it would have come to the knowledge of the Government, and I should have been fleeced of the last farthing, or ended my days in a jail. I have listened for an hour together to my friend Pepe's yarns about Baracoa, of which place he was a native. It must be a delightful spot indeed, and I wish I could have visited it! The land is entirely rocky and mountainous, and celebrated for coffee, but, higher up, the hills are clothed with pine trees (*P. occidentalis*), and their echoes resound to the songs of nightingales, as he called them (rüiseñor), but which, I suppose, are mockingbirds.

An old hand (said Lopez) forming one of a party for catching Apalencados, had managed to separate himself from the rest; being doubly confident, inasmuch as he carried, besides the usual rapier, a double-barreled percussion gun. As he was going along quietly through the wood, he heard the voices of a man and woman in conversation. He immediately burst through the bushes, and stood in front of them, demanding surrender, and presenting his gun. The man, instead of complying, was making off, when the white man, knowing he could not catch him while encumbered with his gun, pulled the trigger, but the cap only exploded! On this the woman, turning round in another direction, called out, "Francisco, come out! white man gun no powder got!" Now behold *three* adversaries; the men armed with swords, the woman with a long knife! However, not this time did his gun prove faithless; he quietly put on a fresh cap, and, as there was no help for it, took a deliberate aim at each of the men, whom he shot in turn, and afterwards capturing the woman, not without some trouble and a few wounds, made his way back to his party.

A good many children are captured in these expeditions, and a friend of mine had a servant who had been one. The rest of the negroes look with supreme contempt on these Palenque people, and really think it a disgrace to have been there. I have often heard them twit this woman on her origin. As for her, she was one of the greatest furies and most completely intractable creatures one could conceive. She had really no end of paramours; and she carried her familiarities with them to such a scandalous degree, that my friend placed her under some restraint or other; in revenge for which she actually set fire to his house, which was burned to the ground, with much valuable property! It was her anxiety to include him in the conflagration, which saved him, for she set fire to the thatch just above where he slept, and the crackling of the flames awoke him, but if she had chosen another part, he might easily have been suffocated. In consideration of this proof of her warm feelings, he disposed of her to a sugar estate, where whe would hardly have a chance to play such pranks, her propensities being known.

SOURCE: J. G. Taylor, *The United States and Cuba* (London: Bentley, 1851), pp. 226–31.

REVOLTS

THE HISTORY of slavery in Latin America and the Caribbean exhibits a continuous record of servile rebellions and revolts. Whenever and wherever they could, the slaves reacted violently against the system that victimized them. The most famous rebellion in the history of the Caribbean—and the only permanently successful one anywhere in the Americas—took place in Saint-Domingue. Beginning in 1791 and lasting more than ten years, the "Revolution of Saint-Domingue" produced a brilliant black leader in Toussaint l'Ouverture and culminated in the creation of the first independent black state in the New World. The best detailed account of it in English is *The Black Jacobins* (1939), by C. L. R. James. Servile conspiracies and plots that never got beyond the planning stage were even more common than actual outbreaks. Most were betrayed before any violence occurred, and many were but figments of the slaveowners' imaginations. But the cumulative effect of attempted rebellions, of frequent uprisings, murders, and acts of arson, and of rumors of massacre and outrage kept the slave-owning class in Latin America and the Caribbean in a more or less permanent state of fear and apprehension.

The following passages have been chosen to illustrate the various forms that violent servile resistance took between the sixteenth and nineteenth centuries. Selection 66 describes what was a very common occurrence, a mutiny during the Middle Passage, that is, the journey from Africa to the Americas. Selections 67 and 68 provide examples of violent reactions to slavery in Mexico and Cuba. Selection 69 recounts the story of the most serious rebellion that ever occurred in Jamaica, and 70 summarizes the history of servile revolts in Brazil.

66 Mutiny during the Middle Passage

The first Mutiny I saw among the Negroes, happened during my first voyage, in the Year 1704. It was on board the Eagle Galley of London, commanded by my Father, with whom I was as Pursar. We had bought our Negroes in the River of Old Callabar in the Bay of Guinea. At the time of their mutinying we were in that River, having four hundred of them on board, and not above ten white Men who were able to do Service: For several of our Ship's Company were dead, and many more sick; besides, two of our Boats were just then gone with Twelve People on Shore to fetch Wood, which lay in sight of the Ship. All these circumstances put the Negroes on consulting how to mutiny, which they did at four o'clock in the Afternoon, just as they went to Supper. But as we had always carefully examined the mens Irons, both Morning and Evening, none had got them off, which in a great measure contributed to our Preservation. Three white Men stood on the Watch and Cutlaces in their Hands. One of them who was on the Forecastle, a stout fellow, seeing some of the Men Negroes take hold of the chief Mate, in order to throw him over board, he laid on them so heartily with the flat side of his Cutlace, that they soon quitted the Mate, who escaped from them, and run on the Quarter Deck to get arms. I was then sick with an Ague, and lying on a Couch in the great Cabbin, the Fit being just come on. However, I no sooner heard the Outcry, That the Slaves were mutinying, than I took two Pistols, and run on the Deck with them; where meeting with my Father and the chief Mate, I delivered a pistol to each of them. Whereupon they went forward on the Booms, calling to the Negroe Men that were on the Forecastle; but they did not regard their Threats, being busy with the Centry, (who had disengaged the chief Mate,) and they would have certainly killed him with his own Cutlace, could they have got it from him; but they could not break the Line wherewith the Handle was fastened to his Wrist. And so, tho' they had seized him, yet they could not make use of his Cutlace. Being thus disappointed, they endeavoured to throw him overboard, but he held so fast by one of them that they could not do it. My Father seeing this stout Man in so much Danger, ventured amongest the Negroes, to save him; and fired his Pistol over the Heads, thinking to frighten them. But a lusty Slave struck him with a Billet so hard, that he was almost stunned. The Slave was going to repeat the Blow, when a young Lad about seventeen years old, whom we had been kind to, interposed his Arm, and received the Blow, by which his arm-bone was fractured. At the same instant the Mate fired his Pistol, and shot the Negroe that had struck my Father. At the sight of this the Mutiny ceased, and all the Men-negroes on the Forecastle threw themselves flat on their Faces, crying out for Mercy.

Upon examining into the matter, we found, there were not above twenty Men slaves concerned in this Mutiny; and the two Ringleaders were missing, having, it seems, jumped overboard as soon as they found their Project defeated, and were drowned.

SOURCE: William Snelgrave, *A New Account of Some Parts of Guinea, and the Slave Trade* (London: Knapton, 1734), pp. 166–67.

67 Revolt in Sixteenth-Century Mexico

Antonio de Mendoza, Viceroy of New Spain, to the Emperor, September 1537:

On the 24th of September I was advised that the Blacks had chosen a king and had reached an agreement to kill all Spaniards and seize the land, and that the Indians were also involved. Since the news was brought to me by one of the Blacks, I did not give it much importance. Nevertheless, I did attempt to find out secretly what truth there was in the rumor, and at the same time I ordered some members of my own household to go among the Indians and, if such were found, to inform me at once. For I had been warned, and although I had not really believed in the existence of danger, I did not want to be unprepared for the possibility that the rumors might be true and the Blacks might overwhelm us. . . . As a result of my efforts I did uncover a few clues, and I immediately ordered the arrest of as many of the principal plotters as could be apprehended. I also sent word to the mines and towns where there are Spaniards living so that they would be forewarned and keep a close watch on the Blacks in those places; and this they did. The Blacks who were arrested confessed that it was true that they had plotted to seize the country. Groups of sentries were formed and stationed in this city and in the mines of Amatepeque, where I sent two dozen of them, together with four Black men and one Black woman, to Francisco Vazquez de Coronado. The Indians killed these Blacks . . . since I had ordered that they be arrested or killed. With this the matter was brought to an end. We have tried to find out all that we could about the complicity of the natives in this, but as of this moment have been unable to establish any more than the fact that they were unaware of the plot, although the Blacks originated it; it would have been unfortunate for us if they had persisted in it.

There is no doubt that among the things which gave the Blacks the courage to plot this revolt were, first of all, the wars and preoccupations which beset Your Majesty. The news from abroad is sent in more detail than is necessary and reaches the ears of the Blacks and the Indians in its entirety, with nothing hidden from them. Secondly, under present conditions ships take such a long time to reach us that one friar was said to have spread the rumor that no ships would be coming from Spain for ten years. He says that this remark was falsely attributed to him, but I am not surprised by what the Blacks have attempted because the Spaniards do betray anxiety about the arrival of ships in spite of the fact that tranquillity has now been restored. Your Majesty should send ships regularly so that news from abroad reaches us regularly. If this were done, it would contribute greatly to the general contentment, and the country would be more peaceful.

In view of all this and in the belief that, if there were fewer Blacks in this land, such plots would not be lightly undertaken, I write to ask Your Majesty to suspend the sending of the Blacks I had requested for the time being, because if there were large numbers of them [here] and another such plot occurred we might be unable to control the situation and the land might be lost.

Since this revolt of the Blacks I have attempted to make the populace more alert to the dangers and also to determine what arms and horses each resident has. We can count on 450 men with horses and an equal number on foot but well armed, and a few others.

SOURCE: José Antonio Saco, *Historia de la Esclavitud de la Raza Africana en el Nuevo Mundo y en especial en los Paises Americo-Hispanos* (4 vols.; Havana: Cultural S.A., 1938), 1:279–81 (extracts). Translated for the present volume by Marion Berdecio.

68 Revolt in Eighteenth-Century Cuba

Don Pedro Morell de Santa Cruz, Canon of the Cathedral of Santiago de Cuba, to the King, 26th August 1731:

In fulfillment of my duty, I inform Your Majesty of the insurrection of black and mulatto slaves in Santiago del Prado on 24 July, and of their retreat into the mountains with their arms. News of the trouble circulated and I expected the Governor to take the appropriate steps, but he, at first, gave it little importance and only later moved to remedy the grave situation. When the ineffectiveness of his measures became apparent, he consulted the municipal government and it was agreed to submit the ordinances to the lawyers of this city for their advice. My counsel was simply to suppress the revolt quickly, applying the sanctions used by previous administrations and suspending more recent provisions.

Everyone agreed with this suggestion and action was begun with the naming of aldermen José de Losada and don José de Hechavarría as peace negotiators. They left for the aforesaid town and, after a number of meetings with the natives, who came down from the hills to see them, found themselves unable to obtain their submission or, indeed, any hope other than the suggestion, which they themselves made, that I should go there to allay some of the fears [of the rebels]. Although I felt that in going I would be doing Your Majesty a particular service, I did not want to leave without informing the Governor of the purpose of my journey. He thanked me and wished me success. I went to the aforementioned village and returned without having accomplished my mission, because I found that with the passage of time and because of their idleness the slaves had become frenzied; they insisted that they were free men and the governors of Cuba had withheld the Royal Edict which had granted them that freedom. Some of them said this, while others, while not contradicting the statement, based their claim to freedom on a misinterpretation of a Royal Edict issued at the time that the mines in question were leased to don Francisco Delgado. Although I explained the Edict to them repeatedly, I was unable to remove their misunderstanding of it; this was because their imperfect comprehension was compounded by their ardent desire for freedom and any remarks of mine which did not encourage this desire caused only laughter. I returned home very discouraged, burdened by the thought of the damage which the whole Island would suffer if they persised in their obstinate attitude. I reported the failure of my efforts to the Governor, and, although his first inclination was to resort to arms, he did, by God's Grace, consult the municipal council again. The council advised him to continue to use gentle methods and urged the need for persuasion by arbitration and lawful means. The governor adopted this suggestion and the village was pacified on the 18th of this month.

I have no doubt that the Governor will try to make amends for this event by reducing these slaves to utter subjection, but I must point out to Your Majesty that the causes of the trouble lie in the severity of his treatment of them. For example, he altered the custom of having squads of 6 to 10 men begin a shift of work in the mines every fortnight; the work is now organized in such a way that all the men he chooses to send, even free men, must work to a continuous schedule that allows them no respite, even during holidays. The families of these men are now utterly abandoned, since they cannot support them on a salary of one *real.* The reason for dividing them into squads was precisely to give them time to take care of their wives and children, and the most practical method of dealing with those who could not report for work was to deduct three pesos from their wages. He further oppressed them by requiring them to contribute to Your Majesty one-fifth of the copper which they wash from the river sediments. This work was usually done by the women, to relieve their economic hardship. An officer from the gaol was sent with 13 riflemen to enforce the orders against these unfortunates with the utmost severity. Some were shackled; others were put in the stocks. They were deprived of their right of access to some hunting grounds, which were sold at public auction. Also, though it seems contrary to Christian charity, they were forbidden, under threat of the severest penalties, to buy meat from the vendors who came through the villages from the interior, and those who went out of the town to meet the meat vendors were brought back bound, which reduced them to the most extreme desperation.

Although the crudeness with which these measures were carried out here saddened me greatly, my distress was even greater when, on going to seek their surrender, I heard the details from the victims themselves. Since the methods of this Governor are very different from those of his predecessors, the slaves were certain to make the mistake of rebelling until earlier policies were restored. There need be no fear that they will persist in [their rebellious attitude], since they are so miserable and wretched that only the most intolerable oppression could have given them the courage to hide in the mountains and to refuse to work. . . .

The service which I have rendered to Your Majesty is extremely valuable for, without being guilty of excessively melancholy reflections, I clearly perceive that the entire island could be lost if the slaves persist in their stubborn attitudes. Since there are so many of them in every region and since their hatred of their masters is so widespread, a general uprising might occur and they would then become the lords of the towns. In confirmation of this I learned after the rebels of Cobre had been subdued that fifty fugitive blacks had come to the rebels' camp to offer their arms and to promise to bring 300 more men within two hours and arouse all the blacks in this city against the residents.

SOURCE: Saco, *Historia de la Esclavitud,* 2:190–94 (extracts). Translated for the present volume by Marion Berdecio.

69 The Jamaica Rebellion, 1831–32

Early in December 1831 rumors of an impending servile war began to spread abroad and agitate the community. The slaves, it was said, had bound themselves by a solemn oath to each other to be slaves no longer. The conspiracy was discovered on *Salt Spring* estate, near Montego Bay, from the mysterious and threatening language of an angry negro to his overseer, which aroused suspicion, led to investigation, and thereby brought to light the whole scheme. The time was near for its being carried into effect, yet nothing seemingly could be done beforehand to prevent it.

The original scheme was simply not to turn out to work after Christmas, without payment for their labor. The idea of a slave revolt in any form was alarming; and the report was received and propagated by the old colonial party with the customary exaggerations of terror. The white people, it was said, would be murdered, the properties burned, and Jamaica become another St. Domingo. The free colored class, indeed, especially about Kingston and other distant parts, made light of the story, as merely one of the old Christmas alarms, got up for some disguised purpose. But there were many, both white and colored, of a moderate middle class, who thought the scheme of passive resistance not incredible, yet believed that, though the slaves meditated no outrage, violence would inevitably ensue. The masters would use it to enforce labor, and the slaves to resist; in which unavoidable struggle property and life would be lost.

But the negroes were not all of one mind. The Creoles—young, strong, and giddy with the new-born hope of liberty, which they said the king had given them and their masters withheld—resolved to stand out for the wages of free labor, and, if needful, to fight for their rights. The old people discouraged the attempt. They had seen worse times, and were sensible of a growing amelioration of their condition. The experience also of former insurrections taught them to dread the consequences of failure. But the counsels of age, attributed to timidity and ignorance, were disregarded. The leaders of the movement,—the captains, colonels, and generals of the insurgents,—fearing that the women first would be persuaded or compelled to resume their hoes, and through them the men, resolved, for their own safety, and the success of their plans, to involve as many as possible, and begin where they knew they must end, by burning down the estates. This would give them time, enable them to complete and extend their arrangements, and increase the number of sworn adherents. Thus the conspiracy was organized over nearly half the island.

Disturbances had often broken out during the Christmas holidays, and were always apprehended. It had been customary, therefore, for the militia to be mustered in every parish at that time. Of late years the negroes had been so peaceable and contented, that confidence had increased, and the Christmas muster became a matter of form, till this new alarm awoke the old fears. Unhappily the means used to prevent only precipitated the confusion, by gathering the forces of the colony into the towns, and leaving the sugar estates throughout the country unprotected, in the hands of the disaffected slaves.

Before any blow had been struck, I admonished my congregation on the subject. One with them, I said, in desiring their freedom, and not doubting they would yet receive it, I assured them it could come to them only in a peaceable and lawful way,—by the efforts of their friends in Britain,—while violence on their part would surely retard its progress, and perhaps insure their own destruction. The game about to be played was too deep for them; they did not understand it, and could not play it like their masters. One false move on their part would be their ruin. If they broke the laws of the country, it was not their masters alone they would have to resist, but the whole power of England, which they could not withstand, when their friends could no longer befriend them, and their enemies would be increased, and enraged against them. In peace, patient continuance in well-doing, yea, and in suffering, lay their power, with such a country as England to look to. They should, therefore, confide in their friends there; prove their fitness for freedom by their continued good conduct; keep far from those who spoke of destroying either life or property; and especially sin not against the Lord for anything in the world. The people were not pleased with this address. Many looked downcast and disappointed; and, as they left the church, said one to another, "Minister give against we." Yet they wisely reflected, and followed my advice. . . .

Christmas day fell on Sabbath, and everything was still quiet. But at Dun's Hole we had no congregation. The people around, not having had the previous day, were employed in receiving their annual allowances on the estates, or in seeking ground provisions in the mountains or the markets. It was bad policy to keep the Saturday from them at such a time, and unjust too; and showed such a want of good feeling on the part of the masters, as aggravated the ill humor of the slaves. They hardly gave the usual "Thankee" for their allowances. Some of them murmured, "And that is my year's pay!" At Cornwall and Cinnamon Hill, however, the people had got their day, and we had a good congregation on the Sabbath.

The following Tuesday was appointed for our customary Christmas church meeting; but religious feelings were for the time in abeyance. At Dun's Hole I was again disappointed. Very few people attended; and only one, my assistant elder, from the *Spring*. All was alarm. The negroes there, it was said, had broken into the overseer's house, and taken away guns and pistols. I hastened thither to seek them, but found only the housewomen. They were terrified, and said that the slaves were ready to cut the head off any person that spoke a word in favor of white people. In the negro houses only the aged and infirm could be seen. Others were watching me and hiding. At length a few were intercepted, through whom I sent word to all, that the possession of these arms would endanger the lives of all found with them, and they must be immediately restored to their place. To relieve their fears of discovery, I proposed that they should be deposited during the night at a certain place, and that next morning I would come, or failing me, my elder, and would gather and replace them in the "busha-house," and make all fast again, without asking any questions. Happily my words were repeated and regarded, and the next day the dangerous weapons were restored, and nothing was again heard of the matter.

It was long past my usual time when I got back to Cornwall, and there I found confusion and dismay. The congregation which had assembled was dispersing in affright, and would not return at my call. The only answer or explanation that could be got was,—*"Palmyra on fire."* It was not an ordinary estate fire they spoke of, which neighboring estates' people would hasten to put out. Were it even so, it need have caused us no alarm, there being a range of wooded hills between it and Cornwall. It was the preconcerted signal for our part of the country that the struggle for freedom had begun; and the volumes of lurid smoke rose high over the hills into the clear air. It was the response to *"Kensington on fire,"* another sugar estate high up the mountains towards the interior. Both were visible to each other, and over a great stretch of intermediate country, richly cultivated, and thickly studded with sugar plantations. The one hoisted the flaming flag of liberty, and the other saluted it, calling on all between and around to follow their example. And it was followed. These were grand beacon-fires, frightful conflagrations, visible far and wide, caused by the burning of the great "trash-houses," with their enormous piles of dry crushed canes, stored up from last year's crop, to supply the furnaces for boiling the next year's sugar. No wonder that even quiet, well-disposed slaves were greatly agitated, when they saw the banner of a great gathering and great conflict floating up to heaven,—a conflict in which they and their children would be deeply interested in its issues of early freedom or prolonged slavery.

When alone that evening, we sat pondering, and saying one to another, "What will the negroes next do? What should we do?" Just then Roderick of Barrett Hall made his appearance, and claimed his Christmas box. He was a New Providence man, a blacksmith by trade, and mulatto by color. He had come from Montego Bay, excited by drink and what he had learned there, and he threw out mysterious hints of what we should soon see. Displeased with his speech, I discouraged it, and advised him to go home quickly and quietly. He wanted his "Christmas" first, he said, a glass of wine or porter to drink my health. But he had got too much of that already, and I urged him to go home and keep quiet, lest he should get into trouble. That was no time, I told him, for a man to make a fool of himself, when the country was on the eve of rebellion. "Well, minister," he replied sharply, "every fool has his own sense"; and he went away offended. Poor man, his sense was insufficent for such a time. When I next saw him he was in irons, weeping bitterly, under an armed guard, and condemned to die, not for crime, but folly; for folly sometimes looks so like crime that it meets the same doom.

Scarcely had night closed in, when the sky towards the interior was illumined by unwonted glares. Our view in that direction was bounded by the Palmyra Hills, but we could not be long ignorant of the cause of these frightful appearances; and as the fires rose here and there in rapid succession, reflected from the glowing heavens, we could guess from their direction, and the character of masters and slaves, what estates were being consumed. Soon the reflections were in clusters, then the sky became a sheet of flame, as if the whole country had become a vast furnace. I dreaded lest the wild spirit of incendiarism should invade our seaside district: and my eyes ever turned towards the *Spring,* where so bad a spirit had already been displayed. But happily the night wore on, and midnight was passed, without a torch being seen in our direction. Then the fires began to die out, and new ones no longer appeared, and we could venture to lie down and rest a little before morning. That was a terrible vengeance which the patient drudges had at length taken on those sugar estates, the causes and scenes of their lifelong toils and degradation, tears and blood. But, be it remembered that, amid the wild excitement of the night, not one freeman's life was taken, not one freewoman molested by the insurgent slaves.

Had the country been quiet, the next day would have seen the resumption of work after the holidays. But that was not to be thought of. The proprietor of our estates might have looked for it from his people, after the great improvement he had effected in their condition; and, indeed, some of them did turn out to the field of their own accord; but he wisely forbore requiring such service then, and told them only to stay at home, keep quiet, and guard the property. Indeed, the rebels had sent threatening messages of fire and blood, if they should turn out to work that day.

In such a state of the country, and not knowing what would follow, Mr. Blyth and I took our families to Falmouth for their greater safety. The Cornwall people earnestly deprecated our leaving them; but we promised soon to return, if they behaved well. At Falmouth every house was crowded with terrified refugees from the interior; but we got a night's lodging in the Rev. Mr. Knibb's; though he had so many of his own brethren with him, that six of us slept on the floor in one room. They had just returned, through Montego Bay, from the opening of a new chapel at *Salter's Hill,* and described the state of the town and country, where they had been, as one of dreadful terror and confusion. His assurances that no "free law" had come for them, were discredited by the assembled thousands,—his exhortations to be quiet and return to their estate duties enraged them. He never thought to see the people so furious; they accused their ministers of deserting them; and the immediate destruction of all the properties in the surrounding districts was their fierce reply to his admonitions. . . .

The next day was the 1st January 1832, and a miserable New-year's day it was. Martial law was proclaimed, and the town was a scene of confusion. It was the Lord's day, but composure of mind for the worship of God was impossible. The weekly market, with its incessant babble, filled the square. The "sets," or "reds and blues," paraded the streets with their horrid din, louder and more discordant than ever—perhaps feigning indifference, to divert suspicion. Companies of estate negroes were driven into town as prisoners before the militia; the men, sturdy and sullen, handcuffed; the women, burdened with infants on their sides, and baskets of household things on their heads; and children, running beside their mothers, crying bitterly. Arrived at the courthouse, they squatted huddled together on the groundfloor, in pitiable plight, for the night, to await the issue of a court-martial on the morrow.

It was soon reported that missionaries must do military duty. The alternative was a painful one—either to take up arms against the people we had come to teach in peace and love, or be regarded and treated as disloyal subjects. We looked to God for guidance in this dilemma. The next day, Mr. R———, a professed but officious "friend of all missionaries," and a magistrate withal, visited the Scottish missionaries to inform us, that we were not free from suspicion, more than Methodists or Baptists, and that to exonerate ourselves we should offer our services to the magistrates, to do some militia duty by keeping guard in town. It would look loyal, he said, and public spirited, disarm suspicion, and afford much satisfaction to the authorities. Though not authorized by the other missionaries in town to speak for them, he could say that they would not be unwilling to do so if we consented. It struck me that if our services could have been rightfully demanded, they would not have been sought in that sly way; and Mr. Blyth had the same idea; for, answering for us all, while he thanked Mr. R—— for the interest he evinced in us, he declined to act on his suggestion, believing that we could prove our loyalty and promote the peace of the island quite as well in some other way, more consistent with our character and office.

We got passports for two days and set off for our several districts, Mr. Blyth and Mr. Cowan to Hampden; Mr. Barrett of Cinnamon Hill and myself to his properties. The commander-in-chief, Sir Willoughby Cotton, had issued a proclamation calling on the disaffected slaves to return to their estates and labors within a certain time, or be treated as rebels. It was needful to make the people acquainted with it. On Mr. Barrett's estate we found everything safe and quiet; the people gathered round us, tired they said of being idle, and ready to return to work at once; and their master was highly pleased.

On *Spot valley* the case was different. The stores had been plundered, and the people were very unruly. Many of them had always been heathenish; and some nominal Christians there were my greatest opponents. Their turbulence on this occasion therefore did not surprise me. They would not come to the overseer's house to meet us, but only to the gate of their own precincts. There they listened to Mr. Barrett reading the proclamation, till it spoke of their returning to work, when they all lifted up their voices and overwhelmed him with clamor. "We have worked enough already, and will work no more. The life we live is too bad; it is the life of a dog. We won't be slaves no more; we won't lift hoe no more; we won't take flog no more. We free now, we free now; no more slaves again." Then they shouted, and laughed, and clapped their hands. It was really so amusing a scene I could not help laughing with them, and my doing so increased their good humor.

After long debating, Mr. Barrett on one side with the head people, and I on the other, with a noisy crowd of women and young men, we let them know the real state of the case, and brought them to reason it with us. Some of them said, "Massa Barrett, your people may work for you. They know who they work for. But we never see for we massa; we no have massa; and we no will work no more for them busha and 'torney." One good old man, however, whom I knew very well, boldly said, "When your people begin work again me and my children will begin too. . . ."

Before leaving Falmouth, I visited the Court House to see the prisoners. There, to my surprise and sorrow, was Roderick, already mentioned, under sentence of death. He seemed stunned and stupified till I spoke to him, when he burst into a passionate flood of tears, and with vehemence protested his innocence, and bewailed his fate. Having inquired of a magistrate concerning him, if a review of his case might be obtained, I was told that nothing could be done for him, his guilt having been clearly proved. His own master, however, told me afterwards that he never knew what he had been guilty of, except rudeness to a militia man, and tearing down a proclamation; and he believed the poor fellow's life had been sworn away by his rival on the property, more guilty but more cunning than he. He died that day.

Ere we reached home, a trooper carrying despatches, and riding a poor jaded horse, overtook us. He saw that my beast looked fresher than his, and proposed an exchange. Civilly he did it; but the *must* lurked under the *please*. "You must if you please, sir," as the Irish bailiff said to the gentleman who wished politely to decline accompanying him. Martial law ruled, and it was useless to contend. The one he rode had been seized, and he knew not its owner. Mine he promised to leave at the next post, where I was glad to recover it the same day, just as another trooper was saddling it to ride off to Montego Bay. The promise was kept.

Missionaries' horses seemed to be fair game at that time. One of Mr. Knibb's best was ridden by troopers from post to post, till it was nearly killed, before he recovered it. A friend of his on a journey brought it to our place, where he left it unable to go further, getting mine instead, and six weeks passed ere it was fit for use again.

The seaside estates continued peaceable, but I did not call Sabbath assemblies till martial law ceased, satisfied with visiting the people on their own estates. A real war was raging, however, at no great distance from our quiet district, and the negroes began to cower under the storm they had raised, terrified by consequences never anticipated.

At the *Spring* I found the people still bold and independent, and ready to debate the question of their right to freedom. They knew that they were safe in doing so with me. They ought to get it, they said. I could only answer that in the way they sought they could never find it; for could they even beat the militia, they could not beat the king's forces, which were then driving the rebels everywhere before them. And were they even free from white people they might still be slaves to one another; for the strongest arm and longest sword would always be master. One of them replied, "Well, minister, what you say is very true; and if we must have masters, better we have white masters; for white men have sense, but black masters have no sense." The head men took my advice to get the people quietly out to work, and keep them together, for their own safety, but without the whip, rather than wait to be driven to it at the point of the bayonet.

Visiting among the estates another day I fell in with a militia officer, who was making an inspection of the estates off work. We rode together to the *Crawle,* but could find none of the people though we went up to the negro houses, and saw signs of recent life among them, doors open, fires burning, and dogs barking. We called aloud, but all in vain. The people had fled, and were hiding in the tall canes behind the village. After a fruitless search we went away, but soon parted company, and I returned to a convenient spot for seeing unseen. Soon the people began to reappear, and I shouted for the head man, John by name. He answered, "hallo," and slowly advanced a little, till assured that I was alone, and then met me halfway.

When I asked why they all had hid from me, when calling them before, he said they were afraid of the "sojer"; but they were not feared for me, he added, and would meet me alone. I sent him to call all the head men, and they came and met me in the millhouse yard.

The people were all at home, they said, and quiet, except one; but were ill-off for want of food; all hungry, being afraid to go to their provision-grounds, lest somebody should meet and kill them. They were not doing any work, and did not know what to do; for "busha never look near them since the war begin."

I advised them to put the people to work, no matter what or how little they might do; and not to run away and hide even from "a sojer," but stand and answer. If they would do so, I should write to their attorney and prevent the mischief the officer's report might otherwise occasion, and they might safely go to their provision grounds. They seemed thankful for the advice, followed it, and were soon relieved from all fears by a commendatory letter from their new attorney. . . .

That revolt was the most serious thing of the kind that ever took place in the British West Indies. What caused it? The severities of the slave system, said some. The teaching of the fanatics, and instigation of abolitionists, said others. We treated our slaves with great indulgence, said the colonial party. We preached the gospel of peace, replied the missionaries. The latter might have added that the character and instructions of their societies, their principles as Christian ministers, and their own safety in the colony, forbade the criminality attributed to them.

The question cannot be answered in one word. Various influences operated. Servile insurrections are not so rare that we need seem surprised when they occur, or be at a loss to account for them. They are, in fact, expected in all countries where a large slave population exists—expected, as a sort of natural consequence of the condition of the people, and guarded against by the most jealous precautions. Hence the strong military organization everywhere of owners and managers, the brutish ignorance in which the bondsmen are kept, the fear of everything like union among them, even prayer meetings in their houses, and the savage ferocity with which the least insubordination is quelled. Slaves have feelings, and resent injuries, like others, and have more to resent than others. Allowed no will, no object of their own, things innumerable must, even unintentionally, cross and irritate them, which, if free, they could easily avoid, redress, or bear. They may grow callous, or cunning enough to seem patient. But the passive and active natures of man cannot both be largely developed at the same time, and slaves cannot be quite broken in unless quite stupefied. Man also is an improvable animal, and the worse his condition is, he must the more desire an improvement of it, to the extent he sees enjoyed by others. Freedom of will and action he naturally regards as the best conditions. It may be hopelessly out of view, and unthought of, but if it comes into view it must be desired, if within reach it will be grasped at. No mere improvement of the state of slavery will fully satisfy those subject to it. They may have less to complain of than formerly, but will see more to desire. Every step in the path of improvement fits them for greater benefits, and increases the longing for them. Some, indeed, under particularly favorable circumstances, may have gained positions of influence and comfort, and may be unwilling to risk what they have gained, by any hazardous attempts. Yet, generally speaking, the rankling of slavery is so incessant—it is so obviously the cause of many and great evils, and it so surely gets the blame of all, while the idea of freedom affords such hope of universal relief—that bondsmen must ever be strongly tempted to use every opportunity of avenging their wrongs, and seizing the coveted prize. Slaveholders know this well, as by instinct; and their assertions and reasonings to the contrary are unnatural and absurd, belied alike by their consciences and their conduct.

Ameliorations both in the law and practice of the slave system had begun in Jamaica, but had been too long of beginning. Nowhere had they got so far as to warrant owners to expect from their people even godly contentment. Emancipation had been spoken of both in the mother country and in the colonies. It was talked of and condemned around the festive board, where prudent reserve seldom presided, even before the colored domestics, and in the public meeting, where temper and common sense were borne down by passionate oratory. The idea was becoming familiar, though the reality seemed distant. The slaves believed that England wished their freedom, while their masters forbade the boon. The wild revilings of the colonists against abolitionists, saints, and missionaries, and their threats to join America, and wade in the blood of their slaves, rather than free them, confirmed the erroneous impressions. The negroes had begun to look for the arrival of the mail packet, and inquire the home news. They had heard of the violent and successful commotions which had agitated Great Britain and Ireland for Catholic emancipation and for Reform, and naturally thought of trying their hands at the same game. Intelligent mulattoes and quadroons, being related to the whites, enjoyed more of their favor and confidence than the negroes, but did not always return it. The information which they gathered above they diffused below them, for sympathy led them to transfer their confidence to fellow-sufferers.

SOURCE: Hope Masterton Waddell, *Twenty-nine Years in the West Indies and Central Africa: A Review of Missionary Work and Adventure, 1829–1858* (London: Nelson, 1863), pp. 50–69 (extracts).

70 Slave Insurrections in Brazil

It is incorrect to state, as so many Brazilian historians and sociologists have done, that the Negro in Brazil, in contrast to the Indian, was a passive social force, quite resigned to the system of slavery. This has sometimes been suggested erroneously as the reason why Negro slavery was substituted for that of the Indian. According to this school of thought, the Indian reacted violently against slavery, taking refuge in the jungle to evade its exactions, while the African Negro, humble and docile, allowed himself to be captured, submitting unprotestingly to a state of servitude.

This interpretation of the situation is untenable from either the historical or sociological point of view. Cultural anthropology has produced convincing evidence that the adaptation of the Negro in Brazil to agriculture was the consequence of the meeting of two social systems. The Indian was an excellent slave prior to the setting up of a strictly agrarian regime which uprooted him from his natural state. The transition from nomadism to a sedentary social order spelt failure for the Indian. On the other hand, the Negro adapted himself marvelously to the agricultural system as a result of a higher level of cultural attainment, distinctly superior to that of the Indian.

It is clear that the Negro was not the docile type, bowed down in submission and incapable of defiance, that he is often depicted. It is quite true that the traditional figure of *Pae João,* mild-tempered and humble is often the concept which we have received of the Negro, although it is far from the general rule. The humble slave of popular fancy is very remote from the historical Negro who gave abundant evidence of a capacity for resistance and even revolt. The Negro, being more capable than the Indian in an agricultural economy, in view of the cultural superiority already mentioned, reacted sometimes with extreme violence to the slave system. He was a good worker but a bad slave. The four centuries of servitude reveal a striking number of insurrections and outbreaks not only in Brazil but in other parts of America. These outbursts of violent antagonism against slavery sometimes took the form of flights, suicide, and at other times of individual protest or mass evasions. In the organized insurrections, as will be noted, the slaves displayed remarkable qualities of leadership, organization, and technical achievement as well as aggressiveness and a high degree of personal pride and dignity.

From the beginnings of slavery, escapes were frequent. The escaped slaves, called locally, *quilombolas,* often gathered together in organized groups, known in Brazil as *quilombos.* These movements were most marked during the seventeenth century when the famous Palmares Republic was formed and to a more or less equal extent in the nineteenth century when the famed holy war of the Moslem Negroes broke out in Bahia. From the beginning, the owners complained of the frequent escapes of the slaves, demanding protection and security from the public authorities. Later the situation was met by the employment of the bush captain and by notices in the press, publicizing the loss of the slaves and urging collective action for their recapture. During the four centuries preceding abolition, *quilombolas* fled singly and in groups, burying themselves in the forest depths, organizing the primitive *quilombos* which enabled them to resist by force, attempts to return them to slavery.

As early as the month of June 1607, the Governor of Bahia, Conde da Ponta, in writing to His Majesty in Lisbon, included mention of the initial insurrection of the Hausa Negroes, calling attention to the fact that they were the most warlike tribe from the West Coast. These same Hausas, together with other Negroes, who had felt the influence of Islam, were responsible for the armed uprisings destined to occur through to the nineteenth century.

During the seventeenth century, from 1630 to 1697 particularly, the Negro slaves of the northeast of Brazil fled in bands, organizing rustic villages, the most notable of which was that of Palmares in the state of Alagoas. . . . Palmares was not, however, the only outstanding case. In 1650 the slaves in Rio de Janeiro organized a number of *quilombos* which caused the police authorities of that region untold difficulties until suppressed by Captain Manoel Jordão da Silva.

In the northeast, other *quilombos* were formed along the general lines of Palmares. One of the most important of these was unquestionably Cumbé in the present state of Parahyba, located at a spot now called Usina Santa Rita. After the destruction of Palmares, many of the Negroes who managed to escape joined their brethren in Parahyba to form a new *quilombo.* A royal decree in 1731 ordered the destruction of this enterprise. An expedition of forty armed men under the command of Jeronymo Tovar de Macedo was defeated and the *quilombo* acquired a reputation for resistance and tenacity. Later, João Tavares de Castro, at the head of an expedition of slaves and mercenaries, overcame this resistance, razing the Cumbé *quilombo* and taking twenty-five Negroes prisoners.

The frequency of the mass flights of the slaves with the consequent establishment of *quilombos* as foci of resistance to the inroads of the colonists, provoked a determined reaction from the Portuguese Crown. Repeated decrees and royal orders described the procedure to be followed in such extermination. The fugitive slave upon recapture was to be branded with the letter F (*fujão* in the Portuguese) and his ear was to be slashed. If he was recalcitrant and fell into the same fault again, he was to be punished by severe whippings as well as other forms of chastisement which the master might see fit to apply. . . .

These energetic measures did not decrease the number of *quilombos.* Toward the middle of the eighteenth century, the Negroes of Minas Geraes formed large *quilombos,* scattered through the Rio Grande and Rio das Mortas valleys. Some historians make mention of the great uprising which the slaves planned for Good Friday, April 15, 1756, at a moment when the masters would be negligent of the ordinary precautions, since the majority would be at mass. The Negroes planned to fall on the heedless owners, slaughtering every white man and mulatto, sparing only the women. This audacious plot was discovered in time, and the terrified slaves fled madly to the forests, ruining all chance of carrying the conspiracy through.

Nevertheless, some scholars, notably the great Bahian Africanist, Nina Rodrigues, deny that there were any large-scale conspiracies by the slaves in which the wholesale murder of the whites was contemplated. There are, in reality, no documents to attest the fact of the existence of such a purpose. The *quilombos* were the points of convergence for discontented slaves, where relative freedom was secured for resistance to reenslavement. To what extent plots for the extermination of the whites developed is open to conjecture in view of the paucity of source materials. In the particular case mentioned, Negroes from the mines and plantations established settlements in the rough hinterland, to the west and south of Sapucahy. Several expeditions were organized to put them down, all of which were defeated. The Negroes had perfected an extraordinarily effective system of vigilance, with spies in the towns, on the roads, and at points where travelers gathered. They worked out a fairly adequate economic system by trade in skins, gold, and other articles which were sold indirectly through agents and exchanged for ammunition and foodstuffs. On this basis the Negroes held out for a surprisingly long time.

After so much uncertainty and delay, Governor José Antonio Freire de Andrade finally ordered expeditions organized under Captains Bartolomeu Bueno do Prado and Diego Bueno da Fonseca. The expeditionary force of Bartolomeu Bueno, the grandson of the well-known Rodrigues do Prado, was organized in March of 1757. It consisted of 400 men and set out into the jungles and hills in search of the *quilombos* of Indaya and Marcella. The whole affair gave the impression of a simple military sortie which would rapidly reduce the Negroes to submission. In fact, it required a persistent and hard-fought campaign in which acts of bravery were matched by the display of tactics. Negro leaders, especially two named Ambrosio and Zundu, distinguished themselves as the leaders of the *quilombos.* Their heroic resistance against overwhelming odds lasted for six months. Pedro Taques, in his *Nobiliarchia Paulistana,* in praising the prowess of his forebear Bartolomeu Bueno, asserts that the commander brought back as trophies of the successful campaign "three thousand nine hundred pairs of ears, with no other reward than the honor of having served the King, carrying out valiantly the orders received to destroy these festering sore spots."

While Bartolomeu Bueno was razing the *quilombos* of Campo Grande, Diego Bueno da Fonseca, during May of 1758, attacked the *quilombos* in the Piumhy region and on the headwaters of São Francisco. Captain Antonio Francisco Franca de Burena undertook to destroy the Negroes of the Sapucahy territory during July of the following year. As the Negroes were decimated, Diego Bueno and his companions pushed into the conquered teritory, establishing themselves in the whole area of the Rio das Mortas.

Other *quilombos* of less importance were formed wherever fugitive slaves were to be found; in the mountains of Cubatão, São Paulo, Leblon, Rio de Janeiro, Maranhão, and Matto Grosso. The insurrections of São Thomé in San José de Maranhão in 1772 were particularly terrible. In this settlement, the fugitive Negroes joined forces with the Indians to attack the populated areas and were subdued only after the most tenacious and costly campaign. The *quilombo* of Carlota in Matto Grosso was destroyed after a bitter and heroic defense in 1770.

During the nineteenth century, from 1807 to 1835, the great city insurrections of the Islamized Negroes of Bahia occurred. These uprisings grew out of causes considerably different from those which provoked the *quilombos* in other provinces. I do not feel that the slave uprisings in Bahia can be attributed exclusively to economic factors. These slaves were Sudanese Negroes who had been converted to Islam and held ascendancy over their fellows, especially the nagos and tapas. The Mohammedans, called *malis* in Brazil, were the Negroes who, having embraced Islam, fought veritable holy wars in Bahia. These outbreaks in Brazil were nothing more or less than a continuation or prolongation of the long and oft-repeated religious struggles and wars of conquest which the Moslem Negroes waged in the Sudan. Uprooted from their habitat, these courageous warlike and aggressive blacks refused to become docile slaves in the new world. Their reaction was not the sorry protest by which so many slaves cried out against their lot. Their aggressiveness was a direct social heritage from the century old wars of religion which had assured the spread of Islam in Africa.

There was a tendency, at least latent, toward revolt everywhere in the province of Bahia where Hausa Negroes were to be found. The preponderant cause, let it be repeated, was religious. In the investigation of the causes and course of these insurrections, the definitely religious factor has been amply demonstrated. It was the Moslem holy war spirit which moved the rebellious Negroes. For this reason, the wars were not conducted solely against the whites, or masters, but also against those Negroes who refused to join the movement. In the revolt of 1835, for example, it was revealed that plans called for the rising of the Negroes under the chief, Arrumá or Alumá and the lands to be taken over. The whites and creole Negroes as well as the African blacks who refused to join the crusade were to be massacred. The mulattoes were to be spared and forced into servitude. Once the uprising was under way, these objectives were even more clear. The hatred of the Moslem Negroes extended to the creole blacks and mulattoes precisely because Islam had never made inroads among them.

The authorities charged with the suppression of these movements were quite ignorant of the religious implications involved. The places where the conspiracies were hatched were Moslem temples where religious propaganda reached its greatest intensity and influence toward the middle of the nineteenth century. The residents of these centers, often chiefs in the movement and called *alufás* or *marabús,* exercised absolute authority over the Negroes under them. The documents which have come down to us, especially those concerning the 1835 insurrection, were written in Arabic script, containing verses from the Koran with cabalistic prayers. For the purpose of this study, attention need be given only to the most important episodes with reference to some of the Negro leaders responsible for them.

The best known outbreaks of the Hausa Negroes took place in 1807, 1809, 1813, and 1816. All had Bahia as their locale. In reality the revolts of 1807 and 1809 were minor skirmishes in preparation for the great uprising of 1813. At the time of the first rebellion, the authorities were informed that the Hausa Negroes were plotting for an uprising on May 28, 1807. In each section of the city was named a captain, agent, or emissary whose task was to aid the slaves from the plantations and within the city to harass the whites. The authorities secured accurate information as to the names of the leaders and the points which had been designated for meeting. On the night of the 27th, patrols were deployed. Aided by the bush captains, they surrounded the houses of the plotters, capturing and imprisoning many of the Negroes. The Governor ordered, as a preventative measure, that henceforth any Negro found on the streets after nine at night, without express permission from his master, was to be taken prisoner and treated to a hundred lashes. These measures proved quite useless, for two years later, in 1809, the revolt of the Hausas and Dahomans broke out. The latter joined forces with the mass of the city Negroes in this memorable uprising. On January 4th, the Negroes launched the revolt, destroying and ravaging everything in their path. Attacked by the government troops, they entrenched themselves in the rough interior country, where they offered fierce resistance. They were finally defeated, losing some eighty prisoners and a much larger number of casualties.

It is important to recall that in the planning of the Negro revolts, the secret Hausa societies, called *Obgoni* or *Ohogobo,* * played a most significant role. These were powerful organizations, following in general the same lines as those in West Africa and eluding completely the vigilance of masters and police. They were developed and kept active in response to the necessity which the transplanted Negroes felt for defense.

The movement of February 28, 1813, was one of the most significant of the Hausa uprisings in Bahia. Some six hundred heavily armed Negroes rose in revolt in the city and at four in the morning burned the houses and slave quarters of their masters. The most stirring events of the revolt took place at Itapoan, a suburb of the capital. The assembled Negroes put the torch to a considerable number of residences and killed every white who offered the slightest resistance. Thirteen were killed outright and some eight wounded. The enraged Negroes fought desperately against the armed force sent to suppress them, dying rather than surrender. The plots and conspiracies continued unabated. A new plot was hatched which was uncovered through betrayal some months before it was due to break. The Governor of Bahia at that time was the Conde dos Arcos, whose personal influence was considerable in the suppression of the movement. Innumerable Negroes were imprisoned, others condemned to forced labor, and still others lashed

* Perhaps *Ogboni,* a Yoruba secret society, is meant; if so, *Ohogobo* would be *Osugbo,* the Ijebu form of the word. Ed.

and deported to the penal settlements in Mozambique, Benguela, and Angola.

In spite of the attention attracted by the Hausa revolts, it should not be surmised that the Yoruba insurrections were unimportant. In 1826 the Yorubas of Bahia set up a *quilombo* in the hinterland at Urubú, not far from the capital. The bush captains, supposing them to be a small band, set out on December 17 to suppress them. The Negroes were more numerous than anticipated and put up a vigorous resistance, converting the initial defense tactics into a counterattack. They invaded a place called Estrada do Cabula, assaulting a number of people and wounding a bush captain badly. It was necessary to rush troops to put them down, an accomplishment which required several sharp engagements. The leading figure in this conflict was a black woman, Zeferina, who was ultimately subdued and her arms taken from her. The confession of some of those captured made it clear that the Negroes had planned a much more elaborate uprising, repercussions of which were to be felt in the future.

In 1827 and 1828 several smaller insurrections broke out, following the usual course of bloodshed, torture, and imprisonments. In 1830 a revolt occurred in the very heart of Bahia. A number of Yorubas broke into the hardware stores, from which they took arms and ammunition, proceeded then to the arming of some hundred more Negroes, and with this considerable band, attacked the police station of Soledade in one of the city's suburbs. Taken completely by surprise, the authorities were helpless. Before aid could be secured and a force organized, the Negroes wrought destruction in the city. The insurrectionists were finally put down with a large loss of life, some fifty perishing and as many more taken prisoners. The rest fled into the fastnesses of the wilderness.

This series of individual uprisings formed part of the broader cycle which reached its historical climax in the great insurrection of January 1835, in Bahia. It would have attained the proportions of a revolution if the authorities had not received word of what was transpiring slightly before the time set for the outbreak. The well-known authority, Nina Rodrigues, describes it as follows:

> As soon as the facts of the situation were communicated to the provincial president, the necessary precautions were taken. The army and police posts were forewarned and reinforcements ar-

ranged for at every crucial point. The chief of police, Dr. Francisco Gonçalves Martins, afterwards, Visconde de São Lorenzo, departed for the Bomfin suburb, where many families resided, in order to prevent the junction of the rebellious city Negroes with those from the nearby plantations.

The search of the Negro quarters began at once. On the charge that in a shop near the square, a large number of Negroes were gathered, the spot was surrounded. In spite of the evasions of the Negro, Domingos Marinho de Sá, the principal tenant, the authorities entered the place at two in the morning and proceeded to a careful search. At this moment, a shot from a blunderbuss was fired through a partly open door, followed by the appearance of sixty noisy blacks armed with swords, lances, pistols, and guns, shouting, "Kill the soldiers." The small police force was easily overcome and Lieutenant Lazaro wounded. The Negroes departed for Ajuda, where they attempted again and again to break down the jail. Failing in this attempt, they continued toward the *Largo do Teatro,* where they dispersed a little force of eight soldiers who fired on them. With shouts and dire threats, attacking and wounding those encountered on the way, including two mulattoes who were killed, the band moved toward the Artillery barracks in the *Forte de São Pedro.* There they killed a sergeant. Since it was clear that they hoped to join a similar force from the Victoria suburb, they hesitated to attack the barracks. Retreating after this threat, they crossed the *Rua do Forte de São Pedro* under the fire from the barracks and joined forces with their comrades from Victoria. From there they proceeded to attack the police and army posts in Mouraria, where considerable gunfire occurred. As the heavy portals were closed and the insurgents handicapped by two dead and numerous wounded, the mob passed on to Barroquinha, coming out finally for a second time at Ajuda. From this point they converged on the *Collegio,* attacking the guard. They killed an artilleryman, who before succumbing dispatched one Negro and wounded several others. The enraged Negroes went down the *Baixa dos Sapateiros,* killed a Negro on the way, went on to the *Coqueiros* and, coming out on the *Aguas de Meninos,* attacked a cavalry detachment.

The chief of police, who had gone to Bomfin, and who proposed to direct the cavalry to that point, received word in time that the city was being attacked and immediately set out for *Aguas de Meninos.* There was scarcely time to take adequate measures for the protection of the families who were herded together in the Bomfin church, a natural point of defense. The police chief returned then, at three in the morning, to the barracks. Infantry detachments were arranged to defend the door and maintain a fire from the windows, while the cavalry deployed to receive the attackers. Scarcely had these measures been taken than a large body of Negroes began the attack on the barracks and cavalry. Driven back and rushed by the fierce charging cavalry, they broke and ran, leaving some forty dead and innumerable wounded. Others, who managed to escape, threw themselves into the sea, or fled into the wilds.[14]

A number of genuine leaders stood out among the Negroes in the insurrections already described, especially in that of 1835. History has recorded the names of Luiza Mahin, Belchior, Gaspar da Silva Cunha, Luiz Sanim, Manoel Calafate, Aprigio, Elesbão de Carmo (Dandara), and Pacifico (Lieutan). All of them were Moslem Hausas in whose huts the ceremonies and teachings of Islam were preserved and the Hausa tongue employed for a more effective diffusion of these precepts or of tidings of the insurrections which were planned.

Luiza Mahin, said to have been an African princess, was the mother of the Negro poet, Luiz Gama. . . . There is very little evidence concerning her. It is supposed that her parents were of royal blood in Africa. Uprooted violently and taken to Brazil, Luiza Mahin was one of the most outstanding of the leaders of the Negro insurrections. Her house in Bahia became a center for the meetings of the leaders of the great revolt in 1835. Her end is shrouded in mystery. Her name has remained, however, in history and legend as a symbol of the courage and audacity of the Negro woman.

The Negro Pacifico, called by his associates Lieutan, was another leader of extraordinary prestige. He was not merely an *alufá,* or Islamic priest, but a practical agitator in whom every discontented slave found an adviser and a counselor as to how freedom might be attained. The *alufá,* Elesbão do Carmo, called popularly Dandara, also attained a really amazing influence among his own people. He was an agent of Islam as well as an agitator for revolutionary change. The authorities were generally quite helpless against such leaders. Dandara, for example, was never arrested. Lieutan was once condemned to 100 lashes. Sanim received six hundred on one occasion. All efforts were in vain against the others.

Historians in recounting these insurrections emphasize the courage and loyalty which distinguished the Negroes. They were stoically loyal to each other, refusing consistently to betray their brethren by so much as a word. Many are the cases of Negroes who were adamant in their refusal to reveal any particle of information which might involve their fellows. In the records of the trials for responsibility in the 1835 insurrection, as described by Professor Nina Rodrigues, one Negro, Joaquim de Mattos, was so obdurate that he "refused even to admit acquaintance with his roommate, Ignacio de Limeira." The heroism of the Yoruban, Henrique, is even more remarkable. Wounded badly in the hand and back, almost speechless from the agony, he managed to assert to his accusers, a few moments before expiring, that "he did not know the Negroes who had brought him into the plot and that he would say nothing, for he was not a person to squeal. What is said is said even in the face of death."

These heroes received a penalty in conformity with their bravery. They were not hanged as common criminals, but shot as soldiers, with full military honors.

Besides the *quilombos* and insurrections already mentioned, the Negro participated in numerous popular movements in Brazil, in cooperation with whites and mulattoes. The uprising of 1832 in Recife was led by a mulatto, Captain Pedro da Fonseca da Silva Pedroso, whose popularity among the soldiery and the Negroes was immense. In the revolt in Pará, known as the *cabanada,* and in the *balaiada* in Maranhão, both Negroes and mulattoes played a significant role. These were both outbreaks during the Regency, expressing a popular discontent with existing conditions. They were in a broad way explosions of liberal, democratic, federalist, and nationalist feeling against the conservative, monarchist, and centralizing tendency of the Government.

The conflict called the *cabanada* fell into two general stages. The first occurred in 1832 in Alagoas and Pernambuco, where 6,000 men were gathered in an uprising against the Regency. The name of *cabanos* was given them by the regular army, in view of the fact that the rebels were humble folk, living in wretched huts or cabins (*cabana* in the Portuguese). These insurgents were often joined by fugitive slaves from the cities and plantations. The second phase of the *cabanada* developed in Pará in 1835 when Eduardo Angelim and Antonio Vinagre, at the head of a band of mulattoes and Indians, invaded the city of Belem. The revolution spread, aided and abetted by slaves from Pará and other provinces. One of the leaders of the movement, Joaquim Antonio, took command of a force of five hundred men and included in his program of action an article calling for the liberation of the slaves.

The struggle between the *cabanos* and the rural landowners and regular troops was violent. The entire Upper and Lower Amazon rose in arms. The reoccupation of Belem in 1839 did not crush the rebellion completely. The *cabanos* took to the forests and only in 1840 did they lay down their arms, after a guarantee of pardon and complete amnesty had been made them. Historians, in describing this incident, have called attention to the spirit of discipline, ability to organize, and real military talent of the Negro leaders.

The *balaiada* broke out in 1839 in the village of Manga in the province of Maranhão. The first leader was the mixed Negro and Indian, Raymundo Gomes, a herdsman from Pianhy, who gathered him a force of some three hundred men. After several skirmishes, hounded relentlessly by the troops, this force took refuge in the fastnesses of Pianhy. With the retirement of Raymundo, other leaders appeared. The best known were the Negro, Cosme, and the Indian, Matroa. The real genius of the *Balaiada* was the Negro, Manoel Francisco dos Anjos Fereira. His nickname of Balião gave rise to the term applied to the whole movement. A Negro chieftain in every sense of the word, Balião organized the revolt so effectively that its suppression required the dispatch of regular troops from the nearby provinces. For three years, the *baliaos* controlled the entire province of Maranhão. Manoel Francisco fought heroically until his death in Caxias from wounds received in action.

In another revolt, known as the *quebra-kilos,* in 1874, renowned in the historical annals of the northeast country, the Negroes and mulattoes played a very considerable role. The introduction into Brazil of the metric decimal system was the original cause of the protest. It broke out on a Saturday, during a fair in the town of Campina Grande in the province of Parahyba, and was led by a mulatto, João Vieira, better known as João Carga d'Agua. The slaves quickly took advantage of the turbulence and, led by the Negro, Manoel do Carmo, marched in a body of three hundred to a place called Timbauba, where they seized several persons and demanded of the local council president their liberty and the "registry books in which the newly born slaves are annotated." Only at the greatest cost were the rebellious Negroes put down, with large numbers fleeing into the forests. The *quebra-kilos* revolt dragged on for some time until the chief, João Vieira, was captured.

During the naval revolt of 1910 in Rio de Janeiro, the Negroes were among the most important participants. One of the leaders of the sailors was the Negro, João Candido, who with his qualities of organization and leadership surprised the authorities seeking to suppress the revolt.

In various other popular and revolutionary movements during the colonial period and since independence, the Negro has invariably played a prominent part.

SOURCE: Arthur Ramos, *The Negro in Brazil* (Washington, D. C.: Associated Publishers, 1939), pp. 24–41.

FREE BLACKS

IN SLAVERY TIMES free blacks who, if of mixed blood, were called "people of color," were discriminated against, both legally and socially, everywhere in Latin America and the Caribbean. The degree of discrimination, however, varied greatly. Much depended on the population balance; where the white slave-owning class was small and the blacks numerous and mostly slaves (as, for example in eighteenth-century Jamaica), free blacks were seen as a danger to public security. The mere fact of their existence, it was believed, tempted their fellows still in bondage to rebel. They were therefore hedged around with legal and customary barriers to advancement and social acceptance. By contrast, in nineteenth-century Brazil and Cuba manumission was common, and a slave could, in certain circumstances, win his freedom fairly easily. Many freedmen in both regions gained positions of distinction and affluence, often merging with the white upper class.

The official documents, historical summaries, and travelers' accounts printed below show the variety of the free black experience. In early eighteenth-century Panamá (Selection 71) militia companies manned and officered by free blacks were crucial to the defense of the settlement against the enemies of Spain. In Peru at about the same time (Selection 72) the authorities felt constrained to reduce the money spent by the lower classes, including the free blacks, on dress. Selections 75 to 77, which refer to Brazil, indicate the high degree of upward social mobility possible to free blacks in that area, and also show the all-important role they played in the Brazilian emancipation movement. The final three passages describe the political influence, social status, and relatively easy path to manumission of the free black population of nineteenth-century Cuba.

71 Panamá: Militia Companies

Recommendation of the War Council of the Indies concerning the claims of the militia companies of Blacks and other castes . . . that captains of their color be established over them, as was previously the practice, Madrid, June 23, 1708:

The President of Panamá, the Marquis of Villarocha, in a letter to Your Majesty of November 20, 1707 . . . described how the numerous companies of *cuarterones* * and blacks (being sons of Spaniards), *zambos,*† and free *morenos* ‡ of this city of Panamá . . . appeared before the Court to petition that their Captains be nominated from among their own ranks. . . .

It has been the practice in the past for colored Captains to serve; this has been done both in this kingdom and in the rest of the Indies. . . . On many occasions [the colored militia companies] have pledged their service to Your Majesty and have served as loyal vassals. [The President of Panamá,] noting that these facts were publicly acknowledged, found it expedient to advise the companies that, owing to the zeal with which they have served and continue to serve, he concurred for the present with their petition, at least during the interim while the Crown decided its policy. . . .

[Your representative] informs Your Majesty that it was these colored militia companies, or sections of them, which were chosen to man the barricades alongside the infantry of this presidio during the attacks launched by the enemy from the sea and the ground assaults made against him; they always comported themselves bravely and zealously in the service of Your Majesty. [Your representative also states] that, to achieve the best results, we have used colored

* Three-quarters white, one-quarter black.
† Negro-American.
‡ Indian and Indian-White.

sergeants to encourage those serving under them. . . . He assures Your Majesty that, judging from his experience of the behavior of the men of these companies on expeditions into the mountains, they are most fit for all aspects of the work.

On due reflection, the Council finds it convenient to concur with the President [of Panamá] that, insofar as there are no reasons or superior orders prohibiting this privilege, the practice should be restored. . . .

It is recommended that Your Majesty order this carried out.

SOURCE: R. Konetzke, ed., *Colección de documentos para la historia de la formación social de Hispano-américa, 1493–1819* (3 vols.; Madrid: 1953–62), 3(1):187. Translated for the present volume by Marion Berdecio.

72 Peru: Sumptuary Legislation

The King of Spain to the Marquis of Castelfuerte, Viceroy, Governor, and Captain-General of the Provinces of Peru, and President of my Royal Audience there, September 7, 1725:

In a letter of April 2nd of last year various testimonies were presented. . . . Don Pedro Antonio de Echeve y Roxas, Judge and Fiscal of the Royal Audience, had published on its behalf a proclamation moderating the scandalous excesses of dress of Negroes, Mulattoes, Indians, and Mestizos of both sexes, from which excesses result the frequent crimes these persons commit in order to maintain their costly ostentation. . . . The decree had little effect, for within a few days the same abuses were repeated with their attendant disorder, owing to the transgressors' receiving countenance and protection from even some officials, this being evident from one of the testimonies which stated that twenty-four hours after the publication of the edict it was transgressed by two female slaves from the household of the Count of Torres, Judge of this same Audience. . . .

In my Council of the Indies, in view of the testimony of the Fiscal, it has been decided that the proclamation referred to was just and should be continued. In respect to this we charge and order you to renew and republish it within fifteen days, together with the penalties established by law and with the admonition and warning that proceedings will be taken against those who contravene it. And thus you have this clarification to hand for your more punctual observance, and you may punish, without distinction of persons, all who fail to fulfill what is here expressed, for such is my will.

SOURCE: Konetzke, *Colección de documentos,* 3(1):108–9. Translated for the present volume by Marion Berdecio.

73 British West Indies: Rights and Disabilities

I proceed now to persons of mixed blood (usually termed *People of Color*) and Native Blacks of free condition. Of the former, all the different classes, or varieties, are not easily discriminated. In the British West Indies they are commonly known by the names of Samboes, Mulattoes, Quadroons, and Mestizes; * but the Spaniards, from whom these appellations are borrowed, have many other and much nicer distinctions, of which the following account is given by Don Anthonio de Ulloa, in his description of the inhabitants of Carthagena:

> Among the tribes which are derived from an intermixture of the Whites with the Negroes, the first are the *Mulattoes;* next to these are the *Tercerones,* produced from a White and a Mulatto, with some approximation to the former, but not so near as to obliterate their origin. After these, follow the *Quarterones,* proceeding from a White and a Terceron. The last are the Quinterons, who owe their origin to a White and Quarteron. This is the last gradation, there being no visible difference between them and the Whites, either in color or features; nay, they are often fairer than the Spaniards. The children of a White and Quinteron consider themselves as free from all taint of the Negro race. Every person is so jealous of the order of their tribe

* A *Sambo* is the offspring of a Black Woman by a Mulatto Man, or *vice versa*.
Mulatto—of a Black Woman by a White Man.
Quadroon—of a Mulatto Woman by a White Man.
Mestize or Mustee—of a Quadroon Woman by a White Man.
The offspring of a Mestize by a White Man are white by law. A Mestize therefore in our island is, I suppose, the *Quinteron* of the Spaniards.

or caste, that if, through inadvertence, you call them by a degree lower than what they actually are, they are highly offended. Before they attain the class of the *Quinterones,* there are several intervening circumstances which throw them back; for between the Mulatto and the Negro, there is an intermediate race, which they call *Samboes,* owing their origin to a mixture between one of these with an Indian, or among themselves. Betwixt the Tercerones and Mulattoes, the Quarterones and the Tercerones, &c. are those called *Tente en el Ayre, Suspended in the air;* because they neither advance nor recede. Children, whose parents are a Quarteron or Quinteron, and a Mulatto or Terceron, are *Salto atras retrogrados;* because, instead of advancing towards being Whites, they have gone backwards towards the Negro race. The children between a Negro and a Quinteron, are called Sambos de Negro, de Mulatto, de Terceron, &c.

In Jamaica, and I believe in the rest of our Sugar Islands, the descendants of Negroes by White people, entitled by birth to all the rights and liberties of White subjects in the full extent, are such as are above three steps removed in lineal digression from the Negro venter. All below this, whether called Mestizes, Quadrons, or Mulattoes, are deemed by law Mulattoes.

Anciently there was a distinction in Jamaica between such of these people as were born of freed mothers (the maxim of the civil law, *partus sequiter ventrem,* prevailing in all our colonies) and such as had been immediately released from slavery by deed or testament of their owners. While the former were allowed a trial by jury in criminal cases, the latter were tried in the same way as the common slaves, by two justices and three freeholders. Neither were the latter admitted as evidences against freeborn persons, until the year 1748, when an act was passed in their favor, putting both classes on the same footing.

At the same time, the legal capacities which they possessed, were very imperfectly defined: The Mulattoes were allowed no other privilege than the freed Negroes, concerning whom (few of them being baptized, or supposed to be sensible of the nature of an oath) the courts of law interpreted the act of manumission by the owner, as nothing more than an abandonment or release of his own proper authority over the person of the slave, which did not, and could not, convey to the object of his bounty, the civil and political rights of a natural-born subject; and the same principle was applied to the issue of freed mothers, until after the third generation from the Negro ancestor.

The principal incapacities to which these people are now subject, as distinct from the Whites, are these;

First; In most of the British Islands, their evidence is not received in criminal cases against a White person, nor even against a person of Color, in whose favor a particular act has been passed by the legislature. In this respect they seem to be placed on a worse footing than the enslaved Negroes, who have masters that are interested in their protection, and who, if their slaves are maltreated, have a right to recover damages, by an action on the case.*

Secondly; They are denied the privilege of being eligible to serve in parochial vestries and general assemblies; or of acting in any office of public trust, even so low as that of a constable; neither are they permitted to hold commissions even in the Black and Mulatto companies of militia. They are precluded also from voting at elections of members to serve in the assembly. It may be urged, however, that the laws of England require baptism, and a certain degree of property, in similar cases.

Thirdly; By an act of the assembly of Jamaica, passed in the year 1762, it is enacted, that a testamentary devise from a White person to a Negro or Mulatto, not born in wedlock, of real or personal estate, exceeding in value £2,000 currency, shall be void, and the property descend to the heir at law.

As some counterbalance however to these restrictions, the assembly, on proper application, is readily enough inclined to pass private acts, granting the privileges of White people, with some limitations, to such persons of Color as have been regularly baptized, and properly educated. On the same ground, private bills are sometimes passed to authorize gentlemen of fortune, under particular circumstances, to devise their estates to their reputed Mulatto children, notwithstanding the act of 1762.

But there is the mischief arising from the system of rigor ostensibly maintained by the laws against this unfortunate race of people; that it tends to degrade them in their own eyes, and in the eyes of the community to which they belong. This is carried so far, as to

* In Jamaica, this grievance has been partly redressed since the publication of the former editions.

make them at once wretched to themselves, and useless to the public. It very frequently happens that the lowest White person, considering himself as greatly superior to the richest and best-educated Free man of Color, will disdain to associate with a person of the latter description; treating him as the Egyptians treated the Israelites, with whom they held it *an abomination to eat bread.* To this evil, arising from public opinion, no partial interposition of the legislature in favor of individuals, affords an effectual remedy; and the consequence is, that instead of a benefit, these unhappy people are a burthen and a reproach to society. They have no motives of sufficient efficacy either to engage them in the service of their country, or in profitable labor for their own advantage. Their progress in civility and knowledge is animated by no encouragement; their attachment is received without approbation; and their diligence exerted without reward.*

I am happy however to assert with truth, that their fidelity and loyalty have hitherto remained unimpeached and unsuspected. To the Negroes they are objects of envy and hatred; for the same or a greater degree of superiority which the Whites assume over *them,* the free Mulattoes lay claim to over the Blacks. These, again, abhor the idea of being slaves to the descendants of slaves. Thus circumstanced, the general character of the Mulattoes is strongly marked by the peculiarity of their situation; and I cannot but think that they are, on the whole, objects of favor and compassion.

In their deportment towards the White people they are humble,

* It would surely be a wise and humane law that should grant to every free Negro and Mulatto, the right of being a competent witness, in all criminal cases, and more especially in those of personal injury to himself. (The Assembly of Jamaica have lately granted this privilege to the freed people in that Island.) Perhaps indeed it might be proper to require of such persons the proof of baptism, and the ability to read and write; and I think that some useful regulations might be made to apportion greater privileges to the colored people according to their approximation to the Whites; a system which would not serve to confound, but to keep up and render useful those distinctions which local causes have created, and which it is not in the power of man to abolish. To the Quadroons and Mestizes for instance (who possess the necessary qualification in *real* property) I would grant the right of voting for representatives in the assembly. Such a privilege would give them an interest in the community, and attach them powerfully to its government. In favor of such persons also, the act of 1762 might be modified. Whether it would be wise to repeal it altogether, is a deep and difficult question. Men who are unacquainted with local manners and customs, are not competent to pronounce an opinion in this case.

submissive, and unassuming. Their spirits seem to sink under the consciousness of their condition. They are accused however of proving bad masters when invested with power; and their conduct towards their slaves is said to be, in a high degree, harsh and imperious. I suspect there is some truth in this representation; for it is the general characteristic of human nature, that men whose authority is most liable to be disputed, are the most jealous of any infringement of it, and the most vigilant in its support.

The accusation generally brought against the free people of Color, is the incontinency of their women; of whom, such as are young, and have tolerable persons, are universally maintained by White men of all ranks and conditions, as kept mistresses. The fact is too notorious to be concealed or controverted; and I trust I have too great an esteem for my fair readers, and too high a respect for myself, to stand forth the advocate of licentiousness and debauchery. Undoubtedly, the conduct of many of the Whites in this respect, is a violation of all decency and decorum; and in insult and injury to society. Let it not offend any modest ear, however, if I add my opinion, that the unhappy females here spoken of, are much less deserving reproach and reprehension than their keepers. I say this, from considering their education and condition in life; for such are the unfortunate circumstances of their birth, that not one in fifty of them is taught to write or read. Profitable instruction therefore, from those who are capable of giving it, is withheld from them; and unhappily, the young men of their own complexion, are in too low a state of degradation, to think of matrimony. On the other hand, no White man of decent appearance, unless urged by the temptation of a considerable fortune, will condescend to give his hand in marriage to a Mulatto! The very idea is shocking. Thus, excluded as they are from all hope of ever arriving to the honor and happiness of wedlock, insensible of its beauty and sanctity; ignorant of all christian and moral obligations; threatened by poverty, urged by their passions, and encouraged by example; upon what principle can we expect these ill-fated women to act otherwise than they do?

Neither should it be forgotten, at the same time, that very few of these poor females, in comparison of the whole, are guilty of that infamous species of profligacy and prostitution, which flourishes, without principle or shame, and in the broad eye of day, throughout all the cities of Europe. In their dress and carriage they are modest, and in conversation reserved; and they frequently manifest a fidelity and attachment towards their keepers, which, if it be not virtue, is something very like it. The terms and manner of their compliance too are commonly as decent, though perhaps not as solemn, as those of marriage; and the agreement they consider equally innocent; giving themselves up to the husband (for so he is called) with faith plighted, with sentiment, and with affection.

That this system ought to be utterly abolished I most readily admit. Justice towards the many beautiful and virtuous young ladies resident in these islands, cries aloud for a thorough reformation of manners: But by whom is such a reform to be begun and accomplished? It can hardly be expected, I think, from the objects of our present enquiries, who are conscious of no vices which their christian instructors have not taught them; and whose good qualities (few and limited as they are) flow chiefly from their own native original character and disposition.

Of those qualities, the most striking is tenderness of heart; a softness or sympathy of mind towards affliction and distress, which I conceive is seldom displayed in either extreme of prosperity or wretchedness. Those who have never experienced any of the vicissitudes and calamities of life, turn averse from the contemplation of them; and those again who are wretched themselves, have no leisure to attend to the sufferings of others: but the benevolence of the poor people of whom I treat, is not merely solitary and contemplative; it is an active principle, in which they may be said particularly to excel; and I have the authority of a great writer before quoted (Don Anthonio De Ulloa) to support me in this representation. Speaking of their kindness to many poor Europeans, who, in the hopes of mending their fortunes, repair to the Spanish West-Indies, where they are utterly unknown, he has the following account of such of them as are called at Carthagena *Pulizones;* being, he says, men without employment, stock, or recommendation. "Many of these (he observes) after traversing the streets until they have nothing left to procure them lodging or food, are reduced to have recourse to the last extremity, the Franciscan hospital; where they receive, in a quantity barely sufficient to preserve life, a kind of pap made of cassada, of which the Natives themselves will not eat. This is their food; their lodging is the porticoes of the squares and churches, until their good fortune throws them in the way of some trader going up the country, who wants a servant. The city merchants, standing in no need of them, discountenance these adventurers. Affected by the difference of the climate, aggravated by bad food, dejected and tortured by the entire disappointment of their romantic hopes, they fall sick; without any other succor to apply to, than Divine Providence. Now it is that the charity of the people of Color becomes conspicuous. The Negro and Mulatto free women, moved at the deplorable condition of these poor wretches, carry them to their houses, and nurse them with the greatest care and affection. If any one die, they bury him by the alms they procure, and even cause masses to be said for his soul."

I believe that no man, who is acquainted with general conduct and disposition of the same class of people in our own islands, will doubt that they would act as benevolently and humanely, under similar circumstances, as those of Carthagena. Their tenderness, as nurses, towards the sick; their disinterested gratitude and attachment where favors are shown them; and their peaceful deportment under a rigorous system of laws, and the influence of manners still more oppressive, afford great room to lament that a more enlightened and liberal policy is not adopted towards them. The enfranchisement of such as are enslaved, Christian instruction to the whole, and encouragement to their industry, would, in time, make them a useful and valuable class of citizens; induce them to intermarry with each other, and render their present relaxed and vicious system of life, as odious in appearance, as it is baneful to society.*

Hitherto I have confined myself to those people who, having some

* The Rev. Mr. Ramsay has enlarged on the same idea concerning these unfortunate people. "Children of Mulatto women," he observes (meaning, I presume, their children by White men) "should be declared free from their birth. Intendants should be appointed to see them placed out in time to such trade or business as may best agree with their inclination and the demands of the colony: this should be done at the expense of their fathers, and a sufficient sum might be deposited in the hands of the churchwardens, soon after their birth to answer the purpose; the intendant keeping the churchwardens to their duty. By these means the number of free citizens would insensibly increase in the colonies, and add to their security and strength. A new rank of citizens, placed between the Black and White races, would be established. They would naturally attach themselves to the White race as the most honorable relation, and so become a barrier against the designs of the Black, &c." All this, however, is easily proposed in theory, but, I am afraid, more difficult to adopt in practice than Mr. Ramsay was aware of.

portion of Christian blood in their veins, pride themselves on that circumstance, and to the conscious value of which it is probable that some part of what is commendable in their conduct is owing. The free Blacks, not having the same advantage, have not the same emulation to excel. In truth, they differ but little from their brethren in bonds.

SOURCE: Bryan Edwards, *The History, Civil and Commercial, of the British Colonies of the West Indies* (3 vols.; London: Stockdale, 1801), 2:18–31.

74 Jamaica: Social Status

If the mother be three degrees removed from the Black, her child by a White man is free, and classes, in point of privilege, with Whites.

White men occasionally give freedom to their mistresses and their children. But this, in all cases where the mistress and her children are not the slaves of the White man, must be effected by purchase, and, of course, with the owner's consent. But such purchases cannot be effected when the estate is mortgaged, or the owner is a minor. White men often complain that the owner is not compelled to give freedom to their children, on his being paid their value. In all cases where slaves are made free, a bond must be given that they shall not become chargeable.

Free Blacks and persons of Color pay all taxes, and perform military duty in the colonial militia, precisely as the Whites. According to the number of Negroes which each planter possesses, he is obliged to have upon his estate a certain number of White persons, or to pay a certain sum for each deficiency. This is with a view to prevent the militia from falling off in numbers. Free people of Color, though they are bound to serve in the militia, yet are of no avail in freeing any estate, on which they may be employed, from this penalty. Indeed, from the prejudice existing against them in the minds of the Whites, it is in very few cases that they are employed on estates, which, considering the perfect competency of many of them, they feel to be a great hardship. So far indeed are they from being encouraged in Jamaica, that their increase is viewed with apprehension, as adding to the danger of insurrection. Much jealousy is entertained of them, especially when they have been educated in England, where they have been treated as men, and on a footing of equality with their White brethren. And yet Mr. Cooper is of opinion, and in that opinion we entirely concur, that "the principle of gradual emancipation," though the subject of so much alarm to West Indians, affords the best means of remedying the evils of the system, with safety to the master and the slave.

It is a strong proof of the degrading light in which free persons of Color are viewed by the Whites, that these last never introduce even their own children into company. It was thought a very extraordinary thing, on one occasion, to see a father riding in a gig with his own Colored daughter. Colored persons reputed to be the children of the owners of the estates are sometimes held as slaves upon them, and have been even sold along with them.

Many of the free Negroes are industrious, and succeed very well, although they never think of hiring themselves to the planters to work in the field. It could not indeed be expected that they should submit to the degradation of working under the lash. They are objects of great respect to the slaves, but are kept at a distance by the free Browns, who consider themselves as rising in rank as they approach to the color of Whites.

Very great difficulty is experienced by Negroes in obtaining their freedom, even when they are able to pay for it, because those who, by their industry and frugality have realized the means of purchasing their freedom, and who, therefore, are most worthy of it, and also likely to employ it most beneficially, are the most valuable hands. Mr. Cooper knew three valuable men who wished to purchase their freedom. They had long applied in vain to the agents of the proprietor resident on the spot. They at length, however, obtained their end, by an application to the proprietor himself, then in England. After this a fourth made many efforts to obtain his freedom by purchase, but they proved unavailing; and he sunk in consequence into a state of despondency, and became of comparatively little value.

The number of Brown slaves, the children of White men, is very considerable. In general, however, they are not employed in the field: Mr. Cooper knew only one estate on which Brown slaves were so employed, viz. Roundhill, in Hanover. They are usually employed as domestics, or taught mechanic arts, as carpenters, coopers, masons, smiths, &c.

SOURCE: *Negro Slavery; or, a View of Some of the More Prominent Features of that State of Society, as It Exists in the United States of America and in the Colonies of the West Indies, especially in Jamaica* (London: Hatchard, 1823), pp. 65–68.

75 Brazil: Opportunities for Advancement

Notwithstanding the relationship of the mulattos on one side to the black race, they consider themselves superior to the mamalucos. They lean to the whites: and from the light in which the Indians are held, pride themselves upon being totally unconnected with them. Still the mulattos are conscious of their connection with men who are in a state of slavery, and that many persons, even of their own color, are under these degraded circumstances. They have therefore always a feeling in the company of white men, if these white men are wealthy and powerful. This inferiority of rank is not so much felt by white persons in the lower walks of life: and these are more easily led to become familiar with individuals of their own color who are in wealthy circumstances. Still the inferiority which the mulatto feels, is more that which is produced by poverty than that which his color has caused; for he will be equally respectful to a person of his own cast, who may happen to be rich.* The degraded state of the people of color in the British colonies is most lamentable. In Brazil, even the trifling regulations which exist against them, remain unattended to. A mulatto enters into holy orders, or is appointed a magistrate, his papers stating him to be a white man, but his appearance plainly denoting the contrary. In conversing on one occasion with a man of color who was in my service, I asked if a certain *Capitam-mor* was not a mulatto man; he answered, "he was, but is not now." I begged him to explain, when he added, "Can a *Capitam-mor* be a mulatto man?" I

* The term *Senhor* or *Senhora* is made use of to all free persons, whites, mulattos, and blacks: and in speaking to a freeman of whatever class or color the manner of address is the same. Dr. Pinckard says, in his "Notes on the West Indies," "the title of Mrs. seems to be reserved solely for the ladies from Europe, and the white creoles, and to form a distinction between them and the women of color of all classes and descriptions."

was intimately acquainted with a priest, whose complexion and hair plainly denoted from whence he drew his origin. I liked him much. He was a well-educated and intelligent man. Besides this individual instance I met with several others of the same description.

The regiments of militia, which are called mulatto regiments, are so named from all the officers and men being of mixed casts; nor can white persons be admitted into them. The principal officers are men of property: and the colonel, like the commander of any other regiment, is only amenable to the governor of the province. In the white militia regiments, the officers ought to be by law white men. But in practice they are rather reputed white men, for very little pains are taken to prove that there is no mixture of blood. Great numbers of the soldiers belonging to the regiments which are officered by white men, are mulattos, and other persons of color. The regiments of the line, likewise (as I have elsewhere said), admit into the ranks all persons excepting negroes and Indians. But the officers of these must prove nobility of birth. However, as certain degrees of nobility have been conferred upon persons in whose families there is much mixture of blood, this proof cannot be regarded as being required against the mulatto or mamaluco part of the population. Thus an European adventurer could not obtain a commission in these regiments, whilst a Brazilian, whose family has distinguished itself in the province in former times, will prove his eligibility without regard to the blood which runs in his veins. He is noble, let that flow from whence it may.*

The late colonel of the mulatto regiment of Recife, by name Nogueira, went to Lisbon, and returned to Pernambuco with the Order of Christ, which the Queen had conferred upon him.† A chief person of one of the provinces is the son of a white man and a woman of color. He has received an excellent education; is of generous disposition; and entertains most liberal views upon all subjects. He has been made a colonel, and a degree of nobility has been con-

* To this statement some explanation is necessary, owing to the regulations of the Portuguese military service. Privates are sometimes raised to commissions by the intermediate steps of corporals, quarter-masters, and sergeants. These men gain their ensigncies without any relation to their birth: and though a decidedly dark-colored mulatto might not be so raised, a European of low birth would. It is to enable a man to become a cadet, and then an officer without serving in the ranks, that requires nobility of birth.

† The son of this man is a priest.

ferred upon him; likewise the Regent is sponsor to one of his children. Many other instances might be mentioned. Thus has Portugal, of late years from policy, continued that system into which she was led by her peculiar circumstances in former times. Some of the wealthy planters of Pernambuco, and of the rich inhabitants of Recife, are men of color. The major part of the best mechanics are also of mixed blood.

It is said that mulattos make bad masters: and this holds good oftentimes with persons of this description, who have been in a state of slavery, and become possessed of slaves of their own, or are employed as managers upon estates. The change of situation would lead to the same consequences in any race of human beings; and cannot be accounted peculiar to the mixed casts. I have seen mulattos of free birth, as kind, as lenient, and as forbearing to their slaves and other dependents, as any white man.

SOURCE: Henry Koster, *Travels in Brazil, 1809 to 1815* (2 vols.; Philadelphia: Carey, 1817), 2:174–78. (Some footnotes omitted.)

76 Brazil: Ownership of Slaves

Next came an old free negress, with a young slave of her own sex and color, carrying a bundle. She was very talkative; and when she found we were English, went on with great volubility, endeavoring to pronounce the names of all the English she had known at Rio, and seemed proud of the extent of her acquaintance. Her young slave was her only property, and she made a good livelihood by hiring her out as a beast of burthen, to whoever wanted her, and for whatever purpose. Many persons, black and white, about Rio, live in the same manner. They possess a single slave, whom they send out in the morning, and exact at night a patac. They themselves do nothing, lying indolently about, and living on this income. Whatever more the slave is able to get, goes to his own support. This mode of life gives rise to infinite dishonesty and petty theft, as the slave, on pain of the severest castigation, is obliged to procure the money *perfas et nefas*.

SOURCE: Robert Walsh, *Notices of Brazil* (2 vols.; London: Westley and Davis, 1830), 2:18–19.

77 Brazil: Abolitionists

The Brazilian Negro has been called the principal architect or agent of his own emancipation. Brief reference has been made to the variety of ways in which the slave contributed to his own freedom. Long before the question reached the halls of parliament, or even in the public press, the Negro ventured his protest against servitude. The original violent reaction which carried with it such disastrous consequences gave way to more thoughtful and cautious ways of achieving the same end. Carrying on his labor, the Negro hoarded the money necessary to purchase his liberty. There are innumerable cases of Negro slaves who managed to buy their liberty. This individual and sometimes sporadic initiative became in due time an organized effort. It was then that the brotherhoods appeared; organizations of Negroes who, in addition to other purposes, paid a fixed quota into the common funds for emancipation.

The brotherhoods inspired with a religious motive were extremely important, the most significant being the Brotherhood of Our Lady and that of Saint Benedict. Even to the present day in some Brazilian states, fraternities of colored men still survive. The need for protection and defense forced the Negro to form these guilds for collective effort toward personal liberty. Certain feasts or celebrations found their origin in this purpose, notably the *reizados* and *congos.* These two feasts combined European and African features and were devoted primarily to the coronation of a king and queen of the Negroes. The first evidences of these ceremonies go back to the seventeenth century. Beginning with a solemn procession with chanting and the accompaniment of African instruments, the symbolic coronation of the king and queen was ended with a visitation to the Church of Our Lady of the Rosary or of Saint Benedict. Aside from the undoubted importance of these festivals as a tradition and as an important element in folklore, the *congos* represented a significant social trend; the grouping together of the Negroes for the purpose of self-emancipation. These same groups devoted considerable attention to the celebration of the great feasts of Christmas and Epiphany. The Catholic leagues and societies among Negroes carried on the same tradition. There existed and still survive in various parts of the country such groups of a purely religious character, devoted to Our Lady of the Rosary, Saint Ephigenia, Saint Domingos de Gusmão, and many others. In these associations, the Negroes contributed a regular quota to be utilized for the purchase of the certificate of emancipation. There are many incidents of Negroes who laboriously and painfully brought together sufficient money for their own liberty and continued in the same weary task to gather the sum necessary for the emancipation of their comrades.

The story of Chico Rei, in the province of Minas Geraes, in the eighteenth century is a case in point which has become almost legendary through tradition and repetition. Chico Rei was a petty king in Africa, taken prisoner with his tribe and sold into slavery in Brazil. His name was Francisco, and it is said that, with the capture of his people, his wife and children accompanied him to the new world. All of the members of the family died in the welter of humanity which came over in the slaver, with the exception of one son. The entire cargo, including Francisco and his son, were sent to the mines of Villa Rica, later the city of Ouro Preto in Minas Geraes. Francisco swore that as a king in his own right, he could continue as a king, even though exiled from his own land. Amassing little by little the necessary money, he purchased the freedom of his son. They labored together to secure the sum for Francisco's liberty. Once this was accomplished, the two applied themselves to the task of redeeming their fellows, working the scheme out as a definite, fixed plan. As each new man was freed, he joined the little group of freemen and worked with them to liberate the entire tribe. Once his own tribe was free, Francisco and his companions performed a similar service for other tribes. In this manner they achieved the freedom of a very considerable number of slaves in Villa Rica, which grew into a veritable colony, a little state within a state, as the local historian Diego de Vasconcellos described it.

Francisco was proclaimed king of this little community and hence passed into legend as Chico Rei, Little King. With his second wife, whom he took in Brazil, his son and daughter-in-law, he formed a royal family in Villa Rica. His wife was popularly accorded the designation of queen and his son and daughter-in-law, prince and princess respectively. Legend has it that the "nation" which Chico Rei created bought the rich mines of Encardideira and Palacio

Velho. With the gold which these mines produced, Chico Rei widened the scope of his plan, freeing more and more Negroes. The "nation" chose as its patron saint, Saint Ephigenia, under whose auspices a fraternity of the same name was founded. The members constructed the magnificant Church of the Rosary which is still to be seen in Ouro Preto.

Every year, on January 6th, the king, queen, and princes, dressed in exquisite finery, adorned with their insignia, took part in the solemn procession to the Church of the Rosary, where high mass was sung. They then paraded through the streets of Villa Rica, to the accompaniment of African instruments and typical dances. They were surrounded by vast multitudes of the common people. The image of Saint Ephigenia was placed close to the holy water fount. The Negro women who comprised the guard of honor of the queen were accustomed, according to the story, to powder their hair with gold dust from the mines. Upon the return of the procession to the church, they shook the dust from their hair into the water, allowing it to settle there, a contribution to the funds of the association. In other cities of Minas Geraes the societies followed this general example. The contributions of all kinds were destined for the primary purpose of purchasing the liberty of less fortunate brethren.

Chico Rei was the first Negro abolitionist in Brazil. His example was followed by many members of his race, who carried through an organized and deliberate program for emancipation. In Bahia, before the existence of funds for emancipation established by the abolitionist societies, the Negroes had organized "loan funds" to facilitate the purchase of freedom. Most of their organizations were converted into emancipation societies as this became the outstanding aim of their existence.

The actual mechanism of these societies is rather interesting. The Negroes in the associations accepted the leadership of the one among them who inspired the greatest confidence and respect. The treasurer of the loan fund, charged with supervising the deposits which the slaves delivered to him, kept a record of what was given in by a special system, since they had no method of writing. This record was maintained by notches on the wooden canes which each contributor possessed. The leader received these funds from a slave who took up the collection at each Sunday's gathering. On the occasion of these meetings, receipts were discussed, payments made, and reports heard on the progress of the fund. These societies took counsel as to the form in which the available resources should be devoted to emancipation. Any member had the privilege of withdrawing whatever amount he might need. If every penny was taken out, a small percentage was charged against the contributor, which went to the treasurer. Since there was no efficient bookkeeping, errors were frequent, as the system of notches gave rise to contradictory contentions, with the result that the discussions often became especially acrimonious. Only the intervention of the leader or chief could bring peace to these turbulent gatherings.

Every year dividends were distributed. It was possible for the slaves to help each other in this co-operative emancipation society. In almost every province of Brazil these societies flourished more or less effectively. As the abolitionist campaign gained headway, the more formal and complex emancipation funds provided by the abolitionist societies were inaugurated, many of them inspired directly in the organization which the slaves themselves had perfected.

During the long and arduous struggle for emancipation, the Negroes were enthusiastic defenders of their own cause. There were few aspects of the abolition movement in which Negroes did not participate. In spite of the restrictions and difficulties, Negro leaders were developed during the years that abolitionism was the all-absorbing question of Brazil. Several of their names have passed into history as energetic and talented leaders of the race.

Luiz Gama stands out among the greatest Negro leaders of Brazil. Born a slave, his activity as an abolitionist leader in the province of São Paulo during the middle nineteenth century is a brilliant chapter in the history of the Brazilian Negro. No story in the annals of the Negro race is touched with greater pathos than the life of this remarkable black man. Gama was born in Bahia in June of 1830, the son of a Portuguese and a free Negro woman, the famous Luiza Mahin, of whom mention has been made in connection with the Hausa uprisings in that region.

Gama was sold by a profligate and dissolute father, ruined by gambling, to a slave trader. At the age of ten the boy was taken to Rio and hence to São Paulo. The unfortunate child was placed aboard the coastal slaver by his own father, who abandoned him without commiseration. It is related that the youngster failed to appreciate the significance of the step his father had taken until the moment before the vessel set sail, when he wailed pitifully that his own father had sold him into bondage.

Fortunately enough, he was placed in a student's residence in São Paulo, where he was enabled to acquire at least a rudimentary education and a smattering of knowledge. In 1848 he fled to enlist in the army. This service was not to his taste, so that after a short period in the barracks, he left to become a copyist in the office of a barrister. In due course he became secretary in the private office of Francisco Maria de Sousa Furtado de Mendonça, who gave him every protection, granting him the opportunity of obtaining a good education. In this new relationship, Gama produced the document which would reveal the illegality of his enslavement; and on presenting it, he was officially declared free. He served as secretary in other offices and later in the police department, a position from which he was evicted in view of his liberalism, in conflict with the prevailing ideas of the moment. He then became proofreader of the review *Ypiranga,* an event which marked the date of his first literary contributions, appearing under the nom de plume of *Afro.*

Within a short time Gama became well known and was almost famous when he joined Ruy Barbosa and other abolitionists on the staff of the newspaper, *Radical Paulistano,* in whose columns appeared many of his principal articles in behalf of abolitionism. He signed the Republican Manifesto in 1869 in company with numerous other intellectuals. A democrat and ardent abolitionist, his voice resounded clearly throughout Brazil. As a lawyer and clerk in São Paulo, he was particularly zealous in defending cases which touched in any way the condition of the slaves. In this ceaseless apostolate, he retrieved some five hundred unfortunates from servitude. He combated, with rare fortitude, every political movement which did not face the slavery question squarely. His office was almost a refuge for persecuted slaves. Antonio Bento followed in the steps of Luiz Gama as a worthy and able successor.

The tradition of his telling eloquence against slavery still lingers in the Club Radical Paulistano. He published relatively little, although several pieces, notably *Primeiras Trovas Burlescas* and *O Moralista,* remain as his literary monument, both consisting of abolitionist poetry. Gama died on August 23, 1882, his name hailed with gratitude in São Paulo and elsewhere in Brazil. He may be called the most representative leader of the Negro race. Forced into slavery, his life was devoted to a single, undeviating purpose, the liberation of his people from the bondage into which he had been sold. Two dominating influences were at work in the formation of the personality of this great Negro abolitionist: the example of his mother in the Negro uprisings of Bahia and the reaction against profound injustice, symbolized by his father's act of selling him into servitude. Zeal and hatred, love and vengeance were the two mainsprings of his thought and action. His love was great for his brethren in misfortune, his hatred bitter against a society which allowed the martyrdom of a portion of humanity which merited better fortune.

Another notable Negro abolitionist was André Rebouças, who struggled in Rio de Janeiro at the side of José de Patrocinio, Joaquim Nabuco, Joaquim Serra, and other personalities of abolitionism, both white and Negro. André Rebouças was born in the town of Cachoeira, in the province of Bahia on January 13, 1838. He studied civil engineering and acquired such a considerable reputation as to be invited to become a member of the Escola Politechnica of Rio de Janeiro. He came to be looked upon in time as one of the foremost figures in Brazilian engineering. He saw service on several government commissions and was in charge of numerous private enterprises. No one was more zealous than he in his devotion to abolitionism with which he became affiliated at an early date. A co-founder of the *Confederação abolicionista, Sociedade Brasileira contra a Escravidão,* and the *Centro Abolicionista da Escola Politecnica,* he collaborated with José de Patrocinio and Arístides Lobo in drawing up the 1883 manifesto of the organization. The fortune which he amassed as an engineer was spent generously for abolitionist propaganda. It was his purse which supported many of the journals, newspapers, and societies which labored so diligently for the cause. Even though of marked republican sympathies, the decree of May 13, 1883, bound Rebouças to the throne and, with the fall of the monarchy, he resigned his post in the polytechnic school to accompany the Emperor into exile. After Dom Pedro's death in Paris, Rebouças took up residence in Funchal, in the Madeira Islands, where he devoted his time to giving gratuitously lessons in mathematics. His tragic death occurred there on May 9, 1898.

José Ferreira de Menezes was another Negro who won high distinction in the abolitionist campaign. Born in Rio de Janeiro in 1845, he studied law and social sciences in the School of Law. His career in law opened the way for activity in writing, speaking, and in politics. His output in the fields of poetry, the novel, and the essay was enormous, while his fame was solidly established as a distinguished and polished speaker. Together with José de Patrocinio, he became a leading member of the little coterie of great abolitionists. Patrocinio esteemed him as one of the most original and fearless of journalists as well as a devoted and faithful colleague.

Among all the Negro abolitionists, José de Patrocinio was beyond doubt the foremost. He was the heart and soul of the entire abolitionist campaign. His activity was spread over a wide field, embracing the press, the rostrum, and the political forum. Of humble origin, José de Patrocinio has gone down in Brazilian history as one of the nation's most effective journalists and social leaders.

His birthplace was Campos, a city in the old province of Rio de Janeiro. He has left us an account of his early environment and experience which may be transcribed very briefly:

> I am the son of a poor Negro vendor of Campos and began life as a serf, an apprentice in the Santa Casa de Misericordia in 1868. I was then between thirteen and fourteen years of age. I left the Misericordia when this establishment passed into the hands of the Sisters of Charity. On this occasion, I would have found myself homeless and without bread, if Albino de Alvarenga had not extended me his protection. He was then assistant Director of the Medical Faculty. I am happy to acknowledge publicly my debt of deepest gratitude to him. In 1868 I was able to undertake my studies. I was earning at the same time some few milreis a month and received sixteen milreis from the parish priest in Campos. I was able to go on thanks to the unexcelled kindness of my teacher, João Pedro de Aquino, who threw open the doors of his classes for preparatory work in pharmacy and medicine. On entering the Medical School, I received an additional aid of twenty milreis from the *Sociedade Beneficente.* I did private tutoring and received room and board through the generosity of my friend, Sebastião Catão Calado. Thus it was that I worked for three years until 1874, when I completed my course in pharmacy.

Patrocinio later married, and with the aid of his father-in-law, Emiliano de Senna, bought the newspaper *Gazeta da Tarde* and the then *Cidade do Rio.* Under these circumstances he revealed himself an able journalist and enthusiastic advocate of emancipation. Early childhood in Campos had afforded him the opportunity to observe the sufferings and vexations of the colored people. Campos was a noted slave center for southern Brazil, an agricultural center where one of the largest concentrations of slaves was to be found, numbering some 30,000. Patrocinio carried with him as a permanent heritage the experiences and scenes of his youth. The bitterness which they produced was reflected in the vigor and energy with which he pleaded the cause of emancipation.

Every step of the way in the progress of abolitionism bears the imprint of José de Patrocinio. He was the spokesman of the movement. No voice surpassed his in eloquence and in the press he played a role comparable to that of Nabuco on the floor of parliament. As a newspaperman, dedicated to a cause, he let no day slip by without something from his pen appearing on emancipation. The *Gazeta da Tarde* and the *Cidade do Rio* were two mighty bulwarks in this campaign of education and conviction.

Patrocinio was the principal collaborator in the manifesto of 1883 of the *Confederacão Abolicionista.* He was the promoter of public meetings, lectures, concerts, benefit functions, and other forms of emancipation propaganda. No phase of the struggle escaped his energetic and variegated activity. Patrocinio, like Rebouças, was intensely loyal to the throne, in recognition of the important part of the Princess Regent and the Emperor himself in making emancipation a reality. When, after abolition was achieved, the opposition to monarchy became stronger, he organized the Black Guard, whose purpose was the defense of the throne at all cost. It was impossible to stem the tide running against the Empire and Patrocinio was forced to witness the heartbreaking spectacle of the departure of the royal family into exile. With the proclamation of the republic, the great journalist was forced into semi-oblivion. He retired into private life, forsaking his former associates and surrounding himself with a few faithful and devoted friends who remained with him even in adversity. It was the end of a brilliant and active life. A grave injustice was committed against a man whose life had been sacrificed to abolitionism. He died in Rio de Janeiro, January 29, 1905, indigent and forgotten. The greatest Negro in abolitionism passed from the scene.

The history of the emancipation movement includes many more names of Negroes who devoted to it much or all of their time and talent. Theodomiro Pereira in Minas Geraes; Manoel Querino in Bahia are among the figures in the provinces who gave unstintingly of their services. Manoel Querino . . . can scarcely be classified as a Negro leader. He was a student of anthropology and sociology as related to the Brazilian Negro. Born in the town of Santo Amaro in the province of Bahia in July of 1851, he lived until 1923. He was a liberal and a republican and took an active part in the abolitionist campaign in Bahia, his native state. He signed the republican manifesto of that province in 1870 in the company of several close friends and founded the papers, *A Provincia* and *O Trabalho,* in which he expressed vigorous abolitionist convictions. He collaborated with several of the societies and contributed a notable series of articles on the suppression of slavery to the *Gazeta da Tarde.*

It would be unjust to let pass without mention the names of mulattoes who contributed effectively to the emancipation of the Negro race. It is difficult to distinguish them in many cases from their white colleagues in the absence of evidence of racial origin and the thin line which prevails in Brazil in the matter of color. In some cases the biographical data at hand are quite insufficient even to determine the race to which the person in question belongs. There are, however, some names which stand out clearly. One of the most significant was Castro Alves. acclaimed as the poet of abolition. Born in Bahia on March 14, 1847, Castro Alves pursued the humanities, studied in the law school in Recife, and later took up residence in São Paulo. He died during the fourth year of his professional training, in 1871. His principal work is *Espumas Fluctuantes,* a book of verse, the first edition of which appeared in 1870. He wrote abundantly in the field of poetry with the emancipation of the slaves as one of his favorite themes. In a more limited way, as a speaker and man of action, he revealed a profound concern for the cause of abolition. Castro Alves was possessed of a deep and lasting appeal which has been reflected in Brazilian letters down to the present day.

In brief, the Negro played a role of decisive importance in achieving abolition. Negro leaders and agitators were not bystanders or onlookers in the great social upheaval which culminated in the emancipation of the race. Negro leadership exerted a wide influence in this struggle for the achievement of human rights.

SOURCE: Arthur Ramos, *The Negro in Brazil* (Washington, D.C.: Associated Publishers, 1939), pp. 66–79.

78 Cuba: Political Power

The Captain-General of Cuba is appointed by Spain, and is commander-general of the army, and governor of the island, president of the royal audiences, and of the provincial assembly, superintendent of the post office, &c.—indeed, a kind of viceroy.

The army is divided into the regular troops and the militia. Of the first, there are seven regiments of infantry of the line, and five regiments of light infantry. One battalion of eight companies of artillery, one of which is of flying artillery, and one company of sappers; also a brigade of two companies, and six of disciplined militia, and four squadrons of Royal Lancers; the disciplined militia includes three battalions of free colored troops, and two regiments of dragoons, whites.

The city militia is composed of eight squadrons of three companies, each containing seventy men. The volunteer *compañias sueltas,* includes eight companies of white infantry, and thirteen of cavalry, and twenty-two of free colored infantry, mulattoes and blacks.

These troops are distributed throughout the island, and as the regular army, with all its officers, is from old Spain, the Creole finds but little sympathy in those who are thus sent to enforce his obedience to the exactions of his unnatural parent. Havana, the key to the whole island, is garrisoned by six regiments of infantry of the regular army, one regiment of infantry, and one of horse of the militia, organized in 1763, and two battalions of free colored troops.

There are three great political parties in Cuba, of which the most powerful are the native Spaniards, of whom, with a few exceptions, are composed the merchants, the army, the priesthood, and all the government officers, from the Captain-General to the Captain of partido. The Creoles form the second class, and are generally planters, farmers, or lawyers, but are, most generally, scrupulously excluded from the army and higher civil offices. The third class is made up of about an equal number of free mulattoes and free negroes, who, although they are not represented, and are by law excluded from all civil offices, still compose a respectable part of the militia, and would play an active part in any revolutionary movement that might occur, either of the whites or of the slaves. To these parties may be added the slaves, who are themselves divided into *bozales,** those recently brought from the coast of Africa; *ladinos,* those who were imported before the passage of the law in 1821, prohibiting the slave trade; and *criollos,* those born on the island. The first retain for a long time all their native vices and ferocity, the second are in a measure civilized, and the third are the most intelligent; but imbibing from their youth all the vices of their African parents, are thereby only the more difficult to govern.

The merchants own a large portion of the wealth of the island, in bonds of planters, in whose estates they are thus largely interested, and with whose prosperity or adversity they deeply sympathize. The free colored have many privileges, and are more kindly treated and respected than the same class in our northern free States. The Spaniard has not the same antipathy to color that the Anglo-Saxon has, and, indeed, a few of the wealthiest and most intelligent, in some parts of the island, mingle in the higher society; these are, however, only of that class in whose veins there is a strong admixture of white blood, the swarthy are totally excluded. They are all permitted to enjoy the advantages of education, but intermarriage between the white and colored races is interdicted by law, by which they are also excluded from all the learned professions. This obstacle is sometimes removed by having the children christened as white by the priest, or by procuring witnesses to give oath to their white extraction, and the fraud is winked at.

The greater portion of this class has procured its freedom by purchase, and is consequently more intelligent and industrious than that remaining in slavery. Its introduction into the army, the many privileges it possesses, and the little sympathy that the African races show for each other, would probably induce it to join the whites in any insurrection among the slaves; whatever effect the promise of equal rights with the former would have on it should the whites themselves revolutionize. During the last fourteen years it has increased 9 percent faster than the whites; its male population already amounts to one-third that of the white.

SOURCE: J. G. F. Wurdeman, *Notes on Cuba* (Boston: Munroe, 1844), pp. 248–50.

* *Bozal* signifies muzzled; *ladino,* versed in an idiom; *criollo,* a creole, applied to any one born on the island, white or colored.

79 Cuba: Social Status

The population of the island bears no proportion to its physical capabilities; yet it is supposed to have doubled in the last fifteen years. No recent census, however, has been taken. It is estimated to be about 800,000, of which the whites are supposed to be as four to five, or nearly 355,000 whites, and 444,000 blacks. The mass of white population is Spanish; there are many French people, particularly in and about Havana. The Americans are next in number among the foreigners, and some suppose them more numerous than the French. There are Scotch, Germans, Dutch, Italians; but my opinion is too conjectural to be worth stating as to the proportion.

It is of more importance to observe that the free blacks are considerably numerous; the number has been stated to exceed 100,000. It is a redeeming circumstance in regard to the Spanish character, that their laws favor emancipation, and the government faithfully executes them. If the slave can present his value, nay, only his *cost,* to his master, however reluctant he may be to part with perhaps the best body servant he has, or an invaluable mechanic, or skillful driver, he cannot retain him. If he attempt to evade the demand, the captain of the Partido must enforce it, and evasion in either case is punished with high pecuniary penalties.

Nor is it so difficult a thing for a smart and saving negro to accomplish the means. Food is furnished to them so abundantly by their masters, that the fruits of their garden may be converted into money. A certain method is to raise a hog, which they can do, to a large size, by corn of their own growing. I have seen swine belonging to slaves, worth two or three ounces (forty or fifty dollars); and there are purchasers enough without their carrying them to market. Live hogs are at this moment sold here at eight dollars per hundred on the hoof. At any rate, negroes make money, and some save and bury it, and at an early period in life may buy their freedom. This very week, splendid funeral was made for a black woman who paid for her freedom, and has left behind her $100,000, collected by her industry, and also an amiable and respectable character. From my chamber window I look down upon a family of freed blacks, who are my laundresses. They sell admirable spruce beer, and I know not what else; and the daughter amuses herself, and the family, and the neighborhood, by singing with a sweet and powerful voice of great compass, and accompanies her singing by the guitar. All this I rejoice to see and hear, and delight to record in honor of the Spanish government. And I would hide my face for shame, that in some of our republican states, a statute forbids manumission, even when the owner is disposed to grant, or the slave is prepared to purchase the blessing.

SOURCE: Abiel Abbot, *Letters Written in the Interior of Cuba . . . 1828* (Boston: Bowles and Dearborn, 1829), pp. 96–98.

80 Cuba: Emancipation Laws

In no part of the world, where slavery exists, is manumission so frequent as in the island of Cuba; for Spanish legislation, directly the reverse of French and English, favors in an extraordinary degree the attainment of freedom, placing no obstacle in its way, nor making it in any manner onerous. The right which every slave has of seeking a new master, or purchasing his liberty, if he can pay the amount of his cost; the religious sentiment that induces many persons in good circumstances to concede by will freedom to a certain number of negroes; the custom of retaining a number of both sexes for domestic service, and the affections that necessarily arise from this familiar intercourse with the whites; and the facilities allowed to slaveworkmen to labor for their own account, by paying a certain stipulated sum to their masters, are the principal causes why so many blacks acquire their freedom in the towns.*

* The customary rate of hire is ten cents on each $100 of the value of the slave for every working day. There are about 290 working days in the year, Sundays and church holidays being considered days of rest. In addition to the above-mentioned facilities for attaining freedom, the slave has the privilege of paying his master small sums of money on account, and thus becoming a co-owner of himself. Thus, if his value be $600, by paying his master $25 he becomes the owner of one twenty-fourth of himself; when he has paid $50, he owns one-twelfth, and so on; and in hiring his time, he pays to his master rent only on the sum remaining due. The law obliges the master to accept these partial payments; and should the owner overvalue the slave at the time of commencing them, the negro can appeal to the syndic, who is annually ap-

The position of the free negroes in Cuba is much better than it is elsewhere, even among those nations which have for ages flattered themselves as being most advanced in civilization. We find there no such barbarous laws as have been invoked, even in our own days, by which free negroes are prohibited from receiving donations from the whites, and can be deprived of their liberty, and sold for the benefit of the State, should they be convicted of affording an asylum to escaped slaves. . . .*

Cuba has received from Africa,

Previous to 1791	93,500
From 1791 to 1825, at least	320,000
	413,500

In 1825, in consequence of the small number of females brought by the traders, there existed in the island only,

Negroes, free and slave	320,000
Mulattoes	70,000
	390,000

A similar calculation was sent to the Cortes of Spain, on the 20 July 1811, based upon numerical elements differing slightly from these, in which it was endeavored to prove that the island of Cuba had received up to 1810, less than 229,000 African negroes, which are represented, in 1811, by a slave and free population of blacks and mulattoes, amounting to 326,000; being an excess of 97,000 over the number imported.† When it is remembered that the whites

pointed to protect the slaves. A slave who has partially manumitted himself is styled *coartado*. Many redeem themselves excepting the sum of $50 or $100; and on this pay a rent to the master for the rest of their lives, no matter how much wealth they may acquire. A careful study of individual reasons, among the blacks in Cuba, for adopting this course, might perhaps develop some unobserved peculiarities of the negro mind. It may sometimes arise from ties of affection, sometimes from interests, and it may be found to result, in some cases, from an intuitive desire, or an idiosyncrasy on the part of the negro to have some immediate and tangible superior, to whose opinion he can look with respect, and from whom he can claim protection in calamity.

* Decision of the Supreme Council of Martinique of 4th July, 1720.—"Decree of 1st March, 1766, No. 7.—II."

† My calculation closes with 1825, and the number of negroes imported since the *conquest* amounts to 413,500. The calculation sent to the Cortes closes with 1810, and gives 229,000 (*Documentos,* p. 119). Difference, 184,500; but, according to the returns

have contributed to the existence of 70,000 mulattoes,* leaving aside the natural increase that has resulted from so many thousand negroes progressively imported, one exclaims, "What other nation, or human society, can give so favorable an account of the results of this *unfortunate trade!*" I respect the sentiments that have dictated these lines, and will again repeat, that if we compare Cuba with Jamaica, the results appear in favor of the Spanish legislation, and the customs of the inhabitants of Cuba. These comparisons demonstrate a state of affairs in the latter island infinitely more favorable to the physical preservation and manumission of the negroes; but what a sorrowful spectacle is presented by Christian and civilized nations disputing which of the two, in three centuries, has destroyed the least number of Africans, by reducing them to slavery!

I will not praise the treatment of the negroes in the southern portion of the United States, but certain it is, that different degrees exist in the sufferings of the human species. The slave who has a cabin and a family, is not so unhappy as he who is folded as if he were one of a flock of sheep. The greater the number of slaves established with their families, in cabins which they deem their own, the more rapid is their multiplication. The slaves in the United States were as follows:—

1770	480,000	1810	1,191,364
1791	676,696	1820	1,541,568
1800	894,444		

The annual increase for the last ten years, has been (without counting the manumission of 100,000), 26,000, which is doubling in

of the Havana custom-house alone, the number of African negroes brought to that port from 1811 to 1820, has been 109,000, and to this we must add, first, according to the principles admitted by the consulado, one-fourth or 27,000 for the licit importations at other ports of the island; and, second, the amount of illicit traffic, from 1811 to 1825.—H.

* The work undertaken by the consulado, in 1811, relative to the probable distribution of 326,000 blacks, free and slave, contains some very interesting matter, which great local knowledge alone could have supplied to that body. A. *Cities.* Western part.—In Havana, 27,000 free colored, and 28,000 slaves; seven towns, with Ayuntamiento, 18,000; from which we have, in the jurisdiction of Havana, 36,000 free colored, and 37,000 slaves. Total, in the cities, 72,000 free colored, and 69,000 slaves, or 141,000. B. *Country.*—Jurisdiction of Havana, 6,000 free colored, and 110,000 slaves. Eastern part, 36,000 free colored, and 33,000 slaves. Total, in the country, 185,000.—*Documentos sobre los negros,* p. 121.—H.

27 years. I will say, therefore . . . that if the slaves in Jamaica and Cuba had multiplied in the same proportion, these two islands would have had, one in 1795, and the other in 1800, very nearly their present population, without any necessity of loading 400,000 negroes with chains, in Africa, and dragging them to Port Royal or Havana.

SOURCE: Alexander Humboldt, *The Islands of Cuba,* J.S. Thrasher, trans. (New York: Derby and Jackson, 1856), pp. 211–13; 222–27 (some footnotes omitted).

NOTES

Introduction: Africa and the Ancient World

1. For a summary of the issues involved, see Robert O. Collins, ed., *Problems in African History* (Englewood Cliffs, N.J.: Prentice-Hall, 1968), Problem 1: "Africa and Egypt"; also, Édouard Naville, "L'origine africaine de la civilisation égyptienne," *Revue Archéologique,* 4th ser. (Jul.–Dec. 1913), 22:47–65, and Thurstan Shaw, "Changes in African Archaeology in the Last Forty Years," in Christopher Fyfe, ed., *African Studies since 1945: A Tribute to Basil Davidson* (London: Longman, 1976), pp. 156–68. Shaw states categorically: "[T]he early cultures of Merimde, the Fayum, Badari and Naqada I and II are essentially African, and early African social customs and religious beliefs were the root and foundation of the ancient Egyptian way of life."

2. Gertrude Caton Thompson and Elizabeth Whittle, "Thermoluminescence Dating of the Badarian," *Antiquity* (June 1975), 49:97.

3. Lester Brooks, *Great Civilizations of Ancient Africa* (New York: Four Winds Press, 1971), p. 29.

4. Thomas W. Africa, "Herodotus and Diodorus on Egypt," *Journal of Near East Studies* (1963), 22(4):254.

5. Henri Lhote, *The Search for the Tassili Frescoes* (1939).

6. Ludwig Friedlander, *Roman Life and Manners under the Early Empire* (7th edition: undated).

7. Gilbert Norwood, *Plautus and Terence* (New York: Longmans, Green, 1932), p. 100.

Part One: Africans in Asia

1. L. Sprague de Camp, "Xerxes' Okapi and Greek Geography," *Isis* (1963), 54(1):124.

2. Jules Leroy, "Les 'Éthiopiens' de Persépolis," *Annales d 'Éthiopie* (1963), 5:293–97.

3. A. T. Olmstead, *History of the Persian Empire* [*Achaemenid Period*] (Chicago: University of Chicago Press, 1948), p. 244.

4. A. Kammerer, *Essai sur l'histoire antique d'Abyssinie* (Paris: Paul Geuthner, 1926), pp. 27, 61–65.

5. Kammerer, *Essai,* p. 109.

6. Since Playfair's time many new sources for the history of sixth-century Arabia have been discovered. These include both manuscripts—see, for example, Axel Moberg, *The Book of the Himyarites* (Lund: Gleerup, 1924)—and rock inscriptions. Recent research has refined the chronology of events accepted by nineteenth-century historians—see Sidney Smith, "Events in Arabia in the 6th Century A.D.," *Bulletin of the School of Oriental and African Studies* (1954), 16:425–68—and has shown that the wars of Christians against Jews in the Yemen were motivated not only by religious antagonisms but also, and more importantly, by competition among rival ruling classes and by the ongoing struggle between the Byzantine and Persian empires (whose clients the Christians and Jews of southern Arabia were) for control of the trade with India—see N. Pigulewskaja, *Byzanz auf den Wegen nach Indien* (Berline: Akademie Verlag; Amsterdam: Hakkert, 1969). For an up-to-date account of the Ethiopian involvement in sixth-century Arabia, see Sergew Hable Sellassie, *Ancient and Medieval Ethiopian History to 1270* (Addis Ababa: United Printers, 1972), pp. 123–58. However, as far as African involvement in sixth-century Arabia is concerned, Playfair's account still gives the feel of the time as well as, if not better than, any more recent work.

7. Régis Blachère, *Histoire de la littérature arabe* (3 vols.; Paris: Adrien-Maisonneuve, 1952–66), 2:272.

8. B. Heller, "Sīrat 'Antar," *Encyclopaedia of Islam,* 2d ed.

9. "Tābi'," *Encyclopaedia of Islam,* 1st ed.

10. " 'Aṭā' b. Abī Rabāḥ," *Encyclopaedia of Islam,* 2d ed.

11. Gernot Rotter, *Die Stellung des Negers in der Islamisch-Arabischen Gesellschaft bis zum XVI. Jahrhundert* (Bonn: Inaugural-Dissertation, Rheinische Friedrich-Wilhelms-Universität, 1967), p. 93.

12. *Kitāb al-aghānī,* cited in Henry George Farmer, *A History of Arabian Music to the XIIIth Century* (London: Luzac & Co., 1929), pp. 120–21.

13. Farmer, *Arabian Music,* p. 147.

14. J. A. Rogers, *World's Great Men of Color,* John Henrik Clarke, ed. (2 vols.; New York: Collier Books, 1972), 1:148–62.

15. "Ibrāhīm b. al-Mahdī," *Encyclopaedia of Islam,* 2d ed.

16. Ali Bey ibn Othman Bey el Abassi [pseud. of Dominigo Badia y Leblish], *Travels of Ali Bey, in Morocco, Tripoli, Cyprus, Egypt, Arabia, Syria, and Turkey: Between the Years 1803 and 1807* (2 vols.; Philadelphia: John Conrad, 1816), 2:380–81, 403.

17. Eyles Irwin, *A Series of Adventures in the Course of a Voyage up the Red-Sea* (London: J. Dodsley, 1780), p. 59.

18. C. J. Cruttenden, "Journal of an Excursion to Sanaa the Capital of Yemen," *Proceedings of the Bombay Geographical Society,* November 1838, p. 48.

19. Ali Bey, *Travels,* 2:46–48.

20. Rotter, *Stellung des Negers,* pp. 111–12.

21. *Ibid.,* p. 112.

22. Most black slaves in ninth-century 'Irāḳ probably came from the Horn of Africa. See Neville Chittick, "East African Trade with the Orient," in D. S. Richards, ed., *Islam and the Trade of Asia: A Colloquium* (Philadelphia: University of Pennsylvania Press, 1970), p. 103.

23. Charles Pellat, *Le milieu baṣrien et la formation de Gāḥiẓ* (Paris: Adrien-Maisonneuve, 1953), p. 41.

24. " 'Alī b. Muḥammad al-Zanjī," *Encyclopaedia of Islam,* 2d ed.

25. Rotter, *Stellung des Negers,* pp. 101–9.

26. J. Spencer Trimingham, "The Arab Geographers and the East African Coast," in H. Neville Chittick and Robert I. Rotberg, eds., *East Africa and the Orient* (New York: Africana, 1975), p. 116.

27. A more modern, but briefer, account appears in E. A. Belyaev, *Arabs, Islam and the Arab Caliphate in the Early Middle Ages* (New York: Praeger, 1969), pp. 239–47.

28. A more highly colored account of the occupation of Baṣra by the Zanj appears in al-Ma'sūdī, *Les prairies d'or,* C. Barbier de Meynard, trans. (9 vols.; Paris: Imprimerie Impériale, 1861–1917), 6:58–61.

29. For a more recent translation of this passage, see Bernard Lewis, ed. and trans., *Islam from the Prophet Muhammad to the Capture of Constantinople* (2 vols.; New York: Walker, 1976), 2:66.

30. Vladimir F. Minorsky, ed., *Ḥudūd al-'Ālam. "The Regions of the World." A Persian Geography. 372 A.H.—982 A.D.* (London: Luzac and Co., 1937), pp. 163, 472.

31. George F. Hourani, *Arab Seafaring in the Indian Ocean in Ancient and Early Medieval Times* (1951; repr., Beirut: Khayats, 1963), p. 79.

32. For another version of this story, see G. S. P. Freeman-Grenville, ed., *The East African Coast: Select Documents from the First to the Earlier Nineteenth Century* (Oxford: Clarendon Press, 1962), pp. 9–13; and for yet another see Lewis, *From the Prophet Muhammad,* 2:82–87.

33. His full name was Abū 'Uthmān 'Amr b. Baḥr al-Fuḳaymi al-Baṣrī

al-Jāḥiẓ. ("Al-Djāḥiẓ," *Encyclopaedia of Islam,* 2d ed.) A tradition exists that one of his grandfathers, named Fazārah, was African. See Bayard Dodge, ed. and trans., *The Fihrist of al-Nadīn: A Tenth-Century Survey of Muslim Culture* (2 vols.; New York: Columbia University Press, 1970), 1:399; Rogers, *World's Great Men of Color,* 1:163–76.

34. Pellat, *Le milieu baṣrien,* passim.

35. Tadeusz Lewicki, *Arabic External Sources for the History of Africa to the South of Sahara* (Warsaw: Polska Akademia Nauk, 1969), p. 19.

36. Charles Pellat, *The Life and Works of Jāḥiẓ: Translations of Selected Texts* (London: Routledge and Kegan Paul, 1969), pp. 7–8.

37. "Al-Djāḥiẓ," *Encyclopaedia of Islam,* 2d ed.

38. Pellat, *Life and Works of Jāḥiẓ,* p. 9.

39. Rotter, *Stellung des Negers,* pp. 99–101; Bernard Lewis, *Race and Color in Islam* (New York: Harper and Row, 1971), pp. 16–18.

40. For a more recent translation of "The Boast of the Blacks," see Lewis, *From the Prophet Muhammad,* 2:210–16.

41. Edward W. Blyden, "Mohammedanism and the Negro Race," *Fraser's Magazine,* November 1875; repr. in *Christianity, Islam and the Negro Race* (London: W. B. Whittingham, 1887), p. 15.

42. 'Abd-al-'Azīz 'Abd-al-Qādir Kāmil, *Islam and the Race Question* (Paris: UNESCO, 1970), p. 63.

43. R. E. Enthoven, *The Tribes and Castes of Bombay,* (3 vols.; Bombay: Government Central Press, 1920–22), 2:234.

44. "Ḥabshī," *Encyclopaedia of Islam,* 2d ed.

45. D. K. Bhattacharya, "Indians of African Origin," *Cahiers d'Études Africaines* (1970), 10(40):579–82.

46. Charles Rathbone Low, *History of the Indian Navy (1613–1863)* (2 vols.; London: Bentley, 1877), 1:62fn. One of the best known caravan leaders of nineteenth-century East Africa—he worked at various times for no fewer than four British explorers (Burton, Speke, Stanley, and Cameron) and retired with a pension from the Royal Geographical Society—was nicknamed "Seedy Bombay." See Donald Simpson, *Dark Companions* (London: Paul Elek, 1975), p. 192.

47. Joseph E. Harris, *The African Presence in Asia: Consequences of the East African Slave Trade* (Evanston, Ill.: Northwestern University Press, 1971), ch. 8.

48. Vasant D. Rao, "The Habshis: India's Unknown Africans," *Africa Report* (September–October 1973), 18(5):35.

49. H. A. R. Gibb, trans., *Ibn Battúta: Travels in Asia and Africa* (London: Routledge and Kegan Paul, 1929), p. 260.

50. "Ḥabshī," *Encyclopaedia of Islam,* 2d ed.

51. Frederick Charles Danvers, *The Portuguese in India* (2 vols.; 1894; repr., London: Frank Cass, 1966), 1:501–2, 524.

52. "Ḥabshī," *Encyclopaedia of Islam,* 2d ed.

53. R. C. Majumdar et al., *An Advanced History of India* (2d ed.; London: Macmillan, 1960), p. 287.

54. Richard Pankhurst, "The History of Ethiopia's Relations with India prior to the Nineteenth Century" (Paper presented to the Fourth Conference of Ethiopian Studies, Rome, 1972), p. 55.

55. *Ibid.*

56. R. C. Majumdar, ed., *The History and Culture of the Indian People* (10 vols.; Bombay: Bharatiya Vidya Bhavan, 1953–), 6:214; Charles Stewart, *The History of Bengal* (London: Black, Parry, 1813), pp. 102–6.

57. *The Cambridge History of India* (6 vols.; Cambridge: Cambridge University Press, 1922–37), 3:269; Stewart, *History of Bengal,* p. 107.

58. "Ḥabshī," *Encyclopaedia of Islam,* 2d ed.

59. *Cambridge History of India,* 3:269–71; Pankhurst, "Ethiopia's Relations with India," p. 56.

60. Majumdar, *History and Culture of the Indian People,* 6:215.

61. K. Bikram Singh, "Did Malik Sarwar of Jaunpur Assume Sovereignty?," *Journal of Indian History* (1965), 43:143–50.

62. Harris, *African Presence in Asia,* p. 79, following R. C. Majumdar and Sir Wolseley Haig.

63. "Ibrāhīm Shāh Sharḳī" and "Djawnpur," *Encyclopaedia of Islam,* 2d ed.

64. Mian Muhammad Saeed, *The Sharqi Sultanate of Jaunpur: A Political and Cultural History* (Karachi: University of Karachi, 1972), pp. 37–38.

65. Majumdar, *History and Culture of the Indian People,* 6:264; Haroon Khan Sherwani, *The Bahmanids of the Deccan* (Hyderabad: Saood Manzil, 1953), pp. 113–14.

66. Iftikhār Aḥmad Ghaurī, "Muslims in the Deccan—An Historical Survey," *Journal of the Research Society of Pakistan* (January 1965), 2(1):6–7.

67. J. S. King, *The History of the Bahmanî Dynasty: Founded on the Burhân-i Ma,âṣir* (London, Luzac, 1900), pp. 120, 123–25.

68. S. K. Sinha, *Medieval History of the Deccan* Vol. I: *Bahmanids* (Hyderabad: Government of Andhra Pradesh, 1964), p. 141.

69. G. Yazdani, *Bidar: Its History and Monuments* (London: Oxford University Press, 1947), p. 49.

70. D. R. Seth, "The Life and Times of Malik Ambar," *Islamic Culture* (1957), 31:155.

71. Harris, *African Presence in Asia,* pp. 91–93; Yar Muhammad Khan, *The Deccan Policy of the Mughuls* (Lahore: United Book Corporation, 1971), pp. 107–9.

72. Seth, "Life and Times," pp. 148, 155; Khan, *Deccan Policy,* p. 9.

73. Edward Grey, ed., *The Travels of Pietro della Valle in India* (2 vols.; London: Hakluyt Society, 1892), 1:147.

74. Cited in J. D. B. Gribble, *A History of the Deccan* (2 vols.; London: Luzac, 1896), 1:256.

75. François Valentyn, *Oud en nieuw Oost-Indien* (5 vols.; Amsterdam: Gerard Onder de Linden, 1724–26), 4:215.

76. B. G. Tamaskar, "An Estimate of Malik Ambar," *Quarterly Review of Historical Studies* (Calcutta, 1968–69), 8:644, n19.

77. "An Account by Richard Predys," [March 15, 1628], in William Foster, ed., *The English Factories in India 1624–1629* (Oxford: Clarendon Press, 1909), p. 253.

78. H. A. R. Gibb, trans., *Ibn Battúta: Travels in Asia and Africa* (London: Routledge and Kegan Paul, 1929) p. 230.

79. K. M. Panikkar, *India and the Indian Ocean* (London: Allen and Unwin, 1945), p. 8.

80. Atul Chandra Roy, *A History of Mughal Navy* (Calcutta: World Press Private Ltd., 1972), p. 145.

81. D. R. Banaji, *Bombay and the Sidis* (London: Macmillan, 1932); Sir William W. Hunter, *A History of British India* (2 vols.; 1889, 1900; repr., New York: A. M. S. Press, 1966), 2:224.

82. C. U. Aitchison, *A Collection of Treaties, Engagements and Sanads relating to India and Neighbouring Countries* (5th ed.; 14 vols.; Calcutta: Government of India Central Publication Branch, 1929–33), 8:85.

83. *Gazetteer of the Bombay Presidency.* Vol. 11: *Kolaba and Janjira* (Bombay: Government Central Press, 1883), p. 447.

84. Richard F. Burton, *Sind Revisited* (2 vols.; London: Richard Bentley, 1877), 1:13.

85. G. S. P. Freeman-Grenville, "The Sidi and Swahili," *Bulletin of the Association of British Orientalists,* n.s., (1971), 6:3–18.

86. *Cambridge History of India,* 5:369.

87. Joseph E. Harris, "The Black Peoples of Asian" *World Encyclopaedia of Black Peoples* (St. Clair Shores, Mich.: Scholarly Press, 1975), p. 272.

88. *Ta Ming t'ai-tsu shih-lu,* 141/4a. Translated for the present volume by L. Carrington Goodrich.

89. C. Martin Wilbur, *Slavery in China during the Former Han Dynasty* (Chicago: Field Museum of Natural History, 1943), p. 93.

90. Kitsuzô Kuwabara, "On P'u Shou-kêng . . . ," *Memoirs of the Research Department of the Toyo Bunko* (1928), 2:63.

91. Austin Coates, *Prelude to Hongkong* (London: Routledge and Kegan Paul, 1966), pp. 4, 13, 68.

92. J. J. L. Duyvendak, *China's Discovery of Africa* (London: Probstain, 1949), p. 23.

93. Paul Wheatley, "The Land of Zanj," in R. W. Steel and R. Mansell Prothero, eds., *Geographers and the Tropics* (London: Longmans, 1964), pp.

153–55, and the same author's "Analecta Sino-Africana Recensa," in Chittick and Rotberg, *East Africa and the Orient,* p. 87.

94. Chang Hsing-lang, "The Importation of Negro Slaves to China under the T'ang Dynasty (A.D. 618–907)," *Bulletin of the Catholic University of Peking* (1930), 7:41.

95. Neville Chittick, "East African Trade with the Orient," in D. S. Richards, ed., *Islam and the Trade of Asia: A Colloquium* (Philadelphia: University of Pennsylvania Press, 1970), p. 101.

96. Edward H. Shafer, *The Golden Peaches of Samarkand: A Study of T'ang Exotics* (Berkeley and Los Angeles: University of California Press, 1963), p. 46, n48.

Part Two: Africans in Latin America and the Caribbean

1. Ibn Faḍl Allāh al-'Umarī, *Masālik al-abṣāṛ fi-mamālik al-amṣār,* cited in Ronald W. Davis, "The Problem of Possible Pre-Columbian Contacts between Africa and the Americas: A Summary of the Evidence," *Ghana Notes and Queries* (June 1970), 11:1.

2. Harold G. Lawrence, "African Explorers of the New World," *The Crisis,* June–July 1962, pp. 322–23; Muhammad Hamidullah, "L'Afrique découvre l'Amérique avant Christophe Colomb," *Présence Africaine* (February–May 1958), 17–18:177; Ronald W. Davis, "Negro Contributions to the Exploration of the Globe," in Joseph S. Roucek and Thomas Kiernan, eds., *The Negro Impact on Western Civilization* (New York: Philosophical Library, 1970), pp. 41–45.

3. Leo Wiener, *Africa and the Discovery of America* (3 vols.; Philadelphia: Innes, 1920–22), 2:365; Lawrence, "African Explorers," pp. 324, 326.

4. Wiener, *Africa and the Discovery of America,* 3:365–70; M. D. W. Jeffreys, "Pre-Columbian Negroes in America," *Scientia* (*Revista di Scienza*) (1953), 88:202–18; John G. Jackson, "Africa and the Discovery of America," in *Introduction to African Civilizations* (2d ed.; New York: University Books, 1970), ch. 5.

5. Rafique Ali Jairazbhoy, *Ancient Egyptians and Chinese in America* (London: Prior, 1974); G. Cauvet, *Les Berbères en Amérique* (Algiers: Bringau, 1930).

6. Samuel Eliot Morison, *The European Discovery of America: The Northern Voyages A.D. 500–1600* (New York: Oxford University Press, 1971), pp. 9–107.

7. Justin Winsor, ed., *Narrative and Critical History of America* (8 vols.; London: Sampson Low, 1884–89), 1:59.

8. Davis, "Possible Pre-Columbian Contacts," pp. 3–4.

9. Alfred W. Crosby, *The Columbian Exchange: Biological and Cultural Consequences of 1492* (Westport, Conn.: Greenwood Publishing Company, 1972), pp. 68–77.

10. It has been suggested that maize was known in Africa before Columbus. (See M. D. W. Jeffreys, "Pre-Columbian Maize in Africa," *Nature,* November 21, 1953, pp. 965–66.) Supporters of this theory, however, say that it was the Arabs who introduced maize into Africa from Spain, and opponents of it believe that references to "maize" in Portuguese and other early records of African agriculture are due to a confusion with sorghum. In any case, it has not been proposed that it was Africans who brought maize from the New World to the old.

11. Crosby, *The Columbian Exchange,* pp. 22–23.

12. Phillip D. Curtin, "Epidemiology and the Slave Trade," *Political Science Quarterly* (June 1968), 83(2):199–200.

13. This account should be read in conjunction with a more recent treatment of the subject: R. K. Kent, "Palmares: An African State in Brazil," *Journal of African History* (1965), 6(1):161–75. On maroons in general, see Richard Price, ed., *Maroon Societies* (Garden City, N.Y.: Anchor Books, 1973).

14. Nina Rodrigues, *Os Africanos no Brasil* (São Paulo: Companhia Editora Nacional, 1932), pp. 79–82.

FOR FURTHER READING

GENERAL WORKS

Armistead, Wilson. *A Tribute for the Negro.* Manchester, England: William Irwin, 1848.

Brown, William Wells. *The Black Man: His Antecedents, His Genius, and His Achievements.* Boston: James Redpath, 1863.

Cunard, Nancy, ed. *Negro: Anthology Made by Nancy Cunard 1931–1933.* London: Wishart, 1934.

Du Bois, W. E. Burghardt. *The World and Africa: An Inquiry into the Part which Africa has Played in World History.* New York: Viking Press, 1947.

Ferris, William H. *The African Abroad: Or, His Evolution in Western Civilization.* 2 vols. New Haven: Tuttle, Morehouse and Taylor, 1913.

Grégoire, Henri Baptiste. *An Enquiry concerning the Intellectual and Moral Faculties, and Literature of Negroes.* Brooklyn, N.Y.: Thomas Kirk, 1810.

Herskovits, Melville J. *The Myth of the Negro Past.* New York: Harper Brothers, 1941.

Irvine, Keith. *The Rise of the Colored Races.* New York: Norton, 1970.

Jackson, John G. *Introduction to African Civilizations.* (Introduction by John Henrik Clarke.) New York: University Books, 1970.

Kilson, Martin L. and Rotberg, Robert I., eds. *The African Diaspora: Interpretive Essays.* Cambridge, Mass.: Harvard University Press, 1976.

Rodney, Walter. "Africa in Europe and the Americas." In *Cambridge History of Africa,* Vol. 4, ch. 9. Cambridge: Cambridge University Press, 1975.

Rogers, Joel A. *World's Great Men of Color.* 2 vols. New York: Collier Books, 1972.

Roucek, Joseph S., and Kiernan, Thomas, eds. *The Negro Impact on Western Civilization.* New York: Philosophical Library, 1970.

Shepperson, George. "The African Abroad or the African Diaspora," in T. O. Ranger, ed., *Emerging Themes of African History* (London: Heinemann, 1968), pp. 152–76.

Williams, Chancellor. *The Destruction of Black Civilization: Great Issues of a Race from 4500 B.C. to 2000 A.D.* Chicago: Third World Press, 1974.

World Encyclopedia of Black Peoples. Vol. 1. "Conspectus." St. Clair Shores, Mich.: Scholarly Press, 1975.

AFRICA AND THE ANCIENT WORLD

Beardsley, Grace M. *The Negro in Greek and Roman Civilization: A Study of the Ethiopian Type.* Baltimore: Johns Hopkins Press, 1929.

Bourgeois, Alain. *La Grèce devant la négritude.* Paris: Présence Africaine, 1971.

Brooks, Lester. *Great Civilizations of Ancient Africa.* New York: Four Winds Press, 1971.

Diop, Cheikh Anta. *The African Origin of Civilization: Myth or Reality.* New York: Lawrence Hill, 1974.

Hansberry, William Leo. *Pillars in Ethiopian History.* Edited by Joseph E. Harris. Washington, D. C.: Howard University Press, 1974.

Junker, Hermann. "The First Appearance of the Negroes in History." *Journal of Egyptian Archeology* (1921), 7:121–32.

Obenga, Théophile. *L'Afrique dans l'antiquité: Égypte pharaonique—Afrique noire.* Paris: Présence Africaine, 1973.

Snowden, Frank M. *Blacks in Antiquity: Ethiopians in the Greco-Roman Experience.* Cambridge, Mass.: Harvard University Press, 1970.

AFRICANS IN ASIA

Banaji, D. R. *Bombay and the Sidis.* Bombay, India: Macmillan, 1932.

Blyden, Edward Wilmot. *Christianity, Islam and the Negro Race.* London: W. B. Whittingham, 1887.

Burton-Page, J. "Ḥabshī," *Encyclopaedia of Islam.* 2d ed.

Chang Hsing-lang. "The Importation of Negro Slaves to China under the T'ang Dynasty (A.D. 618–907)." *Catholic University of Peking Bulletin No. 7,* December 1930, pp. 37–59.

Chou Yi-Liang. "Early Contacts between China and Africa." *Ghana Notes and Queries* (June 1972), 12:1–3.

Duyvendak, J. J. L. *China's Discovery of Africa.* London: Probsthain, 1949.

Filesi, Teobaldo. *China and Africa in the Middle Ages.* London: Frank Cass, 1972.

Goodrich, Luther Carrington. "Negroes in China." *Catholic University of Peking Bulletin No. 8,* 1931, pp. 137–39.
Harris, Joseph E. *The African Presence in Asia: Consequences of the East African Slave Trade.* Evanston, Ill.: Northwestern University Press, 1971.
Jitsuzô Kuwabara, "On P'u Shou-kêng." *Memoirs of the Research Department of the Toyo Bunko* (1928), 2:1–79.
Pankhurst, Richard. "The History of Ethiopia's Relations with India prior to the Nineteenth Century." Paper presented to the Fourth International Conference of Ethiopian Studies, Rome, 1972.
Rubin, Arnold. *Black Nanban: Africans in Japan during the Sixteenth Century.* Bloomington: African Studies Program, Indiana University, 1974.
Seth, D. R. "The Life and Times of Malik Ambar." *Islamic Culture: The Hyderabad Quarterly Review* (1957), 31:142–55.
Tamaskar, B. G. "An Estimate of Malik Ambar." *Quarterly Review of Historical Studies* (Calcutta, 1968–69), 8:247–50.

AFRICANS IN LATIN AMERICA AND THE CARIBBEAN

"Afro-Américains, Les." *Mémoires de l'Institut Français d'Afrique Noire,* no. 27. Dakar, 1952.
Bastide, Roger. *African Civilizations in the New World.* New York: Harper and Row, 1971.
Comitas, Lambros, and Lowenthal, David, eds. *Slaves, Free Men, Citizens: West Indian Perspectives.* Garden City, N.Y.: Anchor Books, 1973.
Davis, David Brion. *The Problem of Slavery in Western Culture.* Ithaca, N.Y.: Cornell University Press, 1966.
Herskovits, Melville J. *The New World Negro: Selected Papers in Afro-American Studies.* Bloomington: Indiana University Press, 1966.
Huggins, Nathan I., Kilson, Martin, and Fox, Daniel M., eds. *Key Issues in the Afro-American Experience.* Vol. 1. "To 1877." New York: Harcourt Brace Jovanovich, 1971.
Knight, Franklin W. *The African Dimension in Latin American Societies.* New York: Macmillan, 1974.
Mörner, Magnus. *Race Mixture in the History of Latin America.* Boston: Little Brown, 1967.
Pescatello, Ann, comp. *The African in Latin America.* New York: Knopf, 1975.
Rout, Leslie B. *The African Experience in Spanish America: 1502 to the Present Day.* New York: Cambridge University Press, 1976.
Toplin, Robert B., ed. *Slavery and Race Relations in Latin America.* Westport, Conn.: Greenwood Press, 1974.
UNESCO. *Introducción a la cultura africana en América Latina.* Paris: UNESCO, 1970.

The Atlantic Slave Trade

Anstey, Roger. *The Atlantic Slave Trade and British Abolition, 1760–1810.* London: Macmillan, 1975.

Atkins, John. *A Voyage to Guinea, Brasil, and the West-Indies.* 2d ed. London: Ward and Chandler, 1737.

Clarkson, Thomas. *An Essay on the Slavery and Commerce of the Human Species, particularly the African.* 2d ed. London: J. Phillips, 1788.

Curtin, Philip D. *The Atlantic Slave Trade: A Census.* Madison: University of Wisconsin Press, 1969.

Curtin, Philip D., ed. *Africa Remembered: Narratives by West Africans from the Era of the Slave Trade.* Madison: University of Wisconsin Press, 1967.

Davidson, Basil. *Black Mother: The Years of the African Slave Trade.* London: Gollancz, 1961.

Donnan, Elizabeth, ed. *Documents Illustrative of the History of the Slave Trade to America.* 4 vols. New York: Octagon Books, 1969.

Du Bois, W. E. Burghardt. *The Suppression of the African Slave-trade to the United States of America 1638–1870.* 1896; repr., Baton Rouge: Louisiana State University Press, 1969.

Jakobsson, Stiv. *Am I Not a Man and a Brother? British Missions and the Abolition of the Slave Trade and Slavery in West Africa and the West Indies 1786–1838.* Uppsala, Sweden: Gleerup, 1972.

Mannix, Daniel P., and Cowley, Malcolm. *Black Cargoes: A History of the Atlantic Slave Trade 1518–1865.* New York: Viking, 1963.

Martin, Bernard, and Spurrell, Mark, eds. *The Journal of a Slave Trader (John Newton) 1750–1754.* London: Epworth Press, 1962.

Pope-Hennessy, James. *Sins of the Fathers: A Study of the Atlantic Slave-traders 1441–1807.* London: Weidenfeld and Nicolson, 1967.

Scelle, Georges. *La traite négrière aux Indes de Castille.* 2 vols. Paris: Société du Recueil, 1906.

Slavery: Comparative Studies

Degler, Carl N. *Neither Black nor White: Slavery and Race Relations in Brazil and the United States.* New York: Macmillan, 1971.

Engerman, Stanley L., and Genovese, Eugene D., eds. *Race and Slavery in the Western Hemisphere: Quantitative Studies.* Princeton, N.J.: Princeton University Press, 1975.

Foner, Laura, and Genovese, Eugene D., eds. *Slavery in the New World: A Reader in Comparative History.* Englewood Cliffs, N.J.: Prentice-Hall, 1969.

Hall, Gwendolyn M. *Social Control in Slave Plantation Societies: A Comparison of St. Domingue and Cuba.* Baltimore: Johns Hopkins Press, 1971.

Hoetink, H. *Slavery and Race Relations in the Americas: Comparative Notes on their Nature and Nexus.* New York: Harper and Row, 1973.

Klein, Herbert S. *Slavery in the Americas: A Comparative Study of Virginia and Cuba.* Chicago: University of Chicago Press, 1967.

Tannenbaum, Frank. *Slave and Citizen: The Negro in the Americas.* New York: Knopf, 1946.

Winks, Robin W., ed. *Slavery, a Comparative Perspective: Readings on Slavery from Ancient Times to the Present.* New York: New York University Press, 1972.

Slavery: Regional and Individual Country Studies

Alcalá y Henke, Agustin. *La esclavitud de los negros en la América española.* Madrid: J. Pueyo, 1919.

Mellafe, Rolando. *Negro Slavery in Latin America.* Berkeley and Los Angeles: University of California Press, 1975.

Saco, José Antonio. *Historia de la esclavitud de la raza africana en el nuevo mundo y en especial en los países américo-hispanos.* 4 vols. Havana: Cultural, s.a., 1938.

British West Indies

Beckford, William. *Remarks upon the Situation of Negroes in Jamaica.* London: T. and J. Egerton, 1788.

Bickell, Richard. *The West Indies as They Are; or, a Real Picture of Slavery.* London: Hatchard, 1825.

Browne, Patrick. *The Civil and Natural History of Jamaica.* London: White, 1789.

Craton, Michael. *Sinews of Empire: A Short History of British Slavery.* London: Temple Smith, 1974.

Craton, Michael, and Walvin, James. *A Jamaican Plantation: The History of Worthy Park, 1670–1970.* Toronto: University of Toronto Press, 1970.

De la Beche, Sir Henry Thomas. *Notes on the Present Condition of the Negroes of Jamaica.* London: Cadell, 1825.

Dunn, Richard S. *Sugar and Slaves: The Rise of the Planter Class in the English West Indies, 1624–1713.* Chapel Hill: University of North Carolina Press, 1972.

Edwards, Bryan. *The History, Civil and Commercial, of the British Colonies of the West Indies.* 3 vols. 3d ed. London: Stockdale, 1801.

Goveia, Elsa V. *Slave Society in the British Leeward Islands at the End of the Eighteenth Century.* New Haven: Yale University Press, 1965.

Jeremie, John. *Four Essays on Colonial Slavery.* London: Hatchard, 1831.

Joseph, Edward L. *History of Trinidad.* Trinidad: H. J. Mills, 1840.

Ligon, Richard. *A True & Exact History of the Island of Barbados.* London: Humphrey Moseley, 1657.

Long, Edward. *The History of Jamaica.* London: Lowndes, 1774.

Luffman, John. *A Brief Account of the Island of Antigua.* London: Ridgeway, n.d. [c. 1788].

Patterson, H. Orlando. *The Sociology of Slavery: An Analysis of the Origins, Development, and Structure of Negro Slave Society in Jamaica.* Rutherford, N. J.: Fairleigh Dickinson University Press, 1969.

Poyer, John. *The History of Barbados.* London: J. Mawman, 1808.

Ramsay, James. *An Essay on the Treatment and Conversion of African Slaves in the British Sugar Colonies.* London: Phillips, 1784.

Renny, Robert. *A History of Jamaica.* London: Cawthorn, 1807.

Roughley, Thomas. *The Jamaica Planter's Guide; or, a System for Planting and Managing a Sugar Estate.* London: Longman, Hurst, Rees, Orme, and Brown, 1823.

Schomburgk, Sir Robert H. *The History of Barbados.* London: Longman, Brown, Green and Longmans, 1848.

Senior, Bernard M. *Jamaica, as It Was, as It Is, and as It May Be.* 1835; repr., New York: Negro Universities Press, 1969.

Shephard, Charles. *A Historical Account of the Island of Saint Vincent.* London: Nicol, 1831.

Sheridan, Richard B. *Sugar and Slavery: An Economic History of the British West Indies 1823–1775.* Baltimore: Johns Hopkins University Press, 1974.

Slave Law of Jamaica: With Proceedings and Documents Relative Thereto. London: Ridgeway, 1828.

Stephen, James. *The Slavery of the British West Indian Colonies Delineated.* 2 vols.; London: Butterworth, 1824, 1830.

Stewart, John. *A View of the Past and Present State of the Island of Jamaica.* Edinburgh: Oliver and Boyd, 1823.

Waddell, Hope Masterton. *Twenty-nine Years in the West Indies and Central Africa.* 2d ed. London: Nelson, 1863.

Williams, Eric. *Capitalism and Slavery.* Chapel Hill: University of North Carolina Press, 1944.

French West Indies

Banbuck, C. A. *Histoire politique, économique et sociale de la Mārtinique sous l'Ancien Régime (1635–1789).* Paris: Rivière, 1935.

Chanualon, Thibault de. *Voyage à la Martinique.* Paris: Bauche, 1763.

Charlevoix, Pierre F. X. de. *Histoire de l'Isle Espagnole ou de S. Domingue.* 2 vols. Paris: Guerin, 1730–31.

Debien, Gabriel. *Plantations et esclaves à Saint-Domingue.* Dakar: Université de Dakar, 1962.

Dessalles, Adrien. *Histoire générale des Antilles.* 5 vols. in 3. Paris: Libraire-Editeur, 1847–48.

Gisler, Antoine. *L'Esclavage aux Antilles Françaises (XVIIe–XIXe siècle).* Fribourg: Editions Universitaires Fribourg Suisse, 1965.

Labat, Jean Baptiste. *Nouveau voyage aux isles de l'Amérique.* 8 vols. Paris: Delespine, 1742.

Martin, Gaston. *Histoire de l'esclavage dans les colonies françaises.* Paris: Presses Universitaires de France, 1948.

Moreau de Saint-Méry, Médéric L. E. *Description topographique, physique, civile, politique et historique de la partie française de l'isle Saint-Domingue.* 3 vols. 1797; repr., Paris: Larose, 1958.

Peytraud, Lucien. *L'Esclavage aux Antilles françaises avant 1789.* Paris: Hachette, 1897.

Satineau, Maurice. *Histoire de la Guadeloupe sous l'Ancien Régime 1635–1789.* Paris: Payot, 1928.

Tertre, Jean-Baptiste du. *Histoire générale des Antilles habitées par les françois.* 3 vols. Paris: Iolly, 1667.

Vaissière, Pierre de. *Saint-Domingue: La société et la vie créoles sous l'ancien régime (1629–1789).* Paris: Perrin, 1909.

Brazil

Carneiro, Edison. *Antologia do negro brasileiro.* Rio de Janeiro: Tecnoprint Gráfica, 1967.

Freyre, Gilberto. *The Masters and the Slaves: A Study in the Development of Brazilian Civilization.* 3d ed. New York: Borzoi Books, 1967.

Nina Rodrigues, Raymundo. *Os africanos no Brasil.* 3d ed. São Paulo: Companhia Editora Nacional, 1945.

Pierson, Donald. *Negroes in Brazil: A Study of Race Contact at Bahia.* Chicago: University of Chicago Press, 1942.

Ramos, Arthur. *The Negro in Brazil.* Washington, D. C.: Associated Publishers, 1939.

Rodrigues, Jose Honorio. *Brazil and Africa.* Berkeley and Los Angeles: University of California Press, 1965.

Toplin, Robert B. *The Abolition of Slavery in Brazil.* New York: Atheneum, 1972.

Verger, Pierre. *Flux et reflux de la traite des nègres entre le golfe de Bénin et Bahia de Todos os Santos du XVIIe au XIXe siècle.* The Hague: Mouton, 1968.

Spanish Caribbean

Aimes, Hubert H. S. *A History of Slavery in Cuba 1511 to 1868.* New York: Putnams, 1907.

Armas y Céspedes, Francisco de. *De la esclavitud en Cuba.* Madrid: Fortanet, 1866.

Corwin, Arthur F. *Spain and the Abolition of Slavery in Cuba, 1817–1886.* Austin: University of Texas Press, 1967.

Díaz Soler, Luis M. *Historia de la esclavitud negra en Puerto Rico.* 3d ed. Rio Piedras: Editorial Universitaria, Universidad de Puerto Rico, 1970.

Knight, Franklin W. *Slave Society in Cuba during the Nineteenth Century.* Madison: University of Wisconsin Press, 1970.

Le Riverend, Julio. *Historia económica de Cuba.* 2d ed. Havana: Editoriel Nacional de Cuba, 1965.

Martínez-Alier, Verena. *Marriage, Class and Color in Nineteenth-century Cuba.* Cambridge: Cambridge University Press, 1974.

Ortiz Fernández, Fernando. *Hampa afro-cubana. Los negros esclavos: estudio sociológico y de derecho publico.* Havana: Revista Bimestre Cubana, 1916.

Mainland Spanish America

Acosta Saignes, Miguel. *Vida de los esclavos negros en Venezuela.* Caracas: Hespérides, 1967.

Aguirre Beltrán, Gonzalo. *La población negra de México, 1519–1810: estudio etnohistórico.* México, D. F.: Ediciones Fuente Cultural, 1946.

Bowser, Frederick P. *The African Slave in Colonial Peru, 1524–1650.* Stanford: Stanford University Press, 1974.

Lombardi, John V. *The Decline and Abolition of Negro Slavery in Venezuela 1820–1854.* Westport, Conn.: Greenwood Press, 1971.

Maroons

Carneiro, Edison. *O quilombo dos Palmares.* 2d ed. São Paulo: Companhia Editora Nacional, 1958.

Dallas, Robert C. *The History of the Maroons.* 2 vols. London: Longman and Rees, 1803.

Montejo, Esteban. *The Autobiography of a Runaway Slave.* New York: Meridian Books, 1970.

Price, Richard, ed. *Maroon Societies: Rebel Slave Communities in the Americas.* Garden City, N. Y.: Anchor Books, 1973.

Proceedings of the Governor and Assembly of Jamaica, in Regard to the Maroon Negroes. London: Stockdale, 1796.

Robinson, Carey. *The Fighting Maroons of Jamaica.* Kingston: William Collins and Sangster (Jamaica), 1969.

Revolts

Arcaya, Pedro M. *Insurrección de los negros de la Serranía de Coro.* Caracas: Instituto Panamericano de Geografía e Historia, 1949.

Brito Figueroa, Federico. *Las insurrecciones de los esclavos negros en la sociedad colonial venezolana.* Caracas: Editorial Cantaclaro, 1961.

Carneiro, Edison. *Guerras de los Palmares.* México: Fondo de Cultura Económica, 1946.

Cole, Hubert. *Christophe, King of Haiti.* New York: VikingPress, 1967.

James, C. L. R. *The Black Jacobins: Toussaint l'Ouverture and the San Domingo Revolution.* 2d ed. New York: Vintage Books, 1963.

—— *A History of Pan-African Revolt.* 2d ed. Washington, D.C.: Drum and Spear Press, 1969.

Korngold, Ralph. *Citizen Toussaint.* New York: Hill and Wang, 1965.

Moura, Clovis. *Rebeliões da senzala: quilombos, insurreições, guerrilhas.* São Paulo: Edições Lumbe, 1959.

Ott, Thomas O. *The Haitian Revolution, 1789–1804.* Knoxville: University of Tennessee Press, 1973.

Reichert, Rolf, ed. *Os documentos arabes do arquivo publico do Estado da Bahia.* Bahia: Universidade Federal da Bahia, 1970.

Free Blacks

Boxer, Charles R. *Race Relations in the Portuguese Colonial Empire, 1415–1825.* Oxford: Clarendon Press, 1963.

Cohen, David W., and Greene, Jack P., eds. *Neither Slave nor Free: The Freedmen of African Descent in the Slave Societies of the New World.* Baltimore: Johns Hopkins University Press, 1972.

Handler, Jerome S. *The Unappropriated People: Freedmen in the Slave Society of Barbados.* Baltimore: Johns Hopkins University Press, 1974.

INDEX

Cornwall (Jamaica), 330-31, 333
Coromantees, 296, 303
Cottawood maroons, 296
Creoles: black, 117, 203, 216-17, 329; white, 193, 203, 228-29, 248-49, 344, 376-77
Cuba, 181, 293-94; slavery in, 223-55; government of, 237-43; sugar plantations in, 223-26, 234-47, 259-62; maroons in, 318-21; revolts in, 323, 326-28; free blacks in, 353, 378-81
Cudjoe, Captain, 295-307

Dāḥis-Ghabrā, 54
Dakhnīs, 146-48
Dāmān, 138
Damascus, 58
Danda-Rājpuri, 157-60
Daylam, 68
Deccan, 142, 145-55
Deccanīs, *see* Dakhnīs
Delhi Sultanate, 137, 139-40, 143, 146, 151-52, 157
Dias, Sebastião, 289, 290, 292
Dīnār Dastūrī Mamālik, Malik, 147
Diodorus Siculus, 16-20
Dutch West Indies, 203, 219-23, 284, 291, 308-16, 314

Egypt, Egyptians, 3-15, 21-24, 31, 33, 131-33, 136, 181
Elesbaas, King, 41
Elesbão do Carmo, Dandara, 348
Emancipation, slave, 242-43, 248-50, 282, 353, 378-81
English East India Company, 155-56, 159, 161-64
Ergamenes, King, 20
Esimiphaeus, 41-42; *see also* Aryāt
Ethiopia, Ethiopians, 3-4, 14-24, 26, 28, 32-36, 39-40, 42, 126, 150; *see also* Abyssinians; Ḥabshīs
Eunuchs, 69, 128, 129, 131
Euphrates, River, 79
Euripides, 26

Farhan, Amīr, 69-72
Fateh Khān, 158-59
al-Fatḥ ibn Khāqān, 116
Fatḥ Shāh, Sulṭān, 141, 144
Fereira Balião, Manoel Francisco dos Anjos, 350
Ferreira de Menezes, José, 372-73
Firishta, 139-40
Fīrūz, Sulṭān, 146
Fonseca da Silva Pedroso, Pedro da, 349
Free blacks, 202-3, 352; in Panamá, 352, 353-54; in Peru, 352, 354-55; in British West Indies, 352, 355-62; in Jamaica, 329, 352, 356-57, 362-64; in Brazil, 352, 364-66; in Cuba, 248-49, 353, 378-82
French West Indies, 185, 203, 223, 225; slavery in, 215-19
Fumiyoon, 45-46
Funerals, 191, 220-21, 263-65

Gama, Luiz, 370-72
Gana (Ghana), 110
Garamantes, 28, 32
Gaur, 142, 144-45
Gebelein, 12-13
Goa, 139, 154
Golconda, 150, 152, 154
Gomes, Raymundo, 350
Greece, Greeks, 13-14, 17-18, 25-27, 29-30, 33-36, 55, 126
Gujarāt, 138, 142, 164-66

Ḥabash Khān (ambassador), 151
Ḥabash Khān (ruler), 142
Ḥabash Khān Sīdī Miftāḥ, 137
Ḥabshī Koṭ, 149

Loheia (Luḥaiya), 70
L'Ouverture, Toussaint, 322
Lūlū, 97, 98

al-Ma'arrī, Abu 'l-'Alā, 122
Madagascar, 137, 217
Mahin, Luiza, 348, 370
Mamlūks, 127, 130, 132-34
al-Ma'mūn, Abū 'l-'Abbās 'Abd Allāh, 67-69
Mandingos, 216, 241
Manīa, 93
Manumission, 242-43, 248-50, 353
Maranhão, 349-50
Marāthās, 151, 156, 158-59, 161-63
Marimbas, 268
Marjān, Malik, 148, 149
Maroons: in Jamaica, 283-84, 293-307; in Cuba, 283-84, 318-21; in Brazil, 283, 284-93, 340-49; in Surinam, 283-84, 308-16
Marriages, slave, 188, 220, 242, 251
Masks, slave, 272
Matanzas, 239, 252
Mawlā, 62, 66, 123, 124
Mawlay Ismā'īl, Sulṭān, 134
Mecca, 51-53, 113
Medina, 44, 61, 73-74
Mello de Castro, Caetano de, 288-93
Memnon, 27
Mên, King, 13
Meroë, 16-20, 28, 40
Mestizes, 354-56, 358
Mexico, 323, 324-26
Mian Raju, 150
Middle Passage, 322-24
Militias, black, 329, 333, 352-54, 365-66, 376
Minas, 241, 273, 274
Minas Geraes, 341, 368-69
Mines, 255-59, 276-80, 327, 368-69
Ming dynasty, 168-70
Missionaries, 205-15, 334-36
Mokhtāra, 85, 93-106
Mo-leh, 172-75
Mongol dynasty, 169
Morocco, 134
Morro Velho, 276-80
Mosquito Shore, 297
Mozambique, 137
Mughals, 137, 150-55, 158, 161-62
Muḥammad 'Alī Pasha, 135
Muḥammad ibn Ṣaṣrā, 61
al-Muḳtadir, Abū 'l-Faḍl Ja'far, 113
Mulattos, 57, 117, 124-25, 355-66, 375-77
Murtaḍā II Niẓām Shāh, 150, 154
Mūsā I, Mansa, 180
Mūsā the Turk, 90
Music, musicians, 58-59, 67-68, 127-28, 166, 188-89, 194, 218-20, 227, 268
al-Mustanṣir, Abū Tamīm Ma'add, 131
al-Mu'tamid, Abu 'l-'Abbās Aḥmad ibn Ja'far, 87, 96
Mutinies, slave, *see* Revolts
al-Muwaffaḳ, 87, 89-94, 96-99, 103-5
al-Muwaffaḳīya, 94, 96, 97, 99, 105

Nāfi' ibn Jubayr, 123
Nagos, 216
Napata, 16, 21, 27
Napoleon Bonaparte, 223
Nāṣir-i-Khusraw, 107
Nawābs of Janjīra, 164-65, 167
Nefertari, 11
Nefertiti, 11
Negus, 49
Nejrān, 45-47
Nero, Emperor, 28
Netherlands East India Company, 152, 161
Niger, River, 28, 31, 32